Lecture Notes in Computer Science 12136

More information about this series at http://www.springer.com/series/7408

Alexey Gotsman · Ana Sokolova (Eds.)

Formal Techniques for Distributed Objects, Components, and Systems

40th IFIP WG 6.1 International Conference, FORTE 2020
Held as Part of the 15th International Federated Conference
on Distributed Computing Techniques, DisCoTec 2020
Valletta, Malta, June 15–19, 2020
Proceedings

 Springer

Editors
Alexey Gotsman
IMDEA Software Institute
Pozuelo de Alarcón, Spain

Ana Sokolova
University of Salzburg
Salzburg, Austria

ISSN 0302-9743   ISSN 1611-3349 (electronic)
Lecture Notes in Computer Science
ISBN 978-3-030-50085-6   ISBN 978-3-030-50086-3   (eBook)
https://doi.org/10.1007/978-3-030-50086-3

LNCS Sublibrary: SL2 – Programming and Software Engineering

This Springer imprint is published by the registered company Springer Nature Switzerland AG
The registered company address is: Gewerbestrasse 11, 6330 Cham, Switzerland

Foreword

The 15th International Federated Conference on Distributed Computing Techniques (DisCoTec 2020) took place during June 15–19, 2020. It was organized by the Department of Computer Science at the University of Malta, but was held online due to the abnormal circumstances worldwide affecting physical travel.

The DisCoTec series is one of the major events sponsored by the International Federation for Information Processing (IFIP). It comprises three conferences:

- The IFIP WG 6.1 22nd International Conference on Coordination Models and Languages (COORDINATION 2020)
- The IFIP WG 6.1 20th International Conference on Distributed Applications and Interoperable Systems (DAIS 2020)
- The IFIP WG 6.1 40th International Conference on Formal Techniques for Distributed Objects, Components and Systems (FORTE 2020)

Together, these conferences cover a broad spectrum of distributed computing subjects, ranging from theoretical foundations and formal description techniques to systems research issues. As is customary, the event also included several plenary sessions in addition to the individual sessions of each conference, that gathered attendants from the three conferences. These included joint invited speaker sessions and a joint session for the best papers from the respective three conferences.

Associated with the federated event, two satellite events took place:

- The 13th International Workshop on Interaction and Concurrency Experience (ICE 2020)
- The First International Workshop on Foundations of Consensus and Distributed Ledgers (FOCODILE 2020)

I would like to thank the Program Committee chairs of the different events for their help and cooperation during the preparation of the conference, and the Steering Committee and Advisory Boards of DisCoTec and their conferences for their guidance and support. The organization of DisCoTec 2020 was only possible thanks to the dedicated work of the Organizing Committee, including Davide Basile and Francisco "Kiko" Fernández Reyes (publicity chairs), Antonis Achilleos, Duncan Paul Attard, and Ornela Dardha (workshop chairs), Lucienne Bugeja (logistics and finances), as well as all the students and colleagues who volunteered their time to help. Finally, I would like to thank IFIP WG 6.1 for sponsoring this event, Springer's *Lecture Notes in Computer Science* team for their support and sponsorship, EasyChair for providing the reviewing framework, and the University of Malta for providing the support and infrastructure to host the event.

June 2020   Adrian Francalanza

Preface

This volume contains the papers presented at the 40th IFIP WG 6.1 International Conference on Formal Techniques for Distributed Objects, Components, and Systems (FORTE 2020), held as one of three main conferences of the 15th International Federated Conference on Distributed Computing Techniques (DisCoTec 2020), during June 15–19, 2020, online due to the coronavirus pandemic.

FORTE is a well-established forum for fundamental research on theory, models, tools, and applications for distributed systems, with special interest in:

- Software quality, reliability, availability, and safety
- Security, privacy, and trust in distributed and/or communicating systems
- Service-oriented, ubiquitous, and cloud computing systems
- Component- and model-based design
- Object technology, modularity, and software adaptation
- Self-stabilization and self-healing/organizing
- Verification, validation, formal analysis, and testing of the above

The Program Committee received a total of 25 submissions, written by authors from 18 different countries. Of these, 11 papers were selected for inclusion in the scientific program. Each submission was reviewed by at least three Program Committee members with the help of 10 external reviewers in selected cases. The selection of accepted submissions was based on electronic discussions via the EasyChair conference management system.

As program chairs, we actively contributed to the selection of the keynote speakers of DisCoTec 2020 (which due to the conference being held online are not all confirmed at the time of writing).

This year DisCoTec also includes a Tutorial Day of six invited tutorials. This volume includes the following tutorial papers:

- Parameterised Verification with Byzantine Model Checker
- Typechecking Java Protocols with [St] Mungo

We wish to thank all the authors of submitted papers, all the members of the Program Committee for their thorough evaluations of the submissions, and the external reviewers who assisted the evaluation process. We are also indebted to the Steering Committee of FORTE for their advice and suggestions. Last but not least, we thank the DisCoTec general chair, Adrian Francalanza, and his organization team for their hard, effective work in providing an excellent environment for FORTE 2020 and all other conferences and workshops, despite of the pandemic troubles.

June 2020

Alexey Gotsman
Ana Sokolova

Organization

Program Committee

Marco Bernardo	University of Urbino, Italy
Nathalie Bertrand	Inria, France
Marco Carbone	IT University of Copenhagen, Denmark
Andrea Corradini	University of Pisa, Italy
Cezara Dragoi	Inria and ENS, France
Constantin Enea	Université Paris-Diderot, France
Javier Esparza	TU Munich, Germany
Alexey Gotsman	IMDEA Software Institute, Spain
Philipp Haller	KTH, Sweden
Bart Jacobs	KU Leuven, Belgium
Radha Jagadeesan	DePaul University, USA
Akash Lal	Microsoft Research, India
Mohsen Lesani	University of California, Riverside, USA
Stephan Merz	Inria, France
Antoine Miné	Sorbonne Université, France
Koko Muroya	RIMS Kyoto University, Japan
Catuscia Palamidessi	Inria and LIX, France
Kirstin Peters	TU Darmstadt, Germany
Tatjana Petrov	University of Konstanz, Germany
Vincent Rahli	University of Birmingham, UK
Ana Sokolova	University of Salzburg, Austria
Tyler Sorensen	Princeton University and University of California, Santa Cruz, USA
Marielle Stoelinga	TU Twente, The Netherlands
Sara Tucci-Piergiovanni	CEA LIST, France
Nikos Tzevelekos	Queen Mary University of London, UK
Viktor Vafeiadis	MPI-SWS, Germany
Josef Widder	TU Vienna and Interchain, Austria

Additional Reviewers

Pranav Ashok	Marco Romanelli
Stephanie Delaune	Ocan Sankur
Maribel Fernandez	Alceste Scalas
Ernst Moritz Hahn	Jacopo Soldani
Yu-Yang Lin	Stefano Tognazzi

Contents

Short Paper

Full Papers

Strategy Synthesis for Autonomous Driving in a Moving Block Railway System with UPPAAL STRATEGO

Davide Basile[1]([✉])[iD], Maurice H. ter Beek[1][iD], and Axel Legay[2][iD]

[1] ISTI–CNR, Pisa, Italy
{davide.basile,maurice.terbeek}@isti.cnr.it
[2] Université Catholique de Louvain, Louvain-la-Neuve, Belgium
axel.legay@uclouvain.be

Abstract. Moving block railway systems are the next generation signalling systems currently under development as part of the Shift2Rail European initiative, including autonomous driving technologies. In this paper, we model a suitable abstraction of a moving block signalling system with autonomous driving as a stochastic priced timed game. We then synthesise safe and optimal driving strategies for the model by applying advanced techniques that combine statistical model checking with reinforcement learning as provided by UPPAAL STRATEGO. Hence, we show the applicability of UPPAAL STRATEGO in this concrete case study.

1 Introduction

Next generation railway systems are based on distributed inter-organisational entities, such as on-board train computers and wayside radio-block centres and satellites, which have to interact to accomplish their tasks. A longstanding effort in the railway domain concerns the use of formal methods and tools for the analysis of railway (signalling) systems in light of the sector's stringent safety requirements [7, 10, 11, 17, 27–31, 41, 42]. Due to their distributed and inter-organisational nature, their formal verification is still an open challenge. Whilst model-checking and theorem-proving techniques are predominant, to the best of our knowledge, applications of controller synthesis techniques are largely lacking.

We describe a formal modelling and analysis experience with UPPAAL STRATEGO of a moving block railway signalling system. This work was conducted in the context of several projects concerned with the use of formal methods and tools for the development of railway systems based on moving block signalling systems, in which train movement is no longer authorised based on sections of the railway track between fixed points, but computed in real time as safe zones around the trains. Most notably, the H2020 Shift2Rail projects ASTRail: SAtellite-based Signalling and Automation SysTems on Railways along with Formal Method and Moving Block Validation (http://www.astrail.eu) and 4SECURail: FORmal Methods and CSIRT for the RAILway sector

Published by Springer Nature Switzerland AG 2020
A. Gotsman and A. Sokolova (Eds.): FORTE 2020, LNCS 12136, pp. 3–21, 2020.
https://doi.org/10.1007/978-3-030-50086-3_1

(http://www.4securail.eu). The European Shift2Rail initiative (http://shift2rail.org) is a joint undertaking of the European Commission and the main railway stakeholders to move the European railway industry forward by increasing its competitiveness. This concerns in particular the transition to next generation signalling systems, including satellite-based train positioning, moving-block distancing, and automatic driving. With a budget of nearly 1 billion euro, it is unique in its kind.

Previously, in [6,8], we introduced a concrete case study of a satellite-based moving block railway signalling system, which was developed in collaboration with industrial partners of the ASTRail project and which was modelled and analysed with SIMULINK and UPPAAL SMC (Statistical Model Checker). While those models offered the possibility to fine tune communication parameters that are fundamental for the reliability of their operational behaviour, they did not account for the synthesis of autonomous driving strategies.

Building on such efforts, in this paper we present a formal model of a satellite-based moving block railway signalling system, which accounts for autonomous driving and which is modelled in UPPAAL STRATEGO as a stochastic priced timed game. The autonomous driving module is not modelled manually, but it is synthesised automatically as a strategy, after which both standard and statistical model checking are applied under the resulting (safe) strategy. The starting point for deriving the strategy is a safety requirement that the model must respect. We moreover consider reliability aspects, and the autonomous driving strategy also provides guarantees for the minimal expected arrival time. The model and experiments are available at https://github.com/davidebasile/FORTE2020.

Related Work. At last year's FORTE, parametric statistical model checking was applied to Unmanned Aerial Vehicles (UAV) [4]. The model was formalised as a parametric Markov chain with the goal of reducing the probability of failure while varying parameters such as precision of the position. The UAV follows a predefined flight plan, whereas we aim at automatically synthesising a strategy to safely drive the train. It would be interesting to investigate the possibility of synthesising flight plans under safety constraints.

A decade ago at FORTE'10, one of the first applications of statistical model checking (using the BIP toolset) to an industrial case study was presented, namely the heterogeneous communication system for cabin communication in civil airplanes [9]. The goal was to study the accuracy of clock synchronisation between different devices running in parallel on a distributed application, i.e. a time bound within which communication must occur. An implementation of this case study in UPPAAL SMC would allow a comparison of the results.

Statistical model checking has also been used to verify the reliability of railway interlocking systems [19] and UPPAAL has been used to verify railway timetables [34]. UPPAAL STRATEGO has been applied to a few other case studies belonging to the transport domain, such as traffic light controllers [3], cruise control [38], and railway scheduling [37]. We conjecture that the UPPAAL STRATEGO model in [37] could be paired with our model to study railway scheduling for autonomous trains, with the goal of synthesising improved strategies for both the scheduler and the autonomous driver.

Finally, there have been several recent attempts at modelling and analysing ERTMS Level 3 signalling systems (in particular Hybrid Level 3 systems with virtual fixed blocks) with Promela/Spin, mCRL2, Alloy/Electrum, iUML, SysML, ProB, Event-B, and real-time Maude [2,5,14,21,25,33,40,43]. None of these concern quantitative modelling and analysis, typically lacking uncertainty, which is fundamental for demonstrating the reliability of the operational behaviour of next generation satellite-based ERTMS Level 3 moving block railway signalling system models. One of the earliest quantitative evaluations of moving block railway signalling systems can be found in [36], based on GSM-R communications.

Structure of the Paper. After some background on UPPAAL STRATEGO in Sect. 2, we describe the setting of the case study from the railway domain in Sect. 3. In Sect. 4, we present the formal model, followed by an extensive description of the conducted analyses in Sect. 5. Finally, we discuss our experience with UPPAAL STRATEGO and provide some ideas for future work in Sect. 6.

2   Background: UPPAAL STRATEGO

In this section, we provide some background of the tools and their input models used in this paper, providing pointers to the literature for more details.

UPPAAL STRATEGO [24] is the latest tool of the UPPAAL [12] suite. It integrates formalisms and algorithms coming from the less recent UPPAAL TIGA [13] (synthesis for timed games), UPPAAL SMC [22] (Statistical Model Checking), and the synthesis of near optimal schedulers proposed in [23].

UPPAAL TIGA [13,20] implements an efficient on-the-fly algorithm for the synthesis of strategies extended to deal with models of *timed games*. These are automata modelling a game between a player (the controller) and an opponent (the environment). Transitions are partitioned into controllable and uncontrollable ones. The controller plays the controllable transitions, while the opponent plays the uncontrollable ones. The controller is only allowed to deactivate controllable transitions. The goal is to synthesise a strategy for the controller such that, no matter the actions of the opponent, a particular property is satisfied. Generally, uncontrollable transitions are used to model events such as delays in communication or other inputs from the environment. On the converse, controllable transitions characterise the logic of the controller, generally related to actuators. The strategy synthesis algorithm uses a suitable abstraction of the real-time part of the model, through *zones* that are constraints over the real-time clocks. Strategy synthesis allows an algorithmic construction of a controller which is guaranteed to ensure that the resulting system satisfies the desired correctness properties, i.e. reachability and safety.

UPPAAL SMC is a statistical model checker based on models of *stochastic timed automata*. These are automata enhanced with real-time modelling through *clock* variables. Moreover, their stochastic extension replaces non-determinism with probabilistic choices and time delays with probability distributions (uniform for bounded time and exponential for unbounded time). These automata may communicate via (broadcast) channels and shared variables. Statistical Model Checking (SMC) [1,39] is based on running a sufficient number of (probabilistic) simulations of a system model to obtain statistical evidence (with a predefined level of statistical confidence) of the quantitative properties to be checked. SMC offers advantages over exhaustive (probabilistic) model checking. Most importantly, SMC scales better since there is no need to generate and possibly explore the full state space of the model under scrutiny, thus avoiding the combinatorial state-space explosion problem typical of model checking, and the required simulations can be easily distributed and run in parallel. This comes at a price: contrary to (probabilistic) model checking, exact results (with 100% confidence) are out of the question.

The method proposed in [23] extends the strategy synthesis of [13] to find near-optimal solutions for *stochastic priced timed games*, which are basically stochastic timed automata enhanced with controllable and uncontrollable transitions, similarly to timed games. In short, the method starts from the most permissive strategy guaranteeing the time bounds, computed with the algorithms in [13]. This strategy is then converted into a stochastic one by substituting non-determinism with uniform distributions. Finally, reinforcement learning is applied iteratively to learn from sampled runs the effect of control choices, to find the near-optimal strategy.

UPPAAL STRATEGO uses stochastic priced timed games as formalism whilst integrating (real-time) model checking, statistical model checking, strategy synthesis, and optimisation. It thus becomes possible to perform model checking and optimisation under strategies, which are first-class objects in the tool. Internally, abstractions that allow to pass from stochastic priced timed games to timed games similar to those in [13] are used to integrate the various algorithms.

3   Context and Case Study

The European Railway Traffic Management System (ERTMS) is a set of international standards for the interoperability, performance, reliability, and safety of modern European rail transport [26]. It relies on the European Train Control System (ETCS), an automatic train protection system that continuously supervises the train, ensuring to not exceed the safety speed and distance. The current standards distinguish four levels (0–3) of operation of ETCS signalling systems, depending largely on the role of trackside equipment and'on the way information is transmitted to and from trains. The ERTMS/ETCS signalling systems currently deployed on railways throughout Europe concern at most Level 2.

Level 2 signalling systems are based on fixed blocks starting and ending at signals. The block sizes are determined based on parameters like the speed limit, the train's speed and braking characteristics, drivers' sighting and reaction times, etc. But the faster trains are allowed to run, the longer the braking distance and the longer the blocks need to be, thus decreasing the line's capacity. This is because the railway sector's stringent safety requirements impose the length of fixed blocks to be based on the worst-case braking distance, regardless of the actual speed of the train. For exact train position detection and train integrity supervision, Level 2 signalling systems make use of trackside equipment (such as track circuits or axle counters). However, communication of the movement authority (MA), i.e. the permission to move to a specific location with supervision of speed, as well as speed information and route data to and from the train is achieved by continuous data transmission via GSM-R or GPRS with a wayside radio block centre. Moreover, an onboard unit continuously monitors the transferred data and the train's maximum permissible speed by determining its position in between the Eurobalises (transponders on the rails of a railway) used as reference points via sensors (axle transducers, accelerometer and radar).

The next generation Level 3 signalling systems currently under investigation and development, no longer rely on trackside equipment for train position detection and train integrity supervision. Instead, an onboard odometry system is responsible for monitoring the train's position and autonomously computing its current speed. The onboard unit frequently sends the train's position to a radio block centre which, in turn, sends each train a MA, computed by exploiting its knowledge of the position of the rear end of the train ahead. For this to work, the precise absolute location, speed, and direction of each train needs to be known, which are to be determined by a combination of sensors: active and passive markers along the track, and trainborne speedometers. The resulting moving block signalling systems allow trains in succession to close up, since a safe zone around the moving trains can be computed, thus considerably reducing headways between trains, in principle to the braking distance. This allows for more trains to run on existing railway tracks, in response to the ever-increasing need to boost the volume of passenger and freight rail transport and the cost and impracticability of constructing new tracks. Furthermore, the removal of trackside equipment results in lower capital and maintenance costs [32].

One of the current challenges in the railway sector is to make moving block signalling systems as effective and precise as possible, including satellite-based positioning systems and leveraging on an integrated solution for signal outages (think, e.g., of the absence of positioning in tunnels) and the problem of multipaths [44]. However, due to its robust safety requirements the railway sector is notoriously cautious about adopting technological innovations. Thus, while GNSS-based positioning systems are in use for some time now in the avionics and automotive sectors, current train signalling systems are still based on fixed blocks. However, experiments are being conducted and case studies are being validated in order to move to Level 3 signalling systems [2,5,6,8,14,15,21,25, 33,40].

The components of the moving block railway signalling case study considered in this paper are depicted in Fig. 1. The train carries the location unit and onboard unit components, while the radio block centre is a wayside component. The location unit receives the train's location from GNSS satellites, sends this location (and the train's integrity) to the onboard unit, which, in turn, sends the

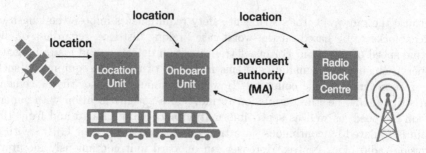

Fig. 1. ERTMS Level 3 moving block railway signalling (adapted from [8,31])

location to the radio block centre. Upon receiving a train's location, the radio block centre sends a MA to the onboard unit (together with speed restrictions and route configurations), indicating the space the train can safely travel based on the safety distance with preceding trains. The radio block centre computes such MA by communicating with neighbouring radio block centres and exploiting its knowledge of the positions of switches and other trains (head and tail position) by communicating with a Route Management System. We abstract from the latter and from communication among neighbouring radio block centres: we consider one train to communicate with one radio block centre, based on a seamless handover when the train moves from one radio block centre supervision area to an adjacent one, as regulated by its Functional Interface Specification [45].

4   Formal Model

In this section, we describe the formal model of the case study introduced before. It consists of a number of SPTGs, which are basically timed automata with prices (a cost function) and stochasticity, composed as a synchronous product.

We briefly describe the model's components, followed by details of the onboard unit. Delays in the communications are exponentially distributed with rate 1:4 to account for possible delays. This is a common way of modelling communication delays. Moreover, all transitions are uncontrollable, except for the controllable actions of the driver in the TRAIN_ATO_T component, which are used to synthesise the safe and optimal strategy.

Component OBU_MAIN_GenerateLocationRequest_T initiates system interactions by generating a request for a new location to send to the location unit. The location unit component LU_MAIN_T receives a new position request from the onboard unit, replying with the current train location (computed via GNSS). The main component OBU_MAIN_SendLocationToRBC_T of the onboard unit performs a variety of operations. It receives the position from the location unit, sends the received position to the radio block centre, and eventually implements a safety mechanism present in the original system specification. In particular, at each instant of time, it checks that the train's position does not exceed the MA received from the radio block centre; if it does, it enters a failure state.

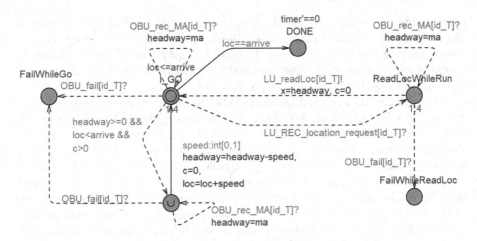

Fig. 2. The `TRAIN_ATO_T` component

The failure is also broadcast to all other components. In fact, all components can enter a failure state if a failure is triggered. The `RBC_Main_T` component model of the radio block centre receives MA requests from the onboard unit. Once received, the radio block centre repeatedly sends a MA message until the corresponding acknowledgement from the onboard unit is received. Also `OBU_MAIN_ReceiveMA_T` models the logic of the onboard unit. It receives a MA from the radio block centre, and sends back a corresponding acknowledgement. Finally, the `TRAIN_ATO_T` component was defined to synthesise a strategy for moving the train in a safe and optimal way. In particular, the position of the train (variable `loc`) is stated in a unidimensional space and identified by one coordinate (representing the position along its route), and the train is allowed at each cycle to either move one unit or stay idle. To allow state-space reduction, the value of `loc` represents a range of the space in which the train is located, rather than a specific point in space. Next, we describe this component, depicted in Fig. 2, in detail.

The initial state of `TRAIN_ATO_T` is the nominal state `I_GO`, drawn with two circles. Two failure states (`FailWhileGo` and `FailWhileReadLoc`) are reached in case the MA is exceeded in `OBU_MAIN_SendLocationToRBC_T`. The initial state has an invariant to guarantee that the train has not passed its destination. Note that invariants can be constraints on clocks or variables. This is done by checking that the location of the train, which is encoded by the integer variable `loc`, is less than or equal to the integer constant `arrive`, which is an input parameter of the model to perform experiments. From the initial state it is possible to transit to state `ReadLocWhileRun`, upon a location request coming from `LU_MAIN_T`, and coming back from `ReadLocWhileRun` to `I_GO` by replying to such a request. Variable `x` is a buffer for value-reading messages. To reduce the model's state space, the value transmitted by `TRAIN_ATO` is the remaining headway, i.e. the difference between the MA and the location. Indeed, such value has a fixed range if compared to the location (under the assumption that the arrival point is greater than the initial headway value, otherwise the train will never exceed its MA before arriving to the destination). In turn, OBU_MAIN_SendLocationToRBC_T checks if such transmitted value (headway) is negative for triggering a failure, since in that case the train has exceeded its MA.

From both states I_GO and ReadLocWhileRun, an inner loop is used to receive the new MA (movaut) from RBC_Main_T. The movaut should be relative to the current location loc of the train, i.e. movaut = loc + fixed number of meters that the train is allowed to travel. However, to reduce the state space, such a message simply resets the headway variable to its initial value, which is an integer constant called ma. Thus, movaut is not stored in the state space because its value can be retrieved as loc+ma. The constant ma is another input parameter of the model. The reason such a loop is also present in state ReadLocWhileRun is that otherwise the MA message would be lost in this state, and similarly for the urgent state (marked with the symbol U, described below).

We now discuss the two controllable transitions in the model. The first is used to move a train. In UPPAAL STRATEGO a controller cannot delay its actions (whereas the environment can), hence the movement of the train is split into an uncontrollable transition followed by a controllable one, with an intermediate urgent state. An intermediate urgent state is such that a transition must be taken without letting time pass. This is a workaround to force the controller to perform an action at that instant of time. From the initial state I_GO, an uncontrollable transition targeting the urgent state is used to check that the conditions for moving the train are met. In particular, if the headway is non-negative and the train has not arrived, the transition for moving the train is enabled. Additionally, a test c>0 on the clock c is used to forbid Zeno behaviour. Indeed the clock c is reset to zero after the train has moved, hence time is forced to pass before the next movement. Such a condition cannot be stated directly on the controllable transition, otherwise a time-lock (i.e. time is not allowed to pass) would be reached in case the condition is not met.

The controllable transition (drawn as a solid arc) from the urgent state can either set the integer speed to 1 or to 0, allowing the train to proceed to the next interval of space or to remain in the previous interval, respectively. Recall that loc is not a coordinate but rather an abstraction of a portion of space. The controllable transition also updates the headway. To reduce the state space, the only negative value allowed for the variable headway is −1.

Finally, the second controllable transition is used to reach a sink state DONE. To further reduce the state space, the train is not allowed to move once loc has reached value arrive. A hybrid clock timer is used as a stop-watch to measure the time it takes for the train to arrive in state DONE. To this aim, the invariant timer'==0 in state DONE sets the derivative of clock timer to zero. A hybrid clock can be abstracted away during the synthesis of a safe strategy.

5   Formal Analysis and Experiments

In this section, we report on analysis of the formal model. The main objective is to synthesise a safe strategy such that the train does not exceed the MA. Additionally, the train should be as fast as possible, within the limits imposed by the safety requirements. To this aim, an optimal and safe strategy is synthesised.

The experiments were carried out on a machine with a processor Intel(R) Core(TM) i7-8500Y CPU at 1.50 GHz, 1601 MHz, 2 cores, and 4 logical processors with 16GB of RAM, running 64 bit Windows 10. The development version of UPPAAL STRATEGO (academic version 4.1.20-8-beta2) was used. Indeed, when developing the model and its analysis, minor issues were encountered (more later). This version of UPPAAL STRATEGO contains some patches resulting from a series of interactions between the first author and the developers team at Aalborg University.

The set-up of the parameters of the statistical model checker was chosen to provide a good confidence in the results and is as follows: probabilistic deviation set to $\delta = 0.01$, probability of false negatives and false positives set to $\alpha = 0.005$ and $\beta = 0.5$, respectively, and the probability uncertainty set to $\epsilon = 0.005$. As anticipated in Sect. 3, we focussed on one radio block centre, one onboard unit, and one location unit, i.e. one train communicating with one radio block centre. Finally, we set ma = 5 and arrive = 20.

To begin with, we want to check if the hazard of exceeding the MA is possible at all in our model. If such a hazard were never possible, the safe strategy would simply allow all behaviour. To analyse this, we perform standard model checking:

A[]   not   (OBU_MAIN_SendLocationToRBC.MAexceededFailure)

This formula checks if for every possible path, the state MAexceededFailure of the component OBU_MAIN_SendLocationToRBC is never visited. Indeed, this particular state is reached exactly when the hazard occurs, i.e. the MA is exceeded, thus triggering a failure. After 0.016 s, using 38,200 KB of memory, UPPAAL STRATEGO reports that this formula is not satisfied, thus such hazard is possible without a proper strategy to drive the train. We would like to check the likelihood to reach this failure, given this specific set-up of parameters. First, the average maximal time in which the train reaches its destination is computed. This is important to fine tune the time bound for further simulations. To do so, we use the statistical model checker to evaluate the following formula:

$$\phi_1 = \text{E[<=700;10000] (max: TRAIN\_ATO.timer)}$$

This formula computes the average maximal value of the TRAIN_ATO.timer stopwatch, i.e. the arrival time. It is computed based on 10000 simulations with an experimental time bound of 700 s. The computed value is 377.235 ± 3.960, and its probability distribution is depicted in Fig. 3. By analysing the probability distribution it is possible to notice that the average value is lower if faults are ignored. Indeed, in case of faults the value of timer is equal to the end of the

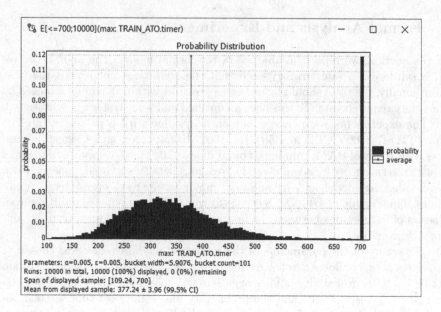

Fig. 3. Probability distribution for average maximal arrival time (ϕ_1)

simulation (i.e. 700 s). Hence, the time bound for the following simulations is set to 500 s, thus considering also worst cases of arrival time.

We now compute the likelihood of the model to reach a failure, using SMC to measure the probability of reaching the failure state with the following formula:

$$\phi_2 = \texttt{Pr[<=500] (<>OBU\_MAIN\_SendLocationToRBC.MAexceededFailure)}$$

UPPAAL STRATEGO executes 33952 simulations and the probability is within the range $[0.117029, 0.127029]$, with confidence 0.995. The probability confidence interval plot for this experiment is depicted in Fig. 4. We conclude that, for this set-up of parameters, there is a relatively high probability for this hazard to occur. This is as expected, due to the absence of a strategy for driving the train and the non-deterministic choice of whether or not to move the train.

After these standard and statistical model-checking experiments, we exploit the synthesis capabilities of UPPAAL STRATEGO to automatically fix the specification to adhere to safety constraints. Indeed, no manual intervention to fix the model is needed: it suffices to compute a driving strategy and compose it with the model. Recall that the only controllable transitions in the model are those for deciding whether or not to move the train (i.e. related to acceleration/deceleration, accordingly). This in turn depends on the stochastic delays in communication. The strategy prunes controllable transitions such that those previously reachable configurations leading to the failure state are no longer

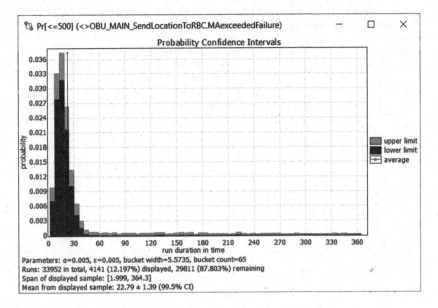

Fig. 4. Probability confidence interval for likelihood of reaching a failure (ϕ_2)

reachable. To compute this strategy, called `safe`, we evaluate the following formula:

```
strategy  safe = control :
          A[] not  (OBU_MAIN_SendLocationToRBC.MAexceededFailure)
```

UPPAAL STRATEGO successfully computes the `safe` strategy in 7.167 s, using 576,888 KB of memory. The strategy allows all possible behaviour that does not violate the above property. To have a glimpse of the strategy at work, we ran 50 simulations of the model composed with the `safe` strategy to visualise the variable `TRAIN_ATO.loc` (i.e. the train's location) with the following command:

```
simulate 50 [<=500] TRAIN_ATO.loc under  safe
```

Figure 5 shows the trajectory of variable `TRAIN_ATO.loc` for 50 simulations, computed in 0.147 s, using 576,984 KB. We see that in all trajectories the train never stops before reaching its destination, i.e. no failure occurs. However, in some simulations the train is relatively slower, when compared to other simulations.

UPPAAL STRATEGO also allows to model check the synthesised strategies. We ran a full state-space exploration by means of standard model checking to formally verify that after composing the model with the `safe` strategy the hazard of exceeding the MA is mitigated. This is checked through the following formula:

```
A[] not (OBU_MAIN_SendLocationToRBC.MAexceededFailure) under  safe
```

This formula checks that in the model composed with the `safe` strategy, the 'bad' state is never reached. After 2.283 s and using 599,268 KB of memory,

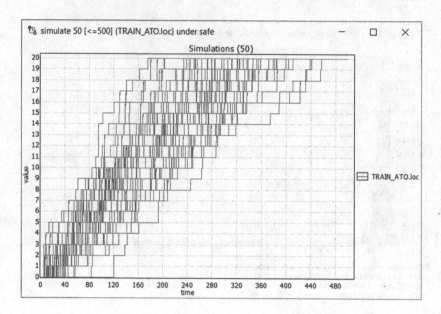

Fig. 5. Simulations of the model under the safe strategy `safe`

UPPAAL STRATEGO reports that the formula is satisfied, thus confirming that we automatically synthesised a strategy for mitigating the hazard. However, even if not showed in Fig. 5, there exist trajectories in the composition where the train never reaches its destination. This can be formally proven with a full state-space exploration of the strategy by standard model checking of the following formula:

$$\texttt{A<> (TRAIN\_ATO.DONE) under safe}$$

This formula checks that in all paths eventually state `TRAIN_ATO.DONE` is reached (i.e. the train reached its destination). After 0.053 s, using 599,268 KB of memory, UPPAAL STRATEGO reports that the formula does not hold. Indeed, as expected, the strategy does not guarantee that such a state is always reached, but it only guarantees to avoid state `OBU_MAIN_SendLocationToRBC.MAexceededFailure`. For example, there exists also a safe strategy that allows the train to remain in its starting position.

To evaluate the probability to reach state `TRAIN_ATO.DONE` under the `safe` strategy, we ran the statistical model checker to evaluate the following formula:

$$\phi_3 = \texttt{Pr[<=500] (<>TRAIN\_ATO.DONE) under safe}$$

UPPAAL STRATEGO executes 10617 runs and estimates the probability to be in the interval $[0.960561, 0.970561]$ with confidence 0.995. The probability distribution of this formula is depicted in Fig. 6. We conclude that the likelihood for the train to not reach its destination within 500 time units under the `safe` strategy is low, and it is mainly due to the possibility of large delays in communications. These delays are indeed the only source of stochastic behaviour in the model.

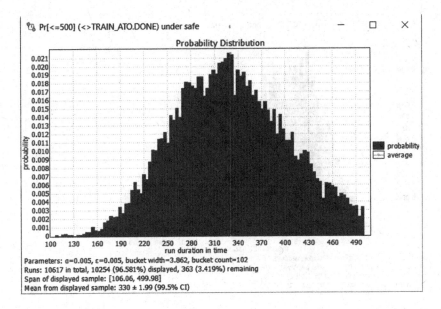

Fig. 6. Probability distribution for reaching the final destination under `safe` (ϕ_3)

We now show how UPPAAL STRATEGO can account for dependability parameters other than safety. In particular, reliability of the system can be related to the capacity of the train to reach its destination quickly. We optimise the safe strategy to minimise the arrival time, thus increasing its reliability whilst satisfying safety. This can be done with the following query, computed in 0.015 s using 580,844 KB of memory:

```
strategy  optsafe = minE (TRAIN_ATO.timer) [<=500] :
                 <> (TRAIN_ATO.DONE) under safe
```

This query creates a new strategy, called `optsafe`, that optimises the strategy `safe` by minimising the average value of the hybrid clock `timer` within 500 time units. Recall that this hybrid clock is used to measure the train's arrival time. The obtained strategy is thus both safe and it has an optimal speed for the train. To check this last improvement, we measure the average maximal arrival time under the strategies `safe` and `optsafe` with the following queries, respectively:

$$\phi_4 = E[<=700;10000] \text{ (max: TRAIN\_ATO.timer) under safe}$$
$$\phi_5 = E[<=700;10000] \text{ (max: TRAIN\_ATO.timer) under optsafe}$$

In particular, both queries run 10000 simulations with time bound of 700 time units. For the `safe` strategy, the estimated value is 338.473 ± 2.264. For the `optsafe` strategy, the estimated value is 331.362 ± 2.250. As expected, the optimised safe strategy has improved the arrival time of the safe strategy. The probability distribution of query ϕ_5 is depicted in Fig. 7.

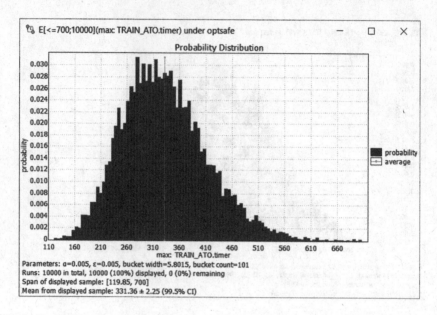

Fig. 7. Probability distribution for average maximal arrival time under optsafe (ϕ_5)

Sensitive Analysis of Maximal Headway. Up to this point, we evaluated the moving block railway signalling system under analysis with a specific parameter set-up. In this set-up, each time the train receives a fresh MA, its headway is reset to 5 (i.e. ma = 5). Thus, this is the maximal possible headway.

The parameters of the model can be tuned in such a way that the analysed properties are within a desired range of values. In particular, we hypothesise that reducing the maximal headway (i.e. ma) results in a deterioration in performance of the optimal strategy and in an increment of the probability of reaching a failure without strategy. Indeed, with a tight headway, the train is forced to move slowly in order not to exceed its MA. In the remainder of this section, we experimentally verify our hypothesis. Table 1 reports the evaluation of properties ϕ_1–ϕ_5 in three different experiments, with values for ma taken from the set $\{3, 5, 10\}$, reporting also the computation times and, where appropriate, the number of runs.

By reducing the maximal headway (i.e. ma = 3), we notice an overall deterioration of the average maximal arrival time (cf. properties ϕ_1, ϕ_4, and ϕ_5). Moreover, without strategy the probability of failure is higher when compared to ma = 5 (cf. property ϕ_2). These results confirm our hypothesis and further corroborate the reliability of our model.

As a final experiment, we enlarged the maximal headway (i.e. ma = 10) to evaluate the improvement in performance in case of a larger headway. We recall that a large headway is not desirable, since it would result in a lower capacity of the railway network. In this experiment, the values of ϕ_2 and ϕ_3 are similar to the case of ma = 5. However, by observing the values of ϕ_1, ϕ_4, and ϕ_5, we note that there is only a slight improvement in arrival time, even if we have doubled the maximal headway. This experiment confirms our intuition that an excessive increment of the maximal headway does not lead to a better performance. This is because the train cannot go faster than its optimal speed. On the converse, an excessive enlargement of the headway results in a deterioration of the overall track capacity. Hence, ma = 5 is a satisfactory set-up for the maximal headway.

Table 1. Three sets of experiments obtained by varying the ma parameter

Headway	Property				
	ϕ_1	ϕ_2	ϕ_3	ϕ_4	ϕ_5
ma = 3	402.869±4.449 14.7 s 708,084 KB	47683 runs [0.179862, 0.189862] 0.3 s 702,676 KB	11197 runs [0.958596, 0.968595] 0.078 s 823,396 KB	346.715± 2.189 28.25 s 823,580 KB	338.470±2.207 36.899 s 823,580 KB
ma = 5	377.235±3.960 14.518 s 38,200 KB	33952 runs [0.117029, 0.127029] 39.124 s 32,856 KB	10617 runs [0.960561, 0.970561] 17.003 s 580,764 KB	338.473±2.264 25.99 s 580,844 KB	331.362±2.250 34.241 s 580,868 KB
ma = 10	374.482±3.935 14.722 s 29,848 KB	32685 runs [0.111755, 0.121755] 0.172 s 30,232 KB	9520 runs [0.964259, 0.974258] 0.187 s 2,301,436 KB	337.087±2.274 26.998 s 2,301,504 KB	329.841±2.282 34.172 s 2,301,688 KB

6   Conclusion and Future Work

We have modelled and analysed an autonomous driving problem for a moving block railway signalling system. Communication between the train and the radio block centre are modelled such that the train is allowed to proceed only within the limits imposed by the radio block centre via the MA, which is based on the position of the train and updated continuously. The goal is to synthesise a strategy for the train to arrive to its destination as quickly as possible without exceeding its limits. We modelled the problem as a stochastic priced timed game. The controller is in charge of moving the train, playing against uncontrollable stochastic delays in communication. We used UPPAAL STRATEGO to compute a strategy to enforce safety in the model. The safe strategy was statistically model checked to evaluate the mean arrival time of the train. This quantity was optimised, and the optimised strategy was compared to the safe one. We observed an improvement in the mean arrival time, whilst retaining safety. As far as we know, this is the first application of synthesis techniques to autonomous driving for next generation railway signalling systems.

This was our first experience with strategy synthesis and optimisation of a case study from the railway domain and also with UPPAAL STRATEGO. Since this is a very recent tool there has not been much experimentation, in particular not outside of the groups involved in its development. The tool is still undergoing testing, and new versions and patches are released frequently. In fact, while developing the model we ran into corner cases that needed interactions with the developers team at Aalborg University. Those interactions led to the release of new versions, with patches fixing the issues discovered through our model.

We did have experience in modelling and analysing railway case studies with UPPAAL SMC [6,8,31]. The original model developed in [8] and statistically model checked had to be simplified considerably (cf. Sect. 4) to undergo strategy synthesis and verification. Indeed, while UPPAAL SMC scales to large systems by applying simulations rather than full state-space exploration, UPPAAL STRATEGO requires full state-space exploration of the timed game for strategy synthesis. For example, using the set-up discussed in Sect. 5 with ma = 10, if we double the constant arrive (i.e. 40 instead of 20) then during the strategy synthesis the tool terminates with an error message due to memory exhaustion.

An interesting future line of research would be to adapt the statistical synthesis techniques described in [16,35] to learn safety objectives, thus avoiding the full state-space exploration (as currently performed in UPPAAL STRATEGO) while guaranteeing the scalability of SMC. This would enable the modelling of more complex ERTMS case studies. Also, further experiments, with different set-ups of the parameters and more trains and radio block centres need to be performed, to investigate the limits of the approach described in this paper in terms of optimisation. Finally, we intend to discuss with our railway project partners the impact of the techniques discussed in this paper.

Acknowledgements. Funding by MIUR PRIN 2017FTXR7S project IT MaTTerS (Methods and Tools for Trustworthy Smart Systems) and H2020 project 4SECURail (FORmal Methods and CSIRT for the RAILway sector). The 4SECURail project received funding from the Shift2Rail Joint Undertaking under EU's H2020 research and innovation programme under grant agreement 881775.

We thank the UPPAAL developers team, in particular Danny Poulsen, Marius Mikucionis, and Peter Jensen, for their assistance with UPPAAL STRATEGO.

References

1. Agha, G., Palmskog, K.: A survey of statistical model checking. ACM Trans. Model. Comput. Simul. **28**(1), 1–39 (2018). https://doi.org/10.1145/3158668
2. Arcaini, P., Ježek, P., Kofron, J.: Modelling the hybrid ERTMS/ETCS level 3 case study in Spin. In: Butler et al. [18], pp. 277–291. https://doi.org/10.1007/978-3-319-91271-4_19
3. Thamilselvam, B., Kalyanasundaram, S., Rao, M.V.P.: Coordinated intelligent traffic lights using Uppaal Stratego. In: 2019 11th International Conference on Communication Systems & Networks (COMSNETS), pp. 789–794. IEEE (2019). https://doi.org/10.1109/COMSNETS.2019.8711457
4. Bao, R., Attiogbe, C., Delahaye, B., Fournier, P., Lime, D.: Parametric statistical model checking of UAV flight plan. In: Pérez, J.A., Yoshida, N. (eds.) FORTE 2019. LNCS, vol. 11535, pp. 57–74. Springer, Cham (2019). https://doi.org/10.1007/978-3-030-21759-4_4
5. Bartholomeus, M., Luttik, B., Willemse, T.: Modelling and analysing ERTMS hybrid level 3 with the mCRL2 toolset. In: Howar, F., Barnat, J. (eds.) FMICS 2018. LNCS, vol. 11119, pp. 98–114. Springer, Cham (2018). https://doi.org/10.1007/978-3-030-00244-2_7

6. Basile, D., ter Beek, M.H., Ciancia, V.: Statistical model checking of a moving block railway signalling scenario with UPPAAL SMC. In: Margaria, T., Steffen, B. (eds.) ISoLA 2018. LNCS, vol. 11245, pp. 372–391. Springer, Cham (2018). https://doi.org/10.1007/978-3-030-03421-4_24

7. Basile, D., et al.: On the industrial uptake of formal methods in the railway domain. In: Furia, C.A., Winter, K. (eds.) IFM 2018. LNCS, vol. 11023, pp. 20–29. Springer, Cham (2018). https://doi.org/10.1007/978-3-319-98938-9_2

8. Basile, D., ter Beek, M.H., Ferrari, A., Legay, A.: Modelling and analysing ERTMS L3 moving block railway signalling with Simulink and UPPAAL SMC. In: Larsen, K.G., Willemse, T. (eds.) FMICS 2019. LNCS, vol. 11687, pp. 1–21. Springer, Cham (2019). https://doi.org/10.1007/978-3-030-27008-7_1

9. Basu, A., Bensalem, S., Bozga, M., Caillaud, B., Delahaye, B., Legay, A.: Statistical abstraction and model-checking of large heterogeneous systems. In: Hatcliff, J., Zucca, E. (eds.) FMOODS/FORTE 2010. LNCS, vol. 6117, pp. 32–46. Springer, Heidelberg (2010). https://doi.org/10.1007/978-3-642-13464-7_4

10. ter Beek, M.H., et al.: Adopting formal methods in an industrial setting: the railways case. In: ter Beek, M.H., McIver, A., Oliveira, J.N. (eds.) FM 2019. LNCS, vol. 11800, pp. 762–772. Springer, Cham (2019). https://doi.org/10.1007/978-3-030-30942-8_46

11. ter Beek, M.H., Gnesi, S., Knapp, A.: Formal methods for transport systems. Int. J. Softw. Tools Technol. Transf. 20(3), 237–241 (2018). https://doi.org/10.1007/s10009-018-0487-4

12. Behrmann, G., et al.: UPPAAL 4.0. In: Quantitative Evaluation of Systems (QEST), pp. 125–126. IEEE (2006). https://doi.org/10.1109/QEST.2006.59

13. Behrmann, G., Cougnard, A., David, A., Fleury, E., Larsen, K.G., Lime, D.: UPPAAL-Tiga: time for playing games!. In: Damm, W., Hermanns, H. (eds.) CAV 2007. LNCS, vol. 4590, pp. 121–125. Springer, Heidelberg (2007). https://doi.org/10.1007/978-3-540-73368-3_14

14. Berger, U., James, P., Lawrence, A., Roggenbach, M., Seisenberger, M.: Verification of the European rail traffic management system in Real-Time Maude. Sci. Comput. Program. 154, 61–88 (2018). https://doi.org/10.1016/j.scico.2017.10.011

15. Biagi, M., Carnevali, L., Paolieri, M., Vicario, E.: Performability evaluation of the ERTMS/ETCS - level 3. Transp. Res. C Emerg. Technol. 82, 314–336 (2017). https://doi.org/10.1016/j.trc.2017.07.002

16. Bønneland, F., Jensen, P., Larsen, K.G., Muñiz, M., Srba, J.: Partial order reduction for reachability games. In: 30th International Conference on Concurrency Theory (CONCUR 2019). LIPIcs, vol. 140, pp. 1–15 (2019). https://doi.org/10.4230/LIPIcs.CONCUR.2019.23

17. Boulanger, J.L. (ed.): Formal Methods Applied to Industrial Complex Systems - Implementation of the B Method. Wiley, New York (2014). https://doi.org/10.1002/9781119002727

18. Butler, M., Raschke, A., Hoang, T.S., Reichl, K. (eds.): ABZ 2018. LNCS, vol. 10817. Springer, Cham (2018). https://doi.org/10.1007/978-3-319-91271-4

19. Cappart, Q., Limbrée, C., Schaus, P., Quilbeuf, J., Traonouez, L., Legay, A.: Verification of interlocking systems using statistical model checking. In: 2017 IEEE 18th International Symposium on High Assurance Systems Engineering (HASE), pp. 61–68. IEEE (2017). https://doi.org/10.1109/HASE.2017.10

20. Cassez, F., David, A., Fleury, E., Larsen, K.G., Lime, D.: Efficient on-the-fly algorithms for the analysis of timed games. In: Abadi, M., de Alfaro, L. (eds.) CONCUR 2005. LNCS, vol. 3653, pp. 66–80. Springer, Heidelberg (2005). https://doi.org/10.1007/11539452_9

21. Cunha, A., Macedo, N.: Validating the hybrid ERTMS/ETCS level 3 concept with Electrum. In: Butler et al. [18], pp. 307–321. https://doi.org/10.1007/978-3-319-91271-4_21

22. David, A., Larsen, K.G., Legay, A., Mikučionis, M., Poulsen, D.B.: Uppaal SMC tutorial. Int. J. Softw. Tools Technol. Transf. 17(4), 397–415 (2015). https://doi.org/10.1007/s10009-014-0361-y

23. David, A., et al.: On time with minimal expected cost!. In: Cassez, F., Raskin, J.-F. (eds.) ATVA 2014. LNCS, vol. 8837, pp. 129–145. Springer, Cham (2014). https://doi.org/10.1007/978-3-319-11936-6_10

24. David, A., Jensen, P.G., Larsen, K.G., Mikučionis, M., Taankvist, J.H.: UPPAAL STRATEGO. In: Baier, C., Tinelli, C. (eds.) TACAS 2015. LNCS, vol. 9035, pp. 206–211. Springer, Heidelberg (2015). https://doi.org/10.1007/978-3-662-46681-0_16

25. Dghaym, D., Poppleton, M., Snook, C.: Diagram-led formal modelling using iUML-B for hybrid ERTMS level 3. In: Butler et al. [18], pp. 338–352. https://doi.org/10.1007/978-3-319-91271-4_23

26. ERTMS/ETCS RAMS Requirements Specification - Chap. 2 - RAM, 30 September 1998. http://www.era.europa.eu/Document-Register/Documents/B1-02s1266-.pdf

27. Fantechi, A.: Twenty-five years of formal methods and railways: what next? In: Counsell, S., Núñez, M. (eds.) SEFM 2013. LNCS, vol. 8368, pp. 167–183. Springer, Cham (2014). https://doi.org/10.1007/978-3-319-05032-4_13

28. Fantechi, A., Ferrari, A., Gnesi, S.: Formal methods and safety certification: challenges in the railways domain. In: Margaria, T., Steffen, B. (eds.) ISoLA 2016. LNCS, vol. 9953, pp. 261–265. Springer, Cham (2016). https://doi.org/10.1007/978-3-319-47169-3_18

29. Fantechi, A., Fokkink, W., Morzenti, A.: Some trends in formal methods applications to railway signaling. In: Gnesi, S., Margaria, T. (eds.) Formal Methods for Industrial Critical Systems: A Survey of Applications, Chap. 4, pp. 61–84. Wiley, New York (2013). https://doi.org/10.1002/9781118459898.ch4

30. Ferrari, A., Fantechi, A., Gnesi, S., Magnani, G.: Model-based development and formal methods in the railway industry. IEEE Softw. 30(3), 28–34 (2013). https://doi.org/10.1109/MS.2013.44

31. Ferrari, A., Mazzanti, F., Basile, D., ter Beek, M.H., Fantechi, A.: Comparing formal tools for system design: a judgment study. In: ICSE. ACM (2020). https://doi.org/10.1145/3377811.3380373

32. Furness, N., van Houten, H., Arenas, L., Bartholomeus, M.: ERTMS level 3: the game-changer. IRSE News 232, 2–9 (2017). https://www.irse.nl/resources/170314-ERTMS-L3-The-gamechanger-from-IRSE-News-Issue-232.pdf

33. Hansen, D., et al.: Validation and real-life demonstration of ETCS hybrid level 3 principles using a formal B model. Int. J. Softw. Tools Technol. Transf. 22(3), 315–332 (2020). https://doi.org/10.1007/s10009-020-00551-6

34. Haxthausen, A.E., Hede, K.: Formal verification of railway timetables - using the UPPAAL model checker. In: ter Beek, M.H., Fantechi, A., Semini, L. (eds.) From Software Engineering to Formal Methods and Tools, and Back. LNCS, vol. 11865, pp. 433–448. Springer, Cham (2019). https://doi.org/10.1007/978-3-030-30985-5_25

35. Jaeger, M., Jensen, P.G., Guldstrand Larsen, K., Legay, A., Sedwards, S., Taankvist, J.H.: Teaching stratego to play ball: optimal synthesis for continuous space MDPs. In: Chen, Y.-F., Cheng, C.-H., Esparza, J. (eds.) ATVA 2019. LNCS, vol. 11781, pp. 81–97. Springer, Cham (2019). https://doi.org/10.1007/978-3-030-31784-3_5

36. Jansen, D.N., Hermanns, H.: Dependability checking with StoCharts: is train radio reliable enough for trains? In: First International Conference on the Quantitative Evaluation of Systems, pp. 250–259. IEEE (2004). https://doi.org/10.1109/QEST.2004.1348039

37. Karra, S.L., Larsen, K.G., Lorber, F., Srba, J.: Safe and time-optimal control for railway games. In: Collart-Dutilleul, S., Lecomte, T., Romanovsky, A. (eds.) RSSRail 2019. LNCS, vol. 11495, pp. 106–122. Springer, Cham (2019). https://doi.org/10.1007/978-3-030-18744-6_7

38. Larsen, K.G., Mikučionis, M., Taankvist, J.H.: Safe and optimal adaptive cruise control. In: Meyer, R., Platzer, A., Wehrheim, H. (eds.) Correct System Design. LNCS, vol. 9360, pp. 260–277. Springer, Cham (2015). https://doi.org/10.1007/978-3-319-23506-6_17

39. Legay, A., Delahaye, B., Bensalem, S.: Statistical model checking: an overview. In: Barringer, H., Falcone, Y., Finkbeiner, B., Havelund, K., Lee, I., Pace, G., Roşu, G., Sokolsky, O., Tillmann, N. (eds.) RV 2010. LNCS, vol. 6418, pp. 122–135. Springer, Heidelberg (2010). https://doi.org/10.1007/978-3-642-16612-9_11

40. Mammar, A., Frappier, M., Tueno Fotso, S.J., Laleau, R.: An Event-B model of the Hybrid ERTMS/ETCS level 3 standard. In: Butler et al. [18], pp. 353–366. https://doi.org/10.1007/978-3-319-91271-4_24

41. Mazzanti, F., Ferrari, A.: Ten diverse formal models for a CBTC automatic train supervision system. In: MARS/VPT. EPTCS, vol. 268, pp. 104–149 (2018). https://doi.org/10.4204/EPTCS.268.4

42. Mazzanti, F., Ferrari, A., Spagnolo, G.O.: Towards formal methods diversity in railways: an experience report with seven frameworks. Int. J. Softw. Tools Technol. Transf. **20**(3), 263–288 (2018). https://doi.org/10.1007/s10009-018-0488-3

43. Nardone, R., et al.: Modeling railway control systems in Promela. In: Artho, C., Ölveczky, P.C. (eds.) FTSCS 2015. CCIS, vol. 596, pp. 121–136. Springer, Cham (2016). https://doi.org/10.1007/978-3-319-29510-7_7

44. Rispoli, F., Castorina, M., Neri, A., Filip, A., Di Mambro, G., Senesi, F.: Recent progress in application of GNSS and advanced communications for railway signaling. In: 2013 23rd International Conference Radioelektronika (RADIOELEKTRONIKA), pp. 13–22. IEEE (2013). https://doi.org/10.1109/RadioElek.2013.6530882

45. UNISIG: FIS for the RBC/RBC handover, 15 June 2016. http://www.era.europa.eu/Document-Register/Pages/set-2-FIS-for-the-RBC-RBC-handover.aspx

Towards Bridging Time and Causal Reversibility

Marco Bernardo and Claudio Antares Mezzina[✉]

Dipartimento di Scienze Pure e Applicate, Università di Urbino, Urbino, Italy
`claudio.mezzina@uniurb.it`

Abstract. Causal consistent reversibility blends causality and reversibility. For a concurrent system, it says that an action can be undone provided this has no consequences, thereby making it possible to bring the system back to a past consistent state. Time reversibility is considered instead in the performance evaluation field. A continuous-time Markov chain is time reversible if its behavior remains the same when the direction of time is reversed. We try to bridge these two theories by showing the conditions under which both causal consistent reversibility and time reversibility can be achieved in the setting of a stochastic process algebra.

1 Introduction

The interest into computation reversibility dates back to the 60's, when it was observed that irreversible computations cause heat dissipation into circuits [16]. This suggested that low energy consumption could be achieved by resorting to *reversible computing*, in which there is no information loss [3]. Nowadays, reversible computing has several applications ranging from biochemical reactions [29,30] and parallel discrete-event simulation [27,32] to robotics [22], control theory [33], fault tolerant systems [6,17,35,36], and program debugging [7,20].

In a reversible system, we can observe two directions of computation: a *forward* one, coinciding with the normal way of computing, and a *backward* one, which is able to undo the effects of the forward one. In the literature, there exist different meanings of reversibility. For instance, in a Petri net model reversibility means that one can always reach the initial marking [2], while in distributed systems it amounts to the capability of returning to a past consistent state [5]. In contrast, in the performance evaluation field, reversibility is intended as time reversibility and is instrumental to develop efficient analysis methods [13].

Our focus is on the relationship between *causal consistent reversibility* and *time reversibility*, from a process algebraic perspective. On the one hand, quantitative aspects have been disregarded in the setting of causal consistent reversibility. On the other hand, the theory of time reversibility has been applied to concurrent systems without explicitly taking causality into account.

In this paper, instead, we aim at bridging these two theories, by showing how causal consistent reversibility and time reversibility can be jointly obtained.

© IFIP International Federation for Information Processing 2020
Published by Springer Nature Switzerland AG 2020
A. Gotsman and A. Sokolova (Eds.): FORTE 2020, LNCS 12136, pp. 22–38, 2020.
https://doi.org/10.1007/978-3-030-50086-3_2

To this purpose, we consider a stochastic process calculus in which every action is equipped with a positive real number expressing the rate at which the action is executed. As is well known in the literature [10], the stochastic process underlying the calculus turns out to be a continuous-time Markov chain (CTMC) [14].

The contribution of this paper is twofold. Firstly, we apply for the first time the technique of [28] to a stochastic process calculus. In particular, we provide forward and backward operational semantic rules – featuring forward and backward actions and rates – and then we show that the resulting calculus is causal consistent reversible. This is accomplished by importing from the reduction semantics setting of [5] the notion of concurrent transitions, which is new in the structural operational semantics framework of [28].

Secondly, after observing that the CTMC underlying the calculus is stationary, we show that time reversibility can be achieved by using, in the operational semantic rules, backward rates equal to the corresponding forward rates. This is quite different from the approaches followed for example in [8,25], where time reversibility is addressed a posteriori, as we instead obtain a calculus in which time reversibility can be guaranteed by construction.

This paper is organized as follows. In Sects. 2 and 3 we recall background information about causal consistent reversibility and time reversibility, respectively. Then, in Sect. 4 we provide and illustrate our results about the integration of these two forms of reversibility in the considered stochastic process calculus. Finally, in Sect. 5 we conclude with some directions for future work.

2   Causal Consistent Reversibility

Reversibility in a system means the possibility of reverting the last performed action. In a sequential system, this is very simple as there exists just one last action. In a concurrent system, the situation is more complex as there is no clear definition of last action. Indeed, there might be several concurrent last actions. One could resort to timestamps to decide which action is the last one, but having synchronised clocks in a distributed system is rather difficult.

A good approximation is to consider as last action each action that has not caused any other action yet. This is at the basis of the so called *causal consistent reversibility* [5], which relates reversibility with causality. Intuitively, the definition says that, in a concurrent system, any action can be undone provided that all of its consequences, if any, are undone beforehand.

In the process algebra literature, there are two reversible variants of CCS [26]. The first one in time order, RCCS [5], uses stack-based memories attached to processes to record all the actions executed by the processes themselves. In contrast, [28] proposes a general method, of which CCSK is a result, to reverse calculi whose operational semantic rules are expressed in the path format [1]. The basic idea of this method is to make all the operators of the calculus static and to univocally identify each executed action with a communication key. Note that, since dynamic operators such as prefixing and choice are forgetful by definition, making them static avoids information loss during a reduction.

Despite these two approaches may seem different, they have been shown to be equivalent in terms of labeled transition system isomorphism [18]. The approach of [5] is more suitable for systems whose operational semantics is given in terms of reduction semantics, hence its application is to be preferred in the case of very expressive calculi [4,19] as well as programming languages [21,24]. On the other hand, the approach of [28] is very handy when it comes to deal with labeled transition systems and CCS-like calculi, which is the case of this paper.

For example, given the process $P + Q$, from $P \xrightarrow{\alpha} P'$ we derive $P + Q \xrightarrow{\alpha} P'$. If we assume the possibility of reverting action α, i.e., $P' \xrightarrow{\alpha_r} P$, we have that P' gets back to a state in which the information about the choice operator and Q is lost. To avoid this, in [28] $+ Q$ is treated as a dead decoration of process P'. In this way, the use of explicit memories of [5] is avoided because the necessary information is syntactically maintained within processes.

3   Time Reversibility

In the field of performance evaluation, a different notion of reversibility, called *time reversibility*, is considered. We illustrate it in the specific case of continuous-time Markov chains, which are discrete-state stochastic processes characterized by the *memoryless property* [14].

A *stochastic process* describes the evolution of some random phenomenon over time through a set of random variables, one for each time instant. A stochastic process $X(t)$ taking values into a discrete state space $\mathcal{S}$ for $t \in \mathbb{R}_{\geq 0}$ is a *continuous-time Markov chain (CTMC)* iff for all $n \in \mathbb{N}$, time instants $t_0 < t_1 < \cdots < t_n < t_{n+1} \in \mathbb{R}_{\geq 0}$, and states $s_0, s_1, \ldots, s_n, s_{n+1} \in \mathcal{S}$ it holds that $\Pr\{X(t_{n+1}) = s_{n+1} \mid X(t_i) = s_i, 0 \leq i \leq n\} = \Pr\{X(t_{n+1}) = s_{n+1} \mid X(t_n) = s_n\}$, i.e., the probability of moving from one state to another does not depend on the particular path that has been followed in the past to reach the current state, hence that path can be forgotten.

A CTMC is *irreducible* iff each of its states can be reached from every other state. A state $s \in \mathcal{S}$ is *recurrent* iff the CTMC will eventually return to s with probability 1, in which case s is called *positive recurrent* iff the expected number of steps until the CTMC returns to it is finite. A CTMC is *ergodic* iff it is irreducible and all of its states are positive recurrent; ergodicity coincides with irreducibility in the case that the CTMC has finitely many states.

A CTMC can be represented as a labeled transition system or as a state-indexed matrix. In the first case, each transition is labeled with some probabilistic information describing the evolution from its source state to its target state. In the second case, the same information is stored into an entry, indexed by those two states, of a matrix. The value of this probabilistic information is, in general, a function of the time at which the state change takes place.

For the sake of simplicity, we restrict ourselves to *time-homogeneous* CTMCs, in which conditional probabilities of the form $\Pr\{X(t + t') = s' \mid X(t) = s\}$ do not depend on t, so that the considered information is simply a positive real number. This is called the *rate* at which the CTMC moves from state s to state s' and uniquely characterizes the exponentially distributed time taken by the considered move. It can be shown that the sojourn time in any state $s \in \mathcal{S}$ is exponentially distributed with rate given by the sum of the rates of the moves of s. The average sojourn time in s is the inverse of such a sum and the probability of moving from s to s' is proportional to the corresponding rate.

Every time-homogeneous, ergodic CTMC $X(t)$ is *stationary*, which means that $(X(t_i + t'))_{1 \leq i \leq n}$ has the same joint distribution as $(X(t_i))_{1 \leq i \leq n}$ for all $n \in \mathbb{N}_{\geq 1}$ and $t_1 < \cdots < t_n, t' \in \mathbb{R}_{\geq 0}$. Specifically, $X(t)$ has a unique *steady-state probability distribution* π that for all $s \in \mathcal{S}$ fulfills $\pi(s) = \lim_{t \to \infty} \Pr\{X(t) = s \mid X(0) = s'\}$ for any $s' \in \mathcal{S}$. These probabilities can be computed by solving the linear system of *global balance equations* $\pi \cdot \mathbf{Q} = \mathbf{0}$ subject to $\sum_{s \in \mathcal{S}} \pi(s) = 1$ and $\pi(s) \in \mathbb{R}_{>0}$ for all $s \in \mathcal{S}$. The *infinitesimal generator matrix* $\mathbf{Q}$ contains for each pair of distinct states the rate of the corresponding move, which is 0 in the absence of a direct move between them, with $q_{s,s} = -\sum_{s' \neq s} q_{s,s'}$ for all $s \in \mathcal{S}$ so that every row of $\mathbf{Q}$ sums up to 0.

Due to state space explosion and numerical stability problems [34], the calculation of the solution of the global balance equation system is not always feasible. However, it can be tackled in the case that the behavior of the considered CTMC remains the same when the direction of time is reversed. A CTMC $X(t)$ is *time reversible* iff $(X(t_i))_{1 \leq i \leq n}$ has the same joint distribution as $(X(t' - t_i))_{1 \leq i \leq n}$ for all $n \in \mathbb{N}_{\geq 1}$ and $t_1 < \cdots < t_n, t' \in \mathbb{R}_{\geq 0}$, in which case $X(t)$ and its reversed version $X^{\mathrm{r}}(t) = X(t' - t)$ are stochastically identical; in particular, $X(t)$ and $X^{\mathrm{r}}(t)$ share the same steady-state probability distribution π if any. In order for a stationary CTMC $X(t)$ to be time reversible, it is necessary and sufficient that the *partial balance equations* $\pi(s) \cdot q_{s,s'} = \pi(s') \cdot q_{s',s}$ are satisfied for all $s, s' \in \mathcal{S}$ such that $s \neq s'$ or, equivalently, that $q_{s_1,s_2} \cdot \ldots \cdot q_{s_{n-1},s_n} \cdot q_{s_n,s_1} = q_{s_1,s_n} \cdot q_{s_n,s_{n-1}} \cdot \ldots \cdot q_{s_2,s_1}$ for all $n \in \mathbb{N}_{\geq 2}$ and distinct $s_1, \ldots, s_n \in \mathcal{S}$ [13].

Time reversibility of CTMC-based compositional models of concurrent systems has been investigated in [8]. More precisely, conditions relying on the conservation of total exit rates of states and of rate products around cycles are examined, which support the hierarchical and compositional reversal of stochastic process algebra terms. These conditions also lead to the efficient calculation of steady-state probability distributions in a product form typical of queueing theory [15], thus avoiding the need of solving the global balance equation system. More recently, in [25] similar conditions have been employed to characterize the class of ρ-reversible stochastic automata. Under certain constraints, the joint steady-state probability distribution of the composition of two such automata is the product of the steady-state probability distributions of the two automata.

4   Integrating Causal and Time Reversibility

In this section, we integrate the two concepts of causal consistent reversibility and time reversibility recalled in the previous two sections. To do so, we start with a simple calculus called RMPC – Reversible Markovian Process Calculus, in which actions are paired with rates, whose syntax and semantics are inspired by the approach of [28]. Then, we show that the reversibility induced by RMPC is causal consistent by importing the notion of concurrent transitions from [5]. Finally, we exhibit the conditions under which time reversibility is achieved too and we compare our setting, in which time reversibility is ensured by construction, with those of [8, 25].

4.1 Syntax and Semantics for RMPC

The syntax of RMPC is shown in Table 1. A *forward process* P can be one of the following: the idle process $\mathbf{0}$; the prefixed process $(a, \lambda).P$, which is able to perform an action a at rate λ and then continues as process P; the nondeterministic choice $P + Q$ between processes P and Q; or the cooperation $P \parallel_L Q$, indicating that processes P and Q execute in parallel and must synchronise only on actions prescribed by the set L.

A *reversible process* R is built on top of forward processes. As in [28], the syntax of reversible processes differs from the one of forward processes by the fact that in the former each prefix (a, λ) can be decorated with a *communication key* i thus becoming $(a, \lambda)[i]$. A process of the form $(a, \lambda)[i].R$ expresses that in the past the process synchronised with the environment and this synchronisation was identified by key i. Keys are thus attached only to already executed actions.

Table 1. Syntax of RMPC forward/standard/initial processes and reversible processes

$$P, Q ::= \mathbf{0} \mid (a, \lambda).P \mid P + Q \mid P \parallel_L Q$$
$$R, S ::= P \mid (a, \lambda)[i].R \mid R + S \mid R \parallel_L S$$

Let $\mathcal{A}$ be the set of actions such that $a, b \in \mathcal{A}$, $\mathcal{R} = \mathbb{R}_{>0}$ be the set of rates such that $\lambda, \mu \in \mathcal{R}$, and $\mathcal{K}$ be the set of keys such that $i, j \in \mathcal{K}$. Let $\mathcal{L} = \mathcal{A} \times \mathcal{R} \times \mathcal{K}$ be the set of labels each formed by an action, a rate, and a communication key. We let ℓ and its decorated versions range over $\mathcal{L}$. Moreover, given a forward label $\ell = (a, \lambda)[i]$, we denote by $\bar{\ell} = (a, \overline{\lambda})[i]$ the corresponding backward label. Finally, $\mathcal{P}$ is the set of processes generated by the production for R in Table 1.

Definition 1 (standard process). *Process $R \in \mathcal{P}$ is standard, written* $\mathrm{std}(R)$, *iff it can be derived from the production for P in Table 1.*

Definition 2 (process key). *The set of keys of process $R \in \mathcal{P}$, written* $\mathrm{key}(R)$, *is inductively defined as follows:*

$$\mathrm{key}(P) = \emptyset \qquad\qquad \mathrm{key}((a, \lambda)[i].R) = \{i\} \cup \mathrm{key}(R)$$
$$\mathrm{key}(R + S) = \mathrm{key}(R) \cup \mathrm{key}(S) \qquad \mathrm{key}(R \parallel_L S) = \mathrm{key}(R) \cup \mathrm{key}(S)$$

The semantics for RMPC is defined as a labeled transition system $(\mathcal{P}, \mathcal{L}, \mapsto)$. Like in [28], the transition relation $\mapsto \subseteq \mathcal{P} \times \mathcal{L} \times \mathcal{P}$ is given by $\rightarrow \cup \rightsquigarrow$, where

Table 2. Structural operational semantic rules for RMPC

$$\text{ACT1} \ \frac{\mathtt{std}(R)}{(a,\lambda).R \xrightarrow{(a,\lambda)[i]} (a,\lambda)[i].R} \qquad \text{ACT1}^{\bullet} \ \frac{\mathtt{std}(R)}{(a,\lambda)[i].R \overset{(a,\overline{\lambda})[i]}{\rightsquigarrow} (a,\lambda).R}$$

$$\text{ACT2} \ \frac{R \xrightarrow{(b,\mu)[j]} R' \quad j \neq i}{(a,\lambda)[i].R \xrightarrow{(b,\mu)[j]} (a,\lambda)[i].R'} \qquad \text{ACT2}^{\bullet} \ \frac{R \overset{(b,\overline{\mu})[j]}{\rightsquigarrow} R' \quad j \neq i}{(a,\lambda)[i].R \overset{(b,\overline{\mu})[j]}{\rightsquigarrow} (a,\lambda)[i].R'}$$

$$\text{CHO} \ \frac{R \xrightarrow{(a,\lambda)[i]} R' \quad \mathtt{std}(S)}{R+S \xrightarrow{(a,\lambda)[i]} R'+S} \qquad \text{CHO}^{\bullet} \ \frac{R \overset{(a,\overline{\lambda})[i]}{\rightsquigarrow} R' \quad \mathtt{std}(S)}{R+S \overset{(a,\overline{\lambda})[i]}{\rightsquigarrow} R'+S}$$

$$\text{PAR} \ \frac{R \xrightarrow{(a,\lambda)[i]} R' \quad a \notin L \quad i \notin \mathtt{key}(S)}{R \parallel_L S \xrightarrow{(a,\lambda)[i]} R' \parallel_L S} \qquad \text{PAR}^{\bullet} \ \frac{R \overset{(a,\overline{\lambda})[i]}{\rightsquigarrow} R' \quad a \notin L \quad i \notin \mathtt{key}(S)}{R \parallel_L S \overset{(a,\overline{\lambda})[i]}{\rightsquigarrow} R' \parallel_L S}$$

$$\text{COO} \ \frac{R \xrightarrow{(a,\lambda)[i]} R' \quad S \xrightarrow{(a,\mu)[i]} S' \quad a \in L}{R \parallel_L S \xrightarrow{(a,\lambda\cdot\mu)[i]} R' \parallel_L S'} \qquad \text{COO}^{\bullet} \ \frac{R \overset{(a,\overline{\lambda})[i]}{\rightsquigarrow} R' \quad S \overset{(a,\overline{\mu})[i]}{\rightsquigarrow} S' \quad a \in L}{R \parallel_L S \overset{(a,\overline{\lambda\cdot\mu})[i]}{\rightsquigarrow} R' \parallel_L S'}$$

the *forward transition relation* $\rightarrow$ and the *backward transition relation* $\rightsquigarrow$ are the least relations respectively induced by the forward rules in the left part and the backward rules in the right part of Table 2.

Rule ACT1 deals with prefixed processes of the form $(a,\lambda).P$, with P written as R subject to $\mathtt{std}(R)$. In addition to transforming the action prefix into a transition label, it generates a fresh key i, which is bound to the action (a,λ) thus yielding the label $(a,\lambda)[i]$. As we can note, the prefix is not discarded by the application of the rule, instead it becomes a key-storing decoration in the target process. Rule ACT1$^{\bullet}$ reverts the action $(a,\lambda)[i]$ of the process $(a,\lambda)[i].R$ provided that R is a standard process, which ensures that $(a,\lambda)[i]$ is the only past action that is left to undo. One of the main design choices of the entire framework is how the rate $\overline{\lambda}$ of the backward action is calculated. For the time being, we leave it unspecified in ACT1$^{\bullet}$ as the value of this rate is not necessary to prove the causal consistency part of reversibility, but as we will see later on it is important in the proof of time reversibility.

The presence of rules ACT2 and ACT2$^{\bullet}$ is motivated by the fact that rule ACT1 does not discard the executed prefix from the process it generates. In particular, rule ACT2 allows a prefixed process $(a,\lambda)[i].R$ to execute if R can itself execute, provided that the action performed by R picks a key j different from i. Rule ACT2$^{\bullet}$ simply propagates the execution of backward actions from inner subprocesses that are not standard as long as key uniqueness is preserved.

Unlike the classical rules of the choice operator [26], rule CHO does not discard the context, i.e., the part of the process that has not contributed to the action. More in detail, if the process $R+S$ does an action, say $(a,\lambda)[i]$, and becomes R', then the entire process becomes $R' + S$. In this way, the information about $+ S$ is preserved. Furthermore, since S is a standard process because of the premise $\mathtt{std}(S)$, it will never execute even if it is present in the process $R' + S$. Hence, the $+ S$ can be seen as a decoration, or a dead context, of process R. Note that, in order to apply rule CHO, at least one of the two processes has to be standard, meaning that it is impossible for two non-standard processes to execute if they are composed by a choice operator. Rule CHO$^\bullet$ has precisely the same structure as rule CHO, but uses the backward transition relation. For both rules, we omit their symmetric variants in which it is S to move.

The semantics of cooperation is inspired by [11]. Rule PAR allows process R within $R \parallel_L S$ to individually perform an action $(a, \lambda)[i]$, provided that $a \notin L$. Rule COO allows R and S to cooperate through any action in the set L, provided that the communication key is the same on both sides. For the sake of simplicity, the rate of the cooperation action is assumed to be the product of the rates of the two involved actions [9]. Rules PAR$^\bullet$ and COO$^\bullet$ respectively have the same structure as PAR and COO; the symmetric variants of PAR and PAR$^\bullet$ are omitted.

Not all the processes generated by the grammar in Table 1 are meaningful as, e.g., there might be several action prefixes sharing the same key in a sequential process, i.e., a process without occurrences of the cooperation operator. We only consider processes that are initial or reachable in the following sense:

Definition 3 (initial and reachable process). *Process $R \in \mathcal{P}$ is initial iff $\mathtt{std}(R)$ holds. Process $R \in \mathcal{P}$ is reachable iff it is initial or can be derived from an initial one via finitely many applications of the rules for $\to$ in Table 2.*

4.2   Properties Preliminary to Reversibility

A basic property to satisfy in order for RMPC to be reversible is the so called loop lemma [5,28], which will be exploited to establish both causal consistent reversibility and time reversibility. This property states that each transition of a reachable process can be undone. Formally:

Lemma 1 (loop lemma). *Let $R \in \mathcal{P}$ be a reachable process. Then $R \xrightarrow{(a,\lambda)[i]} S$ iff $S \xrightsquigarrow{(a,\overline{\lambda})[i]} R$.*

Proof. We proceed by induction on the depth of the derivation of $R \xrightarrow{(a,\lambda)[i]} S$ (resp., $S \xrightsquigarrow{(a,\overline{\lambda})[i]} R$), by noticing that for each forward (resp., backward) rule there exists a corresponding backward (resp., forward) one. ∎

The lemma generalizes as follows. For any sequence σ of $n \in \mathbb{N}_{>0}$ labels $\ell_1, \ldots, \ell_n$, let $R \xrightarrow{\sigma} S$ be the corresponding *forward* sequence of transitions $R \xrightarrow{\ell_1} R_1 \xrightarrow{\ell_2} \cdots \xrightarrow{\ell_n} S$ and $\overline{\sigma}$ be the corresponding *backward* sequence such that, for each ℓ_i occurring in σ, it holds that $R_{i-1} \xrightarrow{\ell_i} R_i$ iff $R_i \xrightsquigarrow{\overline{\ell_i}} R_{i-1}$. A direct consequence of the loop lemma is the following:

Corollary 1. *Let $R \in \mathcal{P}$ be a reachable process. Then $R \xmapsto{\sigma} S$ iff $S \xmapsto{\overline{\sigma}} R$.*

4.3 Causal Consistent Reversibility for RMPC

In order to prove the causal consistent reversibility of RMPC, we borrow some machinery from [5] that needs to be adapted as the reversing method of [28] we are using is different from the one of [5]. In particular, we import the notion of concurrent transitions.

Given a transition $\theta : R \overset{\ell}{\mapsto} S$ with $R, S \in \mathcal{P}$ reachable processes, we call R the *source* of θ and S its *target*. Two transitions are said to be *coinitial* if they have the same source, and *cofinal* if they have the same target. A sequence of pairwise composable transitions is called a *computation*, where *composable* means that the target of any transition in the sequence is the source of the next transition. We let θ and its decorated variants range over transitions, while ω and its decorated variants range over computations. If θ is a forward transition, i.e., $\theta : R \overset{\ell}{\to} S$, we denote its backward version $S \overset{\underline{\ell}}{\to} R$ as $\overline{\theta}$. The notions of source, target, and composability extend naturally to computations. We indicate with ϵ_R the empty computation whose source is R and with $\omega_1; \omega_2$ the composition of two composable computations ω_1 and ω_2.

Before specifying when two transitions are concurrent, we need to define the set of causes – identified by keys – of a given communication key.

Definition 4 (causal set). *Let $R \in \mathcal{P}$ be a reachable process and $i \in \text{key}(R)$. The causal set $\text{cau}(R, i)$ is inductively defined as follows for $j \neq i$:*

$$\text{cau}((a, \lambda)[i].R, i) = \emptyset$$
$$\text{cau}((a, \lambda)[j].R, i) = \{j\} \cup \text{cau}(R, i)$$
$$\text{cau}(R + S, i) \doteq \text{cau}'(R, i) \cup \text{cau}'(S, i)$$
$$\text{cau}(R \parallel_L S, i) = \text{cau}'(R, i) \cup \text{cau}'(S, i)$$

where $\text{cau}'(R, i) = \text{cau}(R, i)$ if $i \in \text{key}(R)$ and $\text{cau}'(R, i) = \emptyset$ otherwise.

If $i \in \text{key}(R)$, then $\text{cau}(R, i)$ represents the set of keys in R that caused i, with $\text{cau}(R, i) \subset \text{key}(R)$ since $i \notin \text{cau}(R, i)$ and keys not causally related to i are not considered. A key j causes i if it appears syntactically before i in R or, said otherwise, i is inside the scope of j. We are now in place to define what we mean by concurrent transitions:

Definition 5 (concurrent transitions). *Two coinitial transitions θ_1 and θ_2 from a reachable process $R \in \mathcal{P}$ are in conflict iff one of the following holds:*

1. *$\theta_1 : R \xrightarrow{(a, \lambda)[j]} S_1$ and $\theta_2 : R \overset{(b, \overline{\mu})[i]}{\rightsquigarrow} S_2$ with $i \in \text{cau}(S_1, j)$.*
2. *$R = R_1 + R_2$ with θ_k deriving from $R_k \xrightarrow{(a_k, \lambda_k)[i_k]} S_k$ for $k = 1, 2$.*

Two coinitial transitions are concurrent when they are not in conflict.

The first condition above just tells that a forward transition is in conflict with a backward one whenever the latter tries to undo a cause of the key of the former. The second condition deems as conflictual two transitions respectively generated by the two subprocesses of a choice operator. Figure 1 shows two related examples. In the first case, the process $(a, \lambda)[i].(b, \mu).P$ can perform two transitions: a backward one and a forward one. They meet the first condition of Definition 5 as the backward transition removes the key i that is in the causal set of j. In the second case, we have that process $(a, \lambda).P + (a, \lambda).P$ is able to trigger two forward transitions. Since they arise from the same choice operator, they are in conflict according to the second condition of Definition 5.

Remark 1. It is worth noting that in a stochastic process calculus like RMPC the semantic treatment of the choice operator is problematic [10] because a process of the form $(a, \lambda).P + (a, \lambda).P$ should produce either a single a-transition whose rate is $\lambda + \lambda$, or two a-transitions each having rate λ that do not collapse into a single one. In our reversible framework, two distinct transitions are generated thanks to the fact that the key associated with the executed action is stored into the derivative process too, as shown in the bottom part of Fig. 1.

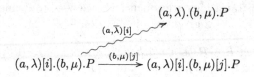

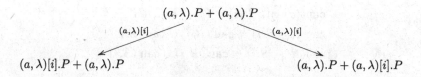

Fig. 1. Examples of conflicting transitions

Concurrent transitions can commute, while conflicting ones cannot. Formally:

Lemma 2 (diamond lemma). *Let $\theta_1 : R \xrightarrow{\ell_1} S_1$ and $\theta_2 : R \xrightarrow{\ell_2} S_2$ be two coinitial transitions from a reachable process $R \in \mathcal{P}$. If θ_1 and θ_2 are concurrent, then there exist two cofinal transitions $\theta_2/\theta_1 : S_1 \xrightarrow{\ell_2} S$ and $\theta_1/\theta_2 : S_2 \xrightarrow{\ell_1} S$.*

Proof. By case analysis on the form of θ_1 and θ_2. ∎

We are now in a position to show that reversibility in our framework is causally consistent. Following [23], we first define a notion of *causal equivalence* between computations that abstracts from the order of concurrent transitions. We formalize $\asymp$ as the least equivalence relation over computations that is closed under composition and obeys the following rules:

$$\theta_1; \theta_2/\theta_1 \asymp \theta_2; \theta_1/\theta_2 \qquad \theta; \overline{\theta} \asymp \epsilon_{\text{source}(\theta)} \qquad \overline{\theta}; \theta \asymp \epsilon_{\text{target}(\overline{\theta})}$$

Equivalence $\asymp$ states that if we have two concurrent transitions, then the two computations obtained by swapping the order of their execution are the same, and that any computation composed by a transition followed by its inverse is equivalent to the empty computation. The proof of causal consistency relying on $\asymp$ follows that of [5], although the arguments are different due to the fact that the notion of concurrent transitions is formalized differently.

The following lemma says that, up to causal equivalence, one can always reach for the maximum freedom of choice among transitions, meaning that it is possible to undo all the executed actions and then restart.

Lemma 3 (rearranging lemma). *For any computation ω there exist two forward computations ω_1 and ω_2 such that $\omega \asymp \overline{\omega_1}; \omega_2$.*

Proof. By induction on the length of ω and on the distance (intended as number of transitions) between the beginning of ω and the earliest pair of consecutive transitions in ω such that the former is forward while the latter is backward. The analysis uses both the loop lemma (Lemma 1) and the diamond lemma (Lemma 2). ∎

The following lemma says that if two computations ω_1 and ω_2 are coinitial and cofinal and ω_2 is made of forward transitions only, then in ω_1 there are some transitions that are later undone. This computation is thus causally equivalent to a forward one in which the undone transitions do not take place at all.

Lemma 4 (shortening lemma). *Let ω_1 and ω_2 be coinitial and cofinal computations, with ω_2 forward. Then there exists a forward computation ω_1' of length at most that of ω_1 such that $\omega_1' \asymp \omega_1$.*

Proof. The proof is by induction on the length of ω_1, using the diamond lemma (Lemma 2) and the rearranging lemma (Lemma 3). In the proof, the forward computation ω_2 is the main guideline for shortening ω_1 into a forward computation. Indeed, the proof relies crucially on the fact that ω_1 and ω_2 share the same source and the same target and that ω_2 is a forward computation. ∎

Theorem 1 (causal consistency). *Let ω_1 and ω_2 be coinitial computations. Then $\omega_1 \asymp \omega_2$ iff ω_1 and ω_2 are cofinal too.*

Proof. The 'if' direction follows by definition of causal equivalence and computation composition. The 'only if' direction exploits the diamond lemma (Lemma 2), the rearranging lemma (Lemma 3), and the shortening lemma (Lemma 4). ∎

With Theorem 1 we have proved that the notion of causal equivalence characterises a space for admissible rollbacks that are (i) consistent in the sense that they do not lead to previously unreachable states and (ii) flexible enough to allow undo operations to be rearranged. This implies that the states reached by a backward computation could be reached by performing forward computations only. We can therefore conclude that RMPC is causal consistent reversible.

4.4   Time Reversibility for RMPC

The rules in Table 2 associate with any initial process $R \in \mathcal{P}$ a labeled transition system $[\![R]\!] = (\mathcal{P}, \mathcal{L}, \mapsto, R)$. To investigate time reversibility, we have to derive from $[\![R]\!]$ the CTMC $\mathcal{M}[\![R]\!]$ underlying R and we have to specify how each backward rate $\overline{\lambda}$ is obtained from the corresponding forward rate λ.

First of all, we observe that every non-terminal state of $[\![R]\!]$ has infinitely many outgoing transitions. The reason is that rules ACT1 and ACT2 generate a transition for each possible admissible key, with the key being part of both the label and the derivative process term. On the one hand, this is useful for avoiding the generation of a single (a, λ)-transition in the case of a process like $(a, \lambda).P + (a, \lambda).P$ whose overall exit rate is $\lambda + \lambda$; even if the key is the same, two different states $(a, \lambda)[i].P + (a, \lambda).P$ and $(a, \lambda).P + (a, \lambda)[i].P$ are reached. On the other hand, it requires considering transition bundles to build $\mathcal{M}[\![R]\!]$.

We call *transition bundle* a set of transitions departing from the same state and labeled with the same action/rate but different keys, whose target states are syntactically identical up to keys. Formally, we denote by $\equiv_\mathcal{K}$ the least equivalence relation over $\mathcal{P}$ induced by $(a, \lambda)[i].S \equiv_\mathcal{K} (a, \lambda)[j].S$. We then define the CTMC underlying an initial process $R \in \mathcal{P}$ as the labeled transition system $\mathcal{M}[\![R]\!] = (\mathcal{P}/\equiv_\mathcal{K}, \mathcal{A} \times \mathcal{R}, \mapsto_\mathcal{K}, [R]_{\equiv_\mathcal{K}})$ where:

- $\mathcal{P}/\equiv_\mathcal{K}$ is the quotient set of $\equiv_\mathcal{K}$ over $\mathcal{P}$, i.e., the set of classes of processes that are equivalent to each other according to $\equiv_\mathcal{K}$.
- $[R]_{\equiv_\mathcal{K}}$ is the equivalence class of R with respect to $\equiv_\mathcal{K}$, which simply is the singleton set $\{R\}$ as R is initial and hence contains no keys.
- $\mapsto_\mathcal{K} \subseteq \mathcal{P}/\equiv_\mathcal{K} \times (\mathcal{A} \times \mathcal{R}) \times \mathcal{P}/\equiv_\mathcal{K}$ is the transition relation given by $\rightarrow_\mathcal{K} \cup \rightsquigarrow_\mathcal{K}$ such that $[R]_{\equiv_\mathcal{K}} \xrightarrow{(a, \lambda)}_\mathcal{K} [R']_{\equiv_\mathcal{K}}$ whenever $R \xrightarrow{(a, \lambda)[i]} R'$ for some $i \in \mathcal{K}$ and $[R]_{\equiv_\mathcal{K}} \xrightsquigarrow{(a, \overline{\lambda})}_\mathcal{K} [R']_{\equiv_\mathcal{K}}$ whenever $R \xrightsquigarrow{(a, \overline{\lambda})[i]} R'$ for some $i \in \mathcal{K}$.

When moving from $[\![R]\!]$ to $\mathcal{M}[\![R]\!]$, individual states are replaced by classes of states that are syntactically identical up to keys in the same positions, moreover keys are removed from transition labels. As a consequence, every state of $\mathcal{M}[\![R]\!]$ turns out to have finitely many outgoing transitions. We also note that $\mathcal{M}[\![R]\!]$ is an *action-labeled* CTMC, as each of its transitions is labeled with both a rate and an action.

As a preliminary step towards time reversibility, we have to show that $\mathcal{M}[\![R]\!]$ is stationary. It holds that $\mathcal{M}[\![R]\!]$ is even ergodic thanks to the loop lemma.

Lemma 5. *Let $R \in \mathcal{P}$ be an initial process. Then $\mathcal{M}[\![R]\!]$ is time homogeneous and ergodic.*

Proof. The time homogeneity of $\mathcal{M}[\![R]\!]$ is a straightforward consequence of the fact that its rates simply are positive real numbers, not time-dependent functions. The ergodicity of $\mathcal{M}[\![R]\!]$ stems from the fact that the graph representation of the considered CTMC is a finite, strongly connected component due to Corollary 1. ∎

We exploit once more the loop lemma to derive that, in the case that $\overline{\lambda} = \lambda$, the steady-state probability distribution of $\mathcal{M}[\![R]\!]$ is the uniform distribution, from which time reversibility will immediately follow.

Lemma 6. *Let $R \in \mathcal{P}$ be an initial process, $\mathcal{S}$ be the set of states of $\mathcal{M}[\![R]\!]$, and $n = |\mathcal{S}|$. If every backward rate is equal to the corresponding forward rate, then the steady-state probability distribution π of $\mathcal{M}[\![R]\!]$ satisfies $\pi(s) = 1/n$ for all $s \in \mathcal{S}$.*

Proof. *If $n = 1$, i.e., R is equal to $\mathbf{0}$ or to the cooperation of several processes whose initial actions have to synchronize but are different from each other, then trivially $\pi(s) = 1/n = 1$ for the only state $s \in \mathcal{S}$.*
Suppose now that $n \geq 2$. From Lemma 5, it follows that $\mathcal{M}[\![R]\!]$ has a unique steady-state probability distribution π. Due to Lemma 1, the global balance equation for an arbitrary $s \in \mathcal{S}$ is as follows:

$$\pi(s) \cdot \sum_{s \xmapsto{(a,\lambda)}_{\mathcal{K}} s'} \lambda = \sum_{s' \xmapsto{(a,\overline{\lambda})}_{\mathcal{K}} s} \pi(s') \cdot \overline{\lambda}$$

Since every backward rate is equal to the corresponding forward rate, the global balance equation for s boils down to:

$$\pi(s) \cdot \sum_{s \xmapsto{(a,\lambda)}_{\mathcal{K}} s'} \lambda = \sum_{s' \xmapsto{(a,\lambda)}_{\mathcal{K}} s} \pi(s') \cdot \lambda$$

Since the two summations have the same number of summands, the equation above is satified when $\pi(s) = \pi(s')$ for all $s' \in \mathcal{S}$ reached by a transition from s. All global balance equations are thus satisfied when $\pi(s) = 1/n$ for all $s \in \mathcal{S}$. ∎

Theorem 2 (time reversibility). *Let $R \in \mathcal{P}$ be an initial process. If every backward rate is equal to the corresponding forward rate, then $\mathcal{M}[\![R]\!]$ is time reversible.*

Proof. *Let $\mathcal{S}$ be the set of states of $\mathcal{M}[\![R]\!]$ and $n = |\mathcal{S}|$. From Lemma 5, it follows that $\mathcal{M}[\![R]\!]$ has a unique steady-state probability distribution π. To avoid trivial cases, suppose $n \geq 2$ and consider $s, s' \in \mathcal{S}$ with $s \neq s'$ connected by a transition. Due to Lemma 1, the partial balance equation for s and s' is as follows:*

$$\pi(s) \cdot \sum_{s \xmapsto{(a,\lambda)}_{\mathcal{K}} s'} \lambda = \pi(s') \cdot \sum_{s' \xmapsto{(a,\overline{\lambda})}_{\mathcal{K}} s} \overline{\lambda}$$

Since every backward rate is equal to the corresponding forward rate, the partial balance equation for s and s' boils down to:

$$\pi(s) \cdot \sum_{s \xmapsto{(a,\lambda)}_{\mathcal{K}} s'} \lambda = \pi(s') \cdot \sum_{s' \xmapsto{(a,\lambda)}_{\mathcal{K}} s} \lambda$$

Since the two summations have the same number of summands and $\pi(s) = \pi(s') = 1/n$ due to Lemma 6, the equation above is satified. The result then follows from the fact that s and s' are two arbitrary distinct states connected by a transition.   ∎

The main difference between our approach to time reversibility and the ones of [8, 25] is twofold. Firstly, our approach is part of a more general framework in which also causal consistent reversibility is addressed. Secondly, our approach is inspired by the idea of [28] of developing a formalism in which it is possible to express models whose reversibility is guaranteed by construction, instead of building a posteriori the time-reversed version of a certain model like in [8] or verifying a posteriori whether a given model is time reversible or not like in [25].

It is worth noting that these methodological differences do not prevent us from adapting to our setting some results from [8, 25], although a few preliminary observations about notational differences are necessary.

Both [8] and [25] make a distinction between active actions, each of which is given a rate, and passive actions, each of which is given a weight, with the constraint that, in case of synchronization, the rate of the active action is multiplied by the weight of the corresponding passive action. In RMPC there is no such distinction, however the same operation, i.e., multiplication, is applied to the rates of two synchronizing actions. A passive action can thus be rendered as an action with rate 1, while a set of alternative passive actions can be rendered as a set of actions whose rates sum up to 1. Moreover, in [25] synchronization is enforced between any active-passive pair of identical actions, whereas in RMPC the cooperation operator is enriched with an explicit synchronization set L, which yields as a special case the aforementioned synchronization discipline when L is equal to the set $\mathcal{A}$ of all the actions. We can therefore conclude that our cooperation operator is a generalization of those used in [8, 25], hence the recalled notational differences do not hamper result transferral.

In [8] the compositionality of a CTMC-based stochastic process calculus is exploited to prove the reversed compound agent theorem (RCAT), which establishes the conditions under which the time-reversed version of the cooperation of two processes is equal to the cooperation of the time-reversed versions of those two processes. The application of RCAT leads to product-form solution results from stochastic process algebraic models, including a new different proof of Jackson theorem for product-form queueing networks [12].

In [25] the notion of ρ-reversibility is introduced for stochastic automata, which are essentially action-labeled CTMCs. Function ρ is a state permutation that ensures (i) for each action the equality of the total exit rate of any state s and $\rho(s)$ and (ii) the conservation of action-related rate products across cycles when considering states in the forward direction and their ρ-counterparts in the backward direction. For any ergodic ρ-reversible automaton, it turns out that $\pi(s) = \pi(\rho(s))$ for every state s. Moreover, the synchronization inspired by [31] of two ρ-reversible stochastic automata is still ρ-reversible and, in case of ergodicity, under certain conditions the steady-state probability of any compound state is the product of the steady-state probabilities of the two constituent states.

Our time reversibility result for RMPC can be rephrased in the setting of [25] in terms of ρ-reversibility with ρ being the identity function over states. As a consequence, the following two results stem from Theorem 2 of the present paper and, respectively, Theorems 2 and 3 of [25]:

Corollary 2 (time reversibility closure). *Let $R, S \in \mathcal{P}$ be initial processes and $L \subseteq \mathcal{A}$. If every backward rate is equal to the corresponding forward rate, then $\mathcal{M}[\![R \parallel_L S]\!]$ is time reversible too.*

Corollary 3 (product form). *Let $R, S \in \mathcal{P}$ be initial processes and $L \subseteq \mathcal{A}$. If every backward rate is equal to the corresponding forward rate and the set of states $\mathcal{S}$ of $\mathcal{M}[\![R \parallel_L S]\!]$ is equal to $\mathcal{S}_R \times \mathcal{S}_S$ where $\mathcal{S}_R$ is the set of states of $\mathcal{M}[\![R]\!]$ and $\mathcal{S}_S$ is the set of states of $\mathcal{M}[\![S]\!]$, then $\pi(r, s) = \pi_R(r) \cdot \pi_S(s)$ for all $(r, s) \in \mathcal{S}_R \times \mathcal{S}_S$.*

The product form result above avoids the calculation of the global balance equations over $\mathcal{M}[\![R \parallel_L S]\!]$, as $\pi(r, s)$ can simply be obtained by multiplying $\pi_R(r)$ with $\pi_S(s)$. However, the condition $\mathcal{S} = \mathcal{S}_R \times \mathcal{S}_S$ requires to check that every state in the full Cartesian product is reachable from $R \parallel_L S$. This means that no compound state is such that its constituent states enable some action, but none of the enabled actions can be executed due to the constraints imposed by the synchronization set L. The condition $\mathcal{S} = \mathcal{S}_R \times \mathcal{S}_S$ implies that $\mathcal{M}[\![R \parallel_L S]\!]$ is ergodic over the full Cartesian product of the two original state spaces, which is the condition used in [25]. Although implicit in the statement of the corollary, the time reversibility of $\mathcal{M}[\![R \parallel_L S]\!]$ is essential for the product form result.

5   Conclusions

Different interpretations of reversibility are present in the literature. In this paper, we have started our research quest towards bridging causal consistent reversibility [5] – developed in concurrency theory – and time reversibility [13] – originated in the field of stochastic processes. We have accomplished this by introducing the stochastic process calculus RMPC, whose syntax and semantics follow the approach of [28], thus paving the way to concurrent system models that are both causal consistent reversible and time reversible by construction. Based on time reversibility, we have also adapted from [25] a product form result that enables the efficient calculation of performance measures.

There are several lines of research that we plan to undergo, ranging from the application of our results to examples and case studies modeled with RMPC to the development of further theoretical results. For instance, we would like to investigate other conditions under which time reversibility is achieved, in addition to the one relying on the equality of forward and backward rates.

Moreover, we observe that the syntax of RMPC does not include recursion. From the point of view of the ergodicity of the underlying CTMC, this is not a problem because every forward transition has the corresponding backward transition by construction. However, there might be situations in which recursion is necessary to appropriately describe the behavior of a system. Because of the use of communication keys, a simple process of the form $P \triangleq (a, \lambda).P$, whose standard labeled transition system features a single state with a self-looping transition, produces a sequence of infinitely many distinct states even if we resort to transition bundles. Our claim is that the specific cooperation operator that we have considered may require a mechanism lighter than communications keys to keep track of past actions, which may avoid the generation of an infinite state space in the presence of recursion.

Acknowledgement. We would like to thank Andrea Marin for the valuable discussions on time reversibility. The second author has been partially supported by the French ANR project *DCore* ANR-18-CE25-0007 and by the Italian INdAM – GNCS project 2020 *Reversible Concurrent Systems: From Models to Languages*.

References

1. Baeten, J.C.M., Verhoef, C.: A congruence theorem for structured operational semantics with predicates. In: Best, E. (ed.) CONCUR 1993. LNCS, vol. 715, pp. 477–492. Springer, Heidelberg (1993). https://doi.org/10.1007/3-540-57208-2_33
2. Barylska, K., Koutny, M., Mikulski, L., Piatkowski, M.: Reversible computation vs. reversibility in Petri nets. Sci. Comput. Program. **151**, 48–60 (2018)
3. Bennett, C.H.: Logical reversibility of computations. IBM J. Res. Dev. **17**, 525–532 (1973)
4. Cristescu, I., Krivine, J., Varacca, D.: A compositional semantics for the reversible π-calculus. In: Proceedings of LICS 2013, pp. 388–397. IEEE-CS Press (2013)
5. Danos, V., Krivine, J.: Reversible communicating systems. In: Gardner, P., Yoshida, N. (eds.) CONCUR 2004. LNCS, vol. 3170, pp. 292–307. Springer, Heidelberg (2004). https://doi.org/10.1007/978-3-540-28644-8_19
6. Danos, V., Krivine, J.: Transactions in RCCS. In: Abadi, M., de Alfaro, L. (eds.) CONCUR 2005. LNCS, vol. 3653, pp. 398–412. Springer, Heidelberg (2005). https://doi.org/10.1007/11539452_31
7. Giachino, E., Lanese, I., Mezzina, C.A.: Causal-consistent reversible debugging. In: Gnesi, S., Rensink, A. (eds.) FASE 2014. LNCS, vol. 8411, pp. 370–384. Springer, Heidelberg (2014). https://doi.org/10.1007/978-3-642-54804-8_26
8. Harrison, P.G.: Turning back time in Markovian process algebra. Theoret. Comput. Sci. **290**(3), 1947–1986 (2003)
9. Hillston, J.: The nature of synchronisation. In: Proceedings of PAPM 1994, pp. 51–70. University of Erlangen, Technical Report 27–4 (1994)
10. Hillston, J.: A Compositional Approach to Performance Modelling. Cambridge University Press, Cambridge (1996)
11. Hoare, C.A.R.: Communicating Sequential Processes. Prentice Hall, Upper Saddle River (1985)
12. Jackson, J.R.: Jobshop-like queueing systems. Manage. Sci. **10**(1), 131–142 (1963)
13. Kelly, F.P.: Reversibility and Stochastic Networks. Wiley, Chichester (1979)
14. Kemeny, J.G., Snell, J.L.: Finite Markov Chains. Van Nostrand, New York (1960)
15. Kleinrock, L.: Queueing Systems. Wiley, New York (1975)
16. Landauer, R.: Irreversibility and heat generated in the computing process. IBM J. Res. Dev. **5**, 183–191 (1961)

17. Lanese, I., Lienhardt, M., Mezzina, C.A., Schmitt, A., Stefani, J.-B.: Concurrent flexible reversibility. In: Felleisen, M., Gardner, P. (eds.) ESOP 2013. LNCS, vol. 7792, pp. 370–390. Springer, Heidelberg (2013). https://doi.org/10.1007/978-3-642-37036-6_21

18. Lanese, I., Medić, D., Mezzina, C.A.: Static versus dynamic reversibility in CCS. Acta Informatica (2019)

19. Lanese, I., Mezzina, C.A., Stefani, J.-B.: Reversing higher-order π. In: Gastin, P., Laroussinie, F. (eds.) CONCUR 2010. LNCS, vol. 6269, pp. 478–493. Springer, Heidelberg (2010). https://doi.org/10.1007/978-3-642-15375-4_33

20. Lanese, I., Nishida, N., Palacios, A., Vidal, G.: CauDEr: a causal-consistent reversible debugger for erlang. In: Gallagher, J.P., Sulzmann, M. (eds.) FLOPS 2018. LNCS, vol. 10818, pp. 247–263. Springer, Cham (2018). https://doi.org/10.1007/978-3-319-90686-7_16

21. Lanese, I., Nishida, N., Palacios, A., Vidal, G.: A theory of reversibility for Erlang. J. Log. Algeb. Meth. Program. **100**, 71–97 (2018)

22. Laursen, J.S., Ellekilde, L.P., Schultz, U.P.: Modelling reversible execution of robotic assembly. Robotica **36**(5), 625–654 (2018)

23. Lévy, J.J.: An algebraic interpretation of the λβK-calculus; and an application of a labelled λ-calculus. Theoret. Comput. Sci. **2**(1), 97–114 (1976)

24. Lienhardt, M., Lanese, I., Mezzina, C.A., Stefani, J.-B.: A reversible abstract machine and its space overhead. In: Giese, H., Rosu, G. (eds.) FMOODS/FORTE -2012. LNCS, vol. 7273, pp. 1–17. Springer, Heidelberg (2012). https://doi.org/10.1007/978-3-642-30793-5_1

25. Marin, A., Rossi, S.: Quantitative analysis of concurrent reversible computations. In: Sankaranarayanan, S., Vicario, E. (eds.) FORMATS 2015. LNCS, vol. 9268, pp. 206–221. Springer, Cham (2015). https://doi.org/10.1007/978-3-319-22975-1_14

26. Milner, R.: Communication and Concurrency. Prentice Hall, Upper Saddle River (1989)

27. Perumalla, K.S., Park, A.J.: Reverse computation for rollback-based fault tolerance in large parallel systems - evaluating the potential gains and systems effects. Cluster Comput. **17**(2), 303–313 (2014)

28. Phillips, I.C.C., Ulidowski, I.: Reversing algebraic process calculi. J. Logic Algeb. Program. **73**(1–2), 70–96 (2007)

29. Phillips, I., Ulidowski, I., Yuen, S.: A reversible process calculus and the modelling of the ERK signalling pathway. In: Glück, R., Yokoyama, T. (eds.) RC 2012. LNCS, vol. 7581, pp. 218–232. Springer, Heidelberg (2013). https://doi.org/10.1007/978-3-642-36315-3_18

30. Michele Pinna, G.: Reversing steps in membrane systems computations. In: Gheorghe, M., Rozenberg, G., Salomaa, A., Zandron, C. (eds.) CMC 2017. LNCS, vol. 10725, pp. 245–261. Springer, Cham (2018). https://doi.org/10.1007/978-3-319-73359-3_16

31. Plateau, B.: On the stochastic structure of parallelism and synchronization models for distributed algorithms. In: Proceedings of SIGMETRICS 1985, pp. 147–154. ACM Press (1985)

32. Schordan, M., Oppelstrup, T., Jefferson, D.R., Barnes Jr., P.D.: Generation of reversible C++ code for optimistic parallel discrete event simulation. New Gener. Comput. **36**(3), 257–280 (2018)

33. Siljak, H., Psara, K., Philippou, A.: Distributed antenna selection for massive MIMO using reversing Petri nets. IEEE Wirel. Commun. Lett. **8**(5), 1427–1430 (2019)

34. Stewart, W.J.: Introduction to the Numerical Solution of Markov Chains. Princeton University Press, Princeton (1994)
35. Vassor, M., Stefani, J.-B.: Checkpoint/rollback vs causally-consistent reversibility. In: Kari, J., Ulidowski, I. (eds.) RC 2018. LNCS, vol. 11106, pp. 286–303. Springer, Cham (2018). https://doi.org/10.1007/978-3-319-99498-7_20
36. de Vries, E., Koutavas, V., Hennessy, M.: Communicating transactions. In: Gastin, P., Laroussinie, F. (eds.) CONCUR 2010. LNCS, vol. 6269, pp. 569–583. Springer, Heidelberg (2010). https://doi.org/10.1007/978-3-642-15375-4_39

Defining and Verifying Durable Opacity: Correctness for Persistent Software Transactional Memory

Eleni Bila[1], Simon Doherty[2], Brijesh Dongol[1]($\boxtimes$), John Derrick[2],
Gerhard Schellhorn[3], and Heike Wehrheim[4]

[1] University of Surrey, Guildford, UK
b.dongol@surrey.ac.uk
[2] University of Sheffield, Sheffield, UK
[3] University of Augsburg, Augsburg, Germany
[4] Paderborn University, Paderborn, Germany

Abstract. Non-volatile memory (NVM), aka persistent memory, is a new paradigm for memory that preserves its contents even after power loss. The expected ubiquity of NVM has stimulated interest in the design of novel concepts ensuring correctness of concurrent programming abstractions in the face of persistency. So far, this has lead to the design of a number of persistent concurrent data structures, built to satisfy an associated notion of correctness: durable linearizability.

In this paper, we transfer the principle of durable concurrent correctness to the area of software transactional memory (STM). Software transactional memory algorithms allow for concurrent access to shared state. Like linearizability for concurrent data structures, opacity is the established notion of correctness for STMs. First, we provide a novel definition of durable opacity extending opacity to handle crashes and recovery in the context of NVM. Second, we develop a durably opaque version of an existing STM algorithm, namely the Transactional Mutex Lock (TML). Third, we design a proof technique for durable opacity based on refinement between TML and an operational characterisation of durable opacity by adapting the TMS2 specification. Finally, we apply this proof technique to show that the durable version of TML is indeed durably opaque. The correctness proof is mechanized within Isabelle.

1 Introduction

Recent technological advances indicate that future architectures will employ some form of *non-volatile memory* (NVM) that retains its contents after a system crash (e.g., power outage). NVM is intended to be used as an intermediate

Bila and Dongol are supported by VeTSS project "Persistent Safety and Security". Dongol is supported by EPSRC grants EP/R019045/2 and EP/R032556/1. Derrick and Doherty are supported by EPSRC grant EP/R032351/1. Wehrheim is supported by DFG grant WE2290/12-1.

Published by Springer Nature Switzerland AG 2020
A. Gotsman and A. Sokolova (Eds.): FORTE 2020, LNCS 12136, pp. 39–58, 2020.
https://doi.org/10.1007/978-3-030-50086-3_3

layer between traditional *volatile memory* (VM) and secondary storage, and has the potential to vastly improve system speed and stability. Software that uses NVM has the potential to be more robust; in case of a crash, a system state before the crash may be recovered using contents from NVM, as opposed to being restarted from secondary storage. However, because the same data is stored in both a volatile and non-volatile manner, and because NVM is updated at a slower rate than VM, recovery to a consistent state may not always be possible. This is particularly true for concurrent systems, where coping with NVM requires introduction of additional synchronisation instructions into a program.

This observation has led to the design of the first *persistent* concurrent programming abstractions, so far mainly concurrent data structures. Together with these, the associated notion of correctness, i.e., linearizability [21], has been transferred to NVM. This resulted in the novel concept of *durable linearizability* [22]. A first proof technique for showing durable linearizability of concurrent data structures has been proposed by Derrick et al. [11].

Besides concurrent data structures, software transactional memory (STM) is the most important synchronization mechanism supporting concurrent access to shared state. STMs provide an *illusion of atomicity* in concurrent programs. The analogy of STM is with database transactions, which perform a series of accesses/updates to shared data (via read and write operations) atomically in an all-or-nothing manner. Similarly with an STM, if a transaction commits, all its operations succeed, and in the aborting case, all its operations fail. The now (mainly) agreed upon correctness criterion for STMs is *opacity* [20]. Opacity requires all transactions (including aborting ones) to agree on a single sequential history of committed transactions and the outcome of transactions has to coincide with this history.

In this paper, we transfer STM and opacity to the novel field of non-volatile memory. This entails a number of steps. First, the correctness criterion of opacity has to be adapted to cope with crashes in system executions. Second, STM algorithms have to be extended to deal with the coexistence of volatile and non-volatile memory during execution and need to be equipped with recovery operations. Third, proof techniques for opacity need to be re-investigated to make them usable for durable opacity. In this paper, we provide contributions to all three steps.

- For the first step, we define *durable opacity* out of opacity in the same way that durable linearizability has been defined based on linearizability. Durable opacity requires the executions of STMs to be opaque even if they are interspersed with crashes. This guarantees that the shared state remains consistent.
- We exemplify the second step by extending the Transactional Mutex Lock (TML) of Dalessandro et al. [8] to durable TML (DTML). To this end, TML needs to be equipped with a recovery operation and special statements to guarantee consistency in case of crashes. We do so by extending TML with a logging mechanism which allows to flush written, but volatile values to NVM during recovery.

– For the third step, we build on a proof technique for opacity based on refinement between IO-automata. This technique uses the automaton TMS2 [15] which has been shown to implement opacity [26] using the PVS interactive theorem prover. This automaton gives us a formal specification, which can be used as the abstract level in a proof of refinement. Furthermore, the IO-automaton framework is part of the standard Isabelle distribution. For use as a proof technique for durable opacity, TMS2 is extended with a crash operation (mimicing system crashes and their effect on memory) to yield DTMS2. The automaton DTMS2 is then proven to only have durably opaque executions. Thereby we obtain an operational characterisation of durable opacity.

Table 1. Events appearing in the histories of TML, where $t \in T$ is a transaction identifier, $x \in L$ is a location, and $v \in V$ a value

Invocations	Possible matching responses
$inv_t(\texttt{TMBegin})$	$res_t(\texttt{TMBegin(ok)})$
$inv_t(\texttt{TMCommit})$	$res_t(\texttt{TMCommit(ok)})$, $res_t(\texttt{TMCommit(abort)})$
$inv_t(\texttt{TMRd}(x))$	$res_t(\texttt{TMRd}(v))$, $res_t(\texttt{TMRd(abort)})$
$inv_t(\texttt{TMWr}(x, v))$	$res_t(\texttt{TMWr(ok)})$, $res_t(\texttt{TMWr(abort)})$

Finally, we bring all three steps together and apply our proof technique to show that durable TML is indeed durably opaque. This proof has been mechanized in the interactive prover Isabelle [32]. Our mechanized proof proceeds by encoding DTMS2 and DTML as IO-automata within Isabelle, then proving the existence of a forward simulation, which in turn has been shown to ensure trace refinement of IO-automata [28], and hence guarantees durable opacity of DTML.

2   Transactional Memory and Opacity

Software Transactional Memory (STM) provides programmers with an easy-to-use synchronisation mechanism for concurrent access to shared data, whereby blocks of code may be treated as transactions that execute with an illusion of atomicity. STMs usually provide a number of operations to programmers: operations to start (`TMBegin`) and commit a transaction (`TMCommit`), and operations to read and write shared data (`TMRd`, `TMWr`). These operations can be called (invoked) from within a client program (possibly with some arguments, e.g., the variable to be read) and then will return with a response. Except for operations that start transactions, all other operations might potentially respond with `abort`, thereby aborting the whole transaction.

A widely accepted correctness condition for STMs that encapsulates transactional phenomena is *opacity* [19,20], which requires all transactions, including aborting transactions to agree on a single sequential global ordering of transactions. Moreover, no transactional read returns a value that is inconsistent with the global ordering.

2.1 Histories

As standard in the literature, opacity is defined on the *histories* of an implementation. Histories are sequences of *events* that record all interactions between the implementation and its clients. An event is either an invocation (*inv*) or a response (*res*) of a transactional operation. For the TML implementation, possible invocation and *matching* response events are given in Table 1, where we assume T is a set of transaction identifiers, L a set of addresses (or locations) mapped to values from a set V.

The type $Mem \cong L \rightarrow V$ describes the possible states of the shared memory. We assume that initially all addresses hold the value $0 \in V$.

We use the following notation on histories: for a history h, $h \upharpoonright t$ is the projection onto the events of transaction t only and $h[i..j]$ the subsequence of h from $h(i)$ to $h(j)$ inclusive. For a response event e, we let $rval(e)$ denote the value returned by e; for instance $rval(\text{TMBegin(ok)}) = \text{ok}$. If e is not a response event, then we let $rval(e) = \bot$.

We are interested in three different types of histories [2]. At the concrete level the TML implementation produces histories where the events are interleaved. At the abstract level we are interested in *sequential histories*, which are ones where there is no interleaving at any level - transactions are atomic: a transaction completes before the next transaction starts. As part of the proof of opacity we use an intermediate specification which has *alternating histories*, in which transactions may be interleaved but operations (e.g., reads, writes) are not interleaved.

A history h is *alternating* if $h = \epsilon$ or is an alternating sequence of invocation and matching response events starting with an invocation. For the rest of this paper, we assume each process invokes at most one operation at a time, and hence, assume that $h \upharpoonright t$ is alternating for any history h and transaction t. Note that this does not necessarily mean h is alternating itself. Opacity is defined for well-formed histories, which formalises the allowable interaction between an STM implementation and its clients. For every t, $h \upharpoonright t = \langle s_0, \ldots, s_m \rangle$ of a well-formed history is an alternating history such that $s_0 = inv_t(\text{TMBegin})$, for all $0 < i < m$, event $s_i \neq inv_t(\text{TMBegin})$ and $rval(s_i) \notin \{\text{commit}, \text{abort}\}$. Note that by definition, well-formedness disallows transaction identifiers from being reused. We say t is *committed* if $rval(s_m) = \text{commit}$ and *aborted* if $rval(s_m) = \text{abort}$. In these cases, the transaction t is *completed*, otherwise t is *live*. A history is *well-formed* if it consists of transactions only and there is at most one live transaction per process.

2.2 Opacity

Opacity [19,20] compares concurrent histories generated by an STM implementation to sequential histories and can be seen as a strengthening of serializability to accommodate aborted transactions. Below, we first formalise the sequential history semantics, then consider opaque histories.

Sequential History Semantics. A sequential history has to ensure that the behaviour is meaningful with respect to the reads and writes of the transactions.

Definition 1 (Valid history). *Let $h = ev_0, \ldots, ev_{2n-1}$ be a sequence of alternating invocation and matching response events starting with an invocation and ending with a response.*

We say h is valid *if there exists a sequence of states $\sigma_0, \ldots, \sigma_n$ such that $\sigma_0(l) = 0$ for all $l \in L$, and for all i such that $0 \leq i < n$ and $t \in T$:*

1. *if $ev_{2i} = inv_t(\textit{TMWr}(l, v))$ and $ev_{2i+1} = res_t(\textit{TMWr}(\text{ok}))$ then $\sigma_{i+1} = \sigma_i[l := v]$,*
2. *if $ev_{2i} = inv_t(\textit{TMRd}(l))$ and $ev_{2i+1} = res_t(\textit{TMRd}(v))$ then $\sigma_i(l) = v$ and $\sigma_{i+1} = \sigma_i$,*
3. *for all other pairs of events (reads and writes with an abort response, as well as begin and commit events) we require $\sigma_{i+1} = \sigma_i$.*

We write $[\![h]\!](\sigma)$ if σ is a sequence of states that makes h valid (since the sequence is unique, if it exists, it can be viewed as the semantics of h).

The point of TM is that the effect of the writes only takes place if the transaction commits. Writes in a transaction that abort do not affect the memory. However, all reads, including those executed by aborted transactions, must be consistent with previously committed writes. Therefore, only some histories of an object reflect ones that could be produced by a TM. We call these the *legal* histories, and they are defined as follows.

Definition 2 (Legal histories). *Let hs be a non-interleaved history and i an index of hs. Let hs' be the projection of $hs[0..(i-1)]$ onto all events of committed transactions plus the events of the transaction to which $hs(i)$ belongs. Then we say hs is legal at i whenever hs' is valid. We say hs is legal iff it is legal at each index i.*

This allows us to define sequentiality for a single history, which we lift to the level of specifications.

Definition 3 (Sequential history). *A well-formed history hs is sequential if it is non-interleaved and legal. We denote by S the set of all possible well-formed sequential histories.*

Opaque Histories. Opacity is defined by matching a concurrent history to a sequential history such that (a) both histories consist of the same events, and (b) the real-time order of transactions is preserved. For (b), the *real-time order* on transactions t_1 and t_2 in a history h is defined as $t_1 \prec_h t_2$ if t_1 is a completed transaction and the last event of t_1 in h occurs before the first event of t_2.

A given concrete history may be incomplete, i.e., it may contain pending operations, represented by invocations that do not have matching responses. Some of these pending operations may have taken effect, and others may not. The corresponding sequential history however must decide: either by adding a suitable matching response event for the pending invocation (the effect has taken place), or by removing the pending invocation (no effect yet). Therefore, we define a function $complete(h)$ that constructs all possible completions of h by appending matching responses for some pending invocations and removing all the other pending invocations. This is similar to the treatment of completions in the formalisation of linearizability [21]. The sequential history then must have the same events as those of one of the results returned by $complete(h)$.

Definition 4 (Opaque history). *A history h is end-to-end opaque iff for some $hc \in complete(h)$, there exists a sequential history $hs \in S$ such that for all $t \in T$, $hc \upharpoonright t = hs \upharpoonright t$ and $\prec_{hc} \subseteq \prec_{hs}$. A history h is opaque iff each prefix h' of h is end-to-end opaque; a set of histories $\mathcal{H}$ is opaque iff each $h \in \mathcal{H}$ is opaque; and an STM implementation is opaque iff its set of histories is opaque.*

3   STMs over Persistent Memory

We now consider STMs over a non-volatile memory model comprising two layers: a *volatile store*, whose contents are wiped clean when a system crashes (e.g., due to power loss), and a *persistent store*, whose state is preserved after a crash and available for use upon reboot. During normal program execution, contents of the volatile store may be transferred to the persistent store by the system. The main idea behind programs for this memory model is to include a *recovery procedure* that executes over the persistent store and resets the system into a consistent (safe) state. To achieve this, a programmer can control transfer of information from volatile to persistent store using a FLUSH(a) operation, ensuring that the information in address a is saved in the persistent store.

For STMs, we introduce a new notion of consistency: *durable opacity* which we define in Sect. 3.1. Durable opacity extends opacity [19,20] in exactly the same way that durable linearizability [22] extends linearizability [21], namely a history that contains crashes is durably opaque precisely when the same history with crashes removed is opaque. We present an example STM implementation that satisfies durable opacity in Sect. 3.2, extending Dalessandro et al.'s Transactional Mutex Lock [9].

3.1   Durable Opacity

Durable opacity is a correctness condition that is defined over *histories* that record the *invocation* and *response* events of operations executed on the transactional memory like opacity. Unlike opacity, durably opaque histories record system crash events, thus may take the form: $H = h_0 c_1 h_1 c_2 ... h_{n-1} c_n h_n$, where each h_i is a history (containing no crash events) and c_i is the ith crash event.

Following Izraelevitz et al. [22], for a history h, we let $ops(h)$ denote h restricted to non-crash events, thus for H above, $ops(H) = h_0 h_1 \ldots h_{n-1} h_n$, which contains no crash events. We call the subhistory h_i the i-th era of h.

The definition of a well-formed history is now updated to include crash events. A history is *durably well-formed* iff $ops(h)$ is well formed and every transaction identifier appears in at most one era. Thus, we assume that when a crash occurs, all running transactions are aborted.

Definition 5 (Durably opaque history). *A history h is durably opaque iff it is durably well-formed and $ops(h)$ is opaque.*

3.2 Example: Durable Transactional Mutex Lock

We now develop a durably opaque STM: a persistent memory version of the Transactional Mutex Lock (TML) [8], as given in Fig. 1. TML adopts a strict policy for transactional synchronisation: as soon as one transaction has successfully written to a variable, all other transactions running concurrently will be aborted when they invoke another read or write operation. To enforce this policy, TML uses a global counter glb (initially 0) and local variable loc, which is used to store a copy of glb. Variable glb records whether there is a *live writing transaction*, i.e., a transaction that has started, has not yet ended nor aborted, and has executed (or is executing) a write operation. More precisely, glb is odd if there is a live writing transaction, and even otherwise. Initially, we have no live writing transaction and thus glb is 0 (and hence even).

A second distinguishing feature of TML is that it performs writes in an *eager* manner, i.e., it updates shared memory during the write operation[1]. This is potentially problematic in a persistent memory context since writes that have completed may not be committed if a crash occurs prior to executing the commit operation. That is, writes of uncommitted transactions should not be seen by any transactions that start after a crash occurs. Our implementation makes use of an *undo log* mapping addresses to their persistent memory values prior to executing the first write operation for that address. Logged values are made persistent before the address is overwritten. Thus, if a crash occurs prior to a transaction committing, it is possible to recover the transaction to a safe state by undoing uncommitted transactional writes.

Operation TMBegin copies the value of glb into its local variable loc and checks whether glb is even. If so, the transaction is started, and otherwise, the process attempts to start again by rereading glb. A TMRead operation succeeds as long as glb equals loc (meaning no writes have occurred since the transaction began), otherwise it aborts the current transaction. The first execution of TMWrite attempts to increment glb using a cas (compare-and-swap), which atomically compares the first and second parameters, and sets the first parameter to the third if the comparison succeeds. If the cas attempt fails, a write

---

[1] This is in contrast to lazy implementations that defer transactional writes until the commit operation is executed (e.g., [9,13]).

by another transaction must have occured, and hence, the current transaction aborts. Otherwise `loc` is incremented (making its value odd) and the write is performed. Note that because `loc` becomes odd after the first successful write, all successive writes that are part of the same transaction will perform the write directly after testing `loc` at line $W1$. Further note that if the `cas` succeeds, `glb` becomes odd, which prevents other transactions from starting, and causes all concurrent live transactions still wanting to read or write to abort. Thus a writing transaction that successfully updates `glb` effectively locks shared memory. Operation `TMEnd` checks to see if a write has occurred by testing whether `loc` is odd. If the test succeeds, `glb` is set to `loc+1`. At line `E2`, `loc` is guaranteed to be equal to `glb`, and therefore this update has the effect of incrementing `glb` to an even value, allowing other transactions to begin.

Our implementation uses a durably linearizable [11, 22] set or map data structure `log`, such as the one described by Zuriel et al. [38]. A durably linearizable operation is guaranteed to take effect in persistent memory prior to the operation returning. In Fig. 1, we use operations `pinsert()`, `pempty()` and `pdelete()` to stress that these operations are durably linearizable.

Our durable TML algorithm (DTML) makes the following adaptations to TML. Note the operations build on a model of a crash that resets volatile memory to persistent memory.

- Within a write operation writing to address `addr`, prior to modifying the value at `addr`, we record the existing address-value pair in `log`, provided that `addr` does not already appear in the undo log (lines `W4` and `W5`). After updating the value (which updates the value of `addr` in the volatile store), the update is flushed to persistent memory prior to the write operation returning (line `W7`).
- We introduce a recovery operation that checks for a non-empty log and transfers the logged values to persistent memory, undoing any writes that have completed (but not committed) before the crash occurred. Since a crash could occur during recovery, we transfer values from the undo log to persistent memory one at a time.
- In the commit operation, we note that we distinguish a committing transaction as one with an odd value for `loc`. For a writing transaction, the log must be cleared by setting it to the empty log (line `E2`). Note that this is the point at which a writing transaction has definitely committed since any subsequent crash and recovery would no longer undo the writes of this transaction.

```
TMBegin:                          TMCommit:
B1 do loc := glb                  E1 if odd(loc) then
B2 until even(loc);               E2    log.pempty();
   return ok;                     E3    glb := loc + 1;
                                        return commit;
TMRead(addr):
R1 val := *addr;                  TMWrite(addr,val):
R2 if (glb = loc) then            W1 if even(loc) then
      return val;                 W2    if ¬ cas(glb,loc,loc+1) then
   else return abort;                      return abort;
                                  W3    else loc++;
                                  W4 if ∀ v. (addr, v) ∉ log then
Recover():                        W5    log.pinsert((addr, *addr));
C1 while ¬ log.isEmpty()          W6 *addr := val;
C2    SOME (addr, val).           W7 FLUSH(addr);
         (addr, val) ∈ log;          return ok;
C3    *addr := val ;
C4    FLUSH(addr) ;
C5    log.pdelete((addr, val));
C6 glb := 0
```

Fig. 1. A durable Transactional Mutex Lock (DTML). Initially: glb = 0, log = emptyLog(). Line numbers for return statements are omitted and we use *addr for the value of addr

4 Proving Durable Opacity

Previous works [1,2,14,17] have considered proofs of opacity using the operational TMS2 specification [15], which has been shown to guarantee opacity [26]. The proofs show refinement of the implementation against the TMS2 specification using either forward or backward simulation. For durable opacity, we use a similar proof strategy. In Sect. 4.3, we develop the DTMS2 operational specification, a durable version of the TMS2 specification, that we prove satisfies durable opacity. Then, in Sect. 5, we establish a simulation between DTML and DTMS2.

4.1 Background: IOA, Refinement and Simulation

We use Input/Output Automata (IOA) [29] to model both the implementation, DTML, and the specification, DTMS2.

Definition 6. *An* Input/Output Automaton *(IOA) is a labeled transition system A with a set of* states states(A), *a set of* actions acts(A), *a set of* start states start(A) ⊆ states(A), *and a* transition relation trans(A) ⊆ states(A) × acts(A) × states(A) *(so that the actions label the transitions).*

The set acts(A) is partitioned into input actions input(A), output actions output(A) and internal actions internal(A). The internal actions represent events of the system that are not visible to the external environment.

The input and output actions are externally visible, representing the automaton's interactions with its environment. Thus, we define the set of *external actions*, $external(A) = input(A) \cup output(A)$. We write $s \xrightarrow{a}_A s'$ iff $(s, a, s') \in trans(A)$.

An *execution* of an IOA A is a sequence $\sigma = s_0 a_0 s_1 a_1 s_2 \ldots s_n a_n s_{n+1}$ of alternating states and actions, such that $s_0 \in start(A)$ and for all states s_i, $s_i \xrightarrow{a_i}_A s_{i+1}$. A *reachable* state of A is a state appearing in an execution of A. An *invariant* of A is any superset of the reachable states of A (equivalently, any predicate satisfied by all reachable states of A). A *trace* of A is any sequence of (external) actions obtained by projecting the external actions of any execution of A. The set of traces of A, denoted $traces(A)$, represents A's externally visible behaviour.

For automata C and A, we say that C is a *refinement* of A iff $traces(C) \subseteq traces(A)$. We show that C is a refinement of A by proving the existence of a *forward simulation*, which enables one to check step correspondence between the transitions of C and those of A. The definition of forward simulation we use is adapted from that of Lynch and Vaandrager [28].

Definition 7. *A* forward simulation *from a concrete IOA C to an abstract IOA A is a relation $R \subseteq states(C) \times states(A)$ such that each of the following holds.*

Initialisation. $\forall cs \in start(C). \; \exists as \in start(A). \; R(cs, as)$

External Step Correspondence.
$\forall cs \in reach(C), as \in reach(A), a \in external(C), cs' \in states(C).$
$$R(cs, as) \wedge cs \xrightarrow{a}_C cs' \Rightarrow \exists as' \in states(A). \; R(cs', as') \wedge as \xrightarrow{a}_A as'$$
Internal Step Correspondence.
$\forall cs \in reach(C), as \in reach(A), a \in internal(C), cs' \in states(C).$
$$R(cs, as) \wedge cs \xrightarrow{a}_C cs' \Rightarrow$$
$$R(cs', as) \vee \exists a' \in internal(A), as' \in states(A). \; R(cs', as') \wedge as \xrightarrow{a'}_A as'$$

Forward simulation is *sound* in the sense that if there is a forward simulation between A and C, then C refines A [28,30].

4.2 IOA for DTML

We now provide the IOA model of DTML. The state of DTML (Fig. 1) comprises global (shared) variables $glb \in \mathbb{N}$ (modelling `glb` in volatile memory); $log \in L \rightarrowtail V$, where $\rightarrowtail$ denotes a partial function (modelling `log` in persistent memory); the volatile memory store $vstore \in L \rightarrow V$; and the persistent memory store $pstore \in L \rightarrow V$. We also use the following transaction-local variables: the program counter $pc \in T \rightarrow PC$, $loc \in T \rightarrow \mathbb{N}$, the input address $addr \in T \rightarrow V$, the input value $val \in T \rightarrow V$. We also make use of an auxiliary variable $writer$ whose value is either the transaction id of the current writing transaction (if one exists), or *None* (if no writing transaction is currently running).

Execution of the program is modelled by defining an IOA transition for each atomic step of Fig. 1, using the values of pc_t (for transaction t) to model control flow. Each action that starts a new operation or returns from a completed operation is an external action. The crash action is also external. All other actions (including flush and recovery) are internal actions.

To model system behaviours (crash, system flush and recovery), we reserve a special transaction id *syst*. A crash and system flush is always enabled, and hence can always be selected for execution. Recovery steps are enabled after a crash has taken place and are only executed by *syst*. The effect of a flush is to copy the value of the address being flushed from *vstore* to *pstore*. Note that a flush can also be executed at specific program locations. In DTML, a flush of `addr` occurs at lines W7 and C5. The effect of a crash is to perform the following:

- set the volatile store to the persistent store (since the volatile store is lost),
- set the program counters of all *in-flight transactions* (i.e., transactions that have started but not yet completed) to *aborted* to ensure that these transaction identifiers are not reused after the system is rebooted, and
- set the status of *syst* to C1 to model that a recovery is now in progress.

In our model, it is possible for a system to crash during recovery. However, no new transaction may start until after the recovery process has completed.

4.3   IOA for DTMS2

In this section, we describe the DTMS2 specification, an operational model that ensures durable opacity, which is based on TMS2 [15]. TMS2 itself has been shown to strictly imply opacity [26], and hence has been widely used as an intermediate specification in the verification of transactional memory implementations [1,2,12,14].

We let $f \oplus g$ denote functional override of f by g, e.g., $f \oplus \{x \mapsto u, y \mapsto v\} = \lambda k.$ if $k = x$ then u elseif $k = y$ then v else $f(k)$.

Formally, DTMS2 is specified by the IOA in Fig. 2, which describes the required ordering constraints, memory semantics and prefix properties. We assume a set L of locations and a set V of values. Thus, a memory is modelled by a function of type $L \to V$. A key feature of DTMS2 (like TMS2) is that it keeps track of a *sequence* of memory states, one for each committed writing transaction. This makes it simpler to determine whether reads are consistent with previously committed write operations. Each committing transaction containing at least one write adds a new memory version to the end of the memory sequence. However, unlike TMS2, following [11], the memory state is considered to be the persistent memory state. Interestingly, the volatile memory state need not be modelled.

The state space of DTMS2 has several components. The first, *mems* is the sequence of *memory* states. For each transaction t there is a program counter variable pc_t, which ranges over a set of *program counter values*, which are used to ensure that each transaction is well-formed, and to ensure that each transactional operation takes effect between its invocation and response. There is also a *begin index* variable $beginIdx_t$, that is set to the index of the most recent memory version when the transaction begins. This variable is critical to ensuring the real-time ordering property between transactions. Finally, there is a *read set*, $rdSet_t$, and a *write set*, $wrSet_t$, which record the values that the transaction has read and written during its execution, respectively.

State variables:
$mems : seq(L \rightarrow V)$, initially satisfying $\text{dom } mems = \{0\}$ and $initMem(mems(0))$
$pc_t : PCVal$, for each $t \in T$, initially $pc_t = \text{notStarted}$ for all $t \in T$
$beginIdx_t : \mathbf{N}$ for each $t \in T$, unconstrained initially
$rdSet_t : L \nrightarrow V$, initially empty for all $t \in T$
$wrSet_t : L \nrightarrow V$, initially empty for all $t \in T$

Transition relation:

$inv_t(\texttt{TMBegin})$
Pre: $pc_t = \text{notStarted}$
Eff: $pc_t := \text{beginPending}$
  $beginIdx_t := len(mems) - 1$

$inv_t(\texttt{TMRd}(l))$
Pre: $pc_t = \text{ready}$
Eff: $pc_t := \text{doRead}(l)$

$inv_t(\texttt{TMWr}(l, v))$
Pre: $pc_t = \text{ready}$
Eff: $pc_t := \text{doWrite}(l, v)$

$inv_t(\texttt{TMCommit})$
Pre: $pc_t = \text{ready}$
Eff: $pc_t := \text{doCommit}$

$resp_t(\text{abort})$
Pre: $pc_t \notin \{\text{notStarted, ready,}$
    $\text{commitResp, committed, aborted}\}$
Eff: $pc_t := \text{aborted}$

$\texttt{DoCommitReadOnly}_t(n)$
Pre: $pc_t = \text{doCommit}$
  $\text{dom}(wrSet_t) = \varnothing$
  $validIdx(t, n)$
Eff: $pc_t := \text{commitResp}$

$\texttt{DoRead}_t(l, n)$
Pre: $pc_t = \text{doRead}(l)$
  $l \in \text{dom}(wrSet_t) \vee validIdx(t, n)$
Eff: if $l \in \text{dom}(wrSet_t)$ then
    $pc_t := \text{readResp}(wrSet_t(l))$
  else $v := mems(n)(l)$
    $pc_t := \text{readResp}(v)$
    $rdSet_t := rdSet_t \oplus \{l \rightarrow v\}$

$resp_t(\texttt{TMBegin})$
Pre: $pc_t = \text{beginPending}$
Eff: $pc_t := \text{ready}$

$resp_t(\texttt{TMRd}(v))$
Pre: $pc_t = \text{readResp}(v)$
Eff: $pc_t := \text{ready}$

$resp_t(\texttt{TMWr})$
Pre: $pc_t = \text{writeResp}$
Eff: $pc_t := \text{ready}$

$resp_t(\texttt{TMCommit})$
Pre: $pc_t = \text{commitResp}$
Eff: $pc_t := \text{committed}$

$\texttt{DoWrite}_t(l, v)$
Pre: $pc_t = \text{doWrite}(l, v)$
Eff: $pc_t := \text{writeResp}$
  $wrSet_t := wrSet_t \oplus \{l \rightarrow v\}$

$\texttt{DoCommitWriter}_t$
Pre: $pc_t = \text{doCommit}$
  $rdSet_t \subseteq last(mems)$
Eff: $pc_t := \text{commitResp}$
  $mems := mems \frown (last(mems) \oplus wrSet_t)$

$crash_t$
Pre: $t = syst$
Eff: $pc := \lambda t : T.$
    if $t \neq syst \wedge$
      $pc_t \notin \{\text{notStarted, committed}\}$
    then $aborted$
  $mems = \langle last(mems) \rangle$

where $validIdx(t, n) \triangleq beginIdx_t \leq n < len(mems) \wedge rdSet_t \subseteq mems(n)$

Fig. 2. The state space and transition relation of DTMS2, which extends TMS2 with a crash event

The read set is used to determine whether the values that have been read by the transaction are consistent with the same version of memory (using *validIdx*). The write set, on the other hand, is required because writes in DTMS2 are modelled using *deferred update* semantics: writes are recorded in the transaction's write set, but are not published to any shared state until the transaction commits.

The *crash* action models both a crash and a recovery. We require that it is executed by the system thread *syst*. It sets the program counter of every in-flight transaction to *aborted*, which prevents these transactions from performing any further actions in the era following the crash (for the generated history). Note that since transaction identifiers are not reused, the program counters of completed transactions need not be set to any special value (e.g., *crashed*) as with durable linearizability [11]. Moreover, after restarting, it must not be possible for any new transaction to interact with memory states prior to the crash. We therefore reset the memory sequence to be a singleton sequence containing the last memory state prior to the crash.

The following theorem ensures that DTMS2 can be used as an intermediate specification in our proof method. We provide a proof sketch below. The full proof may be found in the appendix of [5].

Theorem 1. *Each trace of* DTMS2 *is durably opaque.*

Proof (Sketch). First we recall that TMS2 is exactly the same as the automaton in Fig. 2, but without a crash operation. The proof proceeds by showing that for any history $h \in traces(\text{DTMS2})$, we have that $ops(h) \in traces(\text{TMS2})$. Then since $ops(h)$ is opaque, we have that h is durably opaque. We establish a formal relationship between h and $ops(h)$ by establishing a *weak simulation* between DTMS2 and TMS2 such that $\{ops(h) \mid h \in traces(\text{DTMS2})\} \subseteq traces(\text{TMS2})$. The simulation is weak since the external *crash* action in DTMS2 has no matching counterpart in TMS2.

The simulation relation we use captures the following. Any transaction t of DTMS2 that is aborted due to a crash will set pc_t to *aborted* without executing $resp_t(\text{abort})$. This difference can easily be compensated by the simulation relation. A second difference is that *mems* is reset to *last(mems)* in DTMS2 when a crash occurs, and hence there is a mismatch between *mems* in DTMS2 and in TMS2. Let *ds* be a state of DTMS2 and *as* a state of TMS2. To compensate for the difference between *ds.mems* and *as.mems*, we introduce an auxiliary variable "*allMems*" to *ds* that records memories corresponding to all committed writing transactions in DTMS2. We have the property that *ds.mems* of DTMS2 is a suffix of *ds.allMems* and that *ds.allMems* = *as.mems*.

5   Durable Opacity of DTML

We now describe the simulation relation used in the Isabelle proof.[2]

---

[2] All Isabelle theory files related to this proof may be downloaded from [5].

Our simulation relation is divided into two relations: a *global relation* *globalRel*, and a transactional relation *txnRel*. The global relation describes how the shared states of the two automata are related, and the transaction relation specifies the relationship between the state of each transaction in the concrete automaton, and that of the transaction in the abstract automaton. The simulation relation itself is then given by:

$$simRel(cs, as) = globalRel(cs, as) \land \forall\, t \in T \bullet txnRel(cs, as, t)$$

We first describe *globalRel*, which assumes the following auxiliary definitions where *cs* is the concrete state (of DTML) and *as* is the abstract state (of DTMS2). These definitions are used to compensate for the fact that the commit of a writing transaction in the DTML algorithm takes effect (i.e., linearizes) at line E2 when the log is set to empty.

$$writes(cs, as) = \textbf{if } cs.writer = t \land pc_t \neq E3 \textbf{ then } as.wrSet_t \textbf{ else } \varnothing$$

$$logical\_glb(cs) = \textbf{if } cs.writer = t \land pc_t = E3 \textbf{ then } cs.glb + 1 \textbf{ else } cs.glb$$

$$write\_count(cs) = \left\lfloor \frac{logical\_glb(cs)}{2} \right\rfloor$$

Function $writes(cs, as)$ returns the (abstract) write set of the writing transaction. This is the write set of the writing transaction, t, in the abstract state as provided t hasn't already linearized its commit operation, and is the empty set otherwise. Function $logical\_glb(cs)$ compensates for a lagging value of *glb* after a writing transaction's commit operation is linearized. Namely, it returns the *glb* incremented by 1 if a writer is already at $E3$. Finally, $write\_count(cs)$ is used to determine the number of committed writing transactions in *cs* since the most recent crash since *cs.glb* is initially 0 and reset to 0 by the recovery operation, and moreover, *cs.glb* is incremented twice by each writing transaction: once at line W2 and again at line E2 when the writing transaction commits.

Relation *globalRel* comprises three main parts. We assume a program counter value *RecIdle* which is true for pc_{syst} iff *syst* is not executing the recovery procedure.

$$globalRel(cs, as)$$
$$= (pc_{syst} = RecIdle \Rightarrow cs.vstore = (last(as.mems) \oplus writes(cs, as)) \land \quad (1)$$

$$write\_count(cs) + 1 = length(as.mems))) \land \quad (2)$$

$$(cs.vstore \oplus cs.log) = last(mems(as)) \land \quad (3)$$

$$\forall\, t.t \neq syst \land cs.pc_t = NotStarted \Rightarrow as.pc_t = NotStarted \quad (4)$$

Conditions (1) and (2) assume that a recovery procedure is not in progress. By (1), the concrete volatile store is the last memory in *as.mems* overwritten with the write set of an in-flight writing transaction that has not linearized its commit operation. By (2), the number of memories recorded in the abstract state (since the last crash) is equal to $write\_count(cs) + 1$. By (3), the last abstract (persistent) store can by calculated from $cs.vstore$ by overriding it with the mappings in log. Note that this is equivalent to undoing all uncommitted transactional writes. Finally, (4) ensures that every identifier for a transaction that has not started at the concrete level also has not started at the abstract level.

We turn now to $txnRel$. Its specification is very similar to the specification of $txnRel$ in the proof of TML [10]. Therefore, we only provide a brief sketch below; an interested reader may consult [10] for further details. Part of $txnRel$ maps concrete program counters to their abstract counterparts, which enables steps of the concrete program to be matched with abstract steps. For example, concrete pc values W1, W2, ..., W6 correspond to abstract pc value doWrite($cs.addr_t, cs.val_t$), whereas W7 corresponds to writeResp, indicating that, in our proof, execution of line W6 corresponds to the execution of an abstract $DoWrite_t(cs.addr_t, cs.val_t)$ operation. Moreover, as in the proof of TML [10], a set of assertions are introduced to establish $as.validIdx(t, write\_count(cs))$ for all in-flight transactions t, which ensures that each transactional read and write is valid with respect to some memory snapshot.

Relation $txnRel$ must also provide enough information to enable linearization of a commit operation against the correct abstract step. Note that DTMS2 distinguishes between read-only and writing transactions by checking emptiness of the write set of the committing transaction. To handle this, we exploit the fact that in DTML, writing transactions have an odd loc value if the cas at line W2 is successful and loc is incremented at W3, indicating that a writing transaction is in progress.

Finally, $txnRel$ must ensure that the recovery operation is such that the volatile store matches the last abstract store in $mems$ prior to the crash. To achieve this, we require that $length(as.mems) = 1$ when $syst$ is executing the recovery procedure, and the volatile store for the address being flushed at C3 matches the abstract state before the crash, i.e., $cs.vstore(cs.addr_t) = ((as.mems)(0))(cs.addr_t)$. Since the recovery loop only terminates after the log is emptied, this ensures that the concrete memory state is consistent with the abstract memory prior to executing any transactions after a crash has occurred.

In order to prove that our simulation relation is maintained by each step of the algorithm, we must use certain invariants of the DTML model. These invariants are similar to the corresponding invariants used in a proof of the original TML algorithm for the conventional volatile RAM model (see [10] for details). For example, our invariants imply that there is at most one writing transaction, and there is no such transaction when glb is even. The main additional invariant that we use for DTML constrains the possible differences between volatile and persistent memory: volatile and persistent memory are identical except for any location that has been written by a writer or by the recovery procedure but not yet flushed. This simple invariant combined with the global relation is enough to prove that the memory state after each crash is correct. Our DTML invariants have been verified in Isabelle, and can be found in the Isabelle files.

6   Related Work

Although there is existing research on extending the definition of linearizability to durable systems, there is comparatively less work on extending other notions of transactional memory correctness such as, but not limited to, opacity to durable systems. Various systems attempt to achieve atomic durability, transform general objects to persistent objects and provide a secure interface of persistent memory. The above goals usually require the use of logging which can be software or hardware based. Raad et al have proposed a notion of durable serialisability under relaxed memory [34], but this model does not handle aborted transactions.

ATLAS [6] is a software system that provides durability semantics for NVRAM with lock-base multithreaded code. The system ensures that the outermost critical sections, which are protected by one or more mutexes, are failure-atomic by identifying Failure Atomic Sections (FASEs). These sections ensure that, if at least one update that occurs to a persistent location inside a FASE is durable, then all the updates inside the session are durable. Furthermore, like DTML, ATLAS keeps an persistent undo log, that tracks the synchronisation operations and persistent stores, and allows the recovery of rollback FASEs that were interrupted by crashes.

Koburn et al. [7] integrate persistent objects into conventional programs, and furthermore seek to prevent safety bugs that occur in predominantly persistent memory models, such as multiple frees, pointer errors, and locking errors. This is done by implementing NV-heaps, an interface to the NVRAM based on ACID transactions that guarantees safety and provides reasoning about the order in which changes to the data structures should become permanent. NV-heaps only handle updates to persistent memory inside transactions and critical sections. Other systems based on persistent ACID transactions include Mnemosyne [37], Stasis [36] and BerkeleyDB [33].

Ben-David et al. [4] developed a system that can transform programs that consist of read, write and CAS operations in shared memory, to persistent memory. The system aims to create concurrent algorithms that guarantee consistency after a fault. This is done by introducing checkpoints, which record the current state of the execution and from which the execution can be continued after a crash. Two consecutive checkpoints form a *capsule*, and if a crash occurs inside a capsule, program execution is continued from the previous capsule boundary. We have not applied this technique to develop DTML, but it would be interesting to develop and optimise capsules in an STM context.

Mnemosyne [37] provides a low-level interface to persistent memory with high-level transactions based on TinySTM [18] and a redo log that is purposely chosen to reduce ordering constraints. The log is flushed at the commit of each transaction. As a result, the memory locations that are written to by the transaction remain unmodified until commit. Each read operation checks whether data has been modified and if so, returns the buffered value instead of the value from the memory. The size of the log increases proportionally to the size of the transaction, potentially making the checking time consuming.

Hardware based durable transactional memory has also been proposed [24] with hardware support for redo logging [25]. Other indicative hardware systems help implement atomic durability either by performing accelerated ordering or by performing the logging operation are [27, 31].

7 Conclusions

In this paper we have defined durable opacity, a new correctness condition for STMs, inspired by durable linearizability [22] for concurrent objects. The condition assumes a history with crashes such that in-flight transactions are aborted (i.e., do not continue) after a crash takes place, and simply requires that the history satisfies opacity [19, 20] after the crashes are removed. This is a strong notion of correctness but ensures safety for STMs in the same way that durable linearizability [22] ensures safety for concurrent objects. It is already known that TMS1 [15], which is a weaker condition than opacity [26] is sufficient for contextual refinement [3]; therefore we conjecture that durable opacity can provide similar guarantees in a non-volatile context. For concurrent objects, more relaxed notions such as buffered durable linearizability [22] have also been proposed, which requires causally related operations to be committed in order, but real-time order need not be maintained. Such notions could also be considered in a transactional memory setting [16], but the precise specification of such a condition lies outside the scope of this paper.

To verify durable opacity, we have developed DTMS2, an operational characterisation that extends the TMS2 specification with a crash operation. We establish that all traces of DTMS2 are durably opaque, which makes it possible to prove durable opacity by showing refinement between an implementation and DTMS2. We develop a durably opaque example implementation, DTML, which extends TML [8] with a persistent undo log, and associated modifications such as the introduction of a recovery operation. Finally, we prove durable opacity of DTML by establishing a refinement between it and DTMS2. This proof has been fully mechanised in Isabelle.

Our focus has been on the formalisation of durable opacity and the development of an example algorithm and verification technique. Future work will consider alternative implementations of the algorithm, e.g., using a persistent set [38], or thread-local undo logs [23]. Develop and implement a logging mechanism based on undo and redo log properties named JUSTDO logging. This mechanism aims to reduce the memory size of log entries while preserving data integrity after crash occurrences. Unlike optimistic transactions [6], JUSTDO logging resumes the execution of interrupted FASEs to their last store instruction, and then executes them until completion. A small log is maintained for each thread, that records its most recent store within a FASE, simplifying the log management and reduce the memory requirements. Future work will also consider weakly consistent memory models building on existing works integrating persistency semantics with hardware memory models [34, 35].

References

1. Armstrong, A., Dongol, B.: Modularising opacity verification for hybrid transactional memory. In: Bouajjani, A., Silva, A. (eds.) FORTE 2017. LNCS, vol. 10321, pp. 33–49. Springer, Cham (2017). https://doi.org/10.1007/978-3-319-60225-7_3
2. Armstrong, A., Dongol, B., Doherty, S.: Proving opacity via linearizability: a sound and complete method. In: Bouajjani, A., Silva, A. (eds.) FORTE 2017. LNCS, vol. 10321, pp. 50–66. Springer, Cham (2017). https://doi.org/10.1007/978-3-319-60225-7_4
3. Attiya, H., Gotsman, A., Hans, S., Rinetzky, N.: Safety of live transactions in transactional memory: TMS is necessary and sufficient. In: Kuhn, F. (ed.) DISC 2014. LNCS, vol. 8784, pp. 376–390. Springer, Heidelberg (2014). https://doi.org/10.1007/978-3-662-45174-8_26
4. Ben-David, N., Blelloch, G.E., Friedman, M., Wei, Y.: Delay-free concurrency on faulty persistent memory. In: The 31st ACM Symposium on Parallelism in Algorithms and Architectures, pp. 253–264 (2019)
5. Bila, E., Doherty, S., Dongol, B., Derrick, J., Schellhorn, G., Wehrheim, H.: Defining and verifying durable opacity: correctness for persistent software transactional memory (2020). https://arxiv.org/abs/2004.08200
6. Chakrabarti, D.R., Boehm, H.J., Bhandari, K.: Atlas: leveraging locks for non-volatile memory consistency. ACM SIGPLAN Not. **49**(10), 433–452 (2014)
7. Coburn, J., et al.: Nv-heaps: making persistent objects fast and safe with next-generation, non-volatile memories. ACM SIGARCH Comput. Archit. News **39**(1), 105–118 (2011)
8. Dalessandro, L., Dice, D., Scott, M., Shavit, N., Spear, M.: Transactional mutex locks. In: D'Ambra, P., Guarracino, M., Talia, D. (eds.) Euro-Par 2010. LNCS, vol. 6272, pp. 2–13. Springer, Heidelberg (2010). https://doi.org/10.1007/978-3-642-15291-7_2
9. Dalessandro, L., Spear, M.F., Scott, M.L.: NORec: streamlining STM by abolishing ownership records. In: Govindarajan, R., Padua, D.A., Hall, M.W. (eds.) PPoPP, pp. 67–78. ACM (2010)
10. Derrick, J., Doherty, S., Dongol, B., Schellhorn, G., Travkin, O., Wehrheim, H.: Mechanized proofs of opacity: a comparison of two techniques. Formal Aspects Comput. **30**(5), 597–625 (2017). https://doi.org/10.1007/s00165-017-0433-3
11. Derrick, J., Doherty, S., Dongol, B., Schellhorn, G., Wehrheim, H.: Verifying correctness of persistent concurrent data structures. In: ter Beek, M.H., McIver, A., Oliveira, J.N. (eds.) FM 2019. LNCS, vol. 11800, pp. 179–195. Springer, Cham (2019). https://doi.org/10.1007/978-3-030-30942-8_12
12. Derrick, J., Dongol, B., Schellhorn, G., Travkin, O., Wehrheim, H.: Verifying opacity of a transactional mutex lock. In: Bjørner, N., de Boer, F. (eds.) FM 2015. LNCS, vol. 9109, pp. 161–177. Springer, Cham (2015). https://doi.org/10.1007/978-3-319-19249-9_11
13. Dice, D., Shalev, O., Shavit, N.: Transactional locking II. In: Dolev, S. (ed.) DISC 2006. LNCS, vol. 4167, pp. 194–208. Springer, Heidelberg (2006). https://doi.org/10.1007/11864219_14

14. Doherty, S., Dongol, B., Derrick, J., Schellhorn, G., Wehrheim, H.: Proving opacity of a pessimistic STM. In: Fatourou, P., Jiménez, E., Pedone, F. (eds.) OPODIS. LIPIcs, vol. 70, pp. 35:1–35:17. Schloss Dagstuhl - Leibniz-Zentrum für Informatik (2016)
15. Doherty, S., Groves, L., Luchangco, V., Moir, M.: Towards formally specifying and verifying transactional memory. Formal Asp. Comput. 25(5), 769–799 (2013)
16. Dongol, B., Jagadeesan, R., Riely, J.: Transactions in relaxed memory architectures. PACMPL 2(POPL), 18:1–18:29 (2018)
17. Dongol, B., Derrick, J.: Verifying linearisability: a comparative survey. ACM Comput. Surv. 48(2), 19:1–19:43 (2015)
18. Felber, P., Fetzer, C., Riegel, T.: Dynamic performance tuning of word-based software transactional memory. In: Proceedings of the 13th ACM SIGPLAN Symposium on Principles and Practice of Parallel Programming, pp. 237–246 (2008)
19. Guerraoui, R., Kapalka, M.: On the correctness of transactional memory. In: Chatterjee, S., Scott, M.L. (eds.) PPOPP, pp. 175–184. ACM (2008)
20. Guerraoui, R., Kapalka, M.: Principles of Transactional Memory. Synthesis Lectures on Distributed Computing Theory. Morgan & Claypool Publishers (2010)
21. Herlihy, M., Wing, J.M.: Linearizability: a correctness condition for concurrent objects. ACM TOPLAS 12(3), 463–492 (1990)
22. Izraelevitz, J., Mendes, H., Scott, M.L.: Linearizability of persistent memory objects under a full-system-crash failure model. In: Gavoille, C., Ilcinkas, D. (eds.) DISC 2016. LNCS, vol. 9888, pp. 313–327. Springer, Heidelberg (2016). https://doi.org/10.1007/978-3-662-53426-7_23
23. Izraelevitz, J., Kelly, T., Kolli, A.: Failure-atomic persistent memory updates via justdo logging. ACM SIGARCH Comput. Archit. News 44(2), 427–442 (2016)
24. Joshi, A., Nagarajan, V., Cintra, M., Viglas, S.: DHTM: durable hardware transactional memory. In: 2018 ACM/IEEE 45th Annual International Symposium on Computer Architecture (ISCA), pp. 452–465. IEEE (2018)
25. Joshi, A., Nagarajan, V., Viglas, S., Cintra, M.: Atom: atomic durability in non-volatile memory through hardware logging. In: 2017 IEEE International Symposium on High Performance Computer Architecture (HPCA), pp. 361–372. IEEE (2017)
26. Lesani, M., Luchangco, V., Moir, M.: Putting opacity in its place. In: Workshop on the Theory of Transactional Memory (2012)
27. Lu, Y., Shu, J., Sun, L., Mutlu, O.: Loose-ordering consistency for persistent memory. In: 2014 IEEE 32nd International Conference on Computer Design (ICCD), pp. 216–223. IEEE (2014)
28. Lynch, N., Vaandrager, F.: Forward and backward simulations. Inf. Comput. 121(2), 214–233 (1995)
29. Lynch, N.A., Tuttle, M.R.: Hierarchical correctness proofs for distributed algorithms. In: PODC, pp. 137–151. ACM, New York (1987)
30. Müller, O.: I/O Automata and beyond: temporal logic and abstraction in Isabelle. In: Grundy, J., Newey, M. (eds.) TPHOLs, pp. 331–348. Springer, Heidelberg (1998)
31. Nalli, S., Haria, S., Hill, M.D., Swift, M.M., Volos, H., Keeton, K.: An analysis of persistent memory use with whisper. ACM SIGPLAN Not. 52(4), 135–148 (2017)
32. Nipkow, T., Wenzel, M., Paulson, L.C. (eds.): Isabelle/HOL. LNCS, vol. 2283. Springer, Heidelberg (2002). https://doi.org/10.1007/3-540-45949-9
33. Olson, M.A., Bostic, K., Seltzer, M.I.: Berkeley DB. In: USENIX Annual Technical Conference, FREENIX Track, pp. 183–191 (1999)

34. Raad, A., Wickerson, J., Vafeiadis, V.: Weak persistency semantics from the ground up: formalising the persistency semantics of ARMV8 and transactional models. PACMPL **3**(OOPSLA), 135:1–135:27 (2019)
35. Raad, A., Vafeiadis, V.: Persistence semantics for weak memory: integrating epoch persistency with the TSO memory model. PACMPL **2**(OOPSLA), 137:1–137:27 (2018)
36. Sears, R., Brewer, E., Brewer, E., Brewer, E.: Stasis: flexible transactional storage. In: Proceedings of the 7th symposium on Operating Systems Design and Implementation, pp. 29–44. USENIX Association (2006)
37. Volos, H., Tack, A.J., Swift, M.M.: Mnemosyne: lightweight persistent memory. ACM SIGARCH Comput. Archit. News **39**(1), 91–104 (2011)
38. Zuriel, Y., Friedman, M., Sheffi, G., Cohen, N., Petrank, E.: Efficient lock-free durable sets. PACMPL **3**(OOPSLA), 1281–12826 (2019)

Conformance-Based Doping Detection for Cyber-Physical Systems

Rayna Dimitrova[1], Maciej Gazda[1], Mohammad Reza Mousavi[2(✉)],
Sebastian Biewer[3], and Holger Hermanns[3]

[1] Department of Computer Science, University of Sheffield, Sheffield, UK
[2] School of Informatics, University of Leicester, Leicester, UK
`mm789@le.ac.uk`
[3] Saarland University - Computer Science, Saarland Informatics Campus,
Saarbrücken, Germany

Abstract. We present a novel and generalised notion of doping cleanness for cyber-physical systems that allows for perturbing the inputs and
observing the perturbed outputs both in the time– and value–domains.
We instantiate our definition using existing notions of conformance for
cyber-physical systems. We show that our generalised definitions are
essential in a data-driven method for doping detection and apply our
definitions to a case study concerning diesel emission tests.

1 Introduction

System doping, in our terminology, is an intentional intervention causing a
change in the system's normal behaviour against the interests of the user or
other stakeholders (such as the society at large). Examples of system doping are
widespread and range from vendors' enforcing a monopoly on chargers and spare
parts (by checking for and refusing third-party chargers and spare parts, respectively) to tampering with exhaust emission in order to detect and pass emission
tests. Doping can be the result of embedding a piece of code or smuggling a
piece of electronic circuit into the system and it can be caused by the original
developers or by hackers. Software and system doping has been studied in the
past couple of years and rigorous theories for it have been developed [8,9,15].
These theories were subsequently adopted in order to detect doping, or formally,
to check system cleanness [10,32] (corresponding to the absence of doping).

In the present paper, we extend the theory of doping to the setting of cyber-
physical systems (CPS) by exploiting the notions of conformance testing for
CPS [1,17,33]. The existing theories of software doping define doping in terms
of drastic deviations in output as a result of minor deviations in input, where

This work is partly supported by the ERC Grant 695614 (POWVER) by the Deutsche
Forschungsgemeinschaft (DFG, German Research Foundation) grant 389792660 as part
of TRR 248, see https://perspicuous-computing.science, by the Saarbrücken Graduate
School of Computer Science, and by the Sino-German CDZ project 1023 (CAP).

A. Gotsman and A. Sokolova (Eds.): FORTE 2020, LNCS 12136, pp. 59–77, 2020.
https://doi.org/10.1007/978-3-030-50086-3_4

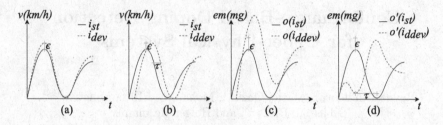

Fig. 1. Running example: specified (a) and actual (b) test cycles and emission footprints obtained from different (fictitious) vehicles (c) and (d).

the term "deviation" refers to differences in validity of propositions or values of variables. However, the current notions come short of properly dealing with the issues of retiming and delays, which are commonly present in the signals of CPS. We observe that this is an essential aspect of detecting doping for cyber-physical systems: often the traces to be tested for doping have subtly different timing behaviour, e.g., due to measurement and calibration errors or due to the slight deviations of human actors in acting upon the planned scenarios. The insufficient treatment of retiming and delays can both lead to false negatives, i.e., missing cases of doping, as well as false positives, i.e., reporting spurious doping cases.

To address these issues, we exploit the notion of conformance to devise a general theory of being clean from doping and instantiate that theory with some existing notions of conformance for hybrid systems. We show how these notions can account for retiming and lead to more precise notions of cleanness.

We illustrate the usefulness of our theory by empirical analysis of diesel engine exhaust emissions in the context of one of the official test cycles, the New European Driving Cycle (NEDC) [42]. In particular, we show that catering for retiming is essential in effectively exploiting the actual driving cycles for performing doping analysis. We thus demonstrate that our new theory remedies a major shortcoming in the existing notions from the literature. To facilitate the presentation, we use throughout the remainder of this paper the following simple running example, which is inspired by our case study.

Example 1. Figure 1.(a) shows two test cycles (evolution of speed over time), designed to detect whether the exhaust emission control of a particular vehicle is doped. The test cycle i_{st}, depicted with a black solid line, is the standard one prescribed by the (fictitious) official regulation, while test cycle i_{dev}, depicted by a red dotted line, is a slight deviation thereof. If the exhaust emissions measured during the test cycle i_{dev} turn out to be significantly higher than the ones measured in test cycle i_{st}, then we can conclude that the exhaust emission system is potentially doped, since it appears tailored to the standard test cycle.

Figure 1.(b) addresses a notorious problem of testing cars: a human tester is supposed to drive the car as just described, however, she can do this only up to a certain imprecision. Assume her driving of i_{dev} exhibits a slight time shift τ relative to the test cycle, as in i_{ddev}, while i_{st} is being driven as intended.

The result of a test is the emission footprint measured at the exhaust pipe of the car. Figure 1.(c) and Fig. 1.(d) show two different possible test results (obtained from different cars) for the scenario in Fig. 1.(b). Intuitively, the footprints in Fig. 1.(c) provide significant evidence for doping – a slightly different test cycle has resulted in significantly larger footprint. However, due to the time shift on the input side Fig. 1.(b) the point-wise difference of the two driven test-cycles has grown very large. As we show in the remainder of this paper, the existing theory of doping fails to detect such a clear evidence, due to the minor delay during the execution of the driving cycle. The emission footprint in Fig. 1.(d) is another (synthetic) example of a significant deviation which cannot be detected for the input in Fig. 1.(b) using existing theories; this latter footprint sheds some light on the intricate design decisions in the theory we develop in this paper.

The contributions for this paper can be summarized as follows:

– We define a *general notion of conformance* that can express different ways of comparing execution traces by allowing deviations both in value and in time.
– We define a general *notion of cleanness for hybrid systems*, and show that it subsumes the existing notion of robust cleanness [15].
– We demonstrate the usefulness of the proposed generic framework by applying it to *software doping tests* in the automotive domain, where we show that the new cleanness definition is able to flag a case of software doping that goes unnoticed when robust cleanness is used.

2 Related Work

The term "software doping" was coined around 2015 [30] in media uncovering the diesel exhaust emissions scandal. An informal problem formulation [8] pointed out the general phenomenon of intentionally added hidden software behaviour, which is not in the interest of the consumer. Shortly after, this observation has been complemented by a set of formal *cleanness* definitions [15] laying the theoretical foundations upon which formal methods to detect such software behaviour can be used. It is possible to detect missing functionality and undesired existing functionality. The definitions support both sequential programs and non-deterministic reactive programs. To check satisfaction of the definitions, it is necessary to compare two (or more) execution traces of the same system. Such properties are called *hyperproperties* [13] (whereas classical properties are *trace properties*). Tool support for analysing hyperproperties typically requires high computational effort [12,25]. There exist several temporal logics for analysing satisfaction of trace properties of various kinds of systems, one of them being *Linear Temporal Logic* (LTL) [39] for systems producing outputs in discrete time steps and properties that do not consider the time passing between outputs. LTL has been extended to the logic HyperLTL, which can express hyperproperties by allowing explicit quantification of execution traces in front of an

LTL formula [12]. Tools for model-checking boolean circuits, satisfiability and monitoring of HyperLTL specifications have been developed [6, 11, 21–25, 29].

Signal Temporal Logic (STL) [36] is an extension of LTL that adds support for time constraints and real-valued signals. Tools exist that automatically try to falsify STL formulas [7, 18]. There has been an extension of STL to HyperSTL in a similar fashion as it was done for HyperLTL [37]. The syntax of HyperSTL, however, is not able to express the cleanness definitions (for deterministic systems) in a way that allows (efficient) falsification. *Robust cleanness* is defined for distance functions on inputs and outputs [15]. When used with temporal logics the distance functions are restricted to those compatible with the logics. To be fully independent, robust cleanness analysis has been embedded into the theory of model-based testing [10] with input-output conformance [40, 41].

Notions of conformance for discrete event systems have been discussed for almost a century. The earliest work on this topic dates back to 1960's when researchers studied model-based testing of digital circuits using Finite State Machine models [31, 35]. Concurrency theory contributed ideas to this field, such as decoupling (i.e., removing the synchronised assumption between) inputs and outputs and observing failures to engage in a communication (and more specifically quiescence) [16, 40]. A theory of conformance testing for systems with continuous dynamics was developed by Michiel van Osch [38]; this theory did not gain much popularity in practice, partly because of its insufficient treatment of approximation (e.g., differences in values and retiming). Pappas and Girard [27, 28] proposed the use of Metric Bisimulation for conformance checking in dynamical systems and Pappas and Fainekos [20] developed a falsification framework for the same purpose. This research led to two notions of conformance used in the present paper, namely hybrid conformance by Abbas and Fainekos [1] and Skorokhod conformance by Deshmukh, Majumdar, and Prabhu [17].

3   Preliminaries

Semantic Domain. In this section, we provide definitions regarding semantic domain, conformance, and robust cleanness. We begin with the definition of our semantic domain, called generalised timed traces [26]. This definition subsumes both discrete-time state sequences and continuous-time trajectories. A generalised timed trace is a function with a discrete or continuous domain (called time domain) and a co-domain which is a metric space. Intuitively, a generalized timed trace maps each element of its time domain to a state. We require that the set of possible states is a metric space since we study conformance notions that compare traces based on the distance between the states of the traces.

Definition 1. *Let* $(\mathcal{Y}, d_{\mathcal{Y}})$ *be a metric space. A* $\mathcal{Y}$-*valued* generalised timed trace (GTT) *is a function* $\mu : \mathcal{T} \to \mathcal{Y}$ *such that* $\mathcal{T} \subseteq \mathbb{R}_{\geq 0}$. *We call* $\mathcal{T}$ *the* time domain *of* μ, *denoted* $dom(\mu)$. $GTT(\mathcal{Y})$ *is the set of all* $\mathcal{Y}$-*valued generalised timed traces.*

For a GTT $\mu : \mathcal{T} \to \mathcal{Y}$ and time $t_0 \in \mathcal{T}$, by $\mu[\ldots t_0]$ we denote the prefix of μ up to t_0, i.e., the restriction $\mu|_{t \in \mathcal{T} : t \leq t_0}$; likewise, by $\mu[t_s \ldots t_e]$, we shall denote the restriction $\mu|_{t \in \mathcal{T} : t_s \leq t \leq t_e}$

A hybrid system is a mapping from generalised (input) traces to sets of generalised (output) timed traces.

Definition 2. *A $\mathcal{Y}$-valued hybrid system is a function $H : GTT(\mathcal{Y}) \to \mathcal{P}(GTT(\mathcal{Y}))$ such that for all $\mu \in GTT(\mathcal{Y})$ and all $\mu' \in H(\mu)$ it holds that $dom(\mu') = dom(\mu)$. We define $\mathcal{H}(\mathcal{Y})$ to be the set of all $\mathcal{Y}$-valued hybrid systems.*

In addition, we distinguish deterministic hybrid systems whose output values range over singleton sets only. In what follows, we identify deterministic hybrid systems with functions of the type $GTT(\mathcal{Y}) \to GTT(\mathcal{Y})$.

For simplicity, we assume that the input and output domain are defined on the same metric spaces. The generalisation to different spaces is straightforward.

Conformance Relations. Recently, a number of notions of conformance for cyber-physical systems have been proposed [3,33]. It turns out that these notions, two of which are quoted below, can provide a rigorous basis for doping detection.

Note that throughout the paper, the variables τ and ϵ (with possible subscripts) always range over non-negative real numbers.

Definition 3. *We say that $\mathcal{Y}$-valued GTTs $\mu_1 : \mathcal{T}_1 \to \mathcal{Y}$ and $\mu_2 : \mathcal{T}_2 \to \mathcal{Y}$ are:*

- *trace conformant with tolerance threshold for signal value ϵ, notation TraceConf$_\epsilon(\mu_1, \mu_2)$, if $\mathcal{T}_1 = \mathcal{T}_2$ and for all $t \in \mathcal{T}_1$, $d_\mathcal{Y}(\mu_1(t), \mu_2(t)) \leq \epsilon$*
- *hybrid conformant with thresholds τ and ϵ, denoted HybridConf$_{\tau,\epsilon}(\mu_1, \mu_2)$, if:*
  - $\forall t_1 \in \mathcal{T}_1 \exists t_2 \in \mathcal{T}_2 : |t_2 - t_1| \leq \tau \land d_\mathcal{Y}(\mu_2(t_2), \mu_1(t_1)) \leq \epsilon$
  - $\forall t_2 \in \mathcal{T}_2 \exists t_1 \in \mathcal{T}_1 : |t_1 - t_2| \leq \tau \land d_\mathcal{Y}(\mu_1(t_1), \mu_2(t_2)) \leq \epsilon$
- *Skorokhod conformant with tolerance thresholds τ and ϵ, notation SkorConf$_{\tau,\epsilon}(\mu_1, \mu_2)$, if $\mathcal{T}_1$ and $\mathcal{T}_2$ are intervals and there is a strictly increasing continuous bijection $r : \mathcal{T}_1 \to \mathcal{T}_2$ called retiming, such that:*
  - *for all $t \in \mathcal{T}_1$, $|r(t) - t| \leq \tau$, and*
  - *for all $t \in \mathcal{T}_1$, $d_\mathcal{Y}(\mu_1(t), \mu_2(r(t))) \leq \epsilon$.*

We show in the proposition below and also in our generalisation results in Sect. 4, that these notions are closely related. However, they also have some fundamental differences, that can be illustrated using the example in Fig. 1.

Example 2. Consider again the example shown in Fig. 1. We can see that in Fig. 1.(a) i_{st} and i_{dev} are trace conformant with value threshold ϵ, as they only exhibit point-wise deviations by values less than ϵ. In contrast, i_{st} and i_{ddev} in Fig. 1.(b) are not trace conformant, yet they are hybrid conformant with time and value margins τ and ϵ, respectively. The key difference is that the inputs depicted in Fig. 1.(b) are very different if compared point-wise, but if one allows for retiming, they are close enough in value after retiming.

The outputs $o'(i_{st})$ and $o'(i_{ddev})$ in Fig. 1.(d) illustrate the fundamental difference between hybrid and Skorokhod conformance: although the order of rising and falling signals are reversed in the two trajectories, they are still hybrid conformant, because hybrid conformance disregards the order. However, Skorokhod conformance requires an order-preserving retiming, and hence distinguishes these two trajectories. On the other hand, such retiming exists, e.g., for i_{st} and i_{ddev} in Fig. 1.(b), witnessing their Skorokhod conformance.

We shall use the following notation. We write $\mathsf{Conf}_1 \sqsubseteq \mathsf{Conf}_2$ whenever for all $\mu_1 : \mathcal{T}_1 \to \mathcal{Y}$ and $\mu_2 : \mathcal{T}_2 \to \mathcal{Y}$, we have $\mathsf{Conf}_1(\mu_1, \mu_2) \implies \mathsf{Conf}_2(\mu_1, \mu_2)$. We write $\mathsf{Conf}_1 \sqsubset \mathsf{Conf}_2$ whenever $\mathsf{Conf}_1 \sqsubseteq \mathsf{Conf}_2$ and $\neg\, \mathsf{Conf}_2 \sqsubseteq \mathsf{Conf}_1$.

Proposition 1. *For any $\tau, \epsilon \in \mathbb{R}_{\geq 0}$, the following relations hold:*

$$TraceConf_\epsilon \sqsubset SkorConf_{\tau,\epsilon} \sqsubset HybridConf_{\tau,\epsilon}$$

Robust Cleanness. We shall now state the original definition of robust cleanness from [15], adapted to our framework of hybrid systems. It is based on Definition 7 and Proposition 19 from [15]; the phrasing below abstracts from the so-called parameters of interest and standard inputs. Moreover it is cast in the setting of generalised timed traces rather than discrete-step programs, and stated using trace conformance with different thresholds for inputs and outputs, κ_I and κ_O.

Intuitively, a hybrid system is robustly clean if for every pair of input prefixes on which no difference in the inputs exceeding κ_I has occurred so far (i.e., all sub-prefixes are trace conformant), the corresponding sets of output prefixes are also conformant with respect to κ_O. As we consider nondeterministic systems, Hausdorff distance is used to compare sets of outputs (see [15] for details).

Definition 4. *A hybrid system H is robustly clean, denoted RobustClean (κ_I, κ_O), whenever:*
$$\forall i_1, i_2 \in GTT(\mathcal{Y}) : \forall t \in dom(i_1) \cup dom(i_2) :$$
$$\bigl(\forall t' \leq t : TraceConf_{\kappa_I}(i_1[\ldots t'], i_2[\ldots t']) \implies$$
$$\bigl((\forall o_1 \in H(i_1)\, \exists o_2 \in H(i_2) : TraceConf_{\kappa_O}(o_1[\ldots t], o_2[\ldots t])) \wedge$$
$$(\forall o_2 \in H(i_2)\, \exists o_1 \in H(i_1) : TraceConf_{\kappa_O}(o_1[\ldots t], o_2[\ldots t])))\bigr)$$

Note that in the above definition we do not require that $dom(i_1) = dom(i_2)$. In practice, robust cleanness is typically applied to pairs of traces that are both defined over $\mathbb{N}$. Here, however, for the sake of generality we impose no such restriction. In particular, when the time domains of two traces are different, for example disjoint, the predicate RobustClean will trivially evaluate to *true*.

Example 3. Consider the traces depicted in Fig. 1. The input prefixes i_{st} and i_{ddev} are given in Fig. 1.(b), and the corresponding pair of outputs is shown in Fig. 1.(c). The trace i_{st} results in output $o(i_{st})$ and i_{ddev} results in $o(i_{ddev})$. Suppose that $\epsilon < |i_{st}(t_0) - i_{ddev}(t_0)|$ and $\epsilon < |o(i_{st})(t_1) - o(i_{ddev})(t_1)|$ at some time t_1. Thus, the left-hand side of the implication in the Definition 4 instantiated with $\kappa_I = \kappa_O = \epsilon$ does not hold for any t'. Hence, regardless of the outputs, this pair of inputs satisfies the condition of RobustClean(ϵ, ϵ), and, if these are the only traces in a hybrid system H then we can conclude that H is RobustClean(ϵ, ϵ).

4   Conformance-Based Cleanness

We now define a general notion of conformance-based cleanness and provide two instantiations based on the conformance notions defined in the previous section. The need for considering disturbance in time as well as in value is motivated by our running example from Fig. 1. One of the challenges in performing doping tests for cyber-physical systems is that in such systems timing is rarely perfectly precise, due to imprecision in measurements, or caused by the interaction with the physical world. As illustrated in Example 1, for instance, when checking for software doping in a car [10], the input to the system is the value of the car's speed over time, which is under the control of a driver, and can thus vary from one execution to the other, even if the driver is trying to execute the same input sequence. Clearly, those variations can be in value, as well as in time.

Example 4. Consider the test setup sketched in Fig. 1. There, i_{st} and i_{ddev}, depicted in Fig. 1.(b) define speed of a car as a function of time. These two input sequences follow a trajectory of values differing by a small margin ϵ (the difference in value allowed by the standard defining the doping tests), but also shifted by a small unit of time τ. Observe further that $|i_{st}(t_0) - i_{ddev}(t_0)| \gg \epsilon$. Thus, without allowing for deviations in time when comparing these input sequences, they will be considered sufficiently different, and as a result their respective exhaust emission outputs will fall out of the comparison when checking for doping according to Definition 4, even if the NO_x emission values in the corresponding outputs $H(i_{st}(t))$ and $H(i_{ddev}(t))$ are vastly different, as depicted in Fig. 1.(c). This results in a false negative, i.e., failing to detect a clearly doped system.

In the above example, we demonstrated that not accounting for timing disturbances when relating input trajectories can result in false negatives in doping detection. Dually, using the traditional comparison for output traces can result in false positives by requiring overly strict matching of outputs.

The above example motivates the need to account for timing deviations in trajectories. Intuitively, for input trajectories this relaxation results in considering more traces as conforming, and thus enforcing more comparisons when checking if a system is clean. For output trajectories this means relaxing the conformance requirement by considering two output sequences as conforming even if their values are not perfectly aligned in time. Furthermore, different types of timing deviations need to be considered in different scenarios, for example, depending on whether the order in which values occur is important or not.

Example 5. Consider the testing workflow from Example 1 and Fig. 1, where inputs i_{st} and i_{ddev} are passed to a car. In the second experiment, depicted in Fig. 1.(d), the car outputs $o'(i_{st})$ and $o'(i_{ddev})$, which are hybrid conformant for ϵ and τ. Hence this observation of the system is classified as clean under hybrid output conformance. However, the output $o'(i_{ddev})$ is clearly suspicious, as the values in $o'(i_{ddev})$ and $o'(i_{st})$ are reversed. This motivates considering conformance notions that require retimings to be order-preserving. Indeed, using Skorokhod conformance we can detect that the system is doped.

The above examples show that in order to be useful in a diverse set of applications, a software cleanness theory should allow for using a variety of conformance notions. To this end, we next take a more general view on conformance notions, in order to be able to develop a generic conformance-based cleanness framework.

So far, we have defined three specific notions of conformance which either coincide, or are closely inspired by ones that have appeared in the literature. In order to define a general framework for cleanness, we also wish to treat notions of conformance in a more generic manner. To this end, we propose an abstract definition of conformance predicates. As conformance predicates admit variations in time, as well as in value, our definition is based on *retimings*, a device that will play a key role in the context of this work. In its general form a retiming is a pair of functions between two time domains. Intuitively, given two GTTs, a retiming will define a mapping from points in each of the traces to points in the other trace. Note that in general the mappings are not required to be injective; this way we can cater for notions of conformance allowing for the so-called local disorder phenomenon (in particular hybrid conformance – see Proposition 2).

Definition 5. *A* retiming *is a pair of functions between two time domains, i.e., a pair of the form* (r_1, r_2)*, where* $r_1 : \mathcal{T}_1 \to \mathcal{T}_2$ *and* $r_2 : \mathcal{T}_2 \to \mathcal{T}_1$*, with time domains* $\mathcal{T}_1, \mathcal{T}_2 \subseteq \mathbb{R}_{\geq 0}$*. Given two time domains* $\mathcal{T}_1$ *and* $\mathcal{T}_2$*, we denote the set of all retimings between* $\mathcal{T}_1$ *and* $\mathcal{T}_2$ *with* $\mathcal{RET}(\mathcal{T}_1, \mathcal{T}_2)$*.*

Retiming is explicitly present in the definition of Skorokhod conformance; there, each Skorokhod retiming is required to be a strictly increasing continuous bijection. We can express a Skorokhod retiming r as an instance of our definition as the pair (r, r^{-1}). In fact, one can also define hybrid conformance, as well as a whole class of conformance notions, using a suitable *family* of retimings.

A family of retimings Ret can be further constrained by τ to a subset Ret_τ of Ret containing only functions that shift time by at most τ time units. In order to use a family of retimings for concrete sequences μ_1 and μ_2, it is necessary to consider only functions that match the domains of the sequences. This leads to a generic notion of conformance associated with a given family of retimings Ret, a given time threshold τ and a given value threshold ϵ.

Definition 6. *Let* Ret *be a family of retimings, and let*

$$\text{Ret}_\tau \quad \triangleq \{(r_1, r_2) \in \text{Ret} \mid \forall t \in dom(r_i) : |r_i(t) - t| \leq \tau \ (i = 1, 2)\},$$
$$\text{Ret}_\tau(\mathcal{T}_1, \mathcal{T}_2) \triangleq \text{Ret}_\tau \cap \mathcal{RET}(\mathcal{T}_1, \mathcal{T}_2).$$

A conformance notion with time threshold τ *and value threshold* ϵ *induced by* Ret *is a predicate* $\text{Conf}_{\tau,\epsilon}^{\text{Ret}}$ *on pairs of GTTs such that, for* $\mu_1 : \mathcal{T}_1 \to \mathcal{Y}$, $\mu_2 : \mathcal{T}_2 \to \mathcal{Y}$:

$$\text{Conf}_{\tau,\epsilon}^{\text{Ret}}(\mu_1, \mu_2) \iff \exists (r_1, r_2) \in \text{Ret}_\tau(\mathcal{T}_1, \mathcal{T}_2) : \forall t \in \mathcal{T}_1 : d_{\mathcal{Y}}(\mu_1(t), \mu_2 \circ r_1(t)) \leq \epsilon$$
$$\wedge \ \forall t \in \mathcal{T}_2 : d_{\mathcal{Y}}(\mu_2(t), \mu_1 \circ r_2(t)) \leq \epsilon.$$

Using the above definition, we can easily express the specific notions of conformance defined in the previous section by selecting a suitable family of retimings.

Proposition 2. *The conformance predicates below coincide with the notions of conformance induced by the corresponding families of retimings:*

- *TraceConf$_\epsilon$ is induced by the family of retimings containing only identity functions:* $\mathsf{Ret_{id}} = \{(\mathrm{id}, \mathrm{id}) \mid \mathrm{id} : \mathcal{T} \to \mathcal{T}$ *is the identity on some* $\mathcal{T} \subseteq \mathbb{R}_{\geq 0}\}$.
- *SkorConf$_{\tau,\epsilon}$ is induced by the family of retimings* $\mathsf{Ret} = \{(r, r^{-1}) \mid r$ *is a strictly increasing continuous bijection*$\}$.
- *HybridConf$_{\tau,\epsilon}$ is induced by pairs of arbitrary functions.*

Definition 6 also enables us to define other notions of conformance, such as, for instance a "shift conformance", which, intuitively, shifts all time points by a given constant $c \in \mathbb{R}$, i.e., $\mathsf{Ret}_c = \{(r, r^{-1}) \mid r(t) = t + c\}$.

Next, we define a generic notion of cleanness, parametrised by conformance predicates for the input and for the output traces. Instantiating these predicates with existing or new conformance notions, yields different conformance-based notions of cleanness that can capture a variety of cleanness specifications.

We now extend the notion of robust cleanness [15] to allow for "small" variations in time, in addition to the variations in value. To this end, the new notion makes use of two conformance predicates, one that postulates when two input traces should be considered close enough, and another one that specifies when two output traces are close enough.

Our starting point, the notion of robust cleanness in Definition 4, is based on comparison of matching prefixes of a pair of input traces and the corresponding prefixes of the associated output traces. As we now want to accommodate for distance in time, we (1) compare prefixes using a conformance relation, and (2) allow for variation in the length of the compared prefixes that is within the corresponding time-distance threshold. More precisely, when comparing two prefixes, we allow for discarding start and end segments of length at most τ.

This intuition is formalized by the predicate PrefConf for relaxed comparison of GTT prefixes using a notion of conformance Conf with tolerance threshold τ for time disturbance. We use cascaded notation to define PrefConf as a higher-order function taking Conf as its first argument. The predicate PrefConf compares two prefixes μ_1 and μ_2 by requiring that there exist traces $\mu_1[t_1^s \ldots t_1^e]$ and $\mu_2[t_2^s \ldots t_2^e]$ obtained from them, that are conformant with respect to Conf. These traces are obtained by possibly removing a sub-prefix of length at most τ, and/or removing extending with a suffix of length at most τ.

Definition 7. *Let* Conf *be a notion of conformance on GTTs with tolerance threshold τ for time disturbance. For any pair of GTTs $\mu_1 : \mathcal{T}_1 \to \mathcal{Y}$, $\mu_2 : \mathcal{T}_2 \to \mathcal{Y}$, and $t \in \mathcal{T} = \mathcal{T}_1 \cup \mathcal{T}_2$, the predicate* PrefConf *is defined as:*

$$\mathsf{PrefConf}(\mu_1, \mu_2, t) \Longleftrightarrow \exists t_1^s \in [0, \tau] \cap \mathcal{T}_1, \exists t_1^e \in [t - \tau, t + \tau] \cap \mathcal{T}_1,$$
$$\exists t_2^s \in [0, \tau] \cap \mathcal{T}_2, \exists t_2^e \in [t - \tau, t + \tau] \cap \mathcal{T}_2 :$$
$$\mathsf{Conf}(\mu_1[t_1^s \ldots t_1^e], \mu_2[t_2^s \ldots t_2^e]).$$

The predicate PrefConf provides a generic notion of prefix-conformance. By instantiating it with conformance relations Conf$_I$ and Conf$_O$ for input and output traces respectively, we define the notion of (Conf$_I$, Conf$_O$)-cleanness.

For deterministic systems $(\mathsf{Conf}_I, \mathsf{Conf}_O)$-cleanness requires that for all pairs of input prefixes for which all sub-prefixes are prefix-conformant w.r.t. Conf_I, the corresponding pair of output prefixes are prefix-conformant w.r.t. Conf_O.

Definition 8. *A deterministic system H is $(\mathsf{Conf}_I, \mathsf{Conf}_O)$-clean if*
$$\forall i_1, i_2 \in GTT(\mathcal{Y}) : \forall t \in dom(i_1) \cup dom(i_2) :$$
$$(\forall t' \leq t : \mathsf{PrefConf}_I(i_1, i_2, t')) \implies \mathsf{PrefConf}_O(H(i_1), H(i_2), t).$$

The above definition naturally generalises to nondeterministic hybrid systems, by comparing sets of possible output prefixes using Hausdorff distance as in [15].

Definition 9. *A system H is $(\mathsf{Conf}_I, \mathsf{Conf}_O)$-clean if*
$$\forall i_1, i_2 \in GTT(\mathcal{Y}) : \forall t \in dom(i_1) \cup dom(i_2) :$$
$$(\forall t' \leq t : \mathsf{PrefConf}_I(i_1, i_2, t')) \implies$$
$$((\forall o_1 \in H(i_1) \exists o_2 \in H(i_2) : \mathsf{PrefConf}_O(o_1, o_2, t)) \wedge$$
$$(\forall o_2 \in H(i_2) \exists o_1 \in H(i_1) : \mathsf{PrefConf}_O(o_1, o_2, t))).$$

Robust cleanness [15] can be now formulated as conformance-based cleanness, which establishes that $(\mathsf{Conf}_I, \mathsf{Conf}_O)$-cleanness is a generalisation. Using hybrid conformance, we define hybrid-conformance cleanness, and similarly, plugging in Skorokhod conformance, we define Skorokhod-conformance cleanness. Formally:

- A hybrid system H is robustly clean, denoted $\mathsf{RobustClean}(\kappa_I, \kappa_O)$, if and only if H is $(\mathsf{TraceConf}_{\kappa_I}, \mathsf{TraceConf}_{\kappa_O})$-clean.
- A hybrid system H is *hybrid-conformance clean with conformance thresholds* $(\tau_I, \epsilon_I, \tau_O, \epsilon_O)$, which we denote by $\mathsf{HybridClean}(\tau_I, \epsilon_I, \tau_O, \epsilon_O)$, if and only if H is $(\mathsf{HybridConf}_{\tau_I, \epsilon_I}, \mathsf{HybridConf}_{\tau_O, \epsilon_O})$-clean.
- A hybrid system H is *Skorokhod-conformance clean with conformance thresholds* $(\tau_I, \epsilon_I, \tau_O, \epsilon_O)$, denoted $\mathsf{SkorClean}(\tau_I, \epsilon_I, \tau_O, \epsilon_O)$, if and only if H is $(\mathsf{SkorConf}_{\tau_I, \epsilon_I}, \mathsf{SkorConf}_{\tau_O, \epsilon_O})$-clean.

We will now establish some key relations between the cleanness notions defined previously. We begin by lifting the implication between conformance relations to implication between cleanness notions defined using those relations.

Proposition 3. *Suppose that $\mathsf{Conf}_I^1 \sqsupseteq \mathsf{Conf}_I^2$ and $\mathsf{Conf}_O^1 \sqsubseteq \mathsf{Conf}_O^2$. Then for any system H: H is $(\mathsf{Conf}_I^1, \mathsf{Conf}_O^1)$-clean $\implies H$ is $(\mathsf{Conf}_I^2, \mathsf{Conf}_O^2)$-clean.*

The proposition above has two important corollaries. The first one explains the relationships between the original robust cleanness, and notions of cleanness based on Skorokhod conformance and hybrid conformance, in particular stating the conservative generalisation property for the latter notions. The second corollary compares cleanness notions with different conformance thresholds.

Corollary 1. *For all $\tau_I, \tau_O, \epsilon_I, \epsilon_O \in \mathbb{R}_{\geq 0}$, the following implications hold:*

1. *$\mathsf{RobustClean}(\epsilon_I, \epsilon_O) \implies \mathsf{SkorClean}(0, \epsilon_I, \tau_O, \epsilon_O) \implies \mathsf{HybridClean}(0, \epsilon_I, \tau_O, \epsilon_O)$,*

2. $HybridClean(\tau_I, \epsilon_I, 0, \epsilon_O) \implies SkorClean(\tau_I, \epsilon_I, 0, \epsilon_O) \implies RobustClean$
   (ϵ_I, ϵ_O).

Also, $RobustClean(\epsilon_I, \epsilon_O) = SkorClean(0, \epsilon_I, 0, \epsilon_O) = HybridClean(0, \epsilon_I, 0, \epsilon_O)$ and hence $SkorClean$ and $HybridClean$ are conservative extensions of robust cleanness.

Corollary 2. *For all* $\epsilon_I, \epsilon'_I, \epsilon_O, \epsilon'_O, \tau_I, \tau'_I, \tau_O, \tau'_O$ *that satisfy the inequalities* $\epsilon'_I \le \epsilon_I, \quad \tau'_I \le \tau_I, \quad \epsilon'_O \ge \epsilon_O, \quad \tau'_O \ge \tau_O$ *the following implications hold:*

1. $RobustClean(\epsilon_I, \epsilon_O) \implies RobustClean(\epsilon'_I, \epsilon'_O);$
2. $HybridClean(\epsilon_I, \tau_I, \epsilon_O, \tau_O) \implies HybridClean(\epsilon'_I, \tau'_I, \epsilon'_O, \tau'_O);$
3. $SkorClean(\epsilon_I, \tau_I, \epsilon_O, \tau_O) \implies SkorClean(\epsilon'_I, \tau'_I, \epsilon'_O, \tau'_O).$

Example 6. Consider the testing workflow in Fig. 1. The inputs passed to a car are i_{st} and i_{ddev}, depicted in Fig. 1.(b). One of the test results is presented in Fig. 1.(c), where i_{st} reveals output $o(i_{st})$ and i_{ddev} reveals $o(i_{ddev})$. We assume that $\epsilon < |i_{st}(t_0) - i_{ddev}(t_0)|$ and $\epsilon < |o(i_{st})(t_1) - o(i_{ddev})(t_1)|$ at some time t_1.

- For inputs i_{st} and i_{ddev}, any output is immediately deemed RobustClean(ϵ, ϵ), as the left-hand side of the implication in Definition 8 does not hold for any t'. Note, that for other inputs the car used for testing might not be RobustClean(ϵ, ϵ).
- As explained in Example 2, i_{st} and i_{ddev} are hybrid conformant for ϵ and τ, i.e., the predicate PrefConf$_I$ on the left-hand side of the implication in Definition 8 holds. PrefConf$_O$, however, fails at time t_1 for signals $o(i_{st})$ and $o(i_{ddev})$. Hence, the system tested in Fig. 1.(c) is not HybridClean$(\epsilon, \tau, \epsilon, \tau)$.

We now discuss testing and falsification of conformance-based cleanness.

For systems with discrete time domains the existing methods for verifying [15] or testing [10] robust cleanness can be readily applied.

In the case of hybrid cleanness, existing methods for testing hybrid conformance, such as [2] and [4] can be extended to testing and falsification of hybrid cleanness of hybrid systems consisting of traces with finite time domains. Methods for checking Skorokhod conformance were presented in [17]. Due to the quantification over all time-points t' in our Definition 8 and Definition 9, it is not clear how to directly extend them to testing Skorokhod cleanness.

5   Case Study

In this section we evaluate the proposed notion of hybrid cleanness in the context of doping detection in relation to the recent Diesel Emissions Scandal.

Conducting software doping tests for cyber-physical systems has a range of applications. A prominent example is the body of recent work [8–10,14,15,32,34] that gives insights into the Diesel Emissions Scandal. This is a world-wide scandal where millions of diesel cars have been equipped with defeat devices reducing the effectiveness of emission cleaning systems during real-world usage – in contrast

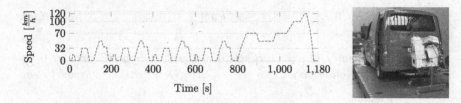

Fig. 2. Left: New European Driving Cycle (NEDC); Right: test setup with Nissan NV200 Evalia on a chassis dynamometer attached to a PEMS.

to the regulator-defined driving scenarios on a chassis dynamometer, where the amount of emitted pollutants are well below the applicable limits.

Assuming the existence of a contract that formalizes when software is considered to be doped, recent work demonstrates how doping tests can be generated automatically and how the characteristic challenges arising with these kinds of tests can be tackled [10]. A major challenge is the distortion of inputs that can occur during test execution. As doping tests have to be conducted on the final product, i.e., a vehicle such as a passenger car, a human driver has to provide the inputs to the car by driving it. It is far from trivial to provide the inputs exactly as defined by the test case. Official regulations, that define the approval process for new car models, precisely specify test cycles for which they allow tolerances in the input of up to 2 km/h (in car speed). But even driving a car within this tolerance requires a very experienced driver. To strengthen the position of consumers against manufacturers, it is necessary to allow manufacturer-independent methods to check the compliance of a car model with the applicable regulations, i.e., the absence of defeat devices. These methods are supposed to require a reasonable amount of effort, and training a driver over months so that she has enough experience to stay within the tolerance of 2 km/h is way beyond reasonable effort. This means that the responsibility for accounting for the driver's imprecision must be shifted to the techniques for checking for software doping.

In this section we give a short summary of recent doping tests with a diesel car and demonstrate how the theory developed in this paper addresses the above challenge. More precisely, it allows us to overcome the imprecise timing leading to minor input distortions, by appropriately accounting for the effect of retiming on the input value error. We further show how using our theory one of the tests reveals strong indications for a defeat device in the car under test – despite a very inexperienced driver conducting the test. This doping detection would not have been possible using the cleanness notions existing prior to this work.

Physical Set-Up of the Experiment. Before a car model can be sold, it must meet the requirements defined in the official regulations. The type approval procedure requires the car to be placed on a chassis dynamometer. Cars have to follow certain standardized test cycles, each defined as a function from time to speed. One of the test cycles, involved in the diesel scandal, was the New European Driving Cycle (NEDC) [42] shown in Fig. 2. For the tests here, we consider the

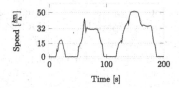 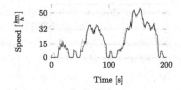

Fig. 3. Initial 200s of PowerNEDC (left) and SineNEDC (right) planned test cycles (red, dotted) and actually driven (black). (Color figure online)

speed of the car as *input*, since this is the parameter defining a test cycle. The *total amount of* NO *and* NO_2 *(abbreviated as* NO_x*)* is the only *output* of interest.

The car under test is a Nissan NV200 Evalia, with Renault 1.5 dci (110hp) diesel engine and approved w.r.t. regulation *Euro 6b*. The test set-up is shown in Fig. 2.

In order to perform a check for defeat devices using a cleanness test, we consider, in addition to the original NEDC, two manually synthesized tests. These test cycles, denoted POWERNEDC and SINENEDC were proposed in previous work [10] and are defined as follows. POWERNEDC is based on the NEDC but slightly deviates from it by enforcing higher accelerations ($1.5\frac{m}{s^2}$ instead of $0.94\frac{m}{s^2}$) after 56 s, 251 s, 446 s and 641 s. The *maximum input deviation from* NEDC *is* $\kappa_I = 10$ km/h. SINENEDC is defined as the NEDC superimposed by a sine curve, formally $SineNEDC(t) = \max\{0, NEDC(t) + 5\sin(0.5t)\}$, with a *maximum input deviation from* NEDC *of* $\kappa_I = 5$ km/h.

These test cycles are defined by specifying the input value (the car's speed) in each second. Both test cases are shown by the red dotted lines in Fig. 3.

Conformance-Based Cleanness Tests for NEDC. We have applied our theory of conformance-based cleanness to check for doping, i.e., the presence of a defeat device, in the car under test. For this, we have at our disposal the raw data obtained from three test drives: (1) Test drive dNEDC is the result of NEDC cycle driven by a human driver. It serves as the reference behaviour of the car, to which we will compare the executions of the other two test cycles. (2) Test drive dPOWERNEDC is the trajectory that is produced as the result of a human driver driving POWERNEDC. (3) Test drive dSINENEDC is the trajectory that is produced as the result of a human driver driving SINENEDC.

The values of the actual sequences of inputs executed by driving the car are sampled in steps of 0.05 s. As mentioned earlier, the human in the loop makes testing considerably more challenging. The maximum deviation of inputs compared to the test specification for NEDC is just below 10 km/h, for POWERNEDC is almost 12 km/h, and for SINENEDC it approaches 16 km/h. This shows that the perturbation introduced by the human driver is clearly noticeable. The amount of NO_x measured for dNEDC is 180 mg/km, for dPOWERNEDC and dSINENEDC the measurements revealed 204 mg/km and 584 mg/km, respectively.

In order to detect doping (by falsifying cleanness), the input sequences of dPOWERNEDC and dSINENEDC have to be each compared to dNEDC, and if the input sequences in the corresponding pair are conforming, then the respective outputs (the total NO_x emission values) have to be checked for conformance.

As we desire for our doping tests to be as strict as possible, we identify hybrid conformance $\mathsf{HybridConf}_{\tau_I,\epsilon_I}$, i.e., the weakest of the conformance relations discussed in Sect. 3, as the most suitable conformance relation for the comparison of input traces. As the outputs are just single values, the choice of output conformance relation is immaterial in this case, so we take $\mathsf{HybridConf}_{0,\epsilon_O}$.

Formally, we consider the deterministic hybrid system H defined by the input GTTs dNEDC, dPOWERNEDC, and dSINENEDC, and check whether H is $\mathsf{HybridClean}(\tau_I,\epsilon_I,0,\epsilon_O)$-clean for given values of τ_I, ϵ_I and ϵ_O.

The driver's imprecision has a significant effect on the values in the input sequences and their timing. This can lead to dismissing pairs of sequences if they are incorrectly deemed too far apart, and thus missing some indications of doping. For instance, a too strict comparison of dSINENEDC to dNEDC will dismiss this pair of executions; however, the measured NO_x emission during the dSINENEDC drive is *three times more* than the one measured during dNEDC.

Testing $\mathsf{HybridClean}(\tau_I,\epsilon_I,0,\epsilon_O)$ allows us to perform a realistic comparison by taking into account the two possible sources of driving errors: the over- or undershooting of the speed, and the timing offsets, where the driver accelerates or decelerates too fast or too slowly. In comparison, prior doping tests based on Robust Cleanness, considered only the former, i.e., the point-wise offset in speed. As we demonstrate, depending on the specified value threshold, there are cases when this is insufficient to identify doping. Indeed, looking into the official regulations, we can see that they allow for a timing variation of one second [19,42]. Thus, essentially, the regulations allow for hybrid conformance with $\tau_I = 1\,$s.

Hybrid Cleanness Testing. In order to test $\mathsf{HybridClean}(\tau_I,\epsilon_I,0,\epsilon_O)$ we have to examine the conformance relations $\mathsf{HybridConf}_{\tau_I,\epsilon_I}(\mathrm{dNEDC},\mathrm{dPOWERNEDC})$ and $\mathsf{HybridConf}_{\tau_I,\epsilon_I}(\mathrm{dNEDC},\mathrm{dSINENEDC})$ between the corresponding input sequences. Recall that since the output of the system measured in each test is the total amount of NO_x emitted during the test, i.e., a single value for the whole execution, timing plays no role when quantifying the value error for the output.

In order to evaluate the power of using hybrid cleanness for detecting doping, we consider different values for ϵ_I and τ_I, and perform two types of analysis of the results of testing $\mathsf{HybridClean}(\tau_I,\epsilon_I,0,\epsilon_O)$, which we describe below.

Effect of τ_I on the Minimal ϵ_I for Which Inputs are Conforming. First, we fix a maximum value that we allow for the time offset τ_I. For this τ_I we analyse our dataset to find the minimal ϵ_I such that for the combination τ_I and ϵ_I the input traces under consideration satisfy hybrid conformance. For $\tau_I = 0$ we get exactly the ϵ_I for which the two traces are trace conformant. Table 1 (left side) shows the computed ϵ_I values for $\tau_I = 0, 0.5, 1, 2, 5, 10$.

As expected, when we increase τ_I, the minimal ϵ_I decreases. At some point (at $\tau_I = 2$ for POWERNEDC and $\tau_I = 5$ for SINENEDC) the decrease in the value error reduces notably. This happens because the error is only partially caused by the incorrect timing of the driver.

From the values reported in Table 1 (left) we see that if, for example, we allow deviation for the input $\tau_I = 1$, as per the official regulation, and set $\epsilon_I = 15$, then we have that both $\mathsf{HybridConf}_{\tau_I,\epsilon_I}(\mathrm{dNEDC}, \mathrm{dPOWERNEDC})$ and $\mathsf{HybridConf}_{\tau_I,\epsilon_I}(\mathrm{dNEDC}, \mathrm{dSINENEDC})$ are true, while, for $\tau_I = 0$ both are false. Thus, under hybrid conformance these pairs of traces will be considered in the cleanness test, while under trace conformance they will be dismissed.

Table 1. Value thresholds for fixed τ_I (left) and time thresholds for fixed ϵ_I (right). Values are given as mg/km and time in seconds.

	$\tau_I = 0$	$\tau_I = 0.5$	$\tau_I = 1$	$\tau_I = 2$	$\tau_I = 5$	$\tau_I = 10$	$\epsilon_I = \kappa_I$	$\epsilon_I = \kappa_I+2$
POWER	$\epsilon_I = 15.88$	$\epsilon_I = 15.03$	$\epsilon_I = 12.41$	$\epsilon_I = 10.10$	$\epsilon_I = 10.07$	$\epsilon_I = 10.07$	$\tau_I = 67.35$	$\tau_I = 10.8$
SINE	$\epsilon_I = 16.17$	$\epsilon_I = 15.46$	$\epsilon_I = 14.24$	$\epsilon_I = 12.91$	$\epsilon_I = 11.67$	$\epsilon_I = 11.37$	$\tau_I = 72.4$	$\tau_I = 4.05$

Since the difference between the outputs measured during dSINENEDC and during dNEDC is vast, we establish that $\mathsf{HybridClean}(1, 15, 0, 180)$ does *not* hold.

Effect of ϵ_I on the Minimal τ_I for Which Inputs are Conforming. Second, we fix the maximum value error ϵ_I and examine what minimal τ_I results in a combination τ_I and ϵ_I for which the analysed data is hybrid conformant. For the synthesized test cases we study the error tolerance ϵ_I set to the respective input thresholds κ_I. As discussed above, this is 10 km/h for POWERNEDC and 5 km/h for SINENEDC. We also consider the scenario where the error tolerance allowed by the official regulation for the test cycle is added, that is, we also consider $\epsilon_I = \kappa_I + 2$ km/h. The two rightmost columns of Table 1 show the necessary time shifts to achieve these value errors. As apparent, they reduce by approximately 84% and 94% when adding the error tolerance of 2 km/h.

These values for τ_I give us the minimal tolerance threshold for time, for which $\mathsf{HybridClean}(\tau_I, \epsilon_I, 0, 180)$ is violated in H for the given ϵ_I; the value of ϵ_O is fixed at 180 mg/km according to the standard [10].

Evaluation and Discussion. The analysis of the data shows that it is indeed necessary to not only consider a deviation of value, but to also allow for timing deviations, especially when the quality of the studied driving tests suffers from the human-caused input distortions. In terms of the theory established in this paper, this means that in scenarios like this one, employing $\mathsf{HybridClean}$ is more adequate than using prior notions such as $\mathsf{RobustClean}$, and without this, the cases of doping we have detected would go unnoticed. Allowing a retiming of up to 10.8 s (for POWERNEDC) and of 4.05 s (for SINENEDC) makes both inputs conformant to the NEDC input, so we are able to detect the violation of SINENEDC for the hybrid cleanness for the specified desired value error tolerance. While these time deviations appear large given the test cycle timeline, they are acceptable when we recall that the tests are executed by human drivers.

If, on the other hand, we want to restrict the tolerance in time to one second, we are able to consider both tests for the hybrid cleanness for value error tolerance of 12.41 km/h for POWERNEDC and 14.24 km/h for SINENEDC.

This demonstrates how conformance-based cleanness notions like HybridClean allow us to some extent to account for human-caused errors related to timing.

Finally, while hybrid cleanness is arguably the appropriate notion for the case study considered here, our generic theory of conformance-based cleanness allows for using other conformance notions as appropriate for the CPS under test.

6   Conclusions

In this paper, we presented a theory of doping detection and cleanness based on the notions of conformance for cyber-physical systems. Our new notion accounts for possible "deviations" of the system output, upon "perturbing" its inputs, both in time and in values. Both notions of "deviation" and "perturbation" turn out to be expressible using a generic notion of retiming. We instantiate our definition with specific notions of retiming from the conformance testing literature. We apply our notions to a case study from the automotive domain and demonstrate how our generalised notions are useful in using actual driving cycles for doping detection according to the New European Driving Cycle (NEDC) [42].

We intend to turn our theory into an automatic tool for doping detection, using hybrid systems models. We intend to use the HyConf tool [4] as the starting point and use our search-based testing implementation in HyConf [5] to automate the process of test-case generation and test-case selection. Once this process is automated, one can generate test-cases that can go beyond a specific standard and detect intelligent defeat devices that cheat the standards and the tests prescribed by them.

We also intend to organise widespread experiments regarding emission detection to put our theory into practice. Our experimental set-up involves instrumenting a large number of cars using low-cost equipments, constructing models of emission behaviour, and generating realistic driving scenarios that are more likely to detect doping.

References

1. Abbas, H., Mittelmann, H.D., Fainekos, G.E.: Formal property verification in a conformance testing framework. In: MEMOCODE 2014, pp. 155–164. IEEE (2014)
2. Abbas, H., Hoxha, B., Fainekos, G., Deshmukh, J.V., Kapinski, J., Ueda, K.: WiP abstract: conformance testing as falsification for cyber-physical systems. In: 2014 ACM/IEEE International Conference on Cyber-Physical Systems (ICCPS), Berlin, p. 211 (2014)
3. Aerts, A., Mousavi, M.R., Reniers, M.A.: Model-based testing of cyber-physical systems. In: Cyber-Physical Systems: Foundations, Principles and Applications. Elsevier (2017). Chap. 19

4. Araujo, H., Carvalho, G., Mohaqeqi, M., Mousavi, M.R., Sampaio, A.: Sound conformance testing for cyber-physical systems: theory and implementation. Sci. Comput. Program. **162**, 35–54 (2018)
5. Araujo, H., Carvalho, G., Mousavi, M.R., Sampaio, A.: Multi-objective search for effective testing of cyber-physical systems. In: Ölveczky, P.C., Salaün, G. (eds.) SEFM 2019. LNCS, vol. 11724, pp. 183–202. Springer, Cham (2019). https://doi.org/10.1007/978-3-030-30446-1_10
6. Agrawal, S., Bonakdarpour, B.: Runtime verification of k-safety hyperproperties in HyperLTL. In: CSF 2016, pp. 239–252. IEEE Computer Society (2016)
7. Annpureddy, Y., Liu, C., Fainekos, G., Sankaranarayanan, S.: S-TaLiRo: a tool for temporal logic falsification for hybrid systems. In: Abdulla, P.A., Leino, K.R.M. (eds.) TACAS 2011. LNCS, vol. 6605, pp. 254–257. Springer, Heidelberg (2011). https://doi.org/10.1007/978-3-642-19835-9_21
8. Barthe, G., D'Argenio, P.R., Finkbeiner, B., Hermanns, H.: Facets of software doping. In: Margaria, T., Steffen, B. (eds.) ISoLA 2016. LNCS, vol. 9953, pp. 601–608. Springer, Cham (2016). https://doi.org/10.1007/978-3-319-47169-3_46
9. Biewer, S., D'Argenio, P.R., Hermanns, H.: Cyber-physical doping tests. In: 3rd Workshop on Monitoring and Testing of Cyber-Physical Systems, MT@CPSWeek, vol. 201, pp. 18–19. IEEE (2018)
10. Biewer, S., D'Argenio, P., Hermanns, H.: Doping tests for cyber-physical systems. In: Parker, D., Wolf, V. (eds.) QEST 2019. LNCS, vol. 11785, pp. 313–331. Springer, Cham (2019). https://doi.org/10.1007/978-3-030-30281-8_18
11. Brett, N., Siddique, U., Bonakdarpour, B.: Rewriting-based runtime verification for alternation-free HyperLTL. In: Legay, A., Margaria, T. (eds.) TACAS 2017. LNCS, vol. 10206, pp. 77–93. Springer, Heidelberg (2017). https://doi.org/10.1007/978-3-662-54580-5_5
12. Clarkson, M.R., Finkbeiner, B., Koleini, M., Micinski, K.K., Rabe, M.N., Sánchez, C.: Temporal logics for hyperproperties. In: Abadi, M., Kremer, S. (eds.) POST 2014. LNCS, vol. 8414, pp. 265–284. Springer, Heidelberg (2014). https://doi.org/10.1007/978-3-642-54792-8_15
13. Clarkson, M.R., Schneider, F.B.: Hyperproperties. In: CSF2008, pp. 51–65 (2008)
14. Contag, M., et al.: How they did it: an analysis of emission defeat devices in modern automobiles SP 2017, pp. 231–250. IEEE Computer Society (2017)
15. D'Argenio, P.R., Barthe, G., Biewer, S., Finkbeiner, B., Hermanns, H.: Is your software on dope? In: Yang, H. (ed.) ESOP 2017. LNCS, vol. 10201, pp. 83–110. Springer, Heidelberg (2017). https://doi.org/10.1007/978-3-662-54434-1_4
16. De Nicola, R., Hennessy, M.: Testing equivalences for processes. Theor. Comput. Sci. **34**, 83–133 (1984)
17. Deshmukh, J.V., Majumdar, R., Prabhu, V.S.: Quantifying conformance using the Skorokhod metric. Formal Methods Syst. Des., 168–206 (2017). https://doi.org/10.1007/s10703-016-0261-8
18. Donzé, A.: Breach, a toolbox for verification and parameter synthesis of hybrid systems. In: Touili, T., Cook, B., Jackson, P. (eds.) CAV 2010. LNCS, vol. 6174, pp. 167–170. Springer, Heidelberg (2010). https://doi.org/10.1007/978-3-642-14295-6_17
19. European Comission: Commission Regulation (EU) 2017/1151 (2017)
20. Fainekos, G.E., Pappas, G.J.: Robustness of temporal logic specifications for continuous-time signals. Theor. Comput. Sci. **410**(42), 4262–4291 (2009)
21. Finkbeiner, B., Hahn, C.: Deciding hyperproperties. In: Desharnais, J., Jagadeesan, R. (eds.) CONCUR 2016 LIPIcs, vol. 59, pp. 13:1–13:14 (2016)

22. Finkbeiner, B., Hahn, C., Stenger, M.: EAHyper: satisfiability, implication, and equivalence checking of hyperproperties. In: Majumdar, R., Kunčak, V. (eds.) CAV 2017. LNCS, vol. 10427, pp. 564–570. Springer, Cham (2017). https://doi.org/10.1007/978-3-319-63390-9_29

23. Finkbeiner, B., Hahn, C., Stenger, M., Tentrup, L.: Monitoring hyperproperties. In: Lahiri, S., Reger, G. (eds.) RV 2017. LNCS, vol. 10548, pp. 190–207. Springer, Cham (2017). https://doi.org/10.1007/978-3-319-67531-2_12

24. Finkbeiner, B., Hahn, C., Stenger, M., Tentrup, L.: RVHyper: a runtime verification tool for temporal hyperproperties. In: Beyer, D., Huisman, M. (eds.) TACAS 2018. LNCS, vol. 10806, pp. 194–200. Springer, Cham (2018). https://doi.org/10.1007/978-3-319-89963-3_11

25. Finkbeiner, B., Rabe, M.N., Sánchez, C.: Algorithms for model checking Hyper-LTL and HyperCTL*. In: Kroening, D., Păsăreanu, C.S. (eds.) CAV 2015. LNCS, vol. 9206, pp. 30–48. Springer, Cham (2015). https://doi.org/10.1007/978-3-319-21690-4_3

26. Gazda, M., Mousavi, M.R.: Logical characterisation of hybrid conformance. In: ICALP 2020 (2020, To appear)

27. Girard, A., Julius, A.A., Pappas, G.J.: Approximate simulation relations for hybrid systems. Discrete Event Dyn. Syst. $18(2)$, 163–179 (2008)

28. Girard, A., Pappas, G.J.: Approximate bisimulation: a bridge between computer science and control theory. Eur. J. Control $17(5–6)$, 568–578 (2011)

29. Hahn, C., Stenger, M., Tentrup, L.: Constraint-based monitoring of hyperproperties. In: Vojnar, T., Zhang, L. (eds.) TACAS 2019. LNCS, vol. 11428, pp. 115–131. Springer, Cham (2019). https://doi.org/10.1007/978-3-030-17465-1_7

30. Hapke, T., Hornung, P., Becker, J.: Schummeln auch in Europa. ARD/Norddeutscher Rundfunk. https://www.tagesschau.de/wirtschaft/vw-schummelsoftware-101.html (2015). Accessed 19 Apr 2019

31. Hennie, F.C.: Fault detecting experiments for sequential circuits. In: 5th Annual Symposium on Switching Circuit Theory and Logical Design, Princeton, New Jersey, USA, 11–13 November 1964, pp. 95–110. IEEE Computer Society (1964)

32. Hermanns, H., Biewer, S., D'Argenio, P.R., Köhl, M.A.: Verification, testing, and runtime monitoring of automotive exhaust emissions. In: LPAR-22. EPiC Series in Computing, vol. 57, pp. 1–17. EasyChair (2018)

33. Khakpour, N., Mousavi, M.R.: Notions of conformance testing for cyber-physical systems: overview and roadmap (invited paper). In: CONCUR 2015 LIPIcs, vol. 42, pp. 18–40 (2015)

34. Köhl, M.A., Hermanns, H., Biewer, S.: Efficient monitoring of real driving emissions. In: Colombo, C., Leucker, M. (eds.) RV 2018. LNCS, vol. 11237, pp. 299–315. Springer, Cham (2018). https://doi.org/10.1007/978-3-030-03769-7_17

35. Lee, D., Yannakakis, M.: Principles and methods of testing finite-state machines - a survey. Proc. IEEE $84(8)$, 1089–1123 (1996)

36. Maler, O., Nickovic, D.: Monitoring temporal properties of continuous signals. In: Lakhnech, Y., Yovine, S. (eds.) FORMATS/FTRTFT -2004. LNCS, vol. 3253, pp. 152–166. Springer, Heidelberg (2004). https://doi.org/10.1007/978-3-540-30206-3_12

37. Nguyen, L.V., Kapinski, J., Jin, X., Deshmukh, J.V., Johnson, T.T.: Hyperproperties of real-valued signals. In: MEMOCODE 2017, pp. 104–113. ACM (2017)

38. van Osch, M.: Hybrid input-output conformance and test generation. In: Havelund, K., Núñez, M., Roşu, G., Wolff, B. (eds.) FATES/RV -2006. LNCS, vol. 4262, pp. 70–84. Springer, Heidelberg (2006). https://doi.org/10.1007/11940197_5

39. Pnueli, A.: The temporal logic of programs. In: 18th Annual Symposium on Foundations of Computer Science, pp. 46–57. IEEE Computer Society (1977)
40. Tretmans, J.: A formal Approach to conformance testing. Ph.D. thesis, University of Twente, The Netherlands (1992)
41. Tretmans, J.: Conformance testing with labelled transition systems: implementation relations and test generation. Comput. Netw. ISDN Syst. **29**(1), 49–79 (1996)
42. United Nations: UN Vehicle Regulations - 1958 Agreement, Revision 2, Addendum 100, Regulation No. 101, Revision 3 – E/ECE/324/Rev. 2/Add.100/Rev.3 (2013)

On Implementable Timed Automata

Sergio Feo-Arenis[1], Milan Vujinović[2], and Bernd Westphal[2(✉)] iD

[1] Airbus Central R&T, Munich, Germany
[2] Albert-Ludwigs-Universität Freiburg, Freiburg im Breisgau, Germany
westphal@informatik.uni-freiburg.de

Abstract. Generating code from networks of timed automata is a well-researched topic with many proposed approaches, which have in common that they not only generate code for the processes in the network, but necessarily generate additional code for a global scheduler which implements the timed automata semantics. For distributed systems without shared memory, this additional component is, in general, undesired.

In this work, we present a new approach to the generation of correct code (without global scheduler) for distributed systems without shared memory yet with (almost) synchronous clocks if the source model does not depend on a global scheduler. We characterise a set of implementable timed automata models and provide a translation to a timed while language. We show that each computation of the generated program has a network computation path with the same observable behaviour.

1 Introduction

Automatic code generation from real-time system models promises to avoid human implementation errors and to be cost and time efficient, so there is a need to automatically derive (at least parts of) an implementation from a model. In this work, we consider a particular class of distributed real-time systems consisting of multiple components with (almost) synchronous clocks, yet without shared memory, a shared clock, or a global scheduler. Prominent examples of such systems are distributed data acquisition systems such as data aggregation in satellite constellations [16,18], the wireless fire alarm system [15], IoT sensors [30], or distributed database systems (e.g. [12]). For these systems, a common notion of time is important (to meet real-time requirements or for energy efficiency) and is maintained up to a certain precision by clock synchronisation protocols, e.g., [17,23,24]. Global scheduling is undesirable because schedulers are expensive in terms of network bandwidth and computational power and the number of components in the system may change dynamically, thus keeping track of all components requires large computational resources.

Timed automata, in particular in the flavour of Uppaal [7], are widely used to model real-time systems (see, for example, [14,32]) and to reason about the

---

Partly supported by the German Research Council (DFG) under grant WE 6198/1-1.

Published by Springer Nature Switzerland AG 2020
A. Gotsman and A. Sokolova (Eds.): FORTE 2020, LNCS 12136, pp. 78–95, 2020.
https://doi.org/10.1007/978-3-030-50086-3_5

correctness of systems as the ones named above. Modelling assumptions of timed automata such as instantaneous updates of variables and zero-time message exchange are often convenient for the analysis of timed system models, yet they, in general, inhibit direct implementations of model behaviour on real-world platforms where, e.g., updating variables take time.

In this work, we aim for the generation of distributed code from networks of timed automata with exactly one program per network component (and no other programs, in particular no implicit global scheduler), where all execution times are considered and modelled (including the selection of subsequent edges), and that comes with a comprehensible notion of correctness. Our work can be seen as the first of two steps towards bridging the gap between timed automata models and code. We propose to firstly consider a simple, iterative programming language with an exact real-time semantics (cf. Sect. 4) as the target for code generation. In this step, which we consider to be the harder one of the two, we deal with the discrepancy between the atomicity of the timed automaton semantics and the non-atomic execution on real platforms. The second step will then be to deal with imprecise timing on real-world platforms.

Our approach is based on the following ideas. We define a short-hand notation (called *implementable timed automata*) for a sub-language of the well-known timed automata (cf. Sect. 3). We assume *independency from a global scheduler* [5] as a sufficient criterion for the existence of a distributed implementation. For the timing aspect, we propose not to use platform clocks directly in, e.g., edge guards (see related work below) but to turn model clocks into program variables and to assume a "sleep" operation with absolute deadlines on the target platform (cf. Sect. 4). In Sect. 5, we establish the strong and concrete notion of correctness that for each time-safe computation of a program obtained by our translation scheme there is a computation path in the network with the same observable behaviour. Section 6 shows that our short-hand notation is sufficiently expressive to support industrial case studies and discusses the remaining gap towards real-world programming languages like C, and Sect. 7 concludes.

Generating code for timed systems from timed automata models has been approached before [3,4,20,25,29]. All these works also generate code for a scheduler (as an additional, explicit component) that corresponds to the implicit, global scheduler introduced by the timed automata semantics [5]. Thus, these approaches do not yield the distributed programs that we aim for. A different approach in the context of timed automata is to investigate discrete sampling of the behaviour [28] and so-called robust semantics [28,33]. A timed automaton model is then called implementable wrt. to certain robustness parameters. Bouyer et al. [11] have shown that each timed automaton (not a network, as in our case) can be sampled and made implementable at the price of a potentially exponential increase in size. A different line of work is [1,2,31]. They use timed automata (in the form of RT-BIP components [6]) as abstract model of the scheduling of tasks. Considering execution times for tasks, a so-called physical model (in a slightly different formalism) is obtained for which an interpreter has been implemented (the *real-time execution engine*) that then realises a scheduling of the tasks. The computation time necessary to choose the subsequent task (including the evaluation of guards) is "hidden" in the execution engine (which at least warns if the available time is exceeded), and they state the unfortunate observation that time-safety does not imply time-robustness with their approach.

There is an enormous amount of work on so-called *synchronous languages* like Esterel [10], SIGNAL [8], Lustre [19] and *time triggered architectures* such as Giotto/HTL [21]. These approaches provide an abstract programming or modelling language such that for each program, a deployable implementation, in particular for signal processing applications, can be generated.

2 Preliminaries

As modelling formalism (and input to code generation), we consider timed automata as introduced in [7]. In the following, we recall the definition of timed automata for self-containedness. Our presentation follows [26] and is standard with the single exception that we exclude strict inequalities in clock constraints.

A *timed automaton* $\mathcal{A} = (L, A, X, V, I, E, \ell_{ini})$ consists of a finite set of *locations* (including the initial location ℓ_{ini}), sets A, X, and V of *channels, clocks,* and *(data) variables*. A *location invariant* $I : L \to \Phi(X)$ assigns a *clock constraint* over X from $\Phi(X)$ to a location. Finitely many *edges* in E are of the form $(\ell, \alpha, \varphi, \vec{r}, \ell') \in L \times A_{!?} \times \Phi(X, V) \times R(X, V)^* \times L$ where $A_{!?}$ consists of input and output actions on channels and the internal action τ, $\Phi(X, V)$ are conjunctions of clock constraints from $\Phi(X)$ and *data constraints* from $\Phi(V)$, and $R(X, V)^*$ are finite sequences of *updates*, an update either resets a clock or updates a data variable. For clock constraints, we exclude strict inequalities as we do not yet support their semantics (of reaching the upper or lower bound arbitrarily close but not inclusive) in the code generation. In the following, we may write $\ell(e)$ etc. to denote the source location of edge e.

The *operational semantics* of a *network* $\mathcal{N} = \mathcal{A}_1 \| \dots \| \mathcal{A}_n$ of timed automata as *components* – and with pairwise disjoint sets of clocks and variables – is the (labelled) transition system $T(\mathcal{N}) = (C, \Lambda, \{\xrightarrow{\lambda} | \lambda \in \Lambda\}, C_{ini})$ over configurations. A configuration $c \in C = \{\langle \vec{\ell}, \nu \rangle \mid \nu \models I(\vec{\ell})\}$ consists of *location vector* $\vec{\ell}$ (an n-tuple whose i-th component is a location of $\mathcal{A}_i$) and a *valuation* $\nu : X(\mathcal{N}) \cup V(\mathcal{N}) \to \mathbb{R}_0^+ \cup \mathcal{D}$ of clocks and variables. The location vector has invariant $I(\vec{\ell}) = \bigwedge_{i=1}^n I(\ell_i)$, and we assume a satisfaction relation between valuations and clock and data constraints as usual. Labels are $\Lambda = \{\tau\} \cup \mathbb{R}_0^+$, and the set of *initial configurations* is $C_{ini} = \{\langle (\ell_{ini,1}, \dots, \ell_{ini,n}), 0 \rangle\} \cap C$. There is a *delay transition* $\langle \vec{\ell}, \nu \rangle \xrightarrow{t} \langle \vec{\ell}, \nu + t \rangle$, $t \in \mathbb{R}_0^+$, if and only if $\nu + t' \models I(\vec{\ell})$ for all $t' \in [0, t]$. There is an *internal transition* $\langle \vec{\ell}, \nu \rangle \xrightarrow{\tau} \langle \vec{\ell}', \nu' \rangle$, if and only if there is an edge $e = (\ell, \tau, \varphi, \vec{r}, \ell')$ enabled in $\langle \vec{\ell}, \nu \rangle$ and ν' is the result of applying e's update vector to ν. An edge is *enabled* in $\langle \vec{\ell}, \nu \rangle$ if and only if its source location occurs in the location vector, its guard is satisfied by ν, and ν' satisfies the destination location's invariant. There is a *rendezvous transition* $\langle \vec{\ell}, \nu \rangle \xrightarrow{\tau} \langle \vec{\ell}', \nu' \rangle$, if and only if there are edges $e_0 = (\ell_0, a!, \varphi_0, \vec{r}_0, \ell_0')$ and $e_1 = (\ell_1, a?, \varphi_1, \vec{r}_1, \ell_1')$ in two different automata enabled in $\langle \vec{\ell}, \nu \rangle$ and ν' is the result of first applying e_0's and then e_1's update vector to ν.

A *transition sequence* of $\mathcal{N}$ is any finite or infinite, initial and consecutive sequence of the form $\langle \vec{\ell_0}, \nu_0 \rangle \xrightarrow{\lambda_1} \langle \vec{\ell_1}, \nu_1 \rangle \xrightarrow{\lambda_2} \cdots$. $\mathcal{N}$ is called deadlock-free if no transition sequence of $\mathcal{N}$ ends in a configuration c such that there are no c', c'' such that $c \xrightarrow{t} c' \xrightarrow{\lambda} c''$ with $t \in \mathbb{R}_0^+$, $\lambda \notin \mathbb{R}_0^+$. A *computation path* of $\mathcal{N}$ is a time stamped transition sequence $\langle \vec{\ell_0}, \nu_0 \rangle, t_0 \xrightarrow{\lambda_1} \langle \vec{\ell_1}, \nu_1 \rangle, t_1 \xrightarrow{\lambda_2} \cdots$ s.t. $t_0 = 0$, $t_{i+1} = t_i + \lambda_{i+1}$ if $\lambda_{i+1} \in \mathbb{R}_0^+$ and $t_{i+1} = t_i$ if $\lambda_{i+1} = \tau$.

Next, Deadline, Boundary. Given an edge e with source location ℓ and clock constraint φ_{clk}, and a configuration $c = \langle \ell, \nu \rangle$, we define $next(c, \varphi_{clk}) = \min\{d \in \mathbb{R}_0^+ \mid \nu + d \models I(\ell) \wedge \varphi_{clk}\}$ and $deadline(c, \varphi_{clk}) = \max\{d \in \mathbb{R}_0^+ \mid \nu + next(c, \varphi_{clk}) + d \models I(\ell) \wedge \varphi_{clk}\}$ if minimum/maximum exist and ∞ otherwise. That is, *next* gives the smallest delay after which e is enabled from c and *deadline* gives the largest delay for which e is enabled after *next*. The *boundary* of a location invariant φ_{clk} is a clock constraint $\partial\varphi_{clk}$ s.t. $\nu + d \models \partial\varphi_{clk}$ if and only if $d = next(c, \varphi_{clk}) + deadline(c, \varphi_{clk})$. A simple sufficient criterion to ensure existence of boundaries is to use location invariants of the form $\varphi_{clk} = x \leq q$, then $\partial\varphi_{clk} = x \geq q$.

3   Implementable Timed Automata

In the following, we introduce *implementable timed automata* that can be seen as a definition of a sub-language of timed automata as recalled in Sect. 2. As briefly discussed in the introduction, a major obstacle with implementing timed automata models is the assumption that actions are instantaneous. The goal of considering the sub-language defined below is to make the execution time of resets and the duration of message transmissions explicit. Other works like, e.g., [13], propose higher-dimensional timed automata where actions take time. We propose to make action times explicit *within* the timed automata formalism.

Definition 1. *An* implementable timed automaton $\mathcal{I} = (L, \ell_{ini}, A, X, V, I, E)$ *consists of locations, initial location, channels, clocks, variables like timed automata, a location invariant* $I : L \rightarrow \Phi(X)$ *s.t. each* $I(\ell)$ *has a boundary* $\partial I(\ell)$, *and a finite set* $E = E_\tau \cup E_! \cup E_?$ *of edges consisting of*

- internal edges $(\ell, \varphi, \vec{r}_{dat}, \vec{r}_{clk}, \ell') \in E_\tau \subseteq L \times \Phi(X, V) \times R(V) \times R(X) \times L$,
- send edges $(\ell, \varphi, a!, \vec{r}_{clk}, \ell') \in E_! \subseteq L \times \Phi(X, V) \times A_! \times R(X) \times L$,
- receive edges $(\ell, \varphi_{clk}, \{(a_1?, \ell_1'), \ldots, (a_n?, \ell_n')\}, \vec{r}_{clk}, \ell')$ $n \geq 0$, in $E_? \subseteq L \times \Phi(X) \times 2^{A_? \times L} \times R(X) \times L$. $\diamondsuit$

Implementable timed automata distinguish internal, send, and receive edges by action *and* update in contrast to timed automata. An internal edge models (only) updates of data variables or sleeping idle (which takes time on the platform), a send edge models (only) the sending of a message (which takes time), and a receive edge (only) models the ability to receive a message with a timeout. All kinds of edges may reset clocks. Figure 1 shows an example implementable timed automaton using double-outline edges to distinguish the graphical representation from timed automata. The edge from ℓ_0 to ℓ_1, for example, models that

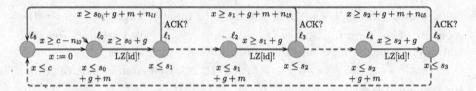

Fig. 1. The LZ-protocol of sensors [15] as implementable timed automaton.

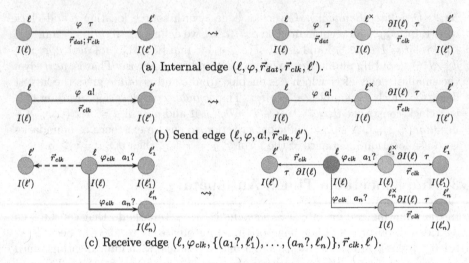

(a) Internal edge $(\ell, \varphi, \vec{r}_{dat}, \vec{r}_{clk}, \ell')$.

(b) Send edge $(\ell, \varphi, a!, \vec{r}_{clk}, \ell')$.

(c) Receive edge $(\ell, \varphi_{clk}, \{(a_1?, \ell_1'), \ldots, (a_n?, \ell_n')\}, \vec{r}_{clk}, \ell')$.

Fig. 2. Edges of the timed automaton of an implementable timed automaton.

message 'LZ[id]' may be transmitted between time $s_0 + g$ (including guard time g and operating time) and $s_0 + g + m$, i.e., the maximal transmission duration here is m. The time n_{l1} would be the operating time budgeted for location ℓ_1.

The semantics of the *implementable network* $\mathcal{N}$ consisting of implementable timed automata $\mathcal{I}_1, \ldots, \mathcal{I}_n$ is the labelled transition system $\mathcal{T}(\mathcal{A}_{\mathcal{I}_1} \| \ldots \| \mathcal{A}_{\mathcal{I}_n})$. The timed automata $\mathcal{A}_{\mathcal{I}_i}$ are obtained from $\mathcal{I}_i$ by applying the translation scheme in Fig. 2 edge-wise. The construction introduces fresh $\ell^\times$-locations. Intuitively, a discrete transition to an $\ell^\times$-location marks the *completion* of a data update or message transmission in $\mathcal{I}$ that started at the *next* time of the considered configuration. After completion of the update or transmission, implementable timed automata always wait up to the deadline. If the update or transmission has a certain time budget, then we need to expect that the time budget may be completely used in some cases. Using the time budget, possibly with a subsequent wait, yields a certain independence from platform speed: if one platform is fast enough to execute the update or transmission in the time budget, then all faster platforms are. Note that the duration of an action may be zero in implementable timed automata (exactly as in timed automata), yet then there will be no time-safe execution of any corresponding program on a real-world platform.

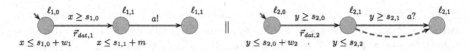

Fig. 3. Artificial example of a non-implementable network if $s_{2,0} + w_2 > s_{1,0} + w_1$.

In [5], the concept of *not to depend on a global scheduler* is introduced. Intuitively, independency requires that sending edges are never blocked because no matching receive edge is enabled or because another send edge in a different component is enabled. That is, the schedule of the network behaviour ensures that at each point in time at most one automaton is ready to send, and that each automaton that is ready to send finds an automaton that is ready for the matching receive. Similar restrictions have been imposed on timed automaton models in [9] to verify the ZeroConf protocol. Whether a network depends on a global scheduler is decidable; for details, we refer the reader to [5].

Figure 3 shows an artificial network of implementable timed automata whose independency from a global scheduler depends on the parameters $s_{1,0} + w_1$ and $s_{2,0} + w_2$. If the location $\ell_{1,1}$ is reached, then the standard semantics of timed automata would (using the implicit global scheduler) block the sending edge until $\ell_{2,1}$ is reached. Yet in a distributed system, the sender should not be assumed to know the current location of the receiver. By choosing the parameters accordingly (i.e., by protocol design), we can ensure that the receiver is always ready *before* the sender so that the sender is never blocked. In this case, we can offer a distributed implementation.

In the following sections, we only consider networks of implementable timed automata that are deadlock-free, *closed component* (no shared clocks or variables, no committed locations (cf. [7])), and do not depend on a global scheduler.

4   Timed While Programs

In this section, we introduce a timed programming language that provides the necessary expressions and statements to implement networks of implementable timed automata as detailed in Sect. 5. The semantics is defined as a structural operational semantics (SOS) [27] that is tailored towards proving the correctness of the implementations obtained by our translation scheme from Sect. 5. We use a dedicated time component in configurations of a program to track the execution times of statements and support a snapshot operator to measure the time that passed since the execution of a particular statement. Due to lack of space, we introduce expressions on a strict as-needed basis, including message, location, edge, and time expressions. In a general purpose programming language, the former kinds of expressions can usually be realised using integers (or enumerations), and time expressions can be realised using platform-specific representations of the current system time.

Syntax. Expressions of our programming language are defined wrt. given network variables V and X. We assume that each constraint from $\Phi(X, V)$ or expression from $\Psi(V)$ over V and X has a corresponding (basic type) program expression and thus that each variable $v \in V$ and each clock $x \in X$ have corresponding (basic type) program variables $\mathtt{v}_v, \mathtt{v}_x \in \mathbb{V}_b$. In addition, we assume typed variables for locations, edges, and messages, and for times (on the target platform). We additionally consider *location variables* $\mathbb{V}_l$ to store the current location, *edge variables* $\mathbb{V}_e$ to store the edge currently worked on, *message variables* $\mathbb{V}_m$ to store the outcome of a receive operation, and *time variables* $\mathbb{V}_t$ to store platform time. *Message expressions* are of the form $mexpr ::= \mathtt{m} \mid a, \mathtt{m} \in \mathbb{V}_m, a \in A$, *location expressions* are of the form $lexpr ::= \mathtt{l} \mid \ell \mid nextloc_{\mathcal{I}}(mexpr), \mathtt{l} \in \mathbb{V}_l$, $\ell \in L$, and *edge expressions* are of the form $eexpr ::= \mathtt{e} \mid e, \mathtt{e} \in \mathbb{V}_e, e \in E$. A *time expression* has the form $texpr ::= \odot \mid \mathtt{t} \mid \mathtt{t} + expr$, where $\odot$ is the *current platform time* and $\mathtt{t} \in \mathbb{V}_t$. Note that time variables are different from clock variables. The values of clock variable $\mathtt{v}_x$ are used to compute a new next time, which is then stored in a time variable, which can be compared to the platform time. Clock variables can be represented by platform integers (given their range is sufficient for the model) while time variables will be represented by platform specific data types like $\mathtt{timespec}$ with C [22] and POSIX. In this way, model clocks are only indirectly connected (and compared) to the platform clock.

Table 1. Statements S, statement sequences $\mathcal{S}$, and programs P.

$$S ::= \mathtt{v} \leftarrow expr \mid \mathtt{t} \leftarrow texpr \mid \mathtt{m} \leftarrow mexpr \mid \mathtt{l} \leftarrow lexpr \mid sleepto(texpr)$$
$$\mid send(mexpr) \mid \mathtt{m} \leftarrow receive(expr) \mid \mathtt{e}, \mathtt{v}_1, \mathtt{v}_2 \leftarrow nextedge_{\mathcal{I}}([mexpr])$$
$$\mid \mathbf{if} \, \square \, \mathtt{e} = eexpr_1 : \mathcal{S}_1 \ldots \square \, \mathtt{e} = eexpr_n : \mathcal{S}_n \, \mathbf{fi} \mid \mathbf{while} \, expr \, \mathbf{do} \, \mathcal{S} \, \mathbf{od}$$
$$\mathcal{S} ::= \epsilon \mid S \mid S\triangleleft \mid S; \mathcal{S} \mid S\triangleleft; \mathcal{S} \qquad (\epsilon; \mathcal{S} \equiv \mathcal{S}; \epsilon \equiv \mathcal{S}), \qquad P ::= \mathcal{S}_1 \| \cdots \| \mathcal{S}_n.$$

The set of *statements*, *statement sequences*, and *timed programs* are given by the grammar in Table 1. The term $nextedge_{\mathcal{I}}([mexpr])$ represents an implementation of the edge selection in an implementable timed automaton that can optionally be called with a message expression. We denote the empty statement sequence by ϵ and introduce $\triangleleft$ as an artificial *snapshot operator* on statements (see below). The particular syntax with snapshot and non-snapshot statements allows us to simplify the semantics definition below. We use *StmSeq* to denote the set of all statement sequences.

Component Configurations and Interpretation of Expressions. A *component configuration* is a tuple $\pi = \langle \mathcal{S}, (\beta, \gamma, w, u), \sigma \rangle$ consisting of a statement sequence $\mathcal{S} \in StmSeq$, the *operating time* of the current statement $\beta \in \mathbb{R}_0^+$ i.e., the time passed since starting to work on the current statement), the *time to completion* of the current statement $\gamma \in \mathbb{R}_0^+ \cup \{\infty\}$ (i.e., the time it will take to complete the work on the current statement), the *snapshot time* $w \in \mathbb{R}_0^+$ (i.e., the time

Table 2. Discrete reductions of the timed programming language. Rules (R2), (R3), and (R4) for time, message, and location assignment are similar to (R1).

$$\text{(R1)}\ \frac{\langle \mathtt{v} \leftarrow expr; \mathcal{S},\ (\beta, 0, w, u),\ \sigma\rangle}{\langle \mathcal{S},\ (0, \gamma', w', u),\ \sigma[\mathtt{v} := \sigma(expr)]\rangle} \qquad \text{(R5)}\ \frac{\langle sleepto(texpr); \mathcal{S},\ (\sigma(texpr), 0, w, u),\ \sigma\rangle}{\langle \mathcal{S},\ (0, \gamma', w', u),\ \sigma\rangle}$$

$$\text{(R6)}\ \frac{\langle send(mexpr); \mathcal{S},\ (\beta, 0, w, u),\ \sigma\rangle}{\langle \mathcal{S},\ (0, \gamma', w', u),\ \sigma\rangle} \qquad \text{(R7)}\ \frac{\langle \mathtt{m} \leftarrow receive(expr); \mathcal{S},\ (\beta, \gamma, w, u), \sigma\rangle}{\langle \mathcal{S},\ (0, \gamma', w', u),\ \sigma[\mathtt{m} := a]\rangle},\ \begin{array}{l} a \in A, \text{ if } \beta \le \sigma(expr), \\ a = \bot, \text{ if } \beta \ge \sigma(expr), \end{array}$$

$$\text{(R8)}\ \frac{\langle \mathtt{e}, \mathtt{v_1}, \mathtt{v_2} \leftarrow nextedge_{\mathcal{I}}([mexpr]); \mathcal{S},\ (\beta, 0, w, u),\ \sigma\rangle}{\langle \mathcal{S},\ (0, \gamma', w', u),\ \sigma[\mathtt{e}, \mathtt{v_1}, \mathtt{v_2} := [\![nextedge_{\mathcal{I}}([mexpr])]\!](\sigma)]\rangle}$$

$$\text{(R9a)}\ \frac{\langle \mathbf{if} \cdots \square\ \mathtt{e} = eexpr_i : S_i \cdots \mathbf{fi}; \mathcal{S},\ (\beta, 0, w, u),\ \sigma\rangle}{\langle S_i; \mathcal{S},\ (0, \gamma', w', u),\ \sigma\rangle},\ \sigma(\mathtt{e}) = \sigma(eexpr_i)$$

$$\text{(R9b)}\ \frac{\langle \mathbf{if}\ \square\ \mathtt{e} = eexpr_1 : S_1 \ldots \square\ \mathtt{e} = eexpr_n : S_n\ \mathbf{fi}; \mathcal{S},\ (\beta, 0, w, u), \sigma\rangle}{\langle \mathcal{S},\ (0, \gamma', w', u),\ \sigma\rangle},\ \begin{array}{l} \forall 0 \le i \le n \bullet \\ \sigma(\mathtt{e}) \ne \sigma(eexpr_i) \end{array}$$

$$\text{(R10a)}\ \frac{\langle \mathbf{while}\ expr\ \mathbf{do}\ S\ \mathbf{od}; \mathcal{S},\ (\beta, 0, w, u),\ \sigma\rangle}{\langle S; \mathbf{while}\ expr\ \mathbf{do}\ S\ \mathbf{od}; \mathcal{S},\ (0, \gamma', w', u),\ \sigma\rangle},\ \sigma(expr) = true$$

$$\text{(R10b)}\ \frac{\langle \mathbf{while}\ expr\ \mathbf{do}\ S\ \mathbf{od}; \mathcal{S},\ (\beta, 0, w, u),\ \sigma\rangle}{\langle \mathcal{S},\ (0, \gamma', w', u),\ \sigma\rangle},\ \sigma(expr) = false$$

since the last snapshot), the *platform clock* value[1] $u \in \mathbb{R}_0^+$, and a type-consistent valuation σ of the program variables. We will use operating time and time to completion to define computations of timed while programs (with discrete transitions when the time to completion is 0), and we will use the snapshot time w as an auxiliary variable in the construction of predicates by which we relate program and network computations. The valuation σ maps basic type variables from $\mathbb{V}_b$ to values from a domain that includes all values of data variables from $\mathcal{D}$ as used in the implementable timed automaton and all values needed to evaluate clock constraints (see below), i.e. $\sigma(\mathbb{V}_b) \subseteq \mathcal{D}_b$. Time variables from $\mathbb{V}_t$ are mapped to non-negative real numbers, i.e., $\sigma(\mathbb{V}_t) \subseteq \mathbb{R}_0^+$, message variables from $\mathbb{V}_m$ are mapped to channels, i.e., $\sigma(\mathbb{V}_m) \subseteq A \cup \{\bot\}$ or the dedicated value $\bot$ representing 'no message', location variables from $\mathbb{V}_l$ are mapped to locations, i.e., $\sigma(\mathbb{V}_l) \subseteq L$, and edge variables from $\mathbb{V}_e$ are mapped to edges, i.e., $\sigma(\mathbb{V}_e) \subseteq E$.

For the interpretation of expressions in a component configuration we assume that, if the valuation σ of the program variables corresponds to the valuation of data variables ν, then the interpretation $[\![expr]\!](\pi)$ of basic type expression $expr$ corresponds to the value of $expr$ under ν. Other variables obtain their values from σ, too, i.e. $[\![\mathtt{t}]\!](\pi) = \sigma(\mathtt{t})$, $[\![\mathtt{m}]\!](\pi) = \sigma(\mathtt{m})$, $[\![\mathtt{l}]\!](\pi) = \sigma(\mathtt{l})$, and $[\![\mathtt{e}]\!](\pi) = \sigma(\mathtt{e})$;

---

[1] Using a real, unbounded value for the platform clock avoids the issue of overflows in executions of programs as defined here. When refining the programs of implementable timed automata to programs on realistic platforms, we need to handle possible overflows in the finitely represented current platform time.

constant symbols are interpreted by their corresponding value, i.e. $[\![a]\!](\pi) = a$, $[\![\ell]\!](\pi) = \ell$, and $[\![e]\!](\pi) = e$, and we have $[\![t + expr]\!](\pi) = [\![t]\!](\pi) + [\![expr]\!](\pi)$.

There are two non-standard cases. The $\odot$-symbol denotes the platform clock value of π, i.e.. $[\![\odot]\!](\pi) = u$, and we assume that $[\![nextloc_{\mathcal{I}}([mexpr])]\!](\pi)$ yields the destination location of the edge that is currently processed (as given by e), possibly depending on a message name given by $mexpr$. If $[\![e]\!](\pi)$ denotes an internal action or send edge e, this is just the destination location $\ell'(e)$, for receive edges it is $\ell'(e)$ if $mexpr$ evaluates to the special value $\perp$, and an ℓ_i from a $(a_i?, \ell_i)$ pair in the edge otherwise. If the receive edge is non-deterministic, we assume that the semantics of $nextloc_{\mathcal{I}}$ resolves the non-determinism.

Program Computations. Table 2 gives an SOS-style semantics with discrete reduction steps of a statement sequence (or component). Note that the rules in Table 2 (with the exception of receive) apply when the time to completion is 0, that is, at the point in time where the current statement completes. Each rule then yields a configuration with the operating time γ' for the new current statement. The new snapshot time w' is 0 if the first statement in $\mathcal{S}$ is a snapshot statement $S\triangleleft$, and w otherwise. Rule (R7) updates m to a, which is a channel or, in case of timeout, the 'no message' indicator '$\perp$'. Rule (R8) is special in that it is supposed to represent the transition relation of an implementable timed automaton. Depending on the program valuation σ, (R8) is supposed to yield a triple of the next edge to work on, this edge's *next* and *deadline*. For simplicity, we assume that the interpretation of $nextedge_{\mathcal{I}}([mexpr])$ is deterministic for a given valuation of program variables.

A *configuration* of program $P = \mathcal{S}_1 \| \cdots \| \mathcal{S}_n$ is an n-tuple

$$\Pi = (\langle \mathcal{S}_1, (\beta_1, \gamma_1, w_1, u_1), \sigma_1 \rangle, \ldots, \langle \mathcal{S}_n, (\beta_n, \gamma_n, w_n, u_n), \sigma_n \rangle)$$

of component configurations; $\mathcal{C}(P)$ denotes the set of all configurations of P.

The operational semantics of a program P is the labelled transition system on system configurations defined as follows. There is a *delay transition*

$$(\langle \mathcal{S}_1, (\beta_1, \gamma_1, w_1, u_1), \sigma_1 \rangle, \ldots) \xrightarrow{\delta}$$
$$(\langle \mathcal{S}_1, (\beta_1 + \delta, \gamma_1 - \delta, w_1 + \delta, u_1 + \delta), \sigma_1 \rangle, \ldots)$$

(by delay $\delta \in \mathbb{R}_0^+$) if, for all i, $1 \leq i \leq n$, $\delta \leq \gamma_i$, i.e. if no current statement completes strictly before δ. There is an *internal transition*

$$(\ldots, \langle \mathcal{S}_i, (\beta_i, 0, w_i, u_i), \sigma_i \rangle, \ldots) \xrightarrow{\tau} (\ldots, \langle \mathcal{S}_i', (0, \gamma_i', w_i', u_i), \sigma_i' \rangle, \ldots)$$

if for some i, $1 \leq i \leq n$, a discrete reduction rule from Table 2 applies, i.e. if

$$\langle \mathcal{S}_i, (\beta_i, 0, w_i, u_i), \sigma_i \rangle \vdash \langle \mathcal{S}_i', (0, \gamma_i', w_i', u_i), \sigma_i' \rangle.$$

There is a *synchronisation transition*

$$(\ldots, \langle \mathcal{S}_i, (\beta_i, 0, w_i, u_i), \sigma_i \rangle, \ldots \langle \mathcal{S}_j, (\beta_j, \gamma_j, w_j, u_j), \sigma_j \rangle, \ldots) \xrightarrow{[\![mexpr]\!](\sigma_i)}$$
$$(\ldots, \langle \mathcal{S}_i', (0, \gamma_i', w_i', u_i), \sigma_i \rangle, \ldots \langle \mathcal{S}_j', (0, \gamma_j', w_j', u_j), \sigma_j' \rangle, \ldots)$$

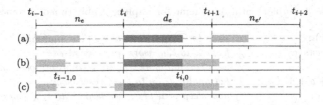

Fig. 4. Scheduling of work and operating time.

if $\langle \mathcal{S}_i, (\beta_i, 0, w_i, u_i), \sigma_i \rangle \vdash \langle \mathcal{S}'_i, (0, \gamma'_i, w'_i, u_i), \sigma_i \rangle$ by (R6), and $\langle \mathcal{S}_j, (\beta_j, \gamma_j, w_j, u_j), \sigma_j \rangle \vdash \langle \mathcal{S}'_j, (0, \gamma'_j, w'_j, u_j), \sigma'_j \rangle$ by (R7), and $\beta_j \geq \beta_i$, i.e. if component j has been listening at least as long as component i has been sending.

Note that this definition of synchronisation allows multiple components to send at the same time (which may cause message collision on a shared medium) and that, similar to the rendezvous communication of timed automata, out of multiple receivers, only one takes the message. In our application domain these cases do not happen because we assume that implementable networks do not depend on a global scheduler. That is, the program of an implementable network never exhibits any of these two behaviours.

A program configuration is called *initial* if and only if the k-th component configuration, $1 \leq k \leq n$, is at $\mathcal{S}_k$, with any β_k, $\gamma_k = 0$, $w_k = 0$, $u_k = 0$, and any σ_k with $\sigma_k(\mathbb{V}_b) = 0$. We use $\mathcal{C}_{ini}(P)$ to denote the set of initial configurations of program P. A *computation* of P is an initial and consecutive sequence of program configurations $\zeta = \Pi_0, \Pi_1, \ldots$, i.e. $\Pi_0 \in \mathcal{C}_{ini}(P)$ and for all $i \in \mathbb{N}_0$ exists $\lambda \in \mathbb{R}_0^+ \cup \{\tau\}$ such that $\Pi_i \xrightarrow{\lambda} \Pi_{i+1}$ as defined above. We need not consider terminating computations of programs here because we assume networks of implementable timed automata without deadlocks.

5   Correct Implementation of Implementable Networks

The program of the network of implementable timed automata $\mathcal{N} = \mathcal{I}_1 \| \ldots \| \mathcal{I}_n$ is $P(\mathcal{N}) = \mathcal{S}(\mathcal{I}_1) \| \ldots \| \mathcal{S}(\mathcal{I}_n)$ (cf. Table 3c). The edges' work is implemented in the corresponding Line 2 of the statement sequences in Tables 3a and 3b. The remaining Lines 3 to 8 include the evaluation of guards to choose the edge to be executed next. The result of choosing the edge is stored in program variable e which (by the while loop and the if-statement) moves to Line 1 of the implementation of that edge. The program's timing behaviour is controlled by variable t and is thus decoupled from clocks in the timed automata model. After Line 8, the value of t denotes the *absolute time* where the execution of the next edge is due. That is, clocks in the program are not directly compared to the platform time (which would raise issues with the precision of platform clocks) but are used to determine points in time that the target platform is supposed to sleep to. By doing so, we also lower the risk of accumulating imprecisions in the sleep operation of the target platform when sleeping for many *relative* durations.

Table 3. Implementation scheme for implementable timed automaton.

```
1: sleepto(t)◁;              // sleep to current next at tᵢ, then snapshot
2: ( r⃗_dat | send(a) );      // from tᵢ to tᵢ,₀, work on τ- or a!-edge
3: l ← ℓ'₀;                  // now fictionally at tᵢ₊₁ in destination location
4: x ← (x + n + d)[r⃗_clk];   // fictionally delay to tᵢ₊₁, reset clocks
5: t ← t + d;                // new sleep goal (1/2, see below): to tᵢ₊₁ (old deadline) ·
6: e, n, d ← nextedge_I();   // choose next edge e based on current component con-
7:                           //    figuration, get next and deadline of e
8: t ← t + n                 // new sleep goal (2/2): and then to tᵢ₊₂ (new next)
```

(a) Implementation $\mathcal{S}(e, \mathcal{I})$ of internal or send edge e in $\mathcal{I}$. Line 2 is the update vector $\vec{r}_{dat}$ if $e \in E_\tau$ (internal edge) and the send action $send(a)$ if $e \in E_!$ (send edge).

```
2: m ← receive(d);           // from tᵢ to tᵢ,₀, work on receive edge, i.e. read message
3: l ← nextloc_I(m);         // at tᵢ,₀, if no m-match: treat like timeout
6: e, n, d ← nextedge_I(m);  // choose next edge e based on current component confi-
7:                           //    guration and message (!), get next and deadline of e
```

(b) Implementation $\mathcal{S}(e, \mathcal{I})$ of receive edge e in $\mathcal{I}$; Lines 1, 4-5, and 8 are as in Figure 3a.

```
1: t ← ⊙;                    // get beginning of time; assume basic type variables are 0
2: l ← ℓ_ini;                // initialise location
3: e, n, d ← nextedge_I();   // choose next edge e based on component configuration
4: t ← t + n;                // new sleep goal: beginning of time plus next of e
5: while true do if □ e = e₀ : S(e₀, I) ··· □ e = eₙ : S(eₙ, I) fi od
```

(c) Implementation $\mathcal{S}(\mathcal{I})$ of implementable timed automaton $\mathcal{I}$.

The idea of scheduling work and operating time is illustrated by the timing diagram in Fig. 4. Row (a) shows a naïve schedule for comparison: From time t_{i-1}, decide on the next edge to execute and determine this edge's *next* time at t_i (light grey phase: operating time, must complete within the next edge's *next* time n_e), then sleep up to the *next* time (dashed grey line), then execute the edge(s) actions (dark grey phase: work time, must complete within the edge's deadline d_e), then sleep up to the edge's deadline at t_{i+1}, and start over. The program obtained by our translation scheme implements the schedule shown in Row (b). The program begins with determining the next edge *right after* the work phase and then has only one sleep phase up to, e.g., t_{i+2} where the next work phase begins. In this manner, we require only one interaction with the execution platform that implements the sleep phases. Row (c) illustrates a possible extension of our approach where operating time is needed right before the work phase, e.g., to prepare the platform's transceiver for sending a message.

We call the program $P(\mathcal{N})$ a correct implementation of network $\mathcal{N}$ if and only if for each observable behaviour of a *time-safe* execution of $P(\mathcal{N})$ there is a *corresponding* computation path of $\mathcal{N}$. In the following, we provide our notion of time-safety and then elaborate on the above mentioned correspondence between program and network computations.

Intuitively, a computation of $P(\mathcal{N})$ is not time-safe if either the execution of an edge's statement sequence takes longer than the admitted deadline or if the *next* time of the subsequent edge is missed, e.g., by an execution platform that is too slow. Note that in a given program computation, the performance of the platform is visible in the operation time β and time to completion γ.

We write $\Pi^k:L_n^e$ to denote that the program counter of component k is at Line n of the statement sequence of edge e. We use $\sigma|_{X\cup V}$ to denote the (network) configuration encoded by the values of the corresponding program variables. We assume[2] that for each program variable v, the old value, i.e., the value before the last assignment in the computation is available as @v.

Definition 2. *A computation $\Pi_0, \Pi_1, \ldots$ of $P(\mathcal{N})$ is* time-safe *if and only if, for each component k, $0 \leq k \leq n$ and all $i \in \mathbb{N}_0$,*

1. *$\Pi_i^k:L_2^e \wedge \gamma_{i,k} = 0 \implies w_k \leq deadline(\langle\sigma_{i,k}(1), \sigma_{i,k}|_{X\cup V}\rangle, \sigma_{i,k}(e))$, i.e., if the i-th configuration completes ($\gamma_{i,k} = 0$) Line 2 of an edge's statement sequence, not more time than admitted by its deadline has been used (w_k),*
2. *$\Pi_i^k:L_1^e \wedge \gamma_{i,k} = 0 \implies w_k = \sigma_{i,k}(@d) + next(\langle\sigma_{i,k}(1), \sigma_{i,k}|_{X\cup V}\rangle, \sigma_{i,k}(e))$, i.e., the sleepto statement in Line 1 completes exactly after the deadline of the previously worked on edge plus the current edge's next time.* ◇

Note that, by Definition 2, operating times may be larger than the subsequent edge's *next* time in a time-safe computation (if the execution of the current edge completes before its deadline). Stronger notions of time-safety are possible.

For correctness of $P(\mathcal{N})$, recall that we introduced Timed While Programs to consider the computation time that is needed to compute the transition relation of an implementable network on the fly. In addition, program computations have a finer granularity than network computations: In network computations, the current location and the valuation of clocks and variables are updated atomically in a transition. In the program $P(\mathcal{N})$, these updates are spread over three lines.

We show that, for each time-safe computation ζ of program $P(\mathcal{N})$, there is a computation of network $\mathcal{N}$ that is related to ζ in a well-defined way. The relation between program and network configurations decouples both computations in the sense that at some times (given by the respective timestamp) the, e.g., clock values in the program configuration are "behind" network clocks (i.e., correspond to an earlier network configuration), at some times they are "ahead", and there are points where they coincide.

Figure 5 illustrates the relation for one edge e. The top row of Fig. 5 gives a timing diagram of the execution of the program for edge e of one component. The rows below show the values over time for each program variable v up to e, n, and d. For example, the value of 1 will denote the source location ℓ of e until Line 3 is completed, and then denotes the destination location ℓ'. Similarly, v' and x' denote the effects of the update vector of e on data variables and clocks. Note that, during the execution of Line 3, we may observe combinations of values

---

[2] Without loss of generality, since the program could be augmented by an auxiliary variable @v for each variable v that provides the old value of v.

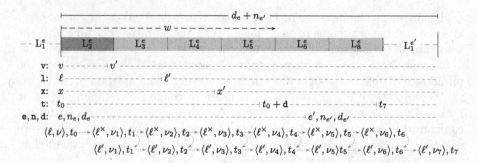

$$\langle \ell, \nu \rangle, t_0 \rightarrow \langle \ell^\times, \nu_1 \rangle, t_1 \rightarrow \langle \ell^\times, \nu_2 \rangle, t_2 \rightarrow \langle \ell^\times, \nu_3 \rangle, t_3 \rightarrow \langle \ell^\times, \nu_4 \rangle, t_4 \rightarrow \langle \ell^\times, \nu_5 \rangle, t_5 \rightarrow \langle \ell^\times, \nu_6 \rangle, t_6$$
$$\langle \ell', \nu_1 \rangle, t_1 \rightarrow \langle \ell', \nu_2 \rangle, t_2 \rightarrow \langle \ell', \nu_3 \rangle, t_3 \rightarrow \langle \ell', \nu_4 \rangle, t_4 \rightarrow \langle \ell', \nu_5 \rangle t_5 \rightarrow \langle \ell', \nu_6 \rangle, t_6 \rightarrow \langle \ell', \nu_7 \rangle, t_7$$

Fig. 5. Relating program and network computations for one component.

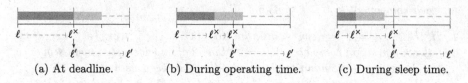

(a) At deadline.   (b) During operating time.   (c) During sleep time.

Fig. 6. Cases of changing from intermediate location to destination location.

for v and 1 that are never observed in a network computation due to the atomic semantics of networks.

The two bottom lines of Fig. 5 show related network configurations aligned with their corresponding program lines. Note that the execution of each line except for Line 1 may be related to two network configurations depending on whether the program timestamp is before or after the current edge's deadline. Figure 6 illustrates the three possible cases: The execution of program Line 2 (work time, dark gray) is related to network configurations with the source location ℓ of the current edge. Right after the work time, the network location $\ell^\times$ is related and at the current edge's deadline the destination location ℓ' is related. In the related network computation, the transition from $\ell^\times$ to ℓ' always takes place at the current edge's deadline. This point in time may, in the program computation, be right after work time (Fig. 6a, no delay in $\ell^\times$), in the operating time (Fig. 6b), or in the sleep time (Fig. 6c).

The relation between program and network configurations as illustrated in Fig. 5 can be formalised by predicates over program and network configurations, one predicate per edge and program line.[3] The following lemma states the described existence of a network computation for each time-safe program computation. The relation gives a precise, component-wise and phase-wise relation of program computations to network computations. In other words, we obtain a precise accounting of *which* phases of a time-safe program computation correspond to a network computation and *how*. We can argue component-wise by the closed component-assumption from Sect. 3.

---

[3] Details on these predicates and a detailed proof of Lemma 1 are provided in a corresponding technical report.

Lemma 1. *For each time-safe computation* $\zeta = \Pi_0, \Pi_1, \ldots$ *of* $P(\mathcal{N})$, *there exists a computation path* $\xi = c_{0,0}, \ldots, c_{0,m_0}, c_{1,0}, \ldots$ *of* $\mathcal{N}$ *s.t. each network configuration* $c_{i,j}$ *is properly related to program configuration* Π_i. $\Diamond$

Proof (sketch). The proof is a technical check of the predicates mentioned above during an inductive construction of computation path ξ. For the base case, we show that the initialisation statements in Lines 1 to 4 of Table 3c reach the Line 2 of a send or receive edge (cf. Table 3a and 3b) and establish a related network configuration. For the induction step, we need to consider delays and discrete steps of the program. From time-safety of ζ we can conclude to possible delays in $\mathcal{N}$ for the related configurations with a case-split wrt. the deadline (cf. Fig. 6). When the program time is at the current edge's deadline, the network may delay up to the deadline in an intermediate location $\ell^{\times}$, take a transition to the successor location ℓ', and possibly delay further. For discrete program steps, we can verify that $\mathcal{N}$ has enabled discrete transitions that reach a network configuration that is related to the next program line. Here, we use our assumptions from the program semantics that update vectors have the same effect in the program and the network. And we use the convenient property of our program semantics that the effects of statements only become visible with the discrete transitions. For synchronisation transitions of the program, we use the assumption that the considered network of implementable timed automata does not depend on a global scheduler, in particular that send actions are never blocked, or, in other words, that whenever a component has a send edge locally enabled, then there is a receiving edge enabled on the same channel.   □

Our main result in Theorem 1 is obtained from Lemma 1 by a projection onto observable behaviour (cf. Definition 3). Intuitively, the theorem states that at each point in time with a discrete transition to Line 2, the program configuration exactly encodes a configuration of network $P(\mathcal{N})$ right before taking an internal, send, or receive edge.

Definition 3. *Let* $\xi^k = \langle \ell^k_{0,0}, \nu^k_{0,0} \rangle \xrightarrow{\lambda_{0,1}} \ldots \xrightarrow{\lambda_{0,m_0}} \langle \ell^k_{1,0}, \nu^k_{1,0} \rangle \ldots$ *be the projection of a computation path* ξ *of the implementable network* $\mathcal{N}$ *onto component* k, $1 \leq k \leq n$, *labelled such that each configuration* $\langle \ell^k_{i,0}, \nu^k_{i,0} \rangle$ *is initial or reached by a discrete transition to a source location of an internal, send, or receive edge.*

The sequence $\xi^k_{obs} = \langle \ell^k_{0,i_0}, \nu^k_{0,i_0} + d_0 \rangle, \langle \ell^k_{1,i_1}, \nu^k_{1,i_1} + d_1 \rangle, \ldots$, $d_j \geq 0$, *where* (j, i_j) *is the largest index such that between* $c := \langle \ell^k_{j,0}, \nu^k_{j,0} \rangle$ *and* $\langle \ell^k_{j,i_j}, \nu^k_{j,i_j} + d_j \rangle$ *exactly* $\mathrm{next}(c)$ *time units have passed, is called the* observable behaviour *of component* k *in* ξ. $\Diamond$

Theorem 1. *Let* $\mathcal{N}$ *be an implementable network and* $\zeta^k = \pi_{0,0}, \ldots, \pi_{0,n_0}, \pi_{1,0}, \ldots$ *the projection onto the* k-*th component of a time-safe computation* ζ *of* $P(\mathcal{N})$ *labelled such that* $\pi_{i,n_i}, \pi_{i+1,0}$ *are exactly those transitions in* ζ *from a Line 1 to the subsequent Line 2. Then* $(\langle \sigma_{i,0}(1), \sigma_{i,0}|_{X \cup V} \rangle, u_{i,0})_{i \in \mathbb{N}_0}$ *is an observable behaviour of component* k *on some computation path of* $\mathcal{N}$. $\Diamond$

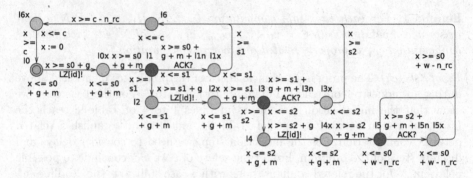

Fig. 7. Timed automaton of the implementable timed automaton (after applying the scheme from Fig. 2) for the LZ-protocol of sensors [15].

6   Evaluation and Discussion

The work presented here was motivated by a project to support the development of a new communication protocol for a distributed wireless fire alarm system [15], without shared memory, only assuming clock synchronisation and message exchange. We provided modelling and analysis of the protocol *a priori*, that is, before the first line of code had been written. In the project, the engineers manually implemented the model and appreciated how the model indicates exactly which action is due in which situation. Later, we were able to study the handwritten code and observed (with little surprise) striking regularities and similarities to the model. So we conjectured that there exists a significant sublanguage of timed automata that is *implementable*. In our previous work [5], we identified independency from a global scheduler as a useful precondition for the existence of a distributed implementation (cf. Sect. 2).

For this work, we have modelled the LZ-protocol of sensors in the wireless fire alarm system from [15] as an implementable timed automaton (cf. Fig. 1; Fig. 7 shows the timed automaton obtained by applying the scheme from Fig. 2). Hence our modelling language supports real-world, industry case-studies. Implementable timed automata also subsume some models of time-triggered, periodic tasks that we would model by internal edges only.

From the program obtained by the translation scheme given in Table 3, we have derived an implementation of the protocol in C. Clock, data, location, edge, and message variables become enumerations or integers, time variables use the POSIX data-structure `timespec`. The implementation runs timely for multiple days. Although our approach with sleeping to absolute times reduces the risk of drift, there is jitter on real-world platforms. The impact of timing imprecision needs to be investigated per application and platform when refining the program of a network to code, e.g., following [11]. In our case study, jitter is much smaller than the model's time unit. Another strong assumption that we use is synchrony of the platform clocks and synchronised starting times of programs which can in general not be achieved on real-world platforms. In the wireless fire alarm system, component clocks are synchronised in an initialisation phase and kept (sufficiently) synchronised using system time information in messages. Robustness against limited clock drift is obtained by including so-called *guard times* [23,24] in the protocol design. In the model, this is constant g: Components are ready to receive g time units before message transmission starts in another component.

Note that Theorem 1 only applies to time-safe computations. Whether an implementation is time-safe needs to be analysed separately, e.g., by conducting worst-case execution time (WCET) analyses of the work code and the code that implements the timed automata semantics. The C code for the LZ-model mentioned above actually implements a *sleepto* function that issues a warning if the target time has already passed (thus indicating non-time-safety). The translation scheme could easily be extended by a statement between Lines 2 and 3 that checks whether the deadline was kept and issues a warning if not. Then, Theorem 1 would strengthen to the statement that all computations of $P(\mathcal{I})$ either correspond to observable behaviour of $\mathcal{I}$ or issue a warning. Note that, in contrast to [1,2,31], our approach has the practically important property that time-safety implies time-robustness, i.e., if a program is time-safe on one platform then it is time-safe on any 'faster' platform. Furthermore, we have assumed a deterministic choice of the next edge to be executed for simplicity and brevity of the presentation. Non-deterministic models can be supported by providing a non-deterministic semantics to the $nextedge_{\mathcal{I}}$ function in the programming language and the correctness proof.

7   Conclusion

We have presented a shorthand notation that defines a subset of timed automata that we call implementable. For networks of implementable timed automata that do not depend on a global scheduler, we have given a translation scheme to a simple, exact-time programming language. We obtain a distributed implementation with one program for each network component, the programs are supposed to be executed concurrently, possibly on different computers. We propose to not substitute (imprecise) platform clocks for (model) clocks in guards and invariants, but to rely on a sleep function with absolute deadlines. The generated programs do not include any "hidden" execution times, but all updates, actions, and the time needed to select subsequent edges are taken into account. For the generated programs, we have established a notion of correctness that closely relates program computations to computation paths of the network. The close relation lowers the mental burden for developers that is induced by other approaches that switch to a slightly different, e.g., robust semantics for the implementation.

Our work decomposes the translation from timed automata models to code into a first step that deals with the discrepancy between atomicity of the timed automaton semantics and the non-atomic execution on real platforms. The second step, to relate the exact-time program to real platforms with imprecise timing is the subject of future work.

References

1. Abdellatif, T., Combaz, J., Sifakis, J.: Model-based implementation of real-time applications. In: Carloni, L.P., Tripakis, S. (eds.) EMSOFT, pp. 229–238. ACM (2010). https://doi.org/10.1145/1879021.1879052
2. Abdellatif, T., Combaz, J., Sifakis, J.: Rigorous implementation of real-time systems - from theory to application. Math. Struct. Comput. Sci. **23**(4), 882–914 (2013). https://doi.org/10.1017/S096012951200028X
3. Abdullah, J., Mohaqeqi, M., Yi, W.: Synthesis of Ada code from graph-based task models. In: Seffah, A., Penzenstadler, B., Alves, C., Peng, X. (eds.) SAC, pp. 1467–1472. ACM (2017). https://doi.org/10.1145/3019612.3019681
4. Amnell, T., Fersman, E., Pettersson, P., Sun, H., Yi, W.: Code synthesis for timed automata. Nord. J. Comput. **9**(4), 269–300 (2002)
5. Feo-Arenis, S., Vujinović, M., Westphal, B.: On global scheduling independency in networks of timed automata. In: Abate, A., Geeraerts, G. (eds.) FORMATS 2017. LNCS, vol. 10419, pp. 42–57. Springer, Cham (2017). https://doi.org/10.1007/978-3-319-65765-3_3
6. Basu, A., Bozga, M., Sifakis, J.: Modeling heterogeneous real-time components in BIP. In: SEFM, pp. 3–12. IEEE (2006). https://doi.org/10.1109/SEFM.2006.27
7. Behrmann, G., David, A., Larsen, K.G.: A tutorial on UPPAAL. In: Bernardo, M., Corradini, F. (eds.) SFM-RT 2004. LNCS, vol. 3185, pp. 200–236. Springer, Heidelberg (2004). https://doi.org/10.1007/978-3-540-30080-9_7
8. Benveniste, A., Le Guernic, P., Jacquemot, C.: Synchronous programming with events and relations: the SIGNAL language and its semantics. Sci. Comput. Program. **16**(2), 103–149 (1991). https://doi.org/10.1016/0167-6423(91)90001-E
9. Berendsen, J., Vaandrager, F.: Compositional abstraction in real-time model checking. In: Cassez, F., Jard, C. (eds.) FORMATS 2008. LNCS, vol. 5215, pp. 233–249. Springer, Heidelberg (2008). https://doi.org/10.1007/978-3-540-85778-5_17
10. Berry, G., Gonthier, G.: The Esterel synchronous programming language: design, semantics, implementation. Sci. Comput. Program. **19**(2), 87–152 (1992). https://doi.org/10.1016/0167-6423(92)90005-V
11. Bouyer, P., Larsen, K.G., Markey, N., Sankur, O., Thrane, C.: Timed automata can always be made implementable. In: Katoen, J.-P., König, B. (eds.) CONCUR 2011. LNCS, vol. 6901, pp. 76–91. Springer, Heidelberg (2011). https://doi.org/10.1007/978-3-642-23217-6_6
12. Corbett, J.C., Dean, J., Epstein, M., et al.: Spanner: Google's globally distributed database. ACM Trans. Comput. Syst. **31**(3), 8:1–8:22 (2013). https://dl.acm.org/citation.cfm?id=2491245
13. Fahrenberg, U.: Higher-dimensional timed automata 51(16), 109–114 (2018). https://doi.org/10.1016/j.ifacol.2018.08.019
14. Fehnker, A., van Glabbeek, R., Höfner, P., McIver, A., Portmann, M., Tan, W.L.: Automated analysis of AODV using UPPAAL. In: Flanagan, C., König, B. (eds.) TACAS 2012. LNCS, vol. 7214, pp. 173–187. Springer, Heidelberg (2012). https://doi.org/10.1007/978-3-642-28756-5_13
15. Feo-Arenis, S., Westphal, B., Dietsch, D., Muñiz, M., Andisha, S., Podelski, A.: Ready for testing: ensuring conformance to industrial standards through formal verification. Formal Aspects Comput. **28**(3), 499–527 (2016). https://doi.org/10.1007/s00165-016-0365-3

16. Feo-Arenis, S., Westphal, B.: Parameterized verification of track topology aggrega-
    tion protocols. In: Beyer, D., Boreale, M. (eds.) FMOODS/FORTE -2013. LNCS,
    vol. 7892, pp. 35–49. Springer, Heidelberg (2013). https://doi.org/10.1007/978-3-
    642-38592-6_4
17. Flammini, A., Ferrari, P.: Clock synchronization of distributed, real-time, indus-
    trial data acquisition systems. In: Vadursi, M. (ed.) Data Acquisition, chap. 3.
    IntechOpen, Rijeka (2010). https://doi.org/10.5772/10458
18. Gobriel, S., Khattab, S.M., Mossé, D., Brustoloni, J.C., Melhem, R.G.: Ridshar-
    ing: fault tolerant aggregation in sensor networks using corrective actions. In:
    SECON, pp. 595–604. IEEE (2006). https://doi.org/10.1109/SAHCN.2006.288516
19. Halbwachs, N., Caspi, P., Raymond, P., Pilaud, D.: The synchronous data flow
    programming language LUSTRE. Proc. IEEE 79(9), 1305–1320 (1991)
20. Hendriks, M.: Translating Uppaal to not quite C (2001). http://repository.ubn.ru.
    nl/bitstream/handle/2066/19058/19058.pdf?sequence=1
21. Henzinger, T.A., Horowitz, B., Kirsch, C.M.: Giotto: a time-triggered language for
    embedded programming. Proc. IEEE 91(1), 84–99 (2003)
22. ISO/IEC: 9899:2018, Programming Languages - C, 4th edn. (2018)
23. Jubran, O., Westphal, B.: Formal approach to guard time optimization for TDMA.
    In: Auguin, M., de Simone, R., Davis, R.I., Grolleau, E. (eds.) RTNS, pp. 223–233.
    ACM (2013). https://doi.org/10.1145/2516821.2516849
24. Jubran, O., Westphal, B.: Optimizing guard time for TDMA in a wireless sen-
    sor network - case study. In: LCN, pp. 597–601. IEEE Computer Society (2014).
    https://doi.org/10.1109/LCNW.2014.6927708
25. Kristensen, J., Mejlholm, A., Pedersen, S.: Automatic translation from Uppaal to
    C (2005). http://mejlholm.org/uni/pdfs/dat4.pdf
26. Olderog, E.R., Dierks, H.: Real-Time Systems - Formal Specification and Auto-
    matic Verification. Cambridge University Press, Cambridge (2008)
27. Plotkin, G.D.: A structural approach to operational semantics. J. Log. Algebr.
    Program. 60–61, 17–139 (2004)
28. Puri, A.: Dynamical properties of timed automata. Discrete Event Dyn. Syst. 10(1–
    2), 87–113 (2000). https://doi.org/10.1023/A:1008387132377
29. Senthooran, I., Watanabe, T.: On generating soft real-time programs for non-real-
    time environments. In: Nishizaki, S.Y., Numao, M., Caro, J., Suarez, M.T. (eds.)
    Theory and Practice of Computation, pp. 1–12. Springer, Tokyo (2013). https://
    doi.org/10.1007/978-4-431-54436-4_1
30. Tirado-Andrés, F., Rozas, A., Araujo, Á.: A methodology for choosing time syn-
    chronization strategies for wireless IoT networks. Sensors 19(16), 3476 (2019).
    https://doi.org/10.3390/s19163476
31. Triki, A., Combaz, J., Bensalem, S., Sifakis, J.: Model-based implementation of
    parallel real-time systems. In: Cortellessa, V., Varró, D. (eds.) FASE 2013. LNCS,
    vol. 7793, pp. 235–249. Springer, Heidelberg (2013). https://doi.org/10.1007/978-
    3-642-37057-1_18
32. Wibling, O., Parrow, J., Pears, A.: Ad Hoc routing protocol verification through
    broadcast abstraction. In: Wang, F. (ed.) FORTE 2005. LNCS, vol. 3731, pp. 128–
    142. Springer, Heidelberg (2005). https://doi.org/10.1007/11562436_11
33. Wulf, M.D., Doyen, L., Raskin, J.: Almost ASAP semantics: from timed models
    to timed implementations. Formal Asp. Comput. 17(3), 319–341 (2005). https://
    doi.org/10.1007/s00165-005-0067-8

Deep Statistical Model Checking

Timo P. Gros, Holger Hermanns, Jörg Hoffmann, Michaela Klauck$^{(\boxtimes)}$,
and Marcel Steinmetz

Saarland University, Saarland Informatics Campus, Saarbrücken, Germany
{timopgros,hermanns,hoffmann,klauck,steinmetz}@cs.uni-saarland.de

Abstract. Neural networks (NN) are taking over ever more decisions
thus far taken by humans, even though verifiable system-level guarantees are far out of reach. Neither is the verification technology available,
nor is it even understood what a formal, meaningful, extensible, and
scalable testbed might look like for such a technology. The present paper
is a modest attempt to improve on both the above aspects. We present
a family of formal models that contain basic features of automated decision making contexts and which can be extended with further orthogonal
features, ultimately encompassing the scope of autonomous driving. Due
to the possibility to model random noise in the decision actuation, each
model instance induces a Markov decision process (MDP) as verification
object. The NN in this context has the duty to actuate (near-optimal)
decisions. From the verification perspective, the externally learnt NN
serves as a determinizer of the MDP, the result being a Markov chain
which as such is amenable to statistical model checking. The combination of a MDP and a NN encoding the action policy is central to what we
call "deep statistical model checking" (DSMC). While being a straightforward extension of statistical model checking, it enables to gain deep
insight into questions like "how high is the NN-induced safety risk?",
"how good is the NN compared to the optimal policy?" (obtained by
model checking the MDP), or "does further training improve the NN?".
We report on an implementation of DSMC inside THE MODEST TOOLSET
in combination with externally learnt NNs, demonstrating the potential
of DSMC on various instances of the model family.

1   Introduction

Neural networks (NN), in particular deep neural networks, promise astounding
advances across a manifold of computing applications across domains as diverse
as image classification [27], natural language processing [21], and game playing [40]. NNs are the technical core of ever more *intelligent systems*, created to
assist or replace humans in decision-making.

This development comes with the urgent need to devise methods to analyze,
and ideally verify, desirable behavioral properties of such systems. Unlike for

---

Authors are listed alphabetically.

© IFIP International Federation for Information Processing 2020
Published by Springer Nature Switzerland AG 2020
A. Gotsman and A. Sokolova (Eds.): FORTE 2020, LNCS 12136, pp. 96–114, 2020.
https://doi.org/10.1007/978-3-030-50086-3_6

traditional programming methods, this endeavor is hampered by the nature of neural networks, whose complex function representation is not suited to human inspection and is highly resistant to mechanical analysis of important properties.

Verification Challenge. As a matter of fact, remarkable progress is being made towards automated NN analysis, be it through specialized reasoning methods of the SAT-modulo-theories family [10,23,25], or through suitable variants of abstract interpretation [13,31] or quantitative analysis [7,42]. All these works thus far focus on the verification of individual NN decision episodes, i.e., the behavior of a single input/output function call. In contrast, the verification of NNs being the decisive (in the literal sense of the word) authorities inside larger systems placed in possibly uncertain contexts, is wide-open scientific territory.

Very many real-world examples, where NNs are expected to become central decision entities – from autonomous driving to medical care robotics – involve discrete decision making in the presence of random phenomena. The former are to be taken in the best possible manner, and it is the NN that decides which decisions to take when and where. A very natural formal model for studying the principles, requirements, efficacy and robustness of such a NN, is the model family of Markov decision processes [38] (MDP). MDPs are a very widely studied class of models in the AI community, as well as in the verification community, where MDPs are the main semantic object of probabilistic model checking [29].

Assume now we are facing a problem for which a NN decision entity has been developed by a different party. If the problem statement can be formally cast as a certain MDP, we may use this MDP as a context to study properties of the NN delivered to us. Concretely, the NN will be put to use as a determinizer of the otherwise non-deterministic choices in the MDP, so that altogether a Markov chain results, which in turn can be evaluated by standard probabilistic model checking techniques. This is the simple idea this paper proposes. The idea can be further extended by making the technology available to a certification authority responsible for NN system approval, or to the party designing the NN, as a valuable feedback mechanism in the design process.

Deep Statistical Model Checking. However, this style of verification is challenged by the complexity of analyzing the participating NN *and* that of analyzing the induced system behaviors and interactions. Already the latter is a notorious practical impediment to successful verification rooted in state space explosion problems. Indeed, standard probabilistic model checking will suffer quickly from this. However, for Markov chains there is a scalable alternative to standard model checking at hand, nowadays referred to as *statistical model checking* [20,43]. The latter method employs efficient sampling techniques to statistically check the validity of a certain formal property. If applicable, it does not suffer from the state space explosion problem, in contrast to standard probabilistic model checking.

The scalable verification method we propose is called *deep statistical model checking* (DSMC) by us. At its core is a straightforward variation of statistical model checking, applied to a MDP, together with a NN that has to take the decisions. For this, DSMC expects a NN that can be queried as a black-box oracle to resolve the non-determinism in the MDP given: The NN receives the state descriptor as input, and it returns as output a decision determining the next step. The DSMC method integrates the pair of NN and MDP, and analyzes the resulting Markov chain statistically. In this way, it is possible to statistically verify properties of the NN itself, as we will discuss.

Racetrack. To study the potential of DSMC, we perform practical experiments with a case study family that remotely resembles the autonomous driving challenge, albeit with some drastic restrictions relative to the grand vision. These restrictions are: (i) We consider a single vehicle, there is no traffic otherwise. (ii) No object or position sensing is in use, instead the vehicle is aware of its exact position and speed. (iii) No speed limits or other traffic regulations are in place. (iv) Fuel consumption is not optimized for. (vi) Weather and road conditions are constant. (vii) The entire problem is discretized in a coarse manner. What remains after all these restrictions (apart from inducing a roadmap of further works beyond what we study) is the problem of navigating a vehicle from start to goal on a discrete map, with actions allowing to accelerate/decelerate in discrete directions, subject to a probabilistic risk of action failing to take effect in each step. The objective is to reach the goal in a minimal number of steps without bumping into a boundary wall. This problem is known as the Racetrack, a benchmark originating in AI autonomous decision making [1,37]. In formal terms, each map and parameter combination induces a MDP.

Racetrack is a simple problem, simple enough to put a neural network in the driver seat: This NN is then the central authority in the vehicle control loop. It needs to take action decisions with the objective to navigate the vehicle safely towards the goal. There are a good number of scientific proposals on how to construct and train a NN for mastering such tasks, and the present paper is not trying at all to innovate in this respect. Instead, *the central contribution of this paper is a scalable method to verify the effectiveness of a NN trained externally for its task.* This technique, DSMC, is by no means bound to the Racetrack problem domain, instead it is generally applicable. We evaluate it in the context of Racetrack because we do think that this is a crisp formal model family, which is of value in ongoing activities to systematize our understanding of NNs that are supposed to take over important decisions from humans.

Our concrete modelling context are MDPs represented in JANI [6], a language interfacing with the leading probabilistic model checkers out there. For the sake of experimentation and for use by third parties, we have implemented a generic connection between NNs and the state-of-the-art statistical model checker MODES [2,5], part of THE MODEST TOOLSET [18]. This extension gives the possibility to use a NN oracle, and to analyze the resulting Markov chain by SMC. We thus establish an initial DSMC tool infrastructure, which we apply on Racetrack benchmarks.

It will become evident by our empirical evaluation that there are a variety of use cases for DSMC, pertaining to end users and domain engineers alike:

- **Quality Assurance.** DSMC can be a tool for end users, or engineers, in system approval or certification, regarding safety, robustness, absence of deadlocks, or performance metrics. The generic connection to model checking furthermore enables the comparison of NN oracles to provably optimal choices, on moderate-size models: taking out the NN, the original MDP results, and can be submitted to standard probabilistic model checking. In our implementation, we use MCSTA [18] for this purpose.
- **Learning Pipeline Assessment.** DSMC can serve as a tool for the NN engineers designing the NN learning pipeline in the first place. This is because the DSMC analysis can reveal specific deficiencies in that pipeline. For example, we show that simple heat maps can highlight *where* the oracles are unsafe. And we exhibit cases where NN oracles turn out highly unsafe despite this phenomenon not being derivable from standard measures of learning performance. Such problems would likely have remained undetected without DSMC.

In summary, our contributions are as follows:

1. We present deep statistical model checking, which statistically evaluated the connection of a NN oracle and a MDP formalizing the problem context.
2. We establish tool infrastructure for DSMC within MODES to connect to NN oracles.
3. We establish infrastructure for Racetrack benchmarking, including parsing, simulation, JANI model export, comparison with optimal behavior, and also for NN learning.
4. We illustrate the use and feasibility of DSMC in Racetrack case studies.

The benchmark and all infrastructure including our modification of MODES as well as our JANI model is archived and publicly available at DOI 10.5281/zenodo.3760098 [14].

The paper is organized as follows. Section 2 briefly covers the necessary background in model checking, neural networks, and the Racetrack benchmark. Section 3 introduces the DSMC connection and discusses our implementation. Section 4 briefly introduces our Racetrack infrastructure, specifically the JANI model and the NN learning machinery. Section 5 describes the case studies, and Sect. 6 closes the paper.

2   Background

Markov Decision Processes. The models we consider are discrete-state Markov Decision Processes (MDP). For any nonempty set S we let $\mathcal{D}(S)$ denote the set of probability distribution over S. We write $\delta(s)$ for the *Dirac distribution* that assigns probability 1 to $s \in S$.

Definition 1 (Markov Decision Process). *A Markov Decision Process (MDP) is a tuple $\mathcal{M} = \langle \mathcal{S}, \mathcal{A}, \mathcal{T}, s_0 \rangle$ consisting of a finite set of states $\mathcal{S}$, a finite set of actions $\mathcal{A}$, a partial transition probability function $\mathcal{T}: \mathcal{S} \times \mathcal{A} \rightarrow \mathcal{D}(\mathcal{S})$, and an initial state $s_0 \in \mathcal{S}$. We say that action $a \in \mathcal{A}$ is applicable in state*

$s \in \mathcal{S}$ if $\mathcal{T}(s, a)$ is defined. We denote by $\mathcal{A}(s) \subseteq \mathcal{A}$ the set of actions applicable in s. We assume that $\mathcal{A}(s)$ is nonempty for each s (which is no restriction).

MDPs are often associated with a *reward* structure, specifying numerical rewards to be accumulated when moving along states sequences. Here we are interested instead in the probability of property satisfaction. Rewards, however, appear in our case study as part of the NN training which aims at optimizing reward expectations during reinforcement learning.

The behavior of a MDP is usually considered together with an entity resolving the otherwise non-deterministic choices in a state. This is effectuated by an *action policy* (or scheduler, or adversary) that determines which applicable action to apply when and where. In full generality this policy may use randomization (picking a distribution over applicable actions), and it may use the past history when picking. The former is of no importance for the setting considered here, while the latter is. Histories are represented as finite sequences of states (i.e. words over $\mathcal{S}$), thus they are drawn from $\mathcal{S}^+$. We use $last(w)$ to denote the last state in $w \in \mathcal{S}^+$.

Definition 2 (Action Policy). *A (deterministic, history-dependent) action policy is a function $\sigma \colon \mathcal{S}^+ \to \mathcal{A}$ such that $\forall w \in \mathcal{S}^+ \colon \sigma(w) \in \mathcal{A}(last(w))$. An action policy is memoryless if it satisfies $\sigma(w) = \sigma(w')$ whenever $last(w) = last(w')$.*

Memoryless policies can equally be represented as $\sigma \colon \mathcal{S} \to \mathcal{A}$ such that $\forall s \in \mathcal{S} \colon \sigma(s) \in \mathcal{A}(s)$.

Definition 3 (Markov Chain). *A Markov Chain is a tuple $\mathcal{C} = \langle \mathcal{S}, \mathcal{T}, s_0 \rangle$ consisting of a set of states $\mathcal{S}$, a transition probability function $\mathcal{T} \colon \mathcal{S} \to \mathcal{D}(\mathcal{S})$ and an initial state $s_0 \in \mathcal{S}$.*

An MDP $\langle \mathcal{S}, \mathcal{A}, \mathcal{T}, s_0 \rangle$ together with an action policy $\sigma \colon \mathcal{S}^+ \to \mathcal{A}$ induces a countable-state Markov chain $\langle \mathcal{S}^+, \mathcal{T}', s_0 \rangle$ over state histories in the obvious way: For any $w \in \mathcal{S}^+$ with $\mathcal{T}(last(w), \sigma(w)) = \mu$, set $\mathcal{T}'(w) = d$ where $d(ws) = \mu(s)$. For memoryless σ the original state space $\mathcal{S}$ can be recovered by setting $\mathcal{T}'(last(w)) = \mu$ in the above, since both are lumping equivalent [4].

Probabilistic and Statistical Model Checking. Model checking of probabilistic models (such as MDPs) nowadays comes in two flavors. *Probabilistic model checking* (PMC) [29] is an algorithmic technique to determine the extremal (maximal or minimal) probability (or expectation) with which an MDP satisfies a certain (temporal logic) property when ranging over all imaginable action policies. For some types of properties (step-bounded reachability, expected number of steps to reach) it does not suffice to restrict to memoryless policies, while for others (inevitability, step-unbounded reachability) it does. At the core of PMC are numerical algorithms that require the full state space to be available upfront (in some way or another) [17,35].

If fixing a particular policy, the MDP turns into a Markov chain. In this setting, *statistical model checking* (SMC [20,43]) is a popular alternative to probabilistic model checking. This is because PMC, requiring the full state space, is limited by the state space explosion problem. SMC is not, even if the underlying model is infinite in size. Furthermore, SMC can extend to non-Markovian formalisms or complex continuous dynamics effectively. At its core, SMC harvests classical Monte Carlo simulation and hypothesis testing techniques. In a nutshell, n finite samples of model executions are generated and evaluated to determine the fraction of executions satisfying a property under study. This yields an estimate q' of the actual value q of the property, together with a statistical statement on the potential error. A typical guarantee is that $\mathbb{P}(|q' - q| < \epsilon) > \delta$, where $1 - \delta$ is the confidence that the result is ϵ-correct. To decrease ϵ and δ, n must be increased. SMC is attractive as it only requires constant memory independent of the size of the state space. When facing rare events, however, the number of samples needed to achieve sufficient confidence may explode.

In the MDP setting (or more complicated settings), SMC analysis is always bound to a particular action policy turning an otherwise non-deterministic model into a stochastic process. Nevertheless, many SMC tools support non-deterministic models, e.g. PRISM [28] and UPPAAL SMC [8]. They use an implicitly defined uniform random action policy to resolve choices. The statistical model checker MODES [5], which is part of THE MODEST TOOLSET [18] instead lets the user choose out of a small set of predefined policies, or provides light-weight support for iterating over policies [5,30] to statistically approximate an optimal policy. In any case, results obtained by SMC are to be interpreted relative to the implicitly or explicitly defined action policy.

Neural Networks. NNs consist of neurons: atomic computational units that typically apply a non-linear function, their *activation function*, to a weighted sum of their inputs [39]. For example, *rectified linear units (ReLu)* use the activation function $f(x) = \max(0, x)$. Here we consider feed-forward NNs, a classical architecture where neurons are arranged in a sequence of layers. Inputs are provided to the first (input) layer, and the computation results are propagated through the layers in sequence until reaching the final (output) layer. In every layer, every neuron receives as inputs the outputs of all neurons in the previous layer. For a given set of possible inputs $\mathcal{I}$ and (final layer) outputs $\mathcal{O}$, a neural network can be considered as an efficient-to-query total function $\pi \colon \mathcal{I} \to \mathcal{O}$.

So-called "deep" neural networks consist of many layers. In tasks such as image recognition, successful NN architectures have become quite sophisticated, involving e.g. convolution and max-pooling layers [27]. Feed-forward NNs are comparatively simple, yet they are in wide-spread use [12], and are in principle able to approximate any function to any desired degree of accuracy [22].

Such NNs can be trained in a multitude of ways. Here we use *deep Q-learning* [33], a successful and nowadays widespread form of reinforcement learning, where the NN is trained by iterative execution and refinement steps. Each step executes the current NN from some state, and updates the NN weights using gradient descent. Deep Q-learning has been shown to learn high-quality NN action policies in a variety of challenging decision-making problems [33].

Racetrack. Originally Racetrack is a pen and paper game [11]. A track is drawn with a start line and a goal line. A vehicle starts with velocity 0 from some positions on the start line, with the objective to reach the goal as fast as possible without crashing into a wall. Nine possible actions modify the current velocity vector by one unit (up, down, left, right, four diagonals, keep current velocity). This simple game lends itself naturally as a benchmark for sequential decision making in risky scenarios. In particular, extending the problem with noise, we obtain MDPs that do not necessarily allow the vehicle to reach the goal with certainty. In a variety of such noisy forms, Racetrack was adopted as a benchmark for MDP algorithms in the AI community [1, 3, 32, 36, 37].

Like in previous work, we consider the single-agent version of the game. We use some of the benchmarks, i.e., track shapes, that are readily available. Specifically, we use the three Racetrack maps illustrated in Fig. 1, originally introduced by Barto et al. [1]. The track itself is defined as a two-dimensional grid, where each cell of the grid can represent a possible starting position "s" (indicated in green), a goal position "g" (red), or can contain a wall "x" (white, crossed). Like Barto et al. [1], we consider a noisy version of Racetrack that emulates slippery road conditions: actions may *fail* with a given probability, in which case the action does not change the velocity and the vehicle instead continues driving with unchanged velocity vector.

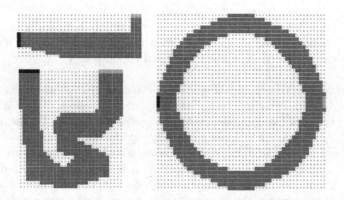

Fig. 1. The maps of our Racetrack benchmarks: Barto-small (left top), Barto-big (left bottom), Ring (right). (Color figure online)

3   Neural Networks as MDP Action Policies

Connecting MDP and Action Oracle. Racetrack is a simple instance of many further examples representing real-world phenomena that involve randomness and decision making. This is the natural scenario where NNs are taking over ever more duties. In essence, their role is very close to that of an action policy: Decide in each situation what options to pick next. If we consider the "situations" (the inputs $\mathcal{I}$) as the states $\mathcal{S}$ of a given MDP, and the "options" (outputs $\mathcal{O}$) as actions $\mathcal{A}$, then the NN is a function $\pi\colon \mathcal{S} \to \mathcal{A}$. We call such a function an *action oracle*. Indeed this is what the reinforcement learning process in Q-learning and other approaches delivers naturally.

Observe that an action oracle can be cast into an action policy except for a subtle problem. Action policies only pick actions (from $\mathcal{A}(s)$, thus) applicable at the current state s, while action oracles may not. A better fitting definition would constrain oracles to always return an applicable action. Yet it is not clear how to guarantee this for NNs – it is easy to see that, even for linear multi-classification, the hard constraints required to guarantee action applicability lead to non-convex optimization problems. An easy fix would use the highest-ranked applicable action instead of the NN classifier output itself. For our purposes however, where we want to analyze the quality of the NN oracle, it makes sense to explicitly distinguish inapplicable actions as a form of low quality.

If an oracle returns an inapplicable action, then no valid behavior is prescribed and in that sense the system can be considered stalled.

Definition 4 (Action Oracle Stalling). *Let $\mathcal{M} = \langle \mathcal{S}, \mathcal{A}, \mathcal{T}, s_0 \rangle$ be an MDP, and $\pi\colon \mathcal{S} \mapsto \mathcal{A}$ be an action oracle. We say that $s \in \mathcal{S}$ is stalled under π if $\pi(s) \notin \mathcal{A}(s)$.*

To accommodate for stalling, we augment the MDP upfront with a fresh action † available at every state, this action is chosen upon stalling, leading to a fresh state ‡ with only that action to continue. So $\mathcal{M} = \langle \mathcal{S}, \mathcal{A}, \mathcal{T}, s_0 \rangle$ is transformed into $\mathcal{M}^{\ddagger} = \langle \mathcal{S} \cup \{\ddagger\}, \mathcal{A} \cup \{\dagger\}, \mathcal{T}', s_0 \rangle$ where for each state s, $\mathcal{T}'(s, \dagger) = \delta(\ddagger)$ and otherwise $\mathcal{T}'(s, a) = \mathcal{T}(s, a)$ wherever the latter is defined.

Definition 5 (Oracle Induced Markov Chain). *Let $\mathcal{M} = \langle \mathcal{S}, \mathcal{A}, \mathcal{T}, s_0 \rangle$ be an MDP, and let π be an action oracle for $\mathcal{M}$. Then the Markov chain $\mathcal{C}^{\pi}$ induced by π is the one induced in $\mathcal{M}^{\ddagger}$ by the memoryless action policy σ defined by $\sigma(w) = \dagger$ whenever $last(w)$ is $\ddagger$ or stalled under π, and otherwise by $\sigma(w) = \pi(last(w))$.*

In words, the oracle induced policy fixes the probability distribution over transitions in each state to that of the chosen action. If that action is inapplicable, then the chain transitions to the fresh state ‡ which represents stalled situations.

Deep Statistical Model Checking. Overall, $\mathcal{C}^{\pi}$ is a Markov chain that uses π as an oracle to determinize the MDP $\mathcal{M}$ whenever possible, and stalls otherwise. With π implemented by a neural network, we can use statistical model checking on $\mathcal{C}^{\pi}$ to analyze the NN behavior in the context of $\mathcal{M}$. This analysis has the potential to deliver deep insights into the effectiveness of the NN applied, allowing for comparisons with other policies and also with optimal policies, the latter obtained from exhaustive model checking. From a practical perspective, an important remark is that in the definitions above and in our implementation of DSMC described below, the inputs to the NN are assumed to be the MDP states $\mathcal{S}$. This captures the scenario where the NN takes the role of a classical system controller, whose inputs are system state attributes, such as program variables. More generally, the connection from the MDP model to the NN input may require an intermediate function f mapping $\mathcal{S}$ to the input domain of the NN. This is in particular the case for NNs processing image sequences, like in vision systems in autonomous driving. In such a scenario, the MDP model states have to represent the relevant aspects of the NN input (e.g. objects and their properties in an image). This advanced form of connection remains a topic for future work. It lacks the crisp nature of the problem considered here.

DSMC Implementation. Deep statistical model checking is based on a pair of NN and MDP operating on the same state space. The NN is assumed to be trained externally prior to the analysis, in which it is combined with the MDP. To experiment with this concept in a real environment, we have developed a DSMC implementation inside THE MODEST TOOLSET [18], which includes the explicit-state model checker MCSTA, and in particular the statistical model checker MODES [5]. MODES thus far offers the options Uniform and Strict to resolve non-determinism. We implemented a novel option called Oracle, which calls an external procedure to resolve non-determinism. With that option in place, every time the next action has to be chosen, MODES provides the current model state s to the Oracle, which then calls the external procedure and returns the chosen action to MODES. In this way, the Oracle can connect to an external NN serving as an action oracle from MODES's perspective.

At the implementation level, connecting to standard NN tools is non-trivial due to the programming languages used. THE MODEST TOOLSET is implemented in C#, whereas standard NN tools are bound to languages like Python or Java. Our key observation to overcome this issue is that a seamless integration is not actually required. Standard NN tools are primarily required for NN *training*, which is computationally intensive and requires highly optimized code. In contrast, implementing our NN Oracle requires only NN *evaluation* (calling the NN on a given input) which is easy – it merely requires to propagate the input values through the network. We thus implemented NN evaluation directly in THE MODEST TOOLSET's code base, as part of our extension. The NNs are learned using standard NN tools. From there, we export a file containing the NN weights and biases. Our extension of MODES reads that file, and uses it to reconstruct the same NN, for use with our evaluation procedure. When the Oracle is called, it connects to that procedure.

MODES contains simulation algorithms specifically tailored to MDP and more advanced models. The tool is implemented in C#. It offers multiple statistical methods including confidence intervals, Okamoto bound [34], and SPRT [41]. As simulation is easily and efficiently parallelizable, MODES can exploit multi-core architectures.

4   Getting Concrete: The Racetrack Case Study

As previously outlined, we consider Racetrack as a simple and discrete, yet highly extensible approximation of real-world phenomena that involve randomness and decision making. In this section we spell out how these benchmarks are made concrete use of.

The JANI *framework.* Central to our practical work is the JANI-*model format* [6,24]. It can express models of distributed and concurrent systems in the form of networks of automata, and supports property specification based on probabilistic computation tree logic (PCTL) [16]. In full generality, JANI models are networks of stochastic timed automata, but we concentrate on MDPs here. Automatic translations from and into other modeling languages are available, connecting among others to the planning language PPDDL [26] and to the PRISM language, and thus to the model checker PRISM [28]. A large set of quantitative verification benchmarks (QVBS) [19] is available in JANI, and many tools offer direct support, among them ePMC, Storm and THE MODEST TOOLSET [9,15,18].

Racetrack Model. For lack of space, the details of the Racetrack encoding in JANI are part of the archive publicly available at [14]. The track itself is represented as a (constant) two-dimensional array whose size equals that of the grid. The JANI files of different Racetrack instances differ only in this array. Vehicle movements and collision checks are represented by separate automata that synchronize using shared actions.

The vehicle automaton keeps track of the current vehicle state via four bounded integer variables (position and directional velocity), and two Boolean variables (indicating whether the vehicle has crashed or reached a goal). The initial automaton location has edges for each of the 9 different acceleration vectors. Each of them updates the velocity accordingly, and sends the current source and next target coordinates to the collision check automaton. It then awaits that automaton to respond with one of three answers: "valid", "crash", or "goal". For the latter two, the automaton moves to a terminal location. For "valid", the vehicle automaton sets the target coordinates as its new source coordinates and moves back to its initial location.

The collision check automaton checks whether the vehicle's next target coordinates lie within the grid. If so, it iterates over the cells on the discretized trajectory from current source to next target, and looks up for each such cell whether it represents a wall or goal cell. Such a result is sent to the vehicle automaton as soon as available. If the entire trajectory is found free of such events, the vehicle automaton's request is answered with "valid", and the automaton location is reset, waiting for the next trajectory to check.

Learning Neural Networks for Racetrack. For the sake of realistic empirical studies, we have drawn on established NN learning techniques to obtain NN oracles for the Racetrack case studies. Here we briefly summarize the main design decisions. Notably, DSMC is entirely independent of the concrete learning process, depth, and shape of the NN employed.

- NNs are learnt for a specific map (cf. Fig. 1), with the inputs being 15 integer values, encoding the two-dimensional position, the two-dimensional velocity, the distance to the nearest wall in eight directions, the x and y differences to the goal coordinates, and Manhattan goal distance (absolute x- and y-difference, summed up). Actions are encoded as classification outputs.

- A crucial design decision is the learning objective, i.e., the rewards used in deep Q-learning. We set the reward for reaching the goal line to 100, and for crashing into a wall to −50. We used a discount factor of 0.99 to encourage short trajectories to the goal. This arrangement was chosen because, empirically, it resulted in an effective learning process. With higher negative rewards for crashing, the policies learn to prefer not to move or to move in circles. Similarly, smaller negative rewards make the learnt policies prefer to crash quickly. Using a discount factor yields better learning performance, but does not match the overall Racetrack setup. This exemplifies that the choice of objectives for learning is governed by learning performance. Both meta-parameters and numeric parameters such as rewards typically require fine-tuning orthogonal to, or at least below the level of abstraction of, the qualities of interest in the application.
- We experimented with a range of NN architectures and hyperparameter settings, the objective being to keep the NNs simple while still able to learn useful oracles in our Racetrack benchmarks. The NNs we settled on have the above described input and output layers, and two hidden layers each of size 64. All neurons use the ReLU activation function.
- NNs are learnt in two variants: (a) starting on the starting line vs. (b) starting from a random point anywhere on the map, each with initial velocity 0. Variant (b) turned out to yield much more effective and robust learning. Intuitively, with (a) it takes the policy a long time to reach the goal at all, while with (b) this happens more quickly yielding earlier and more robust learning also farther away from the goal.

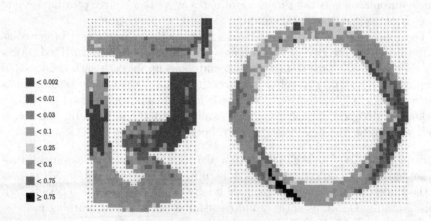

Fig. 2. Heat maps of NN induced crash probabilities for all Racetrack benchmarks. (Color figure online)

5   Getting Practical: DSMC Case Studies in Racetrack

We now demonstrate the statistical model checking approach to NN policy verification through case studies in Racetrack. Section 5.1 illustrates the use of DSMC for quality assurance by human analysts (end users, engineers) in system approval. Section 5.2 illustrates the use of DSMC as a tool for the engineers designing the NN learning pipeline. Section 5.3 evaluates the computational effort incurred by DSMC compared to a conventional SMC setting where the MDP policy is coded in the model itself.

Throughout, we use MODES with an error bound $P(error > \epsilon) < \kappa$, where $\epsilon = 0.01$ and $\kappa = 0.05$, i.e., a confidence of 95%. We set the maximal run length to 10000 steps. Unless otherwise stated, we set the slippery-noise level in Racetrack, i.e. the probability of action failure, to 20%. The NN oracles are learnt by training runs starting anywhere on the map; we will illustrate how DSMC can highlight the deficiencies of the alternate approach (starting on the starting line only). All experiments were run on an Intel(R) Core(TM) i7-4790 CPU @ 3.60 GHz (4 cores, 8 threads) with 32 GB RAM and a 450 GB HDD.

5.1   Quality Assurance in System Approval

The variety in abstract property specification gives versatility to the quality assurance process. This is important in particular because, as previously argued, the relevant quality properties will typically not be identical to the objectives used for NN learning. In the Racetrack example, NN learning optimizes expected reward subject to fine-tuned reward and discount values. For the quality assurance, we consider crash probability and goal probability, expressed as CTL path

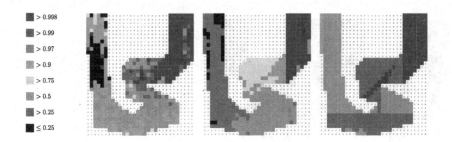

Fig. 3. Goal probability of NN oracle on the Barto-big benchmark trained and executed with 20% noise vs. stress-test executed with 50% noise using the same NN (middle) vs. optimal policies obtained by probabilistic model checking with 50% noise (right). (Color figure online)

formulas in JANI, namely ◊ *crashed* ("eventually crashed") for the former and ¬*crashed* U *goal* ("not crashed until reaching goal") for the latter.[1]

We highlight that the DSMC analysis can not only point out *that* a NN oracle has deficiencies, but also *where*: in which regions of the MDP state space S. Namely, in cyber-physical systems, it is natural to use the spatial dimension underlying S for systematizing the analysis and visualizing its result. This delivers not only a yes/no answer, but an actual quality report. We illustrate this here through the use of simple heat maps over the Racetrack road map.

Figure 2 shows quality assurance results for crash probability in all the Racetrack benchmarks, using for each the best NN oracle from reinforcement learning (i.e. those yielding highest rewards). The heat maps use a simple color scheme as an illustration how the analysis results can be visualized for the human analysts. Similar color schemes will be used in all plots below.

From the displayed DSMC results, quality assurance analysts can directly conclude that the NN oracles are fairly safe in Barto-small (left top), with crash probabilities mostly below 0.1; but not on Barto-large (left bottom) and Ring (right) where crash probabilities are above 0.5 on significant parts of the map. Generally, crash probability increases with distance to the goal line. Some interesting subtleties are also visible, for example that crash probabilities are relatively high in the left-turn before the goal in Barto-small.

Our next results, in Fig. 3, illustrate the quality-assurance versatility afforded by DSMC, through an analysis quite different from the previous one. The human analysts here decide to evaluate goal probability (a quality stronger than not crashing because the latter may be achieved by idling). Apart from the original setting, they consider a stress-test scenario where the road is significantly more slippery than during NN training, namely 50% instead of 20%. They finally decide to compare with optimal goal probabilities, computable via the

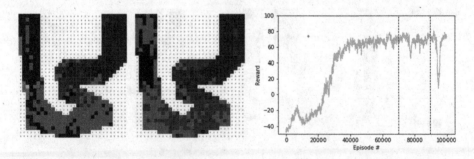

Fig. 4. Goal probabilities on the Barto-big benchmark (color coding as in Fig. 3), for NN oracles learnt over $n = 70000$ (left) and $n = 90000$ (middle) training episodes, together with Q-learning curve (right). (Color figure online)

---

[1] Further properties of interest could be, e.g., bounded goal probability (how likely is it that we will reach the goal within a given number of steps?), expected number of steps to goal, or risk of stalling.

probabilistic model checker MCSTA, so that they can see whether any deficiencies are due to the NN, or are unavoidable given the high amount of noise.

The figure shows the outcome for Barto-large. One of the deficiencies is immediately apparent, the NN policy does not pass the stress test. Its goal probability matches the optimal values only near the goal line, and exhibits significant deficiencies elsewhere. Based on these insights, the quality analysts can now decide whether to relax the stress-test (after all, even optimal behavior here does not reach the goal with certainty), or whether to reject these NN polices and request re-training.

5.2 Learning Pipeline Analysis and Revision

More generally, DSMC can yield important insights not only for quality assurance, but also for the engineers designing the NN learning pipeline in the first place. There are two distinct scenarios:

(i) The engineers run the same success tests as in quality assurance, and re-train if a test is not passed.
(ii) The engineers assess different properties of interest to the learning process itself (e.g. expected length of policy runs), or assess the impact of different hyperparameter settings.

In both scenarios, the DSMC analysis results point to specific state-space regions that require improvement. This can be directly operationalized to revise the learning pipeline, by starting more training runs from states in the critical regions.

Figures 2 and 3 above have already demonstrated (i). Next we demonstrate (ii) through two case studies analyzing different hyperparameter settings.

Our first case study, in Fig. 4, analyzes the number n of training episodes, as a central hyperparameter of the learning pipeline. The only information available in deep Q-learning for the choice of this hyperparameter is the learning curve, i.e., the expected reward as a function of n, depicted on the right. Yet, as our DSMC analysis here shows, this information is insufficient to obtain reliable policies. In Barto-big, the highest reward is obtained after $n = 90000$ episodes. From $n = 70000$ to $n = 90000$, the reward slightly increases. Yet we see in Fig. 4 that the additional 20000 training episodes, while increasing overall goal probability, lead to highly deficient behavior in an area near the start of the map, where goal probability drops below 0.25. If provided with that information, the engineers can focus additional training on that area, for instance.

In our next case study, we assume that the NN engineers decide to analyze the impact of starting training runs on (a) the starting line vs. (b) random points anywhere on the map. Figure 5 shows the results for the Ring map, where they are most striking. In variant (a), the top part of the Racetrack was completely ignored by the learning process. Looking into this issue, one finds that, during training, the first solution happens to be found via the bottom route. From there on, the reinforcement learning process has a strong bias to that route, preventing any further exploration of other routes.

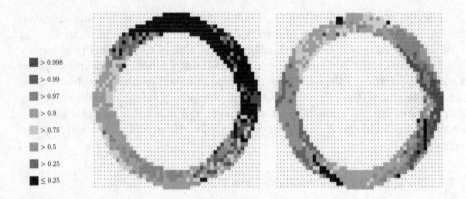

Fig. 5. Goal probabilities in Ring for NN oracles where training was carried out with reinforcing runs from the start line only (left) vs. from anywhere on the map (right). (Color figure online)

Phenomena like this are highly detrimental if the learnt policy needs to be broadly robust, across most of the environment. The deficiency is obvious given the DSMC analysis results, and these results make it obvious how the problem can be fixed. But neither can be seen in the learning curves.

5.3   Computational Effort for the Analysis

As discussed, it can be highly demanding or infeasible to verify the input/output behavior of even a single NN decision episode, and that complexity is potentially compounded by the state space explosion problem when endeavoring to verify the behavior induced by an NN oracle. Deep statistical model checking carries promise as a "light-weight" approach to this formidable problem, as no state space needs to be stored and on the NN side it merely requires to call the NN on sample inputs. In addition, it is efficiently parallelizable, just like SMC. Yet (1) the approach might suffer from an excessive number of sample runs needed to obtain sufficient confidence, and/or (2) the overhead of NN calls might severely hamper its runtime feasibility.

Figure 6 shows data regarding (1). We compare the effort for analyzing our NN policies to that required for analyzing a conventional hand-made policy that we incorporated into our JANI models.[2] As the heat maps show, the latter effort is higher. This is due to a tendency to more risky behavior in the hand-made policy, resulting in higher variance. Regarding (2), the runtime overhead for NN calls is actually negligible in our study. Each call takes between 1 and 4 ms. There is an added overhead for constructing the NN once at the beginning of the analysis, but that takes at most 6 ms.

---

[2] The policy implements a simple reactive controller that brakes if a wall is near and otherwise accelerates towards the goal. Its goal probability is moderately worse than that of the best NN policies.

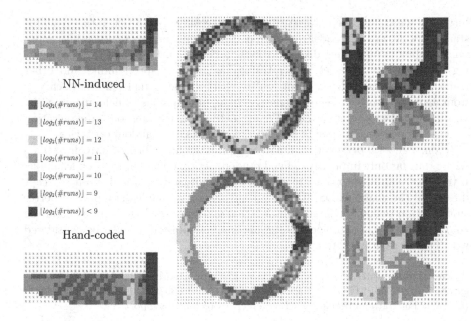

Fig. 6. Heat maps showing computational effort needed by DSMC, measured by the number of sample runs performed by MODES to analyze goal probability for each map location. Results shown for the policies induced by our learnt NN in the top row, vs. a simple hand-coded policy (see text) at the bottom. Each point on the map shows $\lfloor \log_2(\#runs) \rfloor$. (Color figure online)

These results should of course not be over-interpreted, given the limitations of this initial study. But they do provide evidence that the computational overhead may be manageable in practice at least for moderate-size neural networks.

6   Conclusion

This paper has described the cornerstones of an effective methodology to apply statistical model checking as a light-weight approach to checking the behavior of systems incorporating neural networks. The most important aspects of the DSMC approach are its (i) genericity – in that it provides a generic and scalable basis for analyzing learnt action policies; its (ii) openness – since the approach is put into practice using the JANI format, supported by many tools for probabilistic or statistical model checking; and its (iii) focus – on an abstract fragment of the "autonomous driving" challenge. We consider these contributions as a conceptual nucleus of broader activities to foster the scientific understanding of neural network efficacy, by providing the formal and technological framework for precise, yet scalable problem analysis.

We have contributed an initial case study suggesting that this may indeed be useful and feasible. We hope that the study provides a compelling basis for further research on deep statistical model checking. Racetrack forms a viable starting point for this endeavor in that can be made more realistic in a manifold of dimensions: finer discretizations, different surface conditions, appearing/disappearing obstacles, other traffic participants, speed limits and other traffic regulations, different probabilistic perturbances, fuel efficiency, change from map perspective to ego-perspective of an autonomous vehicle, mediated by vision and other sensor systems. We are actually embarking on an exploration of these dimensions, focussing first on speed limits and random obstacles.

From a general perspective, DSMC provides a refined form of SMC for MDPs where thus far only implicitly defined random action policies have been available. If those were applied to Racetrack, goal probabilities <0.1 would result – except directly at the goal line. DSMC instead can harvest available data for a far better suited action policy, in the form of a NN oracle trained on the data at hand. Of course, other forms of oracles (based on, say, random forests) can be considered with DSMC rightaway, too.

Acknowledgements. This work was partially supported by ERC Advanced Investigators Grant 695614 (POWVER), and by DFG Grant 389792660 as part of TRR 248 (CPEC). The authors thank Felix Freiberger for technical support.

References

1. Barto, A.G., Bradtke, S.J., Singh, S.P.: Learning to act using real-time dynamic programming. Artif. Intell. **72**(1–2), 81–138 (1995)
2. Bogdoll, J., Ferrer Fioriti, L.M., Hartmanns, A., Hermanns, H.: Partial order methods for statistical model checking and simulation. In: Bruni, R., Dingel, J. (eds.) FMOODS/FORTE -2011. LNCS, vol. 6722, pp. 59–74. Springer, Heidelberg (2011). https://doi.org/10.1007/978-3-642-21461-5_4
3. Bonet, B., Geffner, H.: Labeled RTDP: improving the convergence of real-time dynamic programming, In: ICAPS, pp. 12–21 (2003)
4. Buchholz, P.: Exact and ordinary lumpability in finite Markov chains. J. Appl. Probab. **31**(1), 59–75 (1994)
5. Budde, C.E., D'Argenio, P.R., Hartmanns, A., Sedwards, S.: A statistical model checker for nondeterminism and rare events. In: Beyer, D., Huisman, M. (eds.) TACAS 2018. LNCS, vol. 10806, pp. 340–358. Springer, Cham (2018). https://doi.org/10.1007/978-3-319-89963-3_20
6. Budde, C.E., Dehnert, C., Hahn, E.M., Hartmanns, A., Junges, S., Turrini, A.: JANI: quantitative model and tool interaction. In: Legay, A., Margaria, T. (eds.) TACAS 2017. LNCS, vol. 10206, pp. 151–168. Springer, Heidelberg (2017). https://doi.org/10.1007/978-3-662-54580-5_9
7. Croce, F., Andriushchenko, M., Hein, M.: Provable robustness of RELU networks via maximization of linear regions, In: AISTATS. pp. 2057–2066. PMLR 89 (2019)
8. David, A., Larsen, K.G., Legay, A., Mikučionis, M., Wang, Z.: Time for statistical model checking of real-time systems. In: Gopalakrishnan, G., Qadeer, S. (eds.) CAV 2011. LNCS, vol. 6806, pp. 349–355. Springer, Heidelberg (2011). https://doi.org/10.1007/978-3-642-22110-1_27

9. Dehnert, C., Junges, S., Katoen, J.-P., Volk, M.: A STORM is Coming: A Modern Probabilistic Model Checker. In: Majumdar, R., Kunčak, V. (eds.) CAV 2017. LNCS, vol. 10427, pp. 592–600. Springer, Cham (2017). https://doi.org/10.1007/978-3-319-63390-9_31

10. Ehlers, R.: Formal Verification of Piece-Wise Linear Feed-Forward Neural Networks. In: D'Souza, D., Narayan Kumar, K. (eds.) ATVA 2017. LNCS, vol. 10482, pp. 269–286. Springer, Cham (2017). https://doi.org/10.1007/978-3-319-68167-2_19

11. Gardner, M.: Mathematical games. Sci. Am. **229**, 118–121 (1973)

12. Gardner, M., Dorling, S.: Artificial neural networks (the multilayer perceptron)-a review of applications in the atmospheric sciences. Atmospheric Environ. **32**(14), 2627–2636 (1998)

13. Gehr, T., Mirman, M., Drachsler-Cohen, D., Tsankov, P., Chaudhuri, S., Vechev, M.T.: AI2: Safety and robustness certification of neural networks with abstract interpretation. IEEE Sympos. Secur. Privacy **2018**, 3–18 (2018)

14. Gros, T.P., Hermanns, H., Hoffmann, J., Klauck, M., Steinmetz, M.: Models and Infrastructure used in "Deep Statistical Model Checking" (2020). https://doi.org/10.5281/zenodo.3760098

15. Hahn, E.M., Li, Y., Schewe, S., Turrini, A., Zhang, L.: ISCASMC: a web-based probabilistic model checker. In: Jones, C., Pihlajasaari, P., Sun, J. (eds.) FM 2014. LNCS, vol. 8442, pp. 312–317. Springer, Cham (2014). https://doi.org/10.1007/978-3-319-06410-9_22

16. Hansson, H., Jonsson, B.: A logic for reasoning about time and reliability. Formal Asp. Comput. **6**(5), 512–535 (1994)

17. Hartmanns, A.: On the analysis of stochastic timed systems. Ph.D. thesis, Saarland University, Germany (2015)

18. Hartmanns, A., Hermanns, H.: The modest toolset: an integrated environment for quantitative modelling and verification. In: Ábrahám, E., Havelund, K. (eds.) TACAS 2014. LNCS, vol. 8413, pp. 593–598. Springer, Heidelberg (2014). https://doi.org/10.1007/978-3-642-54862-8_51

19. Hartmanns, A., Klauck, M., Parker, D., Quatmann, T., Ruijters, E.: The quantitative verification benchmark set. In: Vojnar, T., Zhang, L. (eds.) TACAS 2019. LNCS, vol. 11427, pp. 344–350. Springer, Cham (2019). https://doi.org/10.1007/978-3-030-17462-0_20

20. Hérault, T., Lassaigne, R., Magniette, F., Peyronnet, S.: Approximate probabilistic model checking. In: Steffen, B., Levi, G. (eds.) VMCAI 2004. LNCS, vol. 2937, pp. 73–84. Springer, Heidelberg (2004). https://doi.org/10.1007/978-3-540-24622-0_8

21. Hinton, G., et al.: Deep neural networks for acoustic modeling in speech recognition: the shared views of four research groups. IEEE Signal Process. Mag. **29**(6), 82–97 (2012)

22. Hornik, K., Stinchcombe, M.B., White, H.: Multilayer feedforward networks are universal approximators. Neural Netw. **2**, 359–366 (1989)

23. Huang, X., Kwiatkowska, M., Wang, S., Wu, M.: Safety verification of deep neural networks. In: Majumdar, R., Kunčak, V. (eds.) CAV 2017. LNCS, vol. 10426, pp. 3–29. Springer, Cham (2017). https://doi.org/10.1007/978-3-319-63387-9_1

24. The JANI specification. http://www.jani-spec.org/. Accessed 28 Feb 2020

25. Katz, G., Barrett, C., Dill, D.L., Julian, K., Kochenderfer, M.J.: Reluplex: an efficient SMT solver for verifying deep neural networks. In: Majumdar, R., Kunčak, V. (eds.) CAV 2017. LNCS, vol. 10426, pp. 97–117. Springer, Cham (2017). https://doi.org/10.1007/978-3-319-63387-9_5

26. Klauck, M., Steinmetz, M., Hoffmann, J., Hermanns, H.: Compiling probabilistic model checking into probabilistic planning. In: ICAPS, pp. 150–154 (2018)
27. Krizhevsky, A., Sutskever, I., Hinton, G.E.: Imagenet classification with deep convolutional neural networks. In: NIPS, pp. 1097–1105 (2012)
28. Kwiatkowska, M., Norman, G., Parker, D.: PRISM 4.0: verification of probabilistic real-time systems. In: Gopalakrishnan, G., Qadeer, S. (eds.) CAV 2011. LNCS, vol. 6806, pp. 585–591. Springer, Heidelberg (2011). https://doi.org/10.1007/978-3-642-22110-1_47
29. Kwiatkowska, M., Norman, G., Parker, D.: Stochastic model checking. In: Bernardo, M., Hillston, J. (eds.) SFM 2007. LNCS, vol. 4486, pp. 220–270. Springer, Heidelberg (2007). https://doi.org/10.1007/978-3-540-72522-0_6
30. Legay, A., Sedwards, S., Traonouez, L.-M.: Scalable verification of markov decision processes. In: Canal, C., Idani, A. (eds.) SEFM 2014. LNCS, vol. 8938, pp. 350–362. Springer, Cham (2015). https://doi.org/10.1007/978-3-319-15201-1_23
31. Li, J., Liu, J., Yang, P., Chen, L., Huang, X., Zhang, L.: Analyzing deep neural networks with symbolic propagation: towards higher precision and faster verification. In: Chang, B.-Y.E. (ed.) SAS 2019. LNCS, vol. 11822, pp. 296–319. Springer, Cham (2019). https://doi.org/10.1007/978-3-030-32304-2_15
32. McMahan, H.B., Gordon, G.J.: Fast exact planning in Markov decision processes. In: ICAPS, pp. 151–160 (2005)
33. Mnih, V., et al.: Human-level control through deep reinforcement learning. Nature 518, 529–533 (2015)
34. Okamoto, M.: Some inequalities relating to the partial sum of binomial probabilities. Ann. inst. Stat. Math. 10(1), 29–35 (1959)
35. Parker, D.A.: Implementation of symbolic model checking for probabilistic systems. Ph.D. thesis, University of Birmingham, UK (2003)
36. Pineda, L.E., Lu, Y., Zilberstein, S., Goldman, C.V.: Fault-tolerant planning under uncertainty. In: IJCAI, pp. 2350–2356 (2013)
37. Pineda, L.E., Zilberstein, S.: Planning under uncertainty using reduced models: revisiting determinization. In: ICAPS, 217–225 (2014)
38. Puterman, M.L.: Markov Decision Processes: Discrete Stochastic Dynamic Programming. Wiley, Hoboken (1994)
39. Sarle, W.S.: Neural networks and statistical models (1994)
40. Silver, D., et al.: A general reinforcement learning algorithm that masters chess, shogi, and go through self-play. Science 362(6419), 1140–1144 (2018)
41. Wald, A.: Sequential tests of statistical hypotheses. Ann. Math. Stat. 16(2), 117–186 (1945)
42. Wicker, M., Huang, X., Kwiatkowska, M.: Feature-guided black-box safety testing of deep neural networks. In: Beyer, D., Huisman, M. (eds.) TACAS 2018. LNCS, vol. 10805, pp. 408–426. Springer, Cham (2018). https://doi.org/10.1007/978-3-319-89960-2_22
43. Younes, H.L.S., Simmons, R.G.: Probabilistic verification of discrete event systems using acceptance sampling. In: Brinksma, E., Larsen, K.G. (eds.) CAV 2002. LNCS, vol. 2404, pp. 223–235. Springer, Heidelberg (2002). https://doi.org/10.1007/3-540-45657-0_17

Trace Equivalence and Epistemic Logic to Express Security Properties

Kiraku Minami$^{(\boxtimes)}$ (iD)

Kyoto University, Kyoto 606-8502, Japan
kminami@kurims.kyoto-u.ac.jp

Abstract. In process algebra, we can express security properties using an equivalence on processes. However, it is not clear which equivalence is the most suitable for the purpose. Indeed, several definitions of some properties are proposed. For example, the definition of privacy is not unique. This situation means that we are not certain how to express an intuitive security notion. Namely, there is a gap between an intuitive security notion and the formulation. Proper formalization is essential for verification, and our purpose is to bridge this gap.

In the case of the applied pi calculus, an outputted message is not explicitly expressed. This feature suggests that trace equivalence appropriately expresses indistinguishability for attackers in the applied pi calculus. By chasing interchanging bound names and scope extrusions, we prove that trace equivalence is a congruence. Therefore, a security property expressed using trace equivalence is preserved by application of contexts.

Moreover, we construct an epistemic logic for the applied pi calculus. We show that its logical equivalence agrees with trace equivalence. It means that trace equivalence is suitable in the presence of a non-adaptive attacker. Besides, we define several security properties to use our epistemic logic.

Keywords: Applied pi calculus · Trace equivalence · Epistemic logic

1 Introduction

1.1 Background

In modern society, information technology is indispensable to our daily lives, and many communication protocols are developed to transmit data securely. Verification of security properties of each protocol is essential, but it is not easy.

In the first place, how to formalize security notions is not clear. Various definitions of the same security property have been proposed, we will show an example later. One of our goals is to provide foundations to express these properties in

This work was partly supported by JST ERATO Grant Number JPMJER1603, Japan.

© IFIP International Federation for Information Processing 2020
Published by Springer Nature Switzerland AG 2020
A. Gotsman and A. Sokolova (Eds.): FORTE 2020, LNCS 12136, pp. 115–132, 2020.
https://doi.org/10.1007/978-3-030-50086-3_7

a rigorous way. Besides, how to model communication and concurrency is also not clear; many such models have also been developed. In this work, we focus on process algebra because it allows us to handle parallel composition naturally.

In process calculi, common confidentiality properties such as secrecy are represented to use an equivalence on processes. Many equivalences exist (cf. [18]), but which is the most suitable for expressing confidentiality is not clear. For instance, Delaune et al. [13] defined privacy in electronic voting in terms of the applied pi calculus [1] as follows.

Definition 1 ([13, **Definition 9**]). *A voting protocol respects vote-privacy (or just privacy) if*

$$S[V_A\{a/v\}|V_B\{b/v\}] \approx_l S[V_A\{b/v\}|V_B\{a/v\}]$$

for all possible votes a and b.

V_A and V_B denote the voters containing the free variable v. S is an evaluation context. S denotes other voters and authorities. Intuitively, when the protocol respects privacy, this definition states that an attacker cannot distinguish two situations where votes are swapped. Note that indistinguishability is expressed to use labeled bisimilarity $\approx_l$ in this definition. Is it the most suitable? This question is nontrivial. Indeed, Chadha et al. [7] gave another definition and claimed that trace equivalence is more suitable than bisimilarity to model privacy. We also claim that trace equivalence is more suitable to express security properties in the presence of non-adaptive attackers. Similar arguments are not abundant in previous work.

In the applied pi calculus, a process can send not only names but also terms, but we do not explicitly express sent messages. We indirectly represent them to use alias variables. This feature enables us to handle cryptographic protocols naturally and suggests that trace equivalence means indistinguishability for attackers. This is because attackers whom we consider can observe only labeled transitions. We recall the syntax and semantics of the applied pi calculus in Sect. 2.

Both bisimilarity and trace equivalence on labeled transition systems (LTSs) are well studied. However, trace equivalence in the applied pi calculus (and other variants of the pi calculus [26,27]) has not drawn much attention. This is perhaps because trace equivalence is the coarsest among commonly used equivalences. However, security properties sometimes require that different processes are regarded as the same. For example, consider secrecy. We want to make two processes that send different messages indistinguishable. In the case, trace equivalence is enough, but bisimilarity is not always optimal because it is too strong. Bisimilarity requires that possible actions for each process are the same. However, a non-adaptive attacker cannot detect a difference in feasibility. Here, "non-adaptive" means that the attacker cannot control participants. Thereby, a fine equivalence such as bisimilarity is not always adequate. Bisimilarity is probably suitable for more powerful attackers.

Epistemic logic is often used to express confidentiality directly (e.g. [7,25, 32]). For example, when a message M sent by an agent a is anonymous, we might say that an adversary cannot know who sent M. In epistemic logic, we can express it with a formula such as $\neg K\text{Send}(a, M)$. This logical formulation is close to our intuition. Nevertheless, research into an epistemic logic for the applied pi calculus is not abundant.

In this paper, we assume that attackers can observe only labeled transitions. Especially, they cannot observe what action participants' can do. This assumption is natural because attackers in this paper are non-adaptive. We also assume that an attacker can send messages to participants.

1.2   Contributions

We prove that trace equivalence for the applied pi calculus is a congruence in Sect. 3. Second, we give an epistemic logic that characterizes trace equivalence in Sect. 4. Besides, we define security properties such as role-interchangeability, secrecy [25,32], and openness, using our epistemic logic. Moreover, we show that parallel composition does not generally preserve secrecy and openness.

Whereas, trace equivalence characterizes total secrecy, so application of contexts preserves it. We omit many proofs. See [28] for details.

Our results suggest that trace equivalence is more suitable to express (non-probabilistic) security notions than bisimilarity.

2   The Applied Pi Calculus

The applied pi calculus [1] is an extension of the pi-calculus [26,27]. We can handle cryptographic protocols naturally to use it.

2.1   Syntax

Let Σ be a signature equipped with an equational theory. Terms are made from names, variables, and function symbols. A term is ground when it contains no variables. We recall the syntax of the applied pi-calculus. Here, $M, N...$ range over terms, while n on names and x on variables.

$$P, Q ::= 0 \mid \overline{M}\langle N\rangle.P \mid M(x).P \mid \nu n.P \mid$$
$$\quad \text{if } M = N \text{ then } P \text{ else } Q \mid P + Q \mid P|Q \mid !P$$

$$A, B ::= P \mid \nu n.A \mid \nu x.A \mid A|B \mid \{M/x\}$$

$P, Q, ...$ are plain processes. ν is a binding operator. $\mid$ is a parallel composition operator. $+$ is a nondeterministic choice operator. Plain processes are similar to pi-calculus processes, but they are not the same. A pi-calculus process can send only a name. On the other hand, an applied pi calculus process can send a term. Besides, a channel consists of a term. An object of an input prefix is a variable, so names do not change while the process runs.

$A, B, \ldots$ are extended processes. We call $\{M/x\}$ an active substitution. This notion is peculiar to the applied pi calculus. An active substitution $\{M/x\}$ substitutes M for x in a neighbor process.

fn(A) and bn(A) denote the sets of free names and bound names of a process A, respectively. fv and bv are similar to them. If fn$(A) \cap$ bn$(A) = \emptyset$ and no bound names are restricted twice, we say that A is name-distinct. Variable-distinctness is defined similarly. n(M) denotes the set of names that appear in a term M. v(M) is similar to it.

The domain dom(A) of an extended process A is inductively defined below. If variables in neighbor concurrently running processes are in dom(A), the process A affects those variables. If fv$(A) =$ dom(A), we say that A is closed.

$$\text{dom}(P) = \emptyset, \ \text{dom}(\nu n.A) = \text{dom}(A), \ \text{dom}(\nu x.A) = \text{dom}(A) \setminus \{x\},$$
$$\text{dom}(A|B) = \text{dom}(A) \cup \text{dom}(B), \ \text{dom}(\{M/x\}) = \{x\}$$

2.2   Semantics

A context is an expression containing one hole. An evaluation context is a context whose hole is neither under a replication, a conditional branch, nor an action prefix. Structural equivalence $\equiv$ is the smallest equivalence relation on extended processes that is closed under application of evaluation contexts and α-conversion, such that:

$$A|0 \equiv A \ \ (A|B)|C \equiv A|(B|C) \ \ A|B \equiv B|A$$
$$(\nu u.A)|B \equiv \nu u.(A|B) \ \ \text{if} \ u \notin \text{fn}(B) \cup \text{fv}(B) \ \ \nu u.\nu v.A \equiv \nu v.\nu u.A \ \ !P \equiv P|!P$$
$$P + Q \equiv Q + P \ \ \nu x.\{M/x\} \equiv 0 \ \ A|\{M/x\} \equiv A[M/x]|\{M/x\}$$
$$\{M/x\} \equiv \{N/x\} \ \ \text{if} \ \Sigma \vdash M = N;$$

The second from the last represents how an active substitution $\{M/x\}$ acts.

Definition 2. *Internal reduction* $\rightarrow$ *is the smallest relation on extended processes closed under structural equivalence and application of evaluation contexts, such that:*

$$\text{if} \ M = N \ \text{then} \ P \ \text{else} \ Q \rightarrow P \ \ \text{when} \ \Sigma \vdash M = N$$
$$\text{if} \ M = N \ \text{then} \ P \ \text{else} \ Q \rightarrow Q \ \ \text{when} \ \Sigma \nvdash M = N$$
$$P + Q \rightarrow P$$
$$\overline{M}\langle N \rangle.P \mid M(x).Q \rightarrow P \mid Q[N/x],$$

where terms M and N in the second rule are ground.

The last line represents synchronous communication on a channel M. We emphasize that an environment cannot observe what is interchanged.

Next, we recall labeled semantics and requisite equivalence relations.

$$M(x).P \xrightarrow{M(N)} P[N/x] \qquad \frac{x \notin \mathrm{fv}(\overline{M}\langle N \rangle.P)}{\overline{M}\langle N \rangle.P \xrightarrow{\nu x.\overline{M}\langle x \rangle} P|\{N/x\}}$$

$$\frac{A \xrightarrow{\alpha} A' \quad u \text{ does not appear in } \alpha.}{\nu u.A \xrightarrow{\alpha} \nu u.A'}$$

$$\frac{A \xrightarrow{\alpha} A' \quad \mathrm{bv}(\alpha) \cap \mathrm{fv}(B) = \emptyset}{A|B \xrightarrow{\alpha} A'|B} \qquad \frac{A \equiv A' \quad A' \xrightarrow{\alpha} B' \quad B' \equiv B}{A \xrightarrow{\alpha} B}$$

The second rule represents an output. Note that an active substitution $\{N/x\}$ is generated. The term N does not appear in the action label $\nu x.\overline{M}\langle x \rangle$.

A frame is an extended process generated from 0 and active substitutions to use restriction and parallel composition. $\mathrm{fr}(A)$ denotes a process obtained by replacing plain processes in A with 0, and we call it a frame of A. We can consider that $\mathrm{fr}(A)$ is a list of outputted messages.

μ is an action. We define $\Longrightarrow$ as the transitive reflexive closure of $\longrightarrow$, and $\xRightarrow{\alpha}$ as $\Longrightarrow \xrightarrow{\alpha} \Longrightarrow$. $\xRightarrow{\mu}$ is the former when μ is silent and is the latter otherwise.

Definition 3. $(M = N)\varphi \overset{\mathrm{def}}{\Longleftrightarrow} \mathrm{v}(M) \cup \mathrm{v}(N) \subseteq \mathrm{dom}(\varphi)$ and $M\sigma = N\sigma$ where $\varphi \equiv \nu\tilde{n}.\sigma$ and $\tilde{n} \cap \mathrm{n}(M, N) = \emptyset$ for some names $\tilde{n}$ and active substitutions σ.

$(M = N)\varphi$ means that an attacker cannot distinguish M and N to use φ.

Definition 4. The static equivalence on closed frames is given by

$$\varphi \approx_s \psi \overset{\mathrm{def}}{\Longleftrightarrow} \mathrm{dom}(\varphi) = \mathrm{dom}(\psi) \text{ and } \forall M, N; (M = N)\varphi \Leftrightarrow (M = N)\psi$$

for closed frames φ and ψ. The static equivalence on closed processes is given by

$$A \approx_s B \overset{\mathrm{def}}{\Longleftrightarrow} \mathrm{fr}(A) \approx_s \mathrm{fr}(B)$$

for closed processes A and B.

Static equivalence means that an attacker has the same information about which terms are equal.

Definition 5. A trace $\mathbf{tr}$ is a finite derivation $\mathbf{tr} = A_0 \xRightarrow{\mu_1} \dots \xRightarrow{\mu_n} A_n$ such that every A_i is closed and $\mathrm{fv}(\mu_i) \subseteq \mathrm{dom}(A_{i-1})$ for all i. If A_n can perform no actions, the trace $\mathbf{tr}$ is said to be complete or maximal. Given a trace $\mathbf{tr}$, let $\mathbf{tr}[i]$ be its i-th process A_i, and $\mathbf{tr}[i,j]$ be the trace $A_i \xRightarrow{\mu_{i+1}} \dots \xRightarrow{\mu_j} A_j$ where $0 \le i \le j \le n$. The length of the trace $\mathbf{tr}$ is denoted by $|\mathbf{tr}| = n$.

Definition 6. Let $\mathbf{tr}$ be a trace $A_0 \xRightarrow{\mu_1} \dots \xRightarrow{\mu_n} A_n$ and $\mathbf{tr}'$ be a trace $B_0 \xRightarrow{\mu_1'} \dots \xRightarrow{\mu_m'} B_m$. Static equivalence between $\mathbf{tr}$ and $\mathbf{tr}'$ is defined as below:
$\mathbf{tr} \sim_t \mathbf{tr}' \overset{\mathrm{def}}{\Longleftrightarrow} n = m$ and $\mu_i = \mu_i'$ and $A_i \approx_s B_i$ for all i.

An attacker cannot distinguish statically equivalent traces. $\mathrm{tr}(A)$ is a set of traces of A. $\mathrm{tr}_{\max}(A)$ is a set of maximal traces of A.

Definition 7. *Let A and B be closed processes.*

$$A \subseteq_t B \overset{\text{def}}{\Leftrightarrow} \forall \mathbf{tr} \in \text{tr}(A) \ \exists \mathbf{tr}' \in \text{tr}(B) \text{ s.t. } \mathbf{tr} \sim_t \mathbf{tr}',$$

$$A \approx_t B \overset{\text{def}}{\Leftrightarrow} A \subseteq_t B \text{ and } B \subseteq_t A.$$

Let A and B be two processes. Let σ be a map that maps variables in $(\text{fv}(A) \setminus \text{dom}(A)) \cup (\text{fv}(B) \setminus \text{dom}(B))$ to ground terms. When $A\sigma \approx_t B\sigma$ holds for every such σ, we also denote it as $A \approx_t B$.

$A \subseteq_t B$ means that each trace of A is imitated by some trace of B.

We later show that non-adaptive active attackers cannot distinguish trace equivalent processes.

Trace equivalence is undecidable. However, if processes contain no replications and the equational theory on Σ is a subterm convergent destructor rewriting system, trace equivalence is coNEXP complete [9].

3 Congruency of Trace Equivalence

The theorem below is our main result. It holds that trace equivalence is a congruence even though trace equivalence for the pi-calculus is not a congruence. This is ascribed to the difference between the pi-calculus and the applied pi calculus, namely, to the fact that names and variables are distinguished in the applied pi calculus. This is why adding an input prefix does not break trace equivalence. Besides, a scheme of late instantiation for an input transition is used in pi-calculus [26,27], so parallel composition may break trace equivalence. On the other hand, a scheme of early instantiation is used in the applied pi calculus. This scheme enables us to decompose a trace of a parallel composed process into traces of component processes.

Example 1. We consider pi-calculus. We put

$$P = z(z')|\overline{y}y'.\overline{w}w', \ Q = z(z').\overline{y}y'.\overline{w}w' + \overline{y}y'.z(z').\overline{w}w' + \overline{y}y'.\overline{w}w'.z(z').$$

Then, $x(z).P$ and $x(z).Q$ are trace equivalent, but $\overline{x}y|x(z).P$ and $\overline{x}y|x(z).Q$ are not trace equivalent. On the other hand, $x(z).P$ and $x(z).Q$ are not trace equivalent in the applied pi calculus because instantiation is early.

Abadi et al. [1] defined partial normal forms to prove that labeled bisimilarity is closed by application of closing evaluation contexts. They gave an operational semantics on partial normal forms. They classified transitions between ordinal processes into six cases to use partial normal forms.

To prove the next theorem, we use partial normal forms and define concurrent normal forms of traces. Transitions in a concurrent normal trace have to be particular forms.

Abadi et al. [1] studied decomposition and composition of reductions on partial normal forms. We study decomposition and composition of concurrent normal traces.

Theorem 1. $\approx_t$ *is a congruence.*

The proof is very long and complicated, so we only present an outline of our proof for the proposition below. Other cases are easy. The proof is given in [28].

Proposition 1. $A \approx_t B \Rightarrow A|C \approx_t B|C.$

Proof Outline. First, we define concurrent normal forms. A concurrent normal form is a particular form of a trace of a parallel composed process. A concurrent normal trace captures changes of scopes of bound names. Each process in a concurrent normal trace is of the form $\nu\widetilde{rs}.(\nu\widetilde{x}.(\sigma|P)\rho \mid \nu\widetilde{y}.(\rho|Q)\sigma)$, where σ and ρ are (active) substitutions. Terms sent by the left process are accumulated in σ. Bound names sent by the left process P are accumulated in $\widetilde{s}$. Symmetric cases are similar.

Second, for any trace t of $A|C$, we prove that there exists a concurrent normal trace t' of $A|C$ such that $t \sim_t t'$.

Third, given a concurrent normal trace **tr** of $A|C$, we prove that we can construct traces of A and C which each process in them is of the form $\nu\widetilde{s}.(\sigma|P)\rho$ or $\nu\widetilde{r}.(\rho|Q)\sigma$.

Finally, we take a trace **tr'** of B which is statically equivalent to the extracted trace of A as the above, combine it with **tr'**, and prove that the result is statically equivalent to the given trace **tr**. □

Example 2. Let h be a unary function symbol which cannot be inverted. $\nu m.a(x).\overline{x}\langle m\rangle \approx_t \nu m.a(x).\overline{x}\langle h(m)\rangle$ holds. Then,

$$\nu m.a(x).\overline{x}\langle m\rangle \mid \nu n.\overline{a}\langle n\rangle.n(y).\overline{b}\langle y\rangle \approx_t \nu m.a(x).\overline{x}\langle h(m)\rangle \mid \nu n.\overline{a}\langle n\rangle.n(y).\overline{b}\langle y\rangle$$

is shown as follows.

We arbitrarily take a trace **tr** of the left hand side. We consider

$$\mathbf{tr} : \nu m.a(x).\overline{x}\langle m\rangle \mid \nu n.\overline{a}\langle n\rangle.n(y).\overline{b}\langle y\rangle$$
$$\xrightarrow{\nu z.\overline{a}\langle z\rangle} \nu m.a(x).\overline{x}\langle m\rangle \mid \nu n.(n(y).\overline{b}\langle y\rangle \mid \{n/z\})$$
$$\xrightarrow{a(z)} \nu mn.(\overline{n}\langle m\rangle \mid n(y).\overline{b}\langle y\rangle \mid \{n/z\})$$
$$\longrightarrow \nu mn.(\overline{b}\langle m\rangle \mid \{n/z\})$$
$$\xrightarrow{\nu w.\overline{b}\langle w\rangle} \nu mn.\{n/z, m/w\}$$

as an example. We transform it into a concurrent normal form.

$$\mathbf{tr'} : \nu m.a(x).\overline{x}\langle m\rangle \mid \nu n.\overline{a}\langle n\rangle.n(y).\overline{b}\langle y\rangle$$
$$\xrightarrow{\nu z.\overline{a}\langle z\rangle} \nu n.((\nu m.a(x).\overline{x}\langle m\rangle)[n/z] \mid n(y).\overline{b}\langle y\rangle \mid \{n/z\})$$
$$\xrightarrow{a(z)} \nu n.((\nu m.\overline{z}\langle m\rangle)[n/z] \mid n(y).\overline{b}\langle y\rangle \mid \{n/z\})$$
$$\longrightarrow \nu nm.((\nu v.\{m/v\})[n/z] \mid (\overline{b}\langle v\rangle \mid \{n/z\})[m/v])$$
$$\xrightarrow{\nu w.\overline{b}\langle w\rangle} \nu nm.((\nu v.\{m/v\})[n/z, v/w] \mid \{n/z, v/w\}[m/v])$$

Next, we decompose it into traces of component processes.

$$\textbf{tr}_1 : \nu m.a(x).\overline{x}\langle m\rangle \qquad\qquad \textbf{tr}_2 : \nu n.\overline{a}\langle n\rangle.n(y).\overline{b}\langle y\rangle$$

$$\xrightarrow{a(n)} (\nu m.\overline{z}\langle m\rangle)[n/z] \qquad\qquad \xrightarrow{\nu z.\overline{a}\langle z\rangle} \nu n.(n(y).\overline{b}\langle y\rangle \mid \{n/z\})$$

$$\xrightarrow{\nu v.\overline{n}\langle v\rangle} (\nu m.\{m/v\})[n/z] \qquad\qquad \xrightarrow{z(m)} \nu n.(\overline{b}\langle v\rangle \mid \{n/z\})[m/v]$$

$$\xrightarrow{\nu w.\overline{b}\langle w\rangle} \nu n.\{n/z, v/w\}[m/v]$$

Since $\nu m.a(x).\overline{x}\langle m\rangle \approx_t \nu m.a(x).\overline{x}\langle h(m)\rangle$ holds, we can take a trace of $\nu m.a(x).\overline{x}\langle h(m)\rangle$ which is statically equivalent to the former.

$$\textbf{tr}_3 : \nu m.a(x).\overline{x}\langle h(m)\rangle$$

$$\xrightarrow{a(n)} (\nu m.\overline{z}\langle h(m)\rangle)[n/z]$$

$$\xrightarrow{\nu v.\overline{n}\langle v\rangle} (\nu m.\{h(m)/v\})[n/z]$$

Finally, we compose $\textbf{tr}_2$ and $\textbf{tr}_3$ and obtain a desired trace $\textbf{tr}_4$.

$$\textbf{tr}_4 : \nu m.a(x).\overline{x}\langle h(m)\rangle \mid \nu n.\overline{a}\langle n\rangle.n(y).\overline{b}\langle y\rangle$$

$$\xrightarrow{\nu z.\overline{a}\langle z\rangle} \nu n.((\nu m.a(x).\overline{x}\langle h(m)\rangle)[n/z] \mid n(y).\overline{b}\langle y\rangle \mid \{n/z\})$$

$$\xrightarrow{a(z)} \nu n.((\nu m.\overline{z}\langle h(m)\rangle)[n/z] \mid n(y).\overline{b}\langle y\rangle \mid \{n/z\})$$

$$\longrightarrow \nu nm.((\nu v.\{h(m)/v\})[n/z] \mid (\overline{b}\langle v\rangle \mid \{n/z\})[h(m)/v])$$

$$\xrightarrow{\nu w.\overline{b}\langle w\rangle} \nu nm.((\nu v.\{h(m)/v\})[n/z, v/w] \mid \{n/z, v/w\}[h(m)/v])$$

Cheval et al. [10] established congruence property of trace equivalence for image-finite processes. They proved that trace equivalence is equivalent to may-testing equivalence for image-finite processes. On the other hand, taking all processes into account, may-testing equivalence does not imply trace equivalence. They gave a concrete counterexample. Thus, we cannot use the same technique.

4   An Epistemic Logic for the Applied Pi Calculus

4.1   Syntax

We propose an epistemic logic for the applied pi calculus. It was inspired by [7], but our logic is a bit different. We give syntax of formulas.

$$\delta ::= \top \mid M_1 = M_2 \mid M \in \text{dom} \mid \delta_1 \vee \delta_2 \mid \neg\delta$$

$$\varphi ::= \delta \mid \varphi_1 \vee \varphi_2 \mid \neg\varphi \mid \langle\mu\rangle_{-}\varphi \mid F\varphi \mid K\varphi$$

where M_1, M_2 and M are terms, and μ is an action. We call δ a static formula and φ a modal formula. A static formula δ mentions equality of terms. A modal formula φ mentions traces.

$\langle\mu\rangle_{-}\varphi$ states that the previous action is μ, and φ holds just before observing μ. $F\varphi$ states that φ holds some time or other. The operator K expresses an attacker's knowledge, i.e., $K\varphi$ means an attacker knows that φ holds.

4.2   Semantics

Our logic is an LTL-like logic with an epistemic operator. Let A be a name-variable-distinct process that $\mathrm{fv}(A) \setminus \mathrm{dom}(A) = \widetilde{x}$, ρ be an assignment which maps $\widetilde{x}$ to ground terms, $\mathbf{tr} \in \mathrm{tr}(A\rho)$, $0 \leq i \leq |\mathbf{tr}|$, and M_1 and M_2 be terms. Please remember that $\mathrm{fr}(A)$ is a frame of A.

We suppose that δ and φ contain no variables other than $\widetilde{x} \cup \mathrm{dom}(\mathbf{tr}[i])$. We omit semantics of logical operators. They are defined as expected.

$A, \rho, \mathbf{tr}, i \models M_1 = M_2$ iff $(M_1\rho = M_2\rho)\mathrm{fr}(\mathbf{tr}[i])$

$A, \rho, \mathbf{tr}, i \models M \in \mathrm{dom}$ iff M is a variable x, and $x \in \mathrm{dom}(\mathbf{tr}[i])$

$\qquad A, \rho, \mathbf{tr}, i \models \langle\mu\rangle_{-}\varphi$ iff $\mathbf{tr}[i-1] \overset{\mu}{\Longrightarrow} \mathbf{tr}[i]$ in $\mathbf{tr}$ and $A, \rho, \mathbf{tr}, i-1 \models \varphi$

$\qquad A, \rho, \mathbf{tr}, i \models F\varphi$ iff $\exists j \geq i$ s.t. $A, \rho, \mathbf{tr}, j \models \varphi$

$\qquad A, \rho, \mathbf{tr}, i \models K\varphi$ iff $\forall \rho' \forall \mathbf{tr}' \in \mathrm{tr}(A\rho'); \mathbf{tr}[0, i] \sim_t \mathbf{tr}'[0, i] \Rightarrow A, \rho', \mathbf{tr}', i \models \varphi$

We suppose that an attacker does not know what terms are assigned to free variables before the process runs. Hence, the definition of K contains a quantifier over assignments $\forall\rho'$. Recall that an attacker can observe only labeled transitions, so accessibility is defined based on static equivalence on traces.

We also define satisfiability of formulas containing free variables. We put $\widetilde{y} = \mathrm{dom}(\mathbf{tr}[i])$. We suppose that φ contains no variables other than $\widetilde{x}, \widetilde{y}$, and $\widetilde{z}$.

$$A, \rho, \mathbf{tr}, i \models \varphi(\widetilde{x}, \widetilde{y}, \widetilde{z}) \text{ iff } \forall \widetilde{M}; A, \rho, \mathbf{tr}, i \models \varphi(\widetilde{x}, \widetilde{y}, \widetilde{M}),$$

where $\widetilde{M}$ is a sequence of ground terms.

From now, we suppose that all processes are name-variable-distinct. We often omit restriction of a domain of definition. $D(\rho)$ is a domain of definition of ρ.

When a formula φ is satisfied over all possible runs of a process A, we say that A satisfies φ.

Definition 8. $A \models \varphi \overset{\text{def}}{\Leftrightarrow} \forall \rho \ \forall \mathbf{tr} \in \mathrm{tr}(A\rho); A, \rho, \mathbf{tr}, 0 \models \varphi$, where $D(\rho) = \mathrm{fv}(A) \setminus \mathrm{dom}(A)$.

Definition 9. $A \sqsubseteq_L B \overset{\text{def}}{\Leftrightarrow} \forall \rho \ \forall \mathbf{tr} \in \mathrm{tr}(A\rho) \ \exists \mathbf{tr}' \in \mathrm{tr}(B\rho)$
s.t. $\forall i \ \forall \varphi; [A, \rho, \mathbf{tr}, i \models \varphi \Leftrightarrow B, \rho, \mathbf{tr}', i \models \varphi]$,
where $D(\rho) = (\mathrm{fv}(A) \setminus \mathrm{dom}(A)) \cup (\mathrm{fv}(B) \setminus \mathrm{dom}(B))$.
$A \equiv_L B \overset{\text{def}}{\Leftrightarrow} A \sqsubseteq_L B \text{ and } B \sqsubseteq_L A$.

4.3   Correspondence with Trace Equivalence

We prove that trace equivalent processes satisfy the same formulas.

Theorem 2. *1.* $A \approx_t B \Rightarrow A \sqsubseteq_L B$; *2.* $A \sqsubseteq_L B \Rightarrow A \sqsubseteq_t B$

Proof. Let $\widetilde{x} = (\mathrm{fv}(A) \setminus \mathrm{dom}(A)) \cup (\mathrm{fv}(B) \setminus \mathrm{dom}(B))$.

1) We prove

$$\forall \rho \; \forall \mathbf{tr} \in \mathrm{tr}(A\rho), \mathbf{tr'} \in \mathrm{tr}(B\rho);$$
$$\mathbf{tr} \sim_t \mathbf{tr'} \Rightarrow \forall i \; \forall \varphi; [A, \rho, \mathbf{tr}, i \models \varphi \Leftrightarrow B, \rho, \mathbf{tr'}, i \models \varphi]$$

where $D(\rho) = \widetilde{x}$, by induction on the syntax of formulas.

2) We arbitrarily take an assignment ρ and $\mathbf{tr} \in \mathrm{tr}(A\rho)$.

By $A \sqsubseteq_L B, \exists \mathbf{tr'} \in \mathrm{tr}(B\rho)$ s.t. $\forall i \; \forall \varphi; [A, \rho, \mathbf{tr}, i \models \varphi \Leftrightarrow B, \rho, \mathbf{tr'}, i \models \varphi]$.

Then, we can prove $\mathbf{tr} \sim_t \mathbf{tr'}$.

By arbitrariness of $\mathbf{tr}$, it immediately follows that $A \sqsubseteq_L B \Rightarrow A \sqsubseteq_t B$.   □

Theorem 3. $A \approx_t B \Leftrightarrow A \equiv_L B.$

This theorem suggests that trace equivalence is suitable to define security properties. We give Proposition 2 as an example in the next subsection.

4.4   Applications

In this subsection, we often use abbreviations. Notably, P expresses $\neg K \neg$, and G expresses $\neg F \neg$. $P\varphi$ means that an attacker does not know φ does not hold. In other words, the attacker thinks that the possibility that φ holds remains.

We define minimal secrecy. We regard it as generalized minimal anonymity [25].

Definition 10. *A variable x is minimally secret with respect to δ in A iff $A \models G(\delta(x) \to P(\neg\delta(x)))$.*

This definition means that attackers cannot know that $\delta(x)$ holds.

This property is very weak. For instance, although x is minimally secret with respect to a nontrivial formula δ, x is not always minimally secret with respect to $\neg\delta$. Hereafter, we often omit objects.

Example 3. We put $\delta(z) : z \neq a \land z \neq b$.

We consider a process if $x = a$ then $\overline{c}$ else $\overline{d}$. Then x is minimally secret with respect to δ, but not secret with respect to $\neg\delta$.

Moreover, $\lor$ does not preserve minimally secret. However, $\land$ preserves it.

Although x is minimally secret in A, x is not always secret in $A|A$. Besides, restriction does not always preserve minimal secrecy.

Example 4. We put $\delta(z) : z = a$. We put

$$P = \text{if } x = a \text{ then } (\overline{a}\langle s \rangle + \overline{b}\langle s \rangle) \text{ else } \overline{a}\langle s \rangle, Q = \text{if } x = b \text{ then } \overline{b}\langle s \rangle \text{ else } \overline{c}\langle s \rangle.$$

Then x is minimally secret with respect to δ in $P + Q$, but not secret in $(P + Q)|(P + Q)$.

Example 5. We put $\delta(z) : z = a$. Then, x is minimally secret with respect to δ in $\overline{x} + \overline{a}$, but not secret in $\nu a.(\overline{x} + \overline{a})$. Here, we omitted objects.

We define total secrecy. We can also regard it as generalized total anonymity [25]. Total secrecy states attackers can obtain no information about x.

Definition 11. x *is totally secret in* $A(x, \widetilde{y})$ *iff*

$$\forall \delta(z, \widetilde{z}, \widetilde{w}); A(x, \widetilde{y}) \models G(\delta(x, \widetilde{y}, \widetilde{w}) \rightarrow P(\neg \delta(x, \widetilde{y}, \widetilde{w})))$$

where δ *contains no variables other than ones in* $\{z\} \cup \widetilde{z} \cup \widetilde{w}$ *and satisfies that* $\forall \widetilde{N} \forall \psi \exists M : \text{ground}$ *s.t.* $\psi \models \neg \delta(M, \widetilde{N}, \widetilde{w})$. *Besides,* $|\widetilde{y}| = |\widetilde{z}|$ *and* $\widetilde{w} \cap (\{x\} \cup \widetilde{y}) = \emptyset$.

Proposition 2. x *is totally secret in* $A(x, \widetilde{y})$ *iff* $A(x, \widetilde{y}) \approx_t A(x', \widetilde{y})$.

Proof. $\Rightarrow$) We suppose for the sake of contradiction that $A(x, \widetilde{y}) \not\approx_t A(x', \widetilde{y})$.

There exist M_1, M_2 and $\widetilde{N}$ that are ground such that $A(M_1, \widetilde{N}) \not\approx_t A(M_2, \widetilde{N})$.

We suppose that $A(M_1, \widetilde{N}) \not\sqsubseteq_t A(M_2, \widetilde{N})$. Then, there exists $\mathbf{tr} \in \text{tr}(A(M_1, \widetilde{N}))$ such that any trace of $A(M_2, \widetilde{N})$ is not statically equivalent to $\mathbf{tr}$.

We put $\delta(z, \widetilde{z}) : z \neq M_2 \vee \widetilde{z} \neq \widetilde{N}$. Then

$$A(x, \widetilde{y}), (x \mapsto M_1, \widetilde{y} \mapsto \widetilde{N}), \mathbf{tr}, |\mathbf{tr}| \models K\delta(x, \widetilde{y}).$$

This contradicts total secrecy.

$\Leftarrow$) We arbitrarily take $\delta, \rho, \mathbf{tr}$ and i, where δ meets the demand of Definition 11 and $D(\rho) = \{x\} \cup \widetilde{y}$.

We suppose that $A(x, \widetilde{y}), \rho, \mathbf{tr}, i \models \delta(x, \widetilde{y}, \widetilde{w})$.

We take M such that $\text{fr}(\mathbf{tr}[i]) \models \neg \delta(M, \rho(\widetilde{y}), \widetilde{w})$. Let ρ' be

$$\rho'(y) = \begin{cases} M & (y = x) \\ \rho(y) & (\textit{otherwise}). \end{cases}$$

By assumption, $A(\rho(x), \rho(\widetilde{y})) \approx_t A(M, \rho(\widetilde{y}))$.

Hence, there exists $\mathbf{tr}' \in \text{tr}(A(M, \rho(\widetilde{y})))$ such that $\mathbf{tr} \sim_t \mathbf{tr}'$.

Then, $A(x, \widetilde{y}), \rho', \mathbf{tr}', i \models \neg \delta(M, \rho(\widetilde{y}), \widetilde{w})$.

Therefore, $A(x, \widetilde{y}), \rho, \mathbf{tr}, i \models P(\neg \delta(x, \rho(\widetilde{y}), \widetilde{w}))$.

Then, $A(x, \widetilde{y}) \models G(\delta(x, \widetilde{y}, \widetilde{w}) \rightarrow P(\neg \delta(x, \rho(\widetilde{y}), \widetilde{w})))$. $\qquad \square$

Theorem 4. *If* x *is totally secret in* $A(x, \widetilde{y})$, *then* x *is also totally secret in* $E[A(x, \widetilde{y})]$ *for every context* $E[\_]$ *which does not contain* x.

Our framework can handle role interchangeability [25]. When x_i satisfies a property δ_k and x_l satisfies a property δ_j, an attacker thinks that it is possible that x_l satisfies a property δ_k and x_i satisfies a property δ_j.

Definition 12. *We put* $\text{fv}(A) \setminus \text{dom}(A) = \{x_1, ..., x_p\}$, $J = \{1, ..., q\}$, *and* $I = \{1, ..., p\}$. (x_i, δ_k) *is role interchangeable regarding* $\{\delta_j(z_j, \widetilde{y}_j)\}_{j \in J}$ *in* A *iff*

$$A(x_1, ..., x_p) \models G(\delta_k(x_i, \widetilde{y}_k) \rightarrow \bigwedge_{l \in I} \bigwedge_{j \in J} (\delta_j(x_l, \widetilde{y}_j) \rightarrow P(\delta_k(x_l, \widetilde{y}_k) \wedge \delta_j(x_i, \widetilde{y}_j))))$$

where $\widetilde{y}_j \cap \{x_1, ..., x_p\} = \emptyset$ *for all* $j \in J$.

Proposition 3

$\forall \widetilde{M} \ \forall i \ \forall \mathbf{tr} \in \mathrm{tr}(A(M_1, ..., M_p))$

$\exists \widetilde{N} \ \exists \mathbf{tr'} \in \mathrm{tr}(A(M_i, N_2, ..., N_{i-1}, M_1, N_{i+1}, ..., N_p))$ s.t. $\mathbf{tr} \sim_t \mathbf{tr'}$

$\Leftrightarrow (x_1, \delta_k)$ *is role interchangeable with respect to* $\{\delta_j\}$ *in* A *for all* $\{\delta_j\}$ *and* k.

Corollary 1. $\forall l \in I \setminus \{i\}; A(x_1, ..., x_i, ..., x_l, ..., x_p) \approx_t A(x_1, ..., x_l, ..., x_i, ..., x_p)$
$\Rightarrow (x_i, \delta_k)$ *is role interchangeable with respect to* $\{\delta_j\}$ *in* A *for all* $\{\delta_j\}$ *and* k.

The converse holds only when $p = 2$. We give a counterexample for $p = 3$.

Example 6. We put $A(x, y, z) = $ if $x = y$ then $\overline{x} + \overline{z}$ else if $x = z$ then $\overline{x} + \overline{y}$ else $\overline{y} + \overline{z}$.

Then, (x, δ_k) is role interchangeable regarding $\{\delta_j\}$ in A for all $\{\delta_j\}_{j \in J}$ and k, but $A(a, b, a) \not\approx_t A(b, a, a)$. Thus, $A(x, y, z) \not\approx_t A(y, x, z)$.

We can also consider role permutativity. Mano [24] showed that it is strictly stronger than role interchangeability. Role permutativity states that even if p values are swapped, an attacker cannot notice it.

Definition 13. *We put* $\mathrm{fv}(A) \setminus \mathrm{dom}(A) = \{x_1, ..., x_p\}$, $J = \{1, ..., q\}$, *and* $I = \{1, ..., p\}$. $\{\delta_j\}_{j \in J}$ *is role permutable in* A *iff*

$$\forall n \leq p \ \forall \psi \in \mathfrak{S}_p; A(x_1, ..., x_p) \models G(\bigwedge_{k \leq n} \delta_{i_k}(x_{i_k}, \widetilde{y}_k) \to P(\bigwedge_{k \leq n} \delta_{i_k}(x_{i_{\psi(k)}}, \widetilde{y}_k)))$$

where $\widetilde{y}_j \cap \{x_1, ..., x_p\} = \emptyset$ *for all* j *and each* i_k *differs.*

Proposition 4. $\forall \psi \in \mathfrak{S}_p; A(x_1, ..., x_p) \approx_t A(x_{\psi(1)}, ..., x_{\psi(p)})$
$\Leftrightarrow \{\delta_j\}_{j \in J}$ *is role permutable in* A *for all* $\{\delta_j\}_{j \in J}$.

We define openness. We regard it as generalized identity [32]. Parallel composition does not preserve openness.

Definition 14. x *is open in* A *under* $\Delta(x)$ *iff*

$$\forall \rho \ \forall \mathbf{tr} \in \mathrm{tr_{max}}(A\rho); A, \rho, \mathbf{tr}, |\mathbf{tr}| \models \Delta(x) \to K(\Delta(x) \to (x = x\rho)).$$

Example 7. We put $\Delta(z) : z = r \lor z = s$. We put

$$P = \text{if } x = r \text{ then } \overline{a}\langle n \rangle \text{ else } \overline{b}\langle n \rangle, \ Q = \text{if } x = r \text{ then } \overline{b}\langle n \rangle \text{ else } \overline{a}\langle n \rangle.$$

Then x is open in P and Q under $\Delta(x)$, but x is not open in $P|Q$ under $\Delta(x)$.

Problem 1

Input: An extended process A, an assignment ρ, a trace $\mathbf{tr} \in \mathrm{tr}(A)$, an integer $0 \leq i \leq |\mathbf{tr}|$, and a formula φ.

Question: Does $A, \rho, \mathbf{tr}, i \models \varphi$ hold?

Proposition 5. *Even if the word problem in* Σ *is decidable, Problem 1 can be undecidable.*

Abadi and Cortier [2] proved that static equivalence can be undecidable even if the word problem in Σ is decidable. Proposition 5 follows from it.

We change semantics. We repeat the definition of satisfaction.

$$A \models \varphi \text{ iff } \forall \rho \; \forall \mathbf{tr} \in \text{tr}(A\rho); A, \rho, \mathbf{tr}, 0 \models \varphi$$

Now, we restrict ρ to be an assignment which maps free variables to only names and restrict inputted messages in $\mathbf{tr}$ to be only variables. That is, we assume that an attacker cannot tamper with a message. In other words, the attacker can only transfer messages without any change. Notably, the attacker cannot make a tuple of messages.

Problem 2

Input: An extended process A and a formula φ.
Question: Does $A \models \varphi$ hold?

A convergent subterm theory is an equational theory defined by finite equations whose each right-hand side is a proper subterm of the left-hand side.

Proposition 6. *If the equational theory on Σ is a convergent subterm theory and A contains no replications, Problem 2 is decidable.*

4.5   Comparison with the Work of Chadha et al.

Chadha et al. developed the definition of privacy in e-voting as follows. They considered protocol instances in which two voters Alice and Bob participate, and voting options are **0** and **1**.

Definition 15 ([7, Definition 9]). *The voting process $\mathcal{V}$ respects privacy if $\mathcal{V} \models \mathbf{Aprivacy} \wedge \mathbf{Bprivacy}$ where*

- **Aprivacy** $\overset{\text{def}}{=} \wedge_{v \in \{0,1\}} \Box(\mathbf{K}(\mathbf{Avote}(v)) \rightarrow \mathbf{Bvote}(v))$, *and*
- **Bprivacy** $\overset{\text{def}}{=} \wedge_{v \in \{0,1\}} \Box(\mathbf{K}(\mathbf{Bvote}(v)) \rightarrow \mathbf{Avote}(v))$.

Avote(v) means that Alice voted v, and **Bvote**(v) is similar.

Minimal secrecy of a vote never holds because an attacker trivially knows votes when all votes agree. We consider protocol instances in which m voters participate and n voting options exist. Let v_i be a vote of i. We consider the property below:

$$\vee_{j,k} v_j \neq v_k \rightarrow \wedge_i \wedge_v G(K(v_i = v) \rightarrow v_1 = v \wedge ... \wedge v_{i-1} = v \wedge v_{i+1} = v \wedge ... \wedge v_m = v)$$

The consequence in $G(...)$ implies that $v_i \neq v$ due to the antecedent condition, so we can rewrite the property.

$$\vee_{j,k} v_j \neq v_k \rightarrow \wedge_i \wedge_v G(K(v_i = v) \rightarrow v_i \neq v)$$

Moreover, we take the contraposition in G.

$$\vee_{j,k} v_j \neq v_k \rightarrow \wedge_i \wedge_v G(v_i = v \rightarrow P(v_i \neq v))$$

This consequence is exactly minimal secrecy. Besides, minimal secrecy of voting implies privacy, so privacy and minimal secrecy of voting agree under the disagreement condition $\vee_{j,k} v_j \neq v_k$.

It was shown that $V(\mathbf{0}, \mathbf{1}) \approx_t V(\mathbf{1}, \mathbf{0})$ implies that $\mathcal{V}$ respects privacy, and the partial converse was given in [7]. We give several properties of minimal secrecy.

Proposition 7. *We assume that a voting process $\mathcal{V}$ is equivalent for aborts, and minimal secrecy of each vote in $V(v_1, ..., v_m)$ holds under the disagreement condition $\vee_{j,k} v_j \neq v_k$.*

1. $m = 2 \Rightarrow V(v_1, v_2) \approx_t V(v_2, v_1)$.
2. $m = 3$ and $n = 2 \Rightarrow V(v_1, v_2, v_3) \approx_t V(v_2, v_1, v_3)$.
3. *Otherwise,* $V(v_1, ..., v_i, ..., v_j, ..., v_m) \approx_t V(v_1, ..., v_j, ..., v_i, ..., v_m)$ *does not always hold.*

5   Related Work

Logics about behavior of labeled transition systems originate from Hennessy-Milner logic [20] that is a modal logic characterizing observational congruence. That is, observational equivalent systems satisfy the same modal formulas when these systems are image-finite.

Process algebra is a special LTS. The spi calculus [3] is an extension of the pi-calculus. It enables us to handle symmetric key encryption based on the Dolev-Yao model [14]. In the spi calculus, two ciphertexts obtained by encrypting two different plaintexts are indistinguishable unless an observer gets a secret key. Abadi and Gordon formalized security properties to use testing equivalence.

We focused on the applied pi calculus [1] because it is more powerful than the spi calculus. That is, we intend to handle more various security notions. In the calculus, a process can send not only names but also terms via alias variables. Due to this feature, we can handle not only secrecy but also stricter properties. The authors proved that observational equivalence and labeled bisimilarity correspond.

Chadha et al. [7] already developed an epistemic logic for the applied pi calculus. They defined formulas **Has** and $\widehat{\mathbf{evt}}$. **Has** directly represents attackers' knowledge, and $\widehat{\mathbf{evt}}$ means that a particular event had occurred. Temporal modalities were also used, but they do neither mention the just previous nor next action. The epistemic operator **K** was defined based on static equivalence on traces. Authors suggested that trace equivalence is more suitable than labeled bisimilarity when we consider privacy. However, a correspondent relation between logic and behavior of processes was not provided. As a matter of fact, α-equivalent processes do not always satisfy the same formulas in their framework because secret values are expressed as bound names or through events. In our framework, trace equivalent processes satisfy the same formulas.

Horne [21] introduced quasi-open bisimilarity, and he proved that it coincides open bisimilarity. Moreover, intuitionistic modal logic $\mathcal{FM}$ characterizes quasi-open bisimilarity. The law of excluded middle does not hold in the logic because processes containing a free variable are also considered.

Knight et al. [22] defined an epistemic logic for an LTS. This framework is based on Hennessy-Milner logic, and it handles multiple agents' knowledge. They also proved weak completeness. However, compositionality was not discussed.

Process algebra is one of nominal transition systems. Parrow et al. [29] developed modal logic characterizing bisimilarity for a nominal transition system.

Toninho and Caires [31] proposed a dynamic spatial epistemic logic, which reasons what information a process can obtain. The epistemic operator means not only an attacker's knowledge but also a participant's knowledge, so, for example, the logic can reason a correspondence assertion.

Tsukada et al. [32] studied sequential and parallel compositionality of security notions to use an epistemic logic for a multiagent system. They proved that neither anonymity nor privacy is generally preserved by composition. They also gave a sufficient condition for preservation. However, this word "parallel" merely means that the same agent acts two actions in the paper. That is, concurrency was not considered.

Fiore and Abadi [16] developed symbolic models of processes. They gave a procedure to decide whether an environment can derive a message M. Their technique can be used for verification. However, equivalences on processes were not studied in the paper.

Clarkson and Schneider [12] generalized trace properties to hyperproperties, and Clarkson et al. [11] developed hyperLTL and hyperCTL* for hyperproperties. Hyperproperties can express security properties which cannot be expressed by trace properties. The authors regarded systems as sets of traces, so hyperproperties are properties about systems. Our security properties are also proper hyperproperties. The advantage of our work over these works is to relate trace equivalence to attackers' knowledge. In [11,12], the relation between the equivalence and knowledge is not clear.

Goubault-Larrecq et al. [19] proposed the probabilistic applied pi calculus. In this case, Theorem 1 no longer holds. It is known that trace distribution preorder [30] is not a congruence. On the other hand, it is shown in [5] that probabilistic trace equivalence for nondeterministic and probabilistic LTS is a congruence with respect to parallel composition. Probabilistic trace equivalence is coarser than trace distribution equivalence.

Canetti et al. [6] defined implementation for task-PIOAs. According to their definition, T_1 implements T_2 iff the set of behaviors of T_1 composed with $\mathcal{E}$ is included in the set of behaviors of T_2 composed with $\mathcal{E}$ for every environment $\mathcal{E}$. Here, behavior is the set of trace distributions. The implementation relation is preserved by parallel composition.

Giro and D'Argenio [17] pointed out that ordinary schedulers may give rise to unnatural behavior. A scheduler may leak information if it can look at the whole of the system. To solve this problem, they provided several reasonable subclasses of schedulers. The problem of the scheduler in the formalization of security properties was also pointed out in [4,8], which proposed other approaches.

Eisentraut et al. [15] also studied subclasses of schedulers for probabilistic automata. They defined late distribution bisimulation and proved that late distribution bisimulation with respect to distributed schedulers is compositional. We may need to specify subclasses of schedulers to state a probabilistic variant of Theorem 1.

Knight et al. [23] developed spatial and epistemic process calculus. Their study is for concurrent constraint programming, so their processes can add constraints. They proved that observational equivalence is a congruence. Their processes do not have labeled actions, so observational equivalence means that equivalent processes provide the same results. On the other hand, in the applied pi calculus, trace equivalent processes provide equivalent traces and indistinguishable information.

In this paper, we characterized trace equivalence in terms of our epistemic logic. That is, we showed that a non-adaptive active intruder cannot distinguish trace equivalent processes. We also focused on how composition of systems affects security properties. We proved that any composition preserves total secrecy and role permutativity. This is because trace equivalence is a congruence.

6   Conclusion

6.1   Summary

In this paper, we provided an epistemic logic for the applied pi calculus. This logic is an LTL-like logic, so we can describe security notions. We formulated secrecy, role-interchangeability, and openness. These are generalized security properties regarding multiagent systems.

Moreover, we associated trace equivalence with total secrecy. Application of context does not preserve minimal secrecy, but total secrecy is preserved because trace equivalence is a congruence. We also give a necessary and sufficient condition for role-interchangeability.

We conclude that trace equivalence is suitable to express non-probabilistic indistinguishability in the view of security in the presence of a non-adaptive active adversary.

6.2   Future Work

First, our epistemic logic states an adversary's knowledge. We intend to construct a logic for a process's knowledge. It will bridge a gap between multiagent systems and process calculi.

Second, formalizations of other security properties such as non-malleability are also the next topics.

Finally, what logic is suitable for security in the presence of an adaptive attacker is still open.

Acknowledgments. The author thanks Prof. M. Hasegawa and Prof. N. Yoshida for discussions. He also thanks the anonymous reviewers for helpful comments and suggestions.

References

1. Abadi, M., Blanchet, B., Fournet, C.: The applied pi calculus: mobile values, new names, and secure communication. J. ACM **65**(1), 1–41 (2017). https://doi.org/10.1145/3127586
2. Abadi, M., Cortier, V.: Deciding knowledge in security protocols under equational theories. Theor. Comput. Sci. **367**(1–2), 2–32 (2006). https://doi.org/10.1016/j.tcs.2006.08.032
3. Abadi, M., Gordon, A.D.: A calculus for cryptographic protocols: the spi calculus. Inf. Comput. **148**(1), 1–70 (1999). https://doi.org/10.1006/inco.1998.2740
4. Alvim, M.S., Andrés, M.E., Palamidessi, C., van Rossum, P.: Safe equivalences for security properties. In: Calude, C.S., Sassone, V. (eds.) TCS 2010. IAICT, vol. 323, pp. 55–70. Springer, Heidelberg (2010). https://doi.org/10.1007/978-3-642-15240-5_5
5. Bernardo, M., De Nicola, R., Loreti, M.: Revisiting trace and testing equivalences for nondeterministic and probabilistic processes. Log. Methods Comput. Sci. **10**(1) (2014). https://doi.org/10.2168/LMCS-10(1:16)2014
6. Canetti, R., Cheung, L., Kaynar, D., Liskov, M., Lynch, N., Pereira, O., Segala, R.: Task-structured probabilistic i/o automata. J. Comput. Syst. Sci. **94**, 63–97 (2018). https://doi.org/10.1016/j.jcss.2017.09.007
7. Chadha, R., Delaune, S., Kremer, S.: Epistemic logic for the applied pi calculus. In: Lee, D., Lopes, A., Poetzsch-Heffter, A. (eds.) FMOODS/FORTE -2009. LNCS, vol. 5522, pp. 182–197. Springer, Heidelberg (2009). https://doi.org/10.1007/978-3-642-02138-1_12
8. Chatzikokolakis, K., Palamidessi, C.: Making random choices invisible to the scheduler. In: Caires, L., Vasconcelos, V.T. (eds.) CONCUR 2007. LNCS, vol. 4703, pp. 42–58. Springer, Heidelberg (2007). https://doi.org/10.1007/978-3-540-74407-8_4
9. Cheval, V., Kremer, S., Rakotonirina, I.: DEEPSEC: deciding equivalence properties in security protocols theory and practice. In: SP 2018, pp. 529–546 (2018). https://doi.org/10.1109/SP.2018.00033
10. Cheval, V., Cortier, V., Delaune, S.: Deciding equivalence-based properties using constraint solving. Theor. Comput. Sci. **492**, 1–39 (2013). https://doi.org/10.1016/j.tcs.2013.04.016
11. Clarkson, M.R., Finkbeiner, B., Koleini, M., Micinski, K.K., Rabe, M.N., Sánchez, C.: Temporal logics for hyperproperties. In: Abadi, M., Kremer, S. (eds.) POST 2014. LNCS, vol. 8414, pp. 265–284. Springer, Heidelberg (2014). https://doi.org/10.1007/978-3-642-54792-8_15
12. Clarkson, M.R., Schneider, F.B.: Hyperproperties. J. Comput. Secur. **18**(6), 1157–1210 (2010). https://doi.org/10.3233/JCS-2009-0393
13. Delaune, S., Kremer, S., Ryan, M.: Verifying privacy-type properties of electronic voting protocols. J. Comput. Secur. **17**(4), 435–487 (2009). https://doi.org/10.3233/JCS-2009-0340
14. Dolev, D., Yao, A.C.: On the security of public key protocols. IEEE Trans. Inf. Theory **29**(2), 198–208 (1983). https://doi.org/10.1109/TIT.1983.1056650
15. Eisentraut, C., Godskesen, J.C., Hermanns, H., Song, L., Zhang, L.: Probabilistic bisimulation for realistic schedulers. In: Bjørner, N., de Boer, F. (eds.) FM 2015. LNCS, vol. 9109, pp. 248–264. Springer, Cham (2015). https://doi.org/10.1007/978-3-319-19249-9_16
16. Fiore, M., Abadi, M.: Computing symbolic models for verifying cryptographic protocols. In: CSFW-14, pp. 160–173 (2001). https://doi.org/10.1109/CSFW.2001.930144

17. Giro, S., D'Argenio, P.: On the expressive power of schedulers in distributed probabilistic systems. Electron. Notes Theor. Comput. Sci. **253**(3), 45–71 (2009). https://doi.org/10.1016/j.entcs.2009.10.005
18. Glabbeek, R.J.: The linear time - branching time spectrum. In: Baeten, J.C.M., Klop, J.W. (eds.) CONCUR 1990. LNCS, vol. 458, pp. 278–297. Springer, Heidelberg (1990). https://doi.org/10.1007/BFb0039066
19. Goubault-Larrecq, J., Palamidessi, C., Troina, A.: A probabilistic applied pi-calculus. In: Shao, Z. (ed.) APLAS 2007. LNCS, vol. 4807, pp. 175–190. Springer, Heidelberg (2007). https://doi.org/10.1007/978-3-540-76637-7_12
20. Hennessy, M., Milner, R.: On observing nondeterminism and concurrency. In: de Bakker, J., van Leeuwen, J. (eds.) ICALP 1980. LNCS, vol. 85, pp. 299–309. Springer, Heidelberg (1980). https://doi.org/10.1007/3-540-10003-2_79
21. Horne, R.: A bisimilarity congruence for the applied pi-calculus sufficiently coarse to verify privacy properties. arXiv:1811.02536 (2018)
22. Knight, S., Mardare, R., Panangaden, P.: Combining epistemic logic and hennessy-milner logic. In: Constable, R.L., Silva, A. (eds.) Logic and Program Semantics. LNCS, vol. 7230, pp. 219–243. Springer, Heidelberg (2012). https://doi.org/10.1007/978-3-642-29485-3_14
23. Knight, S., Palamidessi, C., Panangaden, P., Valencia, F.D.: Spatial and epistemic modalities in constraint-based process calculi. In: Koutny, M., Ulidowski, I. (eds.) CONCUR 2012. LNCS, vol. 7454, pp. 317–332. Springer, Heidelberg (2012). https://doi.org/10.1007/978-3-642-32940-1_23
24. Mano, K.: Formal specification and verification of anonymity and privacy. Ph.D. thesis, Nagoya University (2013)
25. Mano, K., Kawabe, Y., Sakurada, H., Tsukada, Y.: Role interchange for anonymity and privacy of voting. J. Logic Comput. **20**(6), 1251–1288 (2010). https://doi.org/10.1093/logcom/exq013
26. Milner, R., Parrow, J., Walker, D.: A calculus of mobile processes, I. Inf. Comput. **100**(1), 1–40 (1992). https://doi.org/10.1016/0890-5401(92)90008-4
27. Milner, R., Parrow, J., Walker, D.: A calculus of mobile processes, II. Inf. Comput. **100**(1), 41–77 (1992). https://doi.org/10.1016/0890-5401(92)90009-5
28. Minami, K.: Trace equivalence and epistemic logic to express security properties. arXiv:1903.03719 (2019)
29. Parrow, J., Borgström, J., Eriksson, L.H., Gutkovas, R., Weber, T.: Modal logics for nominal transition systems. In: CONCUR 2015. LIPIcs, vol. 42, pp. 198–211. Schloss Dagstuhl-Leibniz-Zentrum fuer Informatik (2015). https://doi.org/10.4230/LIPIcs.CONCUR.2015.198
30. Segala, R.: A compositional trace-based semantics for probabilistic automata. In: Lee, I., Smolka, S.A. (eds.) CONCUR 1995. LNCS, vol. 962, pp. 234–248. Springer, Heidelberg (1995). https://doi.org/10.1007/3-540-60218-6_17
31. Toninho, B., Caires, L.: A spatial-epistemic logic for reasoning about security protocols. In: SecCo 2010. EPTCS, vol. 51, pp. 1–15. Open Publishing Association (2011). https://doi.org/10.4204/EPTCS.51.1
32. Tsukada, Y., Sakurada, H., Mano, K., Manabe, Y.: On compositional reasoning about anonymity and privacy in epistemic logic. Ann. Math. Artif. Intell. **78**(2), 101–129 (2016). https://doi.org/10.1007/s10472-016-9516-8

Derivation of Heard-of Predicates from Elementary Behavioral Patterns

Adam Shimi, Aurélie Hurault, and Philippe Queinnec[(✉)]

IRIT – Université de Toulouse, 2 rue Camichel, 31000 Toulouse, France
{adam.shimi,aurelie.hurault,philippe.queinnec}@irit.fr

Abstract. There are many models of distributed computing, and no unifying mathematical framework for considering them all. One way to sidestep this issue is to start with simple communication and fault models, and use them as building blocks to derive the complex models studied in the field. We thus define operations like union, succession or repetition, which makes it easier to build complex models from simple ones while retaining expressivity.

To formalize this approach, we abstract away the complex models and operations in the Heard-Of model. This model relies on (possibly asynchronous) rounds; sequence of digraphs, one for each round, capture which messages sent at a given round are received before the receiver goes to the next round. A set of sequences, called a heard-of predicate, defines the legal communication behaviors – that is to say, a model of communication. Because the proposed operations behave well with this transformation of operational models into heard-of predicates, we can derive bounds, characterizations, and implementations of the heard-of predicates for the constructions.

Keywords: Message-passing · Asynchronous rounds · Failures · Heard-of model

1 Introduction

1.1 Motivation

Let us start with a round-based distributed algorithm; such an algorithm is quite common in the literature, especially in fault-tolerant settings. We want to formally verify this algorithm using the methods of our choice: proof-assistant, model-checking, inductive invariants, abstract interpretation... But how are we supposed to model the context in which the algorithm will run? Even a passing glance at the distributed computing literature shows a plethora of models defined in the mixture of english and mathematics.

Thankfully, there are formalisms for abstracting round-based models of distributed computing. One of these is the Heard-Of model of Charron-Bost and Schiper [4]; it boils down the communication model to a description of all

© IFIP International Federation for Information Processing 2020
Published by Springer Nature Switzerland AG 2020
A. Gotsman and A. Sokolova (Eds.): FORTE 2020, LNCS 12136, pp. 133–149, 2020.
https://doi.org/10.1007/978-3-030-50086-3_8

accepted combinations of received messages. Formally, this is done by considering communications graphs, one for each round, and taking the sets of infinite sequences of graphs that are allowed by the model. Such a set is called a heard-of predicate, and captures a communication model.

An angle of attack for verification is therefore to find the heard-of predicate corresponding to a real-world environment, and use the techniques from the literature to verify an algorithm for this heard-of predicate. But which heard-of predicate should be used? What is the "right" predicate for a given environment? For some cases, the predicates are given in Charron-Bost and Schiper [4]; but this does not solve the general case.

Actually, the answer is quite subtle. This follows from a fundamental part of the Heard-Of model: communication-closedness [7]. This means that for p to use a message from q at round r, p must receive it before or during its own round r. And thus, knowing whether p receives the message from q at the right round or not depends on how p waits for messages. That is, it depends on the specifics of how rounds are implemented on top of it.

Once again, the literature offers a solution: Shimi et al. [12] propose to first find a delivered predicate – a description of which messages will eventually be delivered, without caring about rounds –, and then to derive the heard-of predicate from it. This derivation explicitly studies strategies, the aforementioned rules for how processes waits for messages before changing round.

But this brings us back to square one: now we are looking for the delivered predicate corresponding to a real-world model, instead of the heard-of predicate. Basic delivered predicates for elementary failures are easy to find, but delivered predicates corresponding to combinations of failures are often not intuitive.

In this paper, we propose a solution to this problem: building a complex delivered predicate from simpler ones we already know. For example, consider a system where one process can crash and may recover later, and another process can definitively crash. The delivered predicate for at most one crash is $PDel_1^{crash}$, and the predicate where all the messages are delivered is $PDel^{total}$. Intuitively, a process that can crash and necessarily recover is described by the behavior of $PDel_1^{crash}$ followed by the behavior of $PDel^{total}$. We call this the succession of these predicates, and write it $PDel_1^{recover} \triangleq PDel_1^{crash} \rightsquigarrow PDel^{total}$. In our system, the crashed process may never recover: hence we have either the behavior of $PDel_1^{recover}$ or the behavior of $PDel_1^{crash}$. This amounts to a union (or a disjunction); we write it $PDel_1^{canrecover} \triangleq PDel_1^{recover} \cup PDel_1^{crash}$. Finally, we consider a potential irremediable crash, additionally to the previous predicate. Thus we want the behavior of $PDel_1^{crash}$ and the behavior of $PDel_1^{canrecover}$. We call it the combination (or conjunction) of these predicates, and write it $PDel_1^{crash} \bigotimes PDel_1^{canrecover}$ The complete system is thus described by $PDel_1^{crash} \bigotimes ((PDel_1^{crash} \rightsquigarrow PDel^{total}) \cup PDel_1^{crash})$. In the following, we will also introduce an operator ω to express repetition. For example, a system where, repeatedly, a process can crash and recover is $(PDel_1^{crash} \rightsquigarrow PDel^{total})^\omega$.

Lastly, the analysis of the resulting delivered predicate can be bypassed: its heard-of predicate arises from our operations applied to the heard-of predicates of the elementary building blocks.

1.2   Related Work

The heard-of model was proposed by Charron-Bost and Schiper [4] as a combination of the ideas of two previous work. First, the concept of a fault model where the only information is which message arrives, from Santoro and Widmayer [11]; and second, the idea of abstracting failures in a round per round fashion, from Gafni [8]. Replacing the operational fault detectors of Gafni with the fault model of Santoro and Widmayer gives the heard-of model.

This model was put to use in many ways. Obviously computability and complexity results were proven: new algorithms for consensus in the original paper by Charron-Bost and Schiper [4]; characterizations for consensus solvability by Coulouma et al. [5] and Nowak et al. [10]; a characterization for approximate consensus solvability by Charron-Bost et al. [3]; a study of k set-agreement by Biely et al. [1]; and more.

The clean mathematical abstraction of the heard-of model also works well with formal verification. The rounds provide structure, and the reasoning can be less operational than in many distributed computing abstractions. We thus have a proof assistant verification of consensus algorithms in Charron-Bost et al. [2]; cutoff bounds for the model checking of consensus algorithms by Marić et al. [9]; a DSL to write code following the structure of the heard-of model and verify it with inductive invariants by Drăgoi et al. [6]; and more.

1.3   Contributions

The contributions of the paper are:

- A definition of operations on delivered predicates and strategies, as well as examples using them in Sect. 2.
- The study of oblivious strategies, the strategies only looking at messages for the current round, in Sect. 3. We provide a technique to extract a strategy dominating the oblivious strategies of the built predicate from the strategies of the initial predicates; exact computations of the generated heard-of predicates; and a sufficient condition on the building blocks for the result of operations to be dominated by an oblivious strategy.
- The study of conservative strategies, the strategies looking at everything but messages from future rounds, in Sect. 4. We provide a technique to extract a strategy dominating the conservative strategies of the build predicate from the strategies of the initial predicates; upper bounds on the generated heard-of predicates; and a sufficient condition on the building blocks for the result of operations to be dominated by a conservative strategy.

Due to size constraints, many of the complete proofs are not in the paper itself, and can be found in the full paper [13].

2   Operations and Examples

2.1   Basic Concepts

We start by providing basic definitions and intuitions. The model we consider proceed by rounds, where processes send messages tagged with a round number, wait for some messages with this round number, and then compute the next state and increment the round number. $\mathbb{N}^*$ denotes the non-zero naturals.

Definition 1 (Collections and Predicates). *Let Π a set of processes. An element of $(\mathbb{N}^* \times \Pi) \mapsto \mathcal{P}(\Pi)$ is either a **Delivered collection** c or a **Heard-Of collection** h for Π, depending on the context. c_{tot} is the total collection such that $\forall r > 0, \forall p \in \Pi : c_{tot}(r, p) = \Pi$.*

*An element of $\mathcal{P}((\mathbb{N}^* \times \Pi) \mapsto \mathcal{P}(\Pi))$ is either a **Delivered predicate** PDel or a **Heard-Of predicate** PHO for Π. $\mathcal{P}_{tot} = \{c_{tot}\}$ is the total delivered predicate.*

For a heard-of collection h, $h(r, p)$ are the senders of messages for round r that p has received at or before its round r, and thus has known while at round r. For a delivered collection c, $c(r, p)$ are the senders of messages for round r that p has received, at any point in time. Some of these messages may have arrived early, before p was at r, or too late, after p has left round r. c gives an operational point of view (which messages arrive), and h gives a logical point of view (which messages are used).

Remark 1. We also regularly use the "graph-sequence" notation for a collection c. Let $Graphs_\Pi$ be the set of graphs whose nodes are the elements of Π. A collection gr is an element of $(Graphs_\Pi)^\omega$. We say that c and gr represent the same collection when $\forall r > 0, \forall p \in \Pi : c(r, p) = In_{gr[r]}(p)$, where $In(p)$ is the incoming vertices of p. We will usually not define two collections but use one collection as both kind of objects; the actual type being used in a particular expression can be deduced from the operations on the collection. For example $c[r]$ makes sense for a sequence of graphs, while $c(r, p)$ makes sense for a function.

In an execution, the local state of a process is the pair of its current round and all the received messages up to this point. We disregard any local variable, since our focus is on which messages to wait for. A message is represented by a pair $\langle round, sender \rangle$. For a state q, and a round $r > 0$, $q(r)$ is the set of peers from which the process has received a message for round r.

Definition 2 (Local State). *Let $Q = \mathbb{N}^* \times \mathcal{P}(\mathbb{N}^* \times \Pi)$. Then $q \in Q$ is a **local state**.*

For $q = \langle r, mes \rangle$, we write q.round for r, q.mes for mes and $\forall i > 0 : q(i) \triangleq \{k \in \Pi \mid \langle i, k \rangle \in q.mes\}$.

We then define strategies, which constrain the behavior of processes. A strategy is a set of states from which a process is allowed to change round. It captures rules like "wait for at least F messages from the current round", or "wait for these specific messages". Strategies give a mean to constrain executions.

Definition 3 (Strategy). *$f \in \mathcal{P}(Q)$ is a **strategy**.*

2.2   Definition of Operations

We can now define operations on predicates and their corresponding strategies. The intuition behind these operations is the following:

- The union of two delivered predicates is equivalent to an OR on the two communication behaviors. For example, the union of the delivered predicate for one crash at round r and of the one for one crash at round $r + 1$ gives a predicate where there is either a crash at round r or a crash at round $r + 1$.
- The combination of two behaviors takes every pair of collections, one from each predicate, and computes the intersection of the graphs at each round. Meaning, it adds the loss of messages from both, to get both behaviors at once. For example, combining $PDel_1^{crash}$ with itself gives $PDel_2^{crash}$, the predicate with at most two crashes. Although combination intersects graphs round by round in a local fashion, it actually combines two collections globally, and thus can combine several global predicates like hearing from a given number of process during the whole execution.
- For succession, the system starts with one behavior, then switch to another. The definition is such that the first behavior might never happen, but the second one must appear.
- Repetition is the next logical step after succession: instead of following one behavior with another, the same behavior is repeated again and again. For example, taking the repetition of at most one crash results in a potential infinite number of crash-and-restart, with the constraint of having at most one crashed process at any time.

Definition 4 (Operations on predicates). *Let P_1, P_2 be two delivered or heard-of predicates.*

- *The **union** of P_1 and P_2 is $P_1 \cup P_2$.*
- *The **combination** $P_1 \otimes P_2 \triangleq \{c_1 \otimes c_2 \mid c_1 \in P_1, c_2 \in P_2\}$, where for c_1 and c_2 two collections, $\forall r > 0, \forall p \in \Pi : (c_1 \otimes c_2)(r, p) = c_1(r, p) \cap c_2(r, p)$.*
- *The **succession** $P_1 \rightsquigarrow P_2 \triangleq \bigcup\limits_{c_1 \in P_1, c_2 \in P_2} c_1 \rightsquigarrow c_2$,*

  with $c_1 \rightsquigarrow c_2 \triangleq \{c \mid \exists r \geq 0 : c = c_1[1, r].c_2\}$.
- *The **repetition** of P_1, $(P_1)^\omega \triangleq \{c \mid \exists(c_i)_{i \in \mathbb{N}^*}, \exists(r_i)_{i \in \mathbb{N}^*} : r_1 = 0 \land \forall i \in \mathbb{N}^* : (c_i \in P_1 \land r_i < r_{i+1} \land c[r_i + 1, r_{i+1}] = c_i[1, r_{i+1} - r_i])\}$.*

For all operations on predicates, we provide an analogous one for strategies. We show later that strategies for the delivered predicates, when combined by the analogous operation, retain important properties on the result of the operation on the predicates.

Definition 5 (Operations on strategies). *Let f_1, f_2 be two strategies.*

- *Their **union** $f_1 \cup f_2 \triangleq$ the strategy such that $\forall q$ a local state: $(f_1 \cup f_2)(q) \triangleq f_1(q) \lor f_2(q)$.*

- *Their* **combination** $f_1 \otimes f_2 \triangleq \{q_1 \otimes q_2 \mid q_1 \in f_1 \wedge q_2 \in f_2 \wedge q_1.round \doteq q_2.round\}$, *where for* q_1 *and* q_2 *at the same round* r, $q_1 \otimes q_2 \triangleq \langle r\{\langle r', k \rangle \mid r' > 0 \wedge k \in q_1(r') \cap q_2(r')\}\rangle$
- *Their* **succession** $f_1 \rightsquigarrow f_2 \triangleq f_1 \cup f_2 \cup \{q_1 \rightsquigarrow q_2 \mid q_1 \in f_1 \wedge q_2 \in f_2\}$ *where*

$$q_1 \rightsquigarrow q_2 \triangleq \left\langle \begin{array}{l} q_1.round + q_2.round, \\ \left\{\langle r, k \rangle \mid r > 0 \wedge \left(\begin{array}{ll} k \in q_1(r) & \text{if } r \leq q_1.round \\ k \in q_2(r - q_1.round) & \text{if } r > q_1.round \end{array} \right) \right\} \end{array} \right\rangle$$

- *The* **repetition** *of* f_1, $f_1^\omega \triangleq \{q_1 \rightsquigarrow q_2 \rightsquigarrow ... \rightsquigarrow q_k \mid k \geq 1 \wedge q_1, q_2, ..., q_k \in f_1\}$.

The goal is to derive new strategies for the resulting model by applying operations on strategies for the starting models. This allows, in some cases, to bypass strategies, and deduce the Heard-Of predicate for a given Delivered predicate from the Heard-Of predicates of its building blocks.

2.3 Executions and Domination

Before manipulating predicates and strategies, we need to define what is an execution: a specific ordering of events corresponding to a delivered collection. An execution is an infinite sequence of either delivery of messages ($deliver(r, p, q)$), change to the next round ($next_j$), or a deadlock ($stop$). Message sending is implicit after every change of round. An execution must satisfy three rules: no message is delivered before it is sent, no message is delivered twice, and once there is a $stop$, the rest of the sequence can only be $stop$.

Definition 6 (Execution). *Let* Π *be a set of* n *processes. Let the set of transitions* $T = \{next_j \mid j \in \Pi\} \cup \{deliver(r, k, j) \mid r \in \mathbb{N}^* \wedge k, j \in \Pi\} \cup \{stop\}$. $next_j$ *is the transition for* j *changing round,* $deliver(r, k, j)$ *is the transition for the delivery to* j *of the message sent by* k *in round* r, $stop$ *models a deadlock. Then,* $t \in T^\omega$ *is an* **execution** $\triangleq$

- **(Delivery after sending)**
  $\forall i \in \mathbb{N} : t[i] = deliver(r, k, j) \implies \mathbf{card}(\{l \in [0, i[\mid t[l] = next_k\}) \geq r - 1$
- **(Unique delivery)**
  $\forall \langle r, k, j \rangle \in (\mathbb{N}^* \times \Pi \times \Pi) : \mathbf{card}(\{i \in \mathbb{N} \mid t[i] = deliver(r, k, j)\}) \leq 1$
- **(Once stopped, forever stopped)**
  $\forall i \in \mathbb{N} : t[i] = stop \implies \forall j \geq i : t[j] = stop$

Let c *be a delivered collection. Then,* $execs(c)$, *the* **executions** *of* $c \triangleq$

$$\left\{ t \text{ an execution} \;\middle|\; \begin{array}{l} \forall \langle r, k, j \rangle \in \mathbb{N}^* \times \Pi \times \Pi : \\ (k \in c(r, j) \wedge \mathbf{card}(\{i \in \mathbb{N} \mid t[i] = next_k\}) \geq r - 1) \\ \Longleftrightarrow \\ (\exists i \in \mathbb{N} : t[i] = deliver(r, k, j)) \end{array} \right\}$$

For a delivered predicate $PDel$, $execs(PDel) \triangleq \{execs(c) \mid c \in PDel\}$.

Let t *be an execution,* $p \in \Pi$ *and* $i \in \mathbb{N}$. *The state of* p *in* t *after* i *transitions is* $q_p^t[i] \triangleq \langle \mathbf{card}(\{l < i \mid t[l] = next_p\}) + 1, \{\langle r, k \rangle \mid \exists l < i : t[l] = deliver(r, k, p)\}\rangle$

Notice that such executions do not allow process to "jump" from say round 5 to round 9 without passing by the rounds in-between. The reason is that the Heard-Of model does not give processes access to the decision to change rounds: processes specify only which messages to send depending on the state, and what is the next state depending on the current state and the received messages.

Also, the only information considered here is the round number and the received messages. This definition of execution disregards the message contents and the internal states of processes, as they are irrelevant to the implementation of Heard-Of predicates.

Recall that strategies constrain when processes can change round. Thus, the executions that conform to a strategy change rounds only when allowed by it, and do it infinitely often if possible.

Definition 7 (Executions of a Strategy). *Let f be a strategy and t an execution. t is an **execution of** $f \triangleq t$ satisfies:*

- *(**All nexts allowed**) $\forall i \in \mathbb{N}, \forall p \in \Pi : (t[i] = next_p \implies q_p^t[i] \in f)$*
- *(**Fairness**) $\forall p \in \Pi : \mathbf{card}(\{i \in \mathbb{N} \mid t[i] = next_p\}) < \aleph_0 \implies \mathbf{card}(\{i \in \mathbb{N} \mid q_p^t[i] \notin f\}) = \aleph_0$*

For a delivered predicate PDel, $execs_f(PDel) \triangleq \{t \in execs(PDel) \mid t \text{ is an execution of } f\}$.

The fairness property can approximately be expressed in LTL as $\forall p \in \Pi : \Diamond\Box(q_p^t \in f) \Rightarrow \Box\Diamond next_p$. Note however that executions are here defined as sequences of transitions, whereas LTL models are sequences of states.

An important part of this definition considers executions where processes cannot necessarily change round after each delivery. That is, in the case of "waiting for at most F messages", an execution where more messages are delivered than F at some round is still an execution of the strategy. This hypothesis captures the asynchrony of processes, which are not always scheduled right after deliveries. It is compensated by a weak fairness assumption: if a strategy forever allows the change of round, it must eventually happen.

Going back to strategies, not all of them are equally valuable. In general, strategies that block forever at some round are less useful than strategies that don't – they forbid termination in some cases. The validity of a strategy captures the absence of such an infinite wait.

Definition 8 (Validity).
*An execution t is **valid** $\triangleq \forall p \in \Pi : \mathbf{card}(\{i \in \mathbb{N} \mid t[i] = next_p\}) = \aleph_0$.*
*Let PDel a delivered predicate and f a strategy. f is a **valid strategy** for $PDel \triangleq \forall t \in execs_f(PDel) : t \text{ is a valid execution}$.*

Because in a valid execution no process is ever blocked at a given round, there are infinitely many rounds. Hence, the messages delivered before the changes of round uniquely define a heard-of collection.

Definition 9 (Heard-Of Collection of Executions and Heard-Of Predicate of Strategies). *Let t be a valid execution. h_t is the **heard-of collection** of $t \triangleq$*

$$\forall r \in \mathbb{N}^*, \forall p \in \Pi : h_t(r,p) = \left\{ k \in \Pi \ \middle| \ \exists i \in \mathbb{N} : \left(\begin{array}{l} q_p^t[i].round = r \\ \wedge\ t[i] = next_p \\ \wedge\ \langle r, k \rangle \in q_p^t[i].mes \end{array} \right) \right\}$$

Let PDel be a delivered predicate, and f be a valid strategy for PDel. We write $PHO_f(PDel)$ for the heard-of predicate composed of the collections of the executions of f on PDel: $PHO_f(PDel) \triangleq \{h_t \mid t \in execs_f(PDel)\}$.

Lastly, the heard-of predicate of most interest is the strongest one that can be generated by a valid strategy on the delivered predicate. Here strongest means the one that implies all the other heard-of predicates that can be generated on the same delivered predicate. The intuition boils down to two ideas:

- The strongest predicate implies all the heard-of predicates generated on the same *PDel*, and thus it characterizes them completely.
- When seeing predicates as sets, implication is the reverse inclusion. Hence the strongest predicate is the one included in all the others. Less collections means more constrained communication, which means a more powerful model.

This notion of strongest predicate is formalized through an order on strategies and their heard-of predicates.

Definition 10 (Domination). *Let PDel be a delivered predicate and let f and f' be two valid strategies for PDel. f **dominates** f' for PDel, written $f' \prec_{PDel} f$, $\triangleq PHO_{f'}(PDel) \supseteq PHO_f(PDel)$.*

*A greatest element for $\prec_{PDel}$ is called a **dominating strategy** for PDel. Given such a strategy f, the **dominating predicate** for PDel is $PHO_f(PDel)$.*

2.4 Examples

We now show the variety of models that can be constructed from basic building blocks. Our basic blocks are the model $PDel^{total}$ with only the collection c_{total} where all the messages are delivered, and the model $PDel_{1,r}^{crash}$ with at most one crash that can happen at round r.

Definition 11 (At most 1 crash at round r). $\mathcal{P}_{1,r}^{crash} \triangleq$

$$\left\{ c \text{ a delivered collection} \ \middle| \ \exists \Sigma \subseteq \Pi : \begin{array}{l} |\Sigma| \geq n-1 \\ \wedge\ \forall j \in \Pi \left(\begin{array}{ll} \forall r' \in [1,r[: c(r',j) = \Pi \\ \wedge & c(r,j) \supseteq \Sigma \\ \wedge\ \forall r' \geq r : & c(r',j) = \Sigma \end{array} \right) \end{array} \right\}.$$

From this family of predicates, various predicates can be built. Table 1 show some of them, as well as the Heard-Of predicates computed for these predicates based on the results from Sect. 3.3 and Sect. 3.4. For example the predicate with at most one crash $\mathcal{P}_1^{crash}$ If a crash happens, it happens at one specific round r. We can thus build $\mathcal{P}_1^{crash}$ from a disjunction for all values of r of the predicate with at most one crash at round r; that is, by the union of $\mathcal{P}_{1,r}^{crash}$ for all r.

Table 1. A list of delivered predicate built using our operations, and their corresponding heard-of predicate. The *HOProduct* operator is defined in Definition 16.

Description	Expression	HO	Proof
At most 1 crash	$P_1^{crash} = \bigcup_{i=1}^{\infty} P_{1,i}^{crash}$	$HOProd(\{T \subseteq \Pi \mid |T| \geq n-1\})$	[12]
At most F crashes	$P_F^{crash} = \bigotimes_{j=1}^{F} P_1^{crash}$	$HOProd(\{T \subseteq \Pi \mid |T| \geq n-F\})$	[12]
At most 1 crash, which will restart	$P_1^{recover} = P_1^{crash} \rightsquigarrow P^{total}$	$HOProd(\{T \subseteq \Pi \mid |T| \geq n-1\})$	Theorem 4
At most F crashes, which will restart	$P_F^{recover} = \bigotimes_{j=1}^{F} P_1^{recover}$	$HOProd(\{T \subseteq \Pi \mid |T| \geq n-F\})$	Theorem 4
At most 1 crash, which can restart	$P_1^{canrecover} = P_1^{recover} \cup P_1^{crash}$	$HOProd(\{T \subseteq \Pi \mid |T| \geq n-1\})$	Theorem 4
At most F crashes, which can restart	$P_F^{canrecover} = \bigotimes_{j=1}^{F} P_1^{canrecover}$	$HOProd(\{T \subseteq \Pi \mid |T| \geq n-F\})$	Theorem 4
No bound on crashes and restart, with only 1 crash at a time	$P_1^{recovery} = (P_1^{crash})^\omega$	$HOProd(\{T \subseteq \Pi \mid |T| \geq n-1\})$	Theorem 4
No bound on crashes and restart, with max F crashes at a time	$P_F^{recovery} = \bigotimes_{j=1}^{F} P_1^{recovery}$	$HOProd(\{T \subseteq \Pi \mid |T| \geq n-F\})$	Theorem 4
At most 1 crash, after round r	$P_{1,\geq r}^{crash} = \bigcup_{i=r}^{\infty} P_{1,i}^{crash}$	$\subseteq HOProd(\{T \subseteq \Pi \mid |T| \geq n-1\})$	Theorem 10
At most F crashes, after round r	$P_{F,\geq r}^{crash} = \bigcup_{i=r}^{\infty} P_{F,i}^{crash}$	$\subseteq HOProd(\{T \subseteq \Pi \mid |T| \geq n-F\})$	Theorem 10
At most F crashes with no more than one per round	$P_F^{crash\neq} = \bigcup_{i_1 \neq i_2 ... \neq i_F} \bigotimes_{j=1}^{F} P_{1,i_j}^{crash}$	$\subseteq HOProd(\{T \subseteq \Pi \mid |T| \geq n-F\})$	Theorem 10

2.5 Families of Strategies

Strategies as defined above are predicates on states. This makes them incredibly expressive; on the other hand, this expressivity creates difficulty in reasoning about them. To address this problem, we define families of strategies. Intuitively, strategies in a same family depend on a specific part of the state – for example the messages of the current round. Equality of these parts of the state defines an equivalence relation; the strategies of a family are strategies on the equivalence classes of this relation.

Definition 12 (Families of strategies). *Let $\approx: Q \times Q \to bool$. The family of strategies defined by $\approx$, $family(\approx) \triangleq \{f$ a strategy $\mid \forall q_1, q_2 \in \Pi : q_1 \approx q_2 \implies (q_1 \in f \iff q_2 \in f)\}$.*

3 Oblivious Strategies

The simplest non-trivial strategies use only information from the messages of the current round. These strategies that do not remember messages from previous rounds, do not use messages in advance from future rounds, and do not use the round number itself. These strategies are called oblivious. They are simple, the Heard-Of predicates they implement are relatively easy to compute, and they require little computing power and memory to implement. Moreover, many examples above are dominated by such a strategy. Of course, there is a price to pay: oblivious strategies tend to be coarser than general ones.

3.1 Minimal Oblivious Strategy

An oblivious strategy is defined by the different subsets of Π from which it has to receive a message before allowing a change of round.

Definition 13 (Oblivious Strategy). *Let obliv be the function such that $\forall q \in Q : obliv(q) = \{k \in \Pi \mid \langle q.round, k \rangle \in q.mes\}$. Let $\approx_{obliv}$ the equivalence relation defined by $q_1 \approx_{obliv} q_2 \triangleq obliv(q_1) = obliv(q_2)$. The family of oblivious strategies is $family(\approx_{obliv})$. For f an oblivious strategy, let $Nexts_f \triangleq \{obliv(q) \mid q \in f\}$. It uniquely defines f.*

We will focus on a specific strategy, that dominates the oblivious strategies for a predicate. This follows from the fact that it waits less than any other valid oblivious strategy for this predicate.

Definition 14 (Minimal Oblivious Strategy). *Let $PDel$ be a delivered predicate. The **minimal oblivious strategy** for $PDel$ is $f_{min} \triangleq \{q \mid \exists c \in PDel, \exists p \in \Pi, \exists r > 0 : obliv(q) = c(r,p)\}$.*

Lemma 1 (Domination of Minimal Oblivious Strategy). *Let $PDel$ be a $PDel$ and f_{min} be its minimal oblivious strategy. Then f_{min} is a dominating oblivious strategy for $PDel$.*

Proof (Proof idea). f_{min} is valid, because for every possible set of received messages in a collection of $PDel$, it accepts the corresponding oblivious state by definition of minimal oblivious strategy. It is dominating among oblivious strategies because any other valid oblivious strategy must allow the change of round when f_{min} does it: it contains f_{min}. If an oblivious strategy does not contain f_{min}, then there is a collection of $PDel$ in which at a given round, a certain process might receive exactly the messages for the oblivious state accepted by f_{min} and not by f. This entails that f is not valid.

3.2 Operations Maintain Minimal Oblivious Strategy

As teased above, minimal oblivious strategies behave nicely under the proposed operations. That is, they give minimal oblivious strategies of resulting delivered predicates. One specificity of minimal oblivious strategies is that there is no need for the succession operation on strategies, nor for the repetition. An oblivious strategy has no knowledge about anything but the messages of the current round, and not even its round number, so it is impossible to distinguish a union from a succession, or a repetition from the initial predicate itself.

Theorem 1 (Minimal Oblivious Strategy for Union and Succession).
Let $PDel_1, PDel_2$ be two delivered predicates, f_1 and f_2 the minimal oblivious strategies for, respectively, $PDel_1$ and $PDel_2$. Then $f_1 \cup f_2$ is the minimal oblivious strategy for $PDel_1 \cup PDel_2$ and $PDel_1 \rightsquigarrow PDel_2$.

Proof (Proof idea). Structurally, all proofs in this section consist in showing equality between the strategies resulting from the operations and the minimal oblivious strategy for the delivered predicate.

For a union, the messages that can be received at each round are the messages that can be received at each round in the first predicate or in the second. This is also true for succession. Given that f_1 and f_2 are the minimal oblivious strategies of $PDel_1$ and $PDel_2$, they accept exactly the states with one of these sets of current messages. And thus $f_1 \cup f_2$ is the minimal oblivious strategy for $PDel_1 \cup PDel_2$ and $PDel_1 \rightsquigarrow PDel_2$.

Theorem 2 (Minimal Oblivious Strategy for Repetition). *Let $PDel$ be a delivered predicate, and f be its minimal oblivious strategy. Then f is the minimal oblivious strategy for $PDel^\omega$.*

Proof (Proof idea). The intuition is the same as for union and succession. Since repetition involves only one PDel, the sets of received messages do not change and f is the minimal oblivious strategy.

For combination, a special symmetry hypothesis is needed.

Definition 15 (Totally Symmetric PDel). *Let $PDel$ be a delivered predicate. $PDel$ is **totally symmetric** $\triangleq \forall c \in PDel, \forall r > 0, \forall p \in \Pi, \forall r' > 0, \forall q \in \Pi, \exists c' \in PDel : c(r, p) = c'(r', q)$*

Combination is different because combining collections is done round by round. As oblivious strategies do not depend on the round, the combination of oblivious strategies creates the same combination of received messages for each round. We thus need these combinations to be independent of the round – to be possible at each round – to reconcile those two elements.

Theorem 3 (Minimal Oblivious Strategy for Combination). *Let $PDel_1$, $PDel_2$ be two totally symmetric delivered predicates, f_1 and f_2 the minimal oblivious strategies for, respectively, $PDel_1$ and $PDel_2$. Then $f_1 \otimes f_2$ is the minimal oblivious strategy for $PDel_1 \otimes PDel_2$.*

Proof (Proof idea). The oblivious states of $PDel_1 \otimes PDel_2$ are the combination of an oblivious state of $PDel_1$ and of one of $PDel_2$ at the same round, for the same process. Thanks to total symmetry, this translates into the intersection of any oblivious state of $PDel_1$ with any oblivious state of $PDel_2$. Since f_1 and f_2 are the minimal oblivious strategy, they both accept exactly the oblivious states of $PDel_1$ and $PDel_2$ respectively. Thus, $f_1 \otimes f_2$ accept all combinations of oblivious states of $PDel_1$ and $PDel_2$, and thus is the minimal oblivious strategy of $PDel_1 \otimes PDel_2$.

3.3   Computing Heard-of Predicates

The computation of the heard-of predicate generated by an oblivious strategy is easy thanks to a characteristic of this HO: it is a product of sets of possible messages.

Definition 16 (Heard-Of Product). *Let $S \subseteq \mathcal{P}(\Pi)$. The **heard-of product generated by S**, $HOProd(S) \triangleq \{h \mid \forall p \in \Pi, \forall r > 0 : h(r, p) \in S\}$.*

Lemma 2 (Heard-Of Predicate of an Oblivious Strategy). *Let $PDel$ be a delivered predicate containing c_{tot} and let f be a valid oblivious strategy for $PDel$. Then $PHO_f(PDel) = HOProd(Nexts_f)$.*

Proof. Proved in [12, Theorem 20, Section 4.1].

Thanks to this characterization, the heard-of predicate generated by the minimal strategies for the operations is computed in terms of the heard-of predicate generated by the original minimal strategies.

Theorem 4 (Heard-Of Predicate of Minimal Oblivious Strategies). *Let $PDel, PDel_1, PDel_2$ be delivered predicates containing c_{tot}. Let f, f_1, f_2 be their respective minimal oblivious strategies. Then:*

- $PHO_{f_1 \cup f_2}(PDel_1 \cup PDel_2) = PHO_{f_1 \cup f_2}(PDel_1 \rightsquigarrow PDel_2) = HOProd$ $(Nexts_{f_1} \cup Nexts_{f_2})$.
- *If $PDel_1$ or $PDel_2$ are totally symmetric, $PHO_{f_1 \otimes f_2}(PDel_1 \otimes PDel_2) = HOProd(\{n_1 \cap n_2 \mid n_1 \in Nexts_{f_1} \wedge n_2 \in Nexts_{f_2}\})$.*
- $PHO_f(PDel^\omega) = PHO_f(PDel)$.

Proof (Proof idea). We apply Lemma 2. The containment of c_{tot} was shown in the proof of Theorem 5. As for the equality of the oblivious states, it follows from the intuition in the proofs of the minimal oblivious strategy in the previous section.

3.4   Domination by an Oblivious Strategy

From the previous sections, we can compute the Heard-Of predicate of the dominating oblivious strategies for our examples. We first need to give the minimal oblivious strategy for our building blocks $PDel_1^{crash}$ and $PDel^{total}$.

Definition 17 (Waiting for $n - F$ messages). *The strategy to wait for $n - F$ messages is: $f^{n,F} \triangleq \{q \in Q \mid |obliv(q)| \geq n - F\}$*

For all $F < n$, $f^{n,F}$ is the minimal oblivious strategy for $PDel_F^{crash}$ (shown by Shimi et al. [12, Thm. 17]). For $PDel^{total}$, since every process receives all the messages all the time, the strategy waits for all the messages ($f^{n,0}$).

Using these strategies, we deduce the heard-of predicates of dominating oblivious strategies for our examples.

- For $PDel_1^{recover} \triangleq PDel_1^{crash} \rightsquigarrow PDel^{total}$, the minimal oblivious strategy $f_1^{recover} = f^{n,1} \cup f^{n,0} = f^{n,1}$. This entails that
$PHO_{f_1^{recover}} = HOProd(\{T \subseteq \Pi \mid |T| \geq n-1\})$.
- For $PDel_1^{canrecover} \triangleq PDel_1^{recover} \cup PDel_1^{crash}$, the minimal oblivious strategy $f_1^{canrecover} = f_1^{recover} \cup f^{n,1} = f^{n,1}$. This entails that
$PHO_{f_1^{canrecover}} = HOProd(\{T \subseteq \Pi \mid |T| \geq n-1\})$.
- For $PDel_1^{crash} \otimes PDel_1^{canrecover}$ the minimal oblivious strategy $f = f^{n,1} \otimes f_1^{canrecover} = f^{n,1} \otimes f^{n,1} = f^{n,2}$. This entails that
$PHO_f = HOProd(\{T \subseteq \Pi \mid |T| \geq n-2\})$.

The computed predicate is the predicate of the dominating *oblivious* strategy. But the dominating strategy might not be oblivious, and this predicate might be too weak. The following result shows that $PDel_1^{crash}$ and $PDel^{total}$ satisfy conditions that imply their domination by an oblivious strategy. Since these conditions are invariant by our operations, all PDel constructed with these building blocks are dominated by an oblivious strategy.

Theorem 5 (Domination by Oblivious for Operations). *Let $PDel$, $PDel_1, PDel_2$ be delivered predicates that satisfy:*

- *(Total collection) They contains the total collection c_{tot},*
- *(Symmetry up to a round) $\forall c$ a collection in the predicate, $\forall p \in \Pi, \forall r > 0, \forall r' > 0, \exists c'$ a collection in the predicate: $c'[1, r'-1] = c_{tot}[1, r'-1] \wedge \forall q \in \Pi : c'(r', q) = c(r, p)$*

Then $PDel_1 \cup PDel_2$, $PDel_1 \otimes PDel_2$, $PDel_1 \rightsquigarrow PDel_2$, $PDel^\omega$ satisfy the same two conditions and are dominated by oblivious strategies.

Both $\mathcal{P}_1^{crash}$ from Table 1 and $\mathcal{P}^{total} = \{c_{tot}\}$ satisfy this condition. So do all the first 8 examples from Table 1, since they built from these two.

4 Conservative Strategies

We now broaden our family of considered strategies, by allowing them to consider past and present rounds, as well as the round number itself. This is a generalization of oblivious strategies, that tradeoff simplicity for expressivity, while retaining a nice structure. Even better, we show that both our building blocks and all the predicates built from them are dominated by such a strategy. For the examples then, no expressivity is lost.

4.1 Minimal Conservative Strategy

Definition 18 (Conservative Strategy). *Let $cons$ be the function such that $\forall q \in Q$, $cons(q) \triangleq \langle q.round, \{\langle r, k \rangle \in q.mes \mid r \leq q.round\}\rangle$. Let $\approx_{cons}$ the equivalence relation defined by $q_1 \approx_{cons} q_2 \triangleq cons(q_1) = cons(q_2)$. The family of conservative strategies is $family(\approx_{cons})$. We write $Nexts_f^R \triangleq \{cons(q) \mid q \in f\}$ for the set of conservative states in f. This uniquely defines f.*

In analogy with the case of oblivious strategies, we can define a minimal conservative strategy of $PDel$, and it is a strategy dominating all conservative strategies for this delivered predicate.

Definition 19 (Minimal Conservative Strategy). *Let $PDel$ be a delivered predicate. The **minimal conservative strategy** for $PDel$ is $f_{min} \triangleq$ the conservative strategy such that $f = \{q \in Q \mid \exists c \in PDel, \exists p \in \Pi, \forall r \leq q.round : q(r) = c(r,p)\}$.*

Lemma 3 (Domination of Minimal Conservative Strategy). *Let $PDel$ be a delivered predicate and f_{min} be its minimal conservative strategy. Then f_{min} dominates the conservative strategies for $PDel$.*

Proof (Proof idea). Analogous to the case of minimal oblivious strategies: it is valid because it allows to change round for each possible conservative state (the round and the messages received for this round and before) of collections in $PDel$. And since any other valid conservative strategy f must accept these states (or it would block forever in some execution of a collection of $PDel$), we have that f contains f_{min} and thus that f_{min} dominates f.

4.2   Operations Maintain Minimal Conservative Strategies

Like oblivious strategies, minimal conservative strategies give minimal conservative strategies of resulting delivered predicates.

Theorem 6 (Minimal Conservative Strategy for Union).   *Let $PDel_1, PDel_2$ be two delivered predicates, f_1 and f_2 the minimal conservative strategies for, respectively, $PDel_1$ and $PDel_2$. Then $f_1 \cup f_2$ is the minimal conservative strategy for $PDel_1 \cup PDel_2$.*

Proof (Proof idea). A prefix of a collection in $PDel_1 \cup PDel_2$ comes from either $PDel_1$ or $PDel_2$, and thus is accepted by f_1 or f_2. And any state accepted by $f_1 \cup f_2$ corresponds to some prefix of $PDel_1$ or $PDel_2$.

For the other three operations, slightly more structure is needed on the predicates. More precisely, they have to be independent of the processes. Any prefix of a process p in a collection of the predicate is also the prefix of any other process q in a possibly different collection of the same PDel. Hence, the behaviors (fault, crashes, loss) are not targeting specific processes. This restriction fits the intuition behind many common fault models.

Definition 20 (Symmetric PDel). *Let $PDel$ be a delivered predicate. $PDel$ is **symmetric** $\triangleq \forall c \in PDel, \forall p \in \Pi, \forall r > 0, \forall q \in \Pi, \exists c' \in PDel, \forall r' \leq r : c'(r',q) = c(r',p)$*

Theorem 7 (Minimal Conservative Strategy for Combination).   *Let $PDel_1, PDel_2$ be two symmetric delivered predicates, f_1 and f_2 the minimal conservative strategies for, respectively, $PDel_1$ and $PDel_2$. Then $f_1 \otimes f_2$ is the minimal conservative strategy for $PDel_1 \otimes PDel_2$.*

Proof (Proof idea). Since f_1 and f_2 are the minimal conservative strategies of $PDel_1$ and $PDel_2$, $Nexts^R f_1$ is the set of the conservative states of prefixes of $PDel_1$ and $Nexts^R_{f_2}$ is the set of the conservative states of prefixes of $PDel_2$. Also, the states accepted by $f_1 \otimes f_2$ are the combination of the states accepted by f_1 and the states accepted by f_2. And the prefixes of $PDel_1 \otimes PDel_2$ are the prefixes of $PDel_1$ combined with the prefixes of $PDel_2$ **for the same process**. Thanks to symmetry, we can take a prefix of $PDel_2$ and any process, and find a collection such that the process has that prefix. Therefore the combined prefixes for the same process are the same as the combined prefixes of $PDel_1$ and $PDel_2$. Thus, $Nexts^R_{f_1 \otimes f_2}$ is the set of conservative states of prefixes of $PDel_1 \otimes PDel_2$, and $f_1 \otimes f_2$ is its minimal conservative strategy.

Theorem 8 (Minimal Conservative Strategy for Succession). *Let $PDel_1, PDel_2$ be two symmetric delivered predicates, f_1 and f_2 the minimal conservative strategies for, respectively, $PDel_1$ and $PDel_2$. Then $f_1 \rightsquigarrow f_2$ is the minimal conservative strategy for $PDel_1 \rightsquigarrow PDel_2$.*

Proof (Proof idea). Since f_1 and f_2 are the minimal conservative strategies of $PDel_1$ and $PDel_2$, $Nexts^R f_1$ is the set of the conservative states of prefixes of $PDel_1$ and $Nexts^R_{f_2}$ is the set of the conservative states of prefixes of $PDel_2$. Also, the states accepted by $f_1 \rightsquigarrow f_2$ are the succession of the states accepted by f_1 and the states accepted by f_2. And the prefixes of $PDel_1 \rightsquigarrow PDel_2$ are the successions of prefixes of $PDel_1$ and prefixes of $PDel_2$ **for the same process**. But thanks to symmetry, we can take a prefix of $PDel_2$ and any process, and find a collection such that the process has that prefix.

Therefore the succession of prefixes for the same process are the same as the succession of prefixes of $PDel_1$ and $PDel_2$. Thus, $Nexts^R_{f_1 \rightsquigarrow f_2}$ is the set of conservative states of prefixes of $PDel_1 \rightsquigarrow PDel_2$, and is therefore its minimal conservative strategy.

Theorem 9 (Minimal Conservative Strategy for Repetition). *Let $PDel$ be a symmetric delivered predicate, and f be its minimal conservative strategy. Then f^ω is the minimal conservative strategy for $PDel^\omega$.*

Proof (Proof idea). The idea is the same as in the succession.

4.3 Computing Heard-Of Predicates

Here we split from the analogy with oblivious strategies: the heard-of predicate of conservative strategies is hard to compute, as it depends in intricate ways on the delivered predicate itself.

Yet it is still possible to compute interesting information on this HO: upper bounds. These are overapproximations of the actual HO, but they can serve for formal verification of LTL properties. Indeed, the executions of an algorithm for the actual HO are contained in the executions of the algorithm for any overapproximation of the HO, and LTL properties must be true for all executions of the algorithm. So proving the property on an overapproximation also proves it on the actual HO.

Theorem 10 (Upper Bounds on HO of Minimal Conservative Strategies). *Let $PDel, PDel_1, PDel_2$ be delivered predicates containing c_{tot}. Let $f^{cons}, f_1^{cons}, f_2^{cons}$ be their respective minimal conservative strategies, and $f^{obliv}, f_1^{obliv}, f_2^{obliv}$ be their respective minimal oblivious strategies. Then:*

- $PHO_{f_1^{cons} \cup f_2^{cons}}(PDel_1 \cup PDel_2) \subseteq HOProd(Nexts_{f_1^{obliv}} \cup Nexts_{f_2^{obliv}})$.
- $PHO_{f_1^{cons} \rightsquigarrow f_2^{cons}}(PDel_1 \rightsquigarrow PDel_2) \subseteq HOProd(Nexts_{f_1^{obliv}} \cup Nexts_{f_2^{obliv}})$.
- $PHO_{f_1^{cons} \otimes f_2^{cons}}(PDel_1 \otimes PDel_2) \subseteq HOProd(\{n_1 \cap n_2 \mid n_1 \in Nexts_{f_1^{obliv}} \wedge n_2 \in Nexts_{f_2^{obliv}}\})$.
- $PHO_{(f^{cons})^\omega}(PDel^\omega) \subseteq HOProd(Nexts_{f^{obliv}})$.

Proof (Proof idea). These bounds follow from the fact that an oblivious strategy, is a conservative strategy, and thus the minimal conservative strategy dominates the minimal oblivious strategy.

5   Conclusion

To summarize, we propose operations on delivered predicates that allow the construction of complex predicates from simpler ones. The corresponding operations on strategies behave nicely regarding dominating strategies, for the conservative and oblivious strategies. This entails bounds and characterizations of the dominating heard-of predicate for the constructions.

What needs to be done next comes in two kinds: first, the logical continuation is to look for constraints on delivered predicates for which we can compute the dominating heard-of predicate of conservative strategies. More ambitiously, we will study strategies looking in the future, i.e. strategies that can take into account messages from processes that have already reached a strictly higher round than the recipient. These strategies are useful for inherently asymmetric delivered predicates. For example, message loss is asymmetric, in the sense that we cannot force processes to receive the same set of messages.

Funding. This work was supported by project PARDI ANR-16-CE25-0006.

References

1. Biely, M., Robinson, P., Schmid, M., Schwarz, U., Winkler, K.: Gracefully degrading consensus and k-set agreement in directed dynamic networks. Theor. Comput. Sci. **726**, 41–77 (2018). https://doi.org/10.1016/j.tcs.2018.02.019
2. Charron-Bost, B., Debrat, H., Merz, S.: Formal verification of consensus algorithms tolerating malicious faults. In: Défago, X., Petit, F., Villain, V. (eds.) SSS 2011. LNCS, vol. 6976, pp. 120–134. Springer, Heidelberg (2011). https://doi.org/10.1007/978-3-642-24550-3_11
3. Charron-Bost, B., Függer, M., Nowak, T.: Approximate consensus in highly dynamic networks: the role of averaging algorithms. In: Halldórsson, M.M., Iwama, K., Kobayashi, N., Speckmann, B. (eds.) ICALP 2015. LNCS, vol. 9135, pp. 528–539. Springer, Heidelberg (2015). https://doi.org/10.1007/978-3-662-47666-6_42

4. Charron-Bost, B., Schiper, A.: The heard-of model: computing in distributed systems with benign faults. Distrib. Comput. **22**(1), 49–71 (2009). https://doi.org/10.1007/s00446-009-0084-6
5. Coulouma, É., Godard, E., Peters, J.: A characterization of oblivious message adversaries for which consensus is solvable. Theor. Comput. Sci. **584**, 80–90 (2015). https://doi.org/10.1016/j.tcs.2015.01.024
6. Drăgoi, C., Henzinger, T.A., Zufferey, D.: PSync: a partially synchronous language for fault-tolerant distributed algorithms. SIGPLAN Not. **51**(1), 400–415 (2016). https://doi.org/10.1145/2914770.2837650
7. Elrad, T., Francez, N.: Decomposition of distributed programs into communication-closedlayers. Sci. Comput. Program. **2**(3), 155–173 (1982). https://doi.org/10.1016/0167-6423(83)90013-8
8. Gafni, E.: Round-by-round fault detectors (extended abstract): unifying synchrony and asynchrony. In: 17th ACM Symposium on Principles of Distributed Computing, PODC 1998, pp. 143–152 (1998). https://doi.org/10.1145/277697.277724
9. Marić, O., Sprenger, C., Basin, D.: Cutoff bounds for consensus algorithms. In: Majumdar, R., Kunčak, V. (eds.) CAV 2017. LNCS, vol. 10427, pp. 217–237. Springer, Cham (2017). https://doi.org/10.1007/978-3-319-63390-9_12
10. Nowak, T., Schmid, U., Winkler, K.: Topological characterization of consensus under general message adversaries. In: 2019 ACM Symposium on Principles of Distributed Computing, PODC 2019 (2019). https://doi.org/10.1145/3293611.3331624
11. Santoro, N., Widmayer, P.: Time is not a healer. In: Monien, B., Cori, R. (eds.) STACS 1989. LNCS, vol. 349, pp. 304–313. Springer, Heidelberg (1989). https://doi.org/10.1007/BFb0028994
12. Shimi, A., Hurault, A., Quéinnec, P.: Characterizing asynchronous message-passing models through rounds. In: 22nd International Conference on Principles of Distributed Systems (OPODIS 2018), pp. 18:1–18:17 (2018). https://doi.org/10.4230/LIPIcs.OPODIS.2018.18
13. Shimi, A., Hurault, A., Queinnec, P.: Derivation of heard-of predicates from elementary behavioral patterns (2020). arXiv:2004.10619

Probabilistic Timed Automata with One Clock and Initialised Clock-Dependent Probabilities

Jeremy Sproston[✉]

Dipartimento di Informatica, University of Turin, Turin, Italy
Sproston@di.unito.it

Abstract. Clock-dependent probabilistic timed automata extend classical timed automata with discrete probabilistic choice, where the probabilities are allowed to depend on the exact values of the clocks. Previous work has shown that the quantitative reachability problem for clock-dependent probabilistic timed automata with at least three clocks is undecidable. In this paper, we consider the subclass of clock-dependent probabilistic timed automata that have *one clock*, that have clock dependencies described by affine functions, and that satisfy an *initialisation* condition requiring that, at some point between taking edges with non-trivial clock dependencies, the clock must have an integer value. We present an approach for solving in polynomial time quantitative and qualitative reachability problems of such one-clock initialised clock-dependent probabilistic timed automata. Our results are obtained by a transformation to interval Markov decision processes.

1 Introduction

The diffusion of complex systems with timing requirements that operate in unpredictable environments has led to interest in formal modelling and verification techniques for timed and probabilistic systems. One such formal verification technique is *model checking* [3,12], in which a system model is verified automatically against formally-specified properties. A well-established modelling formalism for timed systems is *timed automata* [2]. A timed automaton consists of a finite graph equipped with a set of real-valued variables called *clocks*, which increase at the same rate as real-time and which can be used to constrain the relative time of events. To model formally probabilistic systems, frameworks such as Markov chains or Markov decision processes are used typically. Model-checking algorithms for these formalisms have been presented in the literature: for overviews of these techniques see, for example, [7] for timed automata, and [3,14] for Markov chains and Markov decision processes. Furthermore, timed automata and Markov decision processes have been combined to obtain the formalism of *probabilistic timed automata* [16,25,28], which can be viewed as timed automata with probabilities associated with their edges (or, equivalently, as Markov decision processes equipped with clocks and their associated constraints).

© IFIP International Federation for Information Processing 2020
Published by Springer Nature Switzerland AG 2020
A. Gotsman and A. Sokolova (Eds.): FORTE 2020, LNCS 12136, pp. 150–168, 2020.
https://doi.org/10.1007/978-3-030-50086-3_9

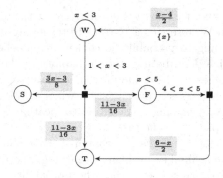

Fig. 1. An example of one-clock clock-dependent probabilistic automaton $\mathcal{P}$.

For the modelling of certain systems, it may be advantageous to model the fact that the probability of some events, in particular those concerning the environment in which the system is operating, vary as time passes. For example, in automotive and aeronautic contexts, the probability of certain reactions of human operators may depend on factors such as fatigue, which can increase over time (see, for example, [13]); an increase in the amount of time that an unmanned aerial vehicle spends performing a search and rescue operation in a hazardous zone may increase the probability that the vehicle incurs damage from the environment; an increase in the time elapsed before a metro train arrives at a station can result in an increase in the number of passengers on the station's platform, which can in turn increase the probability of the doors failing to shut at the station, due to overcrowding of the train (see [4]). A natural way of representing such a dependency of probability of events on time is using a continuous function: for example, for the case in which a task can be completed between 1 and 3 time units in the future, we could represent the successful completion of the task by probability $\frac{x+1}{4}$, where the clock variable x (measuring the amount of time elapsed) ranges over the interval $[1, 3]$. The standard probabilistic timed automaton formalism cannot express such a continuous relationship between probabilities and time, being limited to step functions (where the intervals along which the function is constant have rational-numbered endpoints). This limitation led to the development of an extension of probabilistic timed automata called clock-dependent probabilistic timed automata [32], in which the probabilities of crossing edges can depend on clock values according to piecewise constant functions. Figure 1 gives an example of such a clock-dependent probabilistic timed automaton, using the standard conventions for the graphical representation of (probabilistic) timed automata (the model has one clock denoted by x, and black boxes denote probabilistic choices over outgoing edges). In location W, the system is *working* on a task, which is completed after between 1 and 3 units of time. When the task is completed, it is either *successful* (edge to location S), *fails* (edge to location F) or leads to system *termination* (edge to location T). For the case in which the task completion fails, between 4 and 5 time units after work on the task started the system may either try again to work on the task (edge to location W, resetting x to 0) or to terminate (edge to location T). The edges corresponding to probabilistic choices are labelled with *expressions* over the clock x, which describe how the probability of those edges changes in accordance with changes in the value of x. For example, the longer the time spent in location W, the higher the value of x when location W is left, and the higher the probability of making a transition to location S, which corresponds to the successful completion of the task.

Previous work on clock-dependent probabilistic timed automata showed that a basic *quantitative* reachability problem (regarding whether there is a scheduler of nondeterministic choice such that the probability of reaching a set of target locations exceeds some probability threshold) is undecidable, but that an approach based on the region graph can be employed to approximate optimal reachability probabilities [32]. The undecidability result relied on the presence of at least three clocks: in this paper, following similar precedents in the context of (non-probabilistic and probabilistic) variants of timed automata (for example, [1,5,6,8,23,26]), we restrict our attention to clock-dependent probabilistic timed automata with a *single* clock variable. As in [32], we consider the case in which the dependencies of transition probabilities on the value of the clock are described by affine functions. Furthermore, we assume that, between any two edges with a non-constant dependence on the clock, the clock must have a natural-numbered value, either through being reset to 0 or by increasing as time passes. We call this condition *initialisation*, following the precedents of [1] and [21], in which similar conditions are used to obtain decidability results for stochastic timed systems with one clock, and hybrid automata, respectively; intuitively, the value of the clock is "reinitialised" (either explicitly, through a reset to 0, or implicitly, through the passage of time) to a known, natural value between non-constant dependencies of probability on the value of the clock. Note that the clock-dependent probabilistic timed automaton of Fig. 1 satisfies this assumption (although clock x is not reset on the edge to location F, it must take values 3 and 4 before location F can be left). We show that, for such clock-dependent probabilistic timed automata, quantitative reachability problems can be solved in polynomial time. Similarly, we can also solve in polynomial time *qualitative* reachability problems, which ask whether there exists a scheduler of nondeterminism such that a set of target locations can be reached with probability 1 (or 0), or whether all schedulers of nondeterminism result in the target locations being reached with probability 1 (or 0).

These results rely on the construction of an *interval Markov decision process* from the one-clock clock-dependent probabilistic timed automaton. Interval Markov decision processes have been well-studied in the verification context (for example, in [17,20,30]), and also in other contexts, such as planning [15] and control [27,36]. They comprise a finite state space where transitions between states are achieved in the following manner: for each state, there is a nondeterministic choice between a set of actions, where each action is associated with a decoration of the set of edges from the state with *intervals* in [0, 1]; then a nondeterministic choice as to the exact probabilties associated with each outgoing edge is chosen from the intervals associated with the action chosen in the first step; finally, a probabilistic choice is made over the edges according to the probabilities chosen in the second step, thus determining the next state. In contrast to the standard formulation of interval Markov decision processes, we allow edges corresponding to probabilistic choices to be labelled not only with closed intervals, but also with open and half-open intervals. While (half-)open intervals have been considered previously in the context of interval Markov chains in [9,33], we are unaware of any work considering them in the context of interval Markov decision processes. The presence of open intervals is vital to obtain a precise representation of the one-clock clock-dependent probabilistic timed automaton.

We proceed by giving some preliminary concepts in Sect. 2: this includes a reduction from interval Markov decision processes to interval Markov chains [22, 24,31] with the standard Markov decision process-based semantics, which may be of independent interest. The reduction takes open and half-open intervals into account; while [9] has shown that open interval Markov chains can be reduced to closed Markov chains for the purposes of quantitative properties, [33] shows that the open/closed distinction is critical for the evaluation of qualitative properties. In Sect. 3, we present the definition of one-clock clock-dependent probabilistic timed automata, and present the transformation to interval Markov decision processes in Sect. 4. Proofs of the results can be found in [34].

2   Interval Markov Decision Processes

Preliminaries. We use $\mathbb{R}_{\geq 0}$ to denote the set of non-negative real numbers, $\mathbb{Q}$ to denote the set of rational numbers, and $\mathbb{N}$ to denote the set of natural numbers. A (discrete) probability *distribution* over a countable set Q is a function $\mu : Q \to [0,1]$ such that $\sum_{q \in Q} \mu(q) = 1$. Let $\mathsf{Dist}(Q)$ be the set of distributions over Q. For a (possibly uncountable) set Q and a function $\mu : Q \to [0,1]$, we define $\mathsf{support}(\mu) = \{q \in Q \mid \mu(q) > 0\}$. Then, for an uncountable set Q, we define $\mathsf{Dist}(Q)$ to be the set of functions $\mu : Q \to [0,1]$ such that $\mathsf{support}(\mu)$ is a countable set and μ restricted to $\mathsf{support}(\mu)$ is a distribution. Given a binary function $f : Q \times Q \to [0,1]$ and element $q \in Q$, we denote by $f(q, \cdot) : Q \to [0,1]$ the unary function such that $f(q, \cdot)(q') = f(q, q')$ for each $q' \in Q$.

A *Markov chain* (MC) $\mathcal{C}$ is a pair $(S, \mathbf{P})$ where S is a set of *states* and $\mathbf{P} : S \times S \to [0,1]$ is a *transition probability function*, such that $\mathbf{P}(s, \cdot) \in \mathsf{Dist}(S)$ for each state $s \in S$. A *path* of MC $\mathcal{C}$ is a sequence $s_0 s_1 \cdots$ of states such that $\mathbf{P}(s_i, s_{i+1}) > 0$ for all $i \geq 0$. Given a path $\mathbf{r} = s_0 s_1 \cdots$ and $i \geq 0$, we let $\mathbf{r}(i) = s_i$ be the $(i+1)$-th state along $\mathbf{r}$. The set of paths of $\mathcal{C}$ starting in state $s \in S$ is denoted by $Paths^{\mathcal{C}}(s)$. In the standard manner (see, for example, [3,14]), given a state $s \in S$, we can define a probability measure $\mathrm{Pr}_s^{\mathcal{C}}$ over $Paths^{\mathcal{C}}(s)$.

A *Markov decision process* (MDP) $\mathcal{M} = (S, A, \Delta)$ comprises a set S of *states*, a set A of *actions*, and a *probabilistic transition function* $\Delta : S \times A \to \mathsf{Dist}(S) \cup \{\bot\}$. The symbol $\bot$ is used to represent the unavailability of an action in a state, i.e., $\Delta(s, a) = \bot$ signifies that action $a \in A$ is not available in state $s \in S$.

For each state $s \in S$, let $A(s) = \{a \in A \mid \Delta(s,a) \neq \perp\}$, and assume that $A(s) \neq \emptyset$, i.e., there is at least one available action in each state. Transitions from state to state of an MDP are performed in two steps: if the current state is s, the first step concerns a nondeterministic selection of an action $a \in A(s)$; the second step comprises a probabilistic choice, made according to the distribution $\Delta(s,a)$, as to which state to make the transition (that is, a transition to a state $s' \in S$ is made with probability $\Delta(s,a)(s')$). In general, the sets of states and actions can be uncountable. We say that an MDP is *finite* if S and A are finite sets.

A(n infinite) *path* of an MDP $\mathcal{M}$ is a sequence $s_0 a_0 s_1 a_1 \cdots$ such that $a_i \in A(s_i)$ and $\Delta(s_i, \mu_i)(s_{i+1}) > 0$ for all $i \geq 0$. Given an infinite path $\mathbf{r} = s_0 a_0 s_1 a_1 \cdots$ and $i \geq 0$, we let $\mathbf{r}(i) = s_i$ be the $(i+1)$-th state along $\mathbf{r}$. Let $Paths^{\mathcal{M}}$ be the set of infinite paths of $\mathcal{M}$. A finite path is a sequence $r = s_0 a_0 s_1 a_1 \cdots a_{n-1} s_n$ such that $a_i \in A(s_i)$ and $\Delta(s_i, \mu_i)(s_{i+1}) > 0$ for all $0 \leq i < n$. Let $last(r) = s_n$ denote the final state of r. We use ras to denote the finite path $s_0 a_0 s_1 a_1 \cdots a_{n-1} s_n as$. Let $Paths_*^{\mathcal{M}}$ be the set of finite paths of the MDP $\mathcal{M}$. Let $Paths^{\mathcal{M}}(s)$ and $Paths_*^{\mathcal{M}}(s)$ be the sets of infinite paths and finite paths, respectively, of $\mathcal{M}$ starting in state $s \in S$.

A *scheduler* is a function $\sigma : Paths_*^{\mathcal{M}} \to \bigcup_{s \in S} \mathrm{Dist}(A(s))$ such that $\sigma(r) \in \mathrm{Dist}(A(last(r)))$ for all $r \in Paths_*^{\mathcal{M}}$.[1] Let $\Sigma^{\mathcal{M}}$ be the set of schedulers of the MDP $\mathcal{M}$. We say that infinite path $\mathbf{r} = s_0 a_0 s_1 a_1 \cdots$ is *generated* by σ if $\sigma(s_0 a_0 s_1 a_1 \cdots a_{i-1} s_i)(a_i) > 0$ for all $i \in \mathbb{N}$. Let $Paths^{\sigma}$ be the set of paths generated by σ. The set $Paths_*^{\sigma}$ of finite paths generated by σ is defined similarly. Let $Paths^{\sigma}(s) = Paths^{\sigma} \cap Paths^{\mathcal{M}}(s)$ and $Paths_*^{\sigma}(s) = Paths_*^{\sigma} \cap Paths_*^{\mathcal{M}}(s)$. Given a scheduler $\sigma \in \Sigma^{\mathcal{M}}$, we can define a countably infinite-state MC $\mathcal{C}^{\sigma}$ that corresponds to the behaviour of the scheduler σ: we let $\mathcal{C}^{\sigma} = (Paths_*^{\sigma}, \mathbf{P})$, where, for $r, r' \in Paths_*^{\sigma}$, we have $\mathbf{P}(r, r') = \sigma(r)(a) \cdot \Delta(last(r), a)(s)$ if $r' = ras$ and $a \in A(last(r))$, and $\mathbf{P}(r, r') = 0$ otherwise. For $r = s_0 a_0 s_1 a_1 \cdots a_{n-1} s_n$, we denote the $(i+1)$-th prefix of r by r_i, i.e., $r_i = s_0 a_0 s_1 a_1 \cdots a_{i-1} s_i$, for $i \leq n$. Then, given $s \in S$ and $r \in Paths_*^{\sigma}$, we let $\mathrm{Pr}_{*,s}^{\sigma}(r) = \mathbf{P}(r_0, r_1) \cdot \ldots \cdot \mathbf{P}(r_{n-1}, r_n)$. Let $\mathrm{Cyl}(r) \subseteq Paths^{\mathcal{M}}(s)$ be the set of infinite paths starting in s that have the finite path r as a prefix. Then we let Pr_s^{σ} be the unique probability measure over $Paths^{\sigma}(s)$ such that $\mathrm{Pr}_s^{\sigma}(\mathrm{Cyl}(r)) = \mathrm{Pr}_{*,s}^{\sigma}(r)$ (for more details, see [3,14]).

Given a set $T \subseteq S$, we define $\Diamond T = \{\mathbf{r} \in Paths^{\mathcal{M}} \mid \exists i \in \mathbb{N} . \mathbf{r}(i) \in T\}$ as the set of infinite runs of $\mathcal{M}$ such that some state of T is visited along the run. Let $s \in S$. We define the *maximum probability of reaching T from s* as $\mathbb{P}_{\mathcal{M},s}^{\max}(\Diamond T) = \sup_{\sigma \in \Sigma^{\mathcal{M}}} \mathrm{Pr}_s^{\sigma}(\Diamond T)$. Similarly, the *minimum probability of reaching T from s* is defined as $\mathbb{P}_{\mathcal{M},s}^{\min}(\Diamond T) = \inf_{\sigma \in \Sigma^{\mathcal{M}}} \mathrm{Pr}_s^{\sigma}(\Diamond T)$. The *maximal reachability problem* for $\mathcal{M}$, $T \subseteq S$, $s \in S$, $\unrhd \in \{\geq, >\}$ and $\lambda \in [0,1]$ is to decide whether $\mathbb{P}_{\mathcal{M},s}^{\max}(\Diamond T) \unrhd \lambda$. Similarly, the *minimal reachability problem* for $\mathcal{M}$, $T \subseteq S$, $s \in S$, $\unlhd \in \{\leq, <\}$ and $\lambda \in [0,1]$ is to decide whether $\mathbb{P}_{\mathcal{M},s}^{\min}(\Diamond T) \unlhd \lambda$. The maximal and minimal reachability problems are called *quantitative* problems. We also consider

---

[1] From [18, Lemma 4.10], without loss of generality we can assume henceforth that schedulers map to distributions assigning positive probability to *finite* sets of actions, i.e., schedulers σ for which $|\mathrm{support}(\sigma(r))|$ is finite for all $r \in Paths_*^{\mathcal{M}}$.

the following *qualitative* problems: ($\forall 0$) decide whether $\Pr_s^\sigma(\Diamond T) = 0$ for all $\sigma \in \Sigma^\mathcal{M}$; ($\exists 0$) decide whether there exists $\sigma \in \Sigma^\mathcal{M}$ such that $\Pr_s^\sigma(\Diamond T) = 0$; ($\exists 1$) decide whether there exists $\sigma \in \Sigma^\mathcal{M}$ such that $\Pr_s^\sigma(\Diamond T) = 1$; ($\forall 1$) decide whether $\Pr_s^\sigma(\Diamond T) = 1$ for all $\sigma \in \Sigma^\mathcal{M}$.

Interval Markov Chains. We let $\mathcal{I}$ denote the set of (open, half-open or closed) intervals that are subsets of $[0, 1]$ and that have rational-numbered endpoints. Given an interval $I \in \mathcal{I}$, we let $\mathsf{left}(I)$ (respectively, $\mathsf{right}(I)$) be the left (respectively, right) endpoint of I. Note that $\mathsf{left}(I), \mathsf{right}(I) \in [0, 1] \cap \mathbb{Q}$.

An *interval distribution* over a finite set Q is a function $\mathfrak{d} : Q \to \mathcal{I}$ such that (1) $\sum_{q \in Q} \mathsf{left}(\mathfrak{d}(q)) \leq 1 \leq \sum_{q \in Q} \mathsf{right}(\mathfrak{d}(q))$, (2a) $\sum_{q \in Q} \mathsf{left}(\mathfrak{d}(q)) = 1$ implies that $\mathfrak{d}(q)$ is left-closed for all $q \in Q$, and (2b) $\sum_{q \in Q} \mathsf{right}(\mathfrak{d}(q)) = 1$ implies that $\mathfrak{d}(q)$ is right-closed for all $q \in Q$. We define $\mathfrak{Dist}(Q)$ as the set of interval distributions over Q. An *assignment for interval distribution* $\mathfrak{d}$ is a distribution $\alpha \in \mathsf{Dist}(Q)$ such that $\alpha(q) \in \mathfrak{d}(q)$ for each $q \in Q$. Note that conditions (1), (2a) and (2b) in the definition of interval distributions guarantee that there exists at least one assignment for each interval distribution. Let $\mathfrak{G}(\mathfrak{d})$ be the set of assignments for $\mathfrak{d}$.

An (open) *interval Markov chain* (IMC) $\mathfrak{C}$ is a pair $(S, \mathfrak{P})$, where S is a finite set of *states*, and $\mathfrak{P} : S \times S \to \mathcal{I}$ is a *interval-based transition function* such that $\mathfrak{P}(s, \cdot)$ is an interval distribution for each $s \in S$ (formally, $\mathfrak{P}(s, \cdot) \in \mathfrak{Dist}(S)$). An IMC makes a transition from a state $s \in S$ in two steps: first an assignment α is chosen from the set $\mathfrak{G}(\mathfrak{P}(s, \cdot))$ of assignments for $\mathfrak{P}(s, \cdot)$, then a probabilistic choice over target states is made according to α. The semantics of an IMC corresponds to an MDP that has the same state space as the IMC, and for which each state is associated with a set of distributions, the precise transition probabilities of which are chosen from the interval distribution of the state. Formally, the semantics of an IMC $\mathfrak{C} = (S, \mathfrak{P})$ is the MDP $[\![\mathfrak{C}]\!] = (S, \mathfrak{G}(\mathfrak{P}), \Delta)$, where $\mathfrak{G}(\mathfrak{P}) = \bigcup_{s \in S} \mathfrak{G}(\mathfrak{P}(s, \cdot))$, and for which $\Delta(s, \alpha) = \alpha$ for all states $s \in S$ and assignments $\alpha \in \mathfrak{G}(\mathfrak{P}(s, \cdot))$ for $\mathfrak{P}(s, \cdot)$. In previous literature (for example, [10,11,31]), this semantics is called the "IMDP semantics".

Computing $\mathbb{P}_{[\![\mathfrak{C}]\!], s}^{\max}(\Diamond T)$ and $\mathbb{P}_{[\![\mathfrak{C}]\!], s}^{\min}(\Diamond T)$ can be done for an IMC $\mathfrak{C}$ simply by transforming the IMC by closing all of its (half-)open intervals, then employing a standard maximum/minimum reachability probability computation on the new, "closed" IMC (for example, the algorithms of [11,31]): the correctness of this approach is shown in [9]. Algorithms for qualitative problems of IMCs (with open, half-open and closed intervals) are given in [33]. All of the aforementioned algorithms run in polynomial time in the size of the IMC, which is obtained as the sum over all states $s, s' \in S$ of the binary representation of the endpoints of $\mathfrak{P}(s, s')$, where rational numbers are encoded as the quotient of integers written in binary.

Interval Markov Decision Processes. An (open) *interval Markov decision process* (IMDP) $\mathfrak{M} = (S, \mathfrak{A}, \mathfrak{D})$ comprises a finite set S of states, a finite set $\mathfrak{A}$ of actions, and an *interval-based transition function* $\mathfrak{D} : S \times \mathfrak{A} \to \mathfrak{Dist}(S) \cup \{\bot\}$.

Let $\mathfrak{A}(s) = \{\mathfrak{a} \in \mathfrak{A} \mid \mathfrak{D}(s, \mathfrak{a}) \neq \bot\}$, and assume that $\mathfrak{A}(s) \neq \emptyset$ for each state $s \in S$. In contrast to IMCs, an IMDP makes a transition from a state $s \in S$ in *three* steps: (1) an action $\mathfrak{a} \in \mathfrak{A}(s)$ is chosen, then (2) an assignment α for $\mathfrak{D}(s, \mathfrak{a})$ is chosen, and finally (3) a probabilistic choice over target states to make the transition to is performed according to α. Formally, the semantics of an IMDP $\mathfrak{M} = (S, \mathfrak{A}, \mathfrak{D})$ is the MDP $[\![\mathfrak{M}]\!] = (S, A, \Delta)$ where $A(s) = \{(\mathfrak{a}, \alpha) \in \mathfrak{A} \times \mathrm{Dist}(S) \mid \mathfrak{a} \in \mathfrak{A}(s) \text{ and } \alpha \in \mathfrak{G}(\mathfrak{D}(s, \mathfrak{a}))\}$ for each state $s \in S$, and $\Delta(s, (\mathfrak{a}, \alpha)) = \alpha$ for each state $s \in S$ and action/assignment pair $(\mathfrak{a}, \alpha) \in A(s)$. Note that (as in, for example, [17,20,30]) we adopt a *cooperative* resolution of nondeterminism for IMDPs, in which the choice of action and assignment (steps (1) and (2) above) is combined into a *single* nondeterministic choice in the semantic MDP.

— Given the cooperative nondeterminism for IMDPs, we can show that, given an IMDP, an IMC can be constructed such that the maximal and minimal reachability probabilities for the IMDP and IMC coincide, and furthermore qualitative properties agree on the IMDP and the IMC. Formally, given the IMDP $\mathfrak{M} = (S, \mathfrak{A}, \mathfrak{D})$, we construct an IMC $\mathfrak{C}[\mathfrak{M}] = (\tilde{S}, \tilde{\mathfrak{P}})$ in the following way:

- the set of states is defined as $\tilde{S} = S \cup (S \otimes \mathfrak{A})$, where $S \otimes \mathfrak{A} = \bigcup_{s \in S} \{(s, \mathfrak{a}) \in S \times \mathfrak{A} \mid \mathfrak{a} \in \mathfrak{A}(s)\}$;
- for $s \in S$ and $\mathfrak{a} \in \mathfrak{A}(s)$, let $\tilde{\mathfrak{P}}(s, (s, \mathfrak{a})) = [0, 1]$, and let $\tilde{\mathfrak{P}}((s, \mathfrak{a}), \cdot) = \mathfrak{D}(s, \mathfrak{a})$.

The following proposition states the correctness of this construction with respect to quantitative and qualitative problems.

Proposition 1. *Let $\mathfrak{M} = (S, \mathfrak{A}, \mathfrak{D})$ be an IMDP, and let $s \in S$, $T \subseteq S$ and $\lambda \in \{0, 1\}$. Then:*

- $\mathbb{P}_{[\![\mathfrak{M}]\!],s}^{\max}(\Diamond T) = \mathbb{P}_{[\![\mathfrak{C}[\mathfrak{M}]]\!],s}^{\max}(\Diamond T)$ *and* $\mathbb{P}_{[\![\mathfrak{M}]\!],s}^{\min}(\Diamond T) = \mathbb{P}_{[\![\mathfrak{C}[\mathfrak{M}]]\!],s}^{\min}(\Diamond T)$;
- *there exists* $\sigma \in \Sigma^{[\![\mathfrak{M}]\!]}$ *such that* $\mathrm{Pr}_s^{\sigma}(\Diamond T) = \lambda$ *if and only if there exists* $\sigma' \in \Sigma^{[\![\mathfrak{C}[\mathfrak{M}]]\!]}$ *such that* $\mathrm{Pr}_s^{\sigma'}(\Diamond T) = \lambda$;
- $\mathrm{Pr}_s^{\sigma}(\Diamond T) = \lambda$ *for all* $\sigma \in \Sigma^{[\![\mathfrak{M}]\!]}$ *if and only if* $\mathrm{Pr}_s^{\sigma'}(\Diamond T) = \lambda$ *for all* $\sigma' \in \Sigma^{[\![\mathfrak{C}[\mathfrak{M}]]\!]}$.

3   Clock-Dependent Probabilistic Timed Automata with One Clock

In this section, we introduce the formalism of clock-dependent probabilistic timed automata. The definition of clock-dependent probabilistic timed automata of [32] features an arbitrary number of clock variables. In contrast, we consider models with only *one* clock variable, which will be denoted x for the remainder of the paper.

A *clock valuation* is a value $v \in \mathbb{R}_{\geq 0}$, interpreted as the current value of clock x. Following the usual notational conventions for modelling formalisms based on timed automata, for clock valuation $v \in \mathbb{R}_{\geq 0}$ and $X \in \{\{x\}, \emptyset\}$, we write $v[X := 0]$ to denote the clock valuation in which clocks in X are reset to 0; in the one-clock setting, we have $v[\{x\}:=0] = 0$ and $v[\emptyset:=0] = v$. In the following, we write $2^{\{x\}}$ rather than $\{\{x\}, \emptyset\}$.

The set Ψ of *clock constraints* over x is defined as the set of conjunctions over atomic formulae of the form $x \sim c$, where $\sim \in \{<, \leq, \geq, >\}$ and $c \in \mathbb{N}$. A clock valuation v satisfies a clock constraint ψ, denoted by $v \models \psi$, if ψ resolves to **true** when substituting each occurrence of clock x with v.

For a set Q, a *distribution template* $\wp : \mathbb{R}_{\geq 0} \to \mathsf{Dist}(Q)$ gives a distribution over Q for each clock valuation. In the following, we use notation $\wp[v]$, rather than $\wp(v)$, to denote the distribution corresponding to distribution template $\wp$ and clock valuation v. Let $\mathsf{Temp}(Q)$ be the set of distribution templates over Q.

A *one-clock clock-dependent probabilistic timed automaton* (1c-cdPTA) $\mathcal{P} = (L, inv, prob)$ comprises the following components:

- a finite set L of *locations*;
- a function $inv : L \to \Psi$ associating an *invariant condition* with each location;
- a set $prob \subseteq L \times \Psi \times \mathsf{Temp}(2^{\{x\}} \times L)$ of *probabilistic edges*.

A probabilistic edge $(l, g, \wp) \in prob$ comprises: (1) a source location l; (2) a clock constraint g, called a *guard*; and (3) a distribution template $\wp$ with respect to pairs of the form $(X, l') \in 2^{\{x\}} \times L$ (i.e., pairs consisting of a first element indicating whether x should be reset to 0 or not, and a second element corresponding to a target location l'). We refer to pairs $(X, l') \in 2^{\{x\}} \times L$ as *outcomes*.

The behaviour of a 1c-cdPTA takes a similar form to that of a standard (one-clock) probabilistic timed automaton [16,23,25]: in any location time can advance as long as the invariant condition holds, and the choice as to how much time elapses is made nondeterministically; a probabilistic edge can be taken if its guard is satisfied by the current value of the clock, and the choice as to which probabilistic edge to take is made nondeterministically; for a taken probabilistic edge, the choice of whether to reset the clock and which target location to make the transition to is *probabilistic*. In comparison with one-clock probabilistic timed automata, the key novelty of 1c-cdPTAs is that the distribution used to make this probabilistic choice depends on the probabilistic edge taken *and* on the current clock valuation.

A *state* of a 1c-cdPTA is a pair comprising a location and a clock valuation satisfying the location's invariant condition, i.e., $(l, v) \in L \times \mathbb{R}_{\geq 0}$ such that $v \models inv(l)$. In any state (l, v), a certain amount of time $t \in \mathbb{R}_{\geq 0}$ elapses, then a probabilistic edge is traversed. The choice of t requires that the invariant $inv(l)$ remains continuously satisfied while time passes. The resulting state after the elapse of time is $(l, v+t)$. A probabilistic edge $(l', g, \wp) \in prob$ can then be chosen from $(l, v + t)$ if $l = l'$ and it is *enabled*, i.e., the clock constraint g is satisfied by $v + t$. Once a probabilistic edge $(l, g, \wp)$ is chosen, a successor location, and whether to reset the clock to 0, is chosen at random, according to the distribution $\wp[v + t]$.

We make the following assumptions on 1c-cdPTAs, in order to simplify the definition of their semantics. Firstly, we consider 1c-cdPTAs featuring invariant conditions that prevent the clock from exceeding some bound, and impose no lower bound: formally, for each location $l \in L$, we have that $inv(l)$ is a constraint

$x \leq c$ for some $c \in \mathbb{N}$, or a constraint $x < c$ for some $c \in \mathbb{N} \setminus \{0\}$. Secondly, we restrict our attention to 1c-cdPTAs for which it is always possible to take a probabilistic edge, either immediately or after letting time elapse. Formally, for each location $l \in L$, if $inv(l) = (x \leq c)$ then (viewing c as a clock valuation) $c \models g$ for some $(l, g, \wp) \in prob$; instead, if $inv(l) = (x < c)$ then $c - \varepsilon \models g$ for all $\varepsilon \in (0, 1)$ and $(l, g, \wp) \in prob$. Thirdly, we assume that all possible target states of probabilistic edges satisfy their invariants. Observe that, given the first assumption, this may not be the case only when the clock is *not* reset. Formally, for all probabilistic edges $(l, g, \wp) \in prob$, for all clock valuations $v \in \mathbb{R}_{\geq 0}$ such that $v \models g$, and for all $l' \in L$, we have that $\wp[v](\emptyset, l') > 0$ implies $v[\emptyset :=0] \models inv(l')$, i.e., $v \models inv(l')$. Note that we relax some of these assumptions when depicting 1c-cdPTAs graphically (for example, the 1c-cdPTA of Fig. 1 can be made to satisfy these assumptions by adding invariant conditions and self-looping probabilistic edges to locations S and T).

The semantics of the 1c-cdPTA $\mathcal{P} = (L, inv, prob)$ is the MDP $[\![\mathcal{P}]\!] = (S, A, \Delta)$ where:

- $S = \{(l, v) \in L \times \mathbb{R}_{\geq 0} \mid v \models inv(l)\}$;
- $A = \mathbb{R}_{\geq 0} \times prob$;
- for $(l, v) \in S$, $\tilde{v} \in \mathbb{R}_{\geq 0}$ and $(l, g, \wp) \in prob$ such that (1) $\tilde{v} \geq v$, (2) $\tilde{v} \models g$ and (3) $w \models inv(l)$ for all $v \leq w \leq \tilde{v}$, then we let $\Delta((l, v), (\tilde{v}, (l, g, \wp)))$ be the distribution such that, for $(l', v') \in S$:

$$\Delta((l, v), (\tilde{v}, (l, g, \wp)))(l', v') = \begin{cases} \wp[\tilde{v}](\{x\}, l') + \wp[\tilde{v}](\emptyset, l') & \text{if } v' = \tilde{v} = 0 \\ \wp[\tilde{v}](\emptyset, l') & \text{if } v' = \tilde{v} > 0 \\ \wp[\tilde{v}](\{x\}, l') & \text{if } v' = 0 \text{ and } \tilde{v} > 0 \\ 0 & \text{otherwise.} \end{cases}$$

Let $F \subseteq L$ be a set of locations, and let $T_F = \{(l, v) \in S \mid l \in F\}$ be the set of states of $[\![\mathcal{P}]\!]$ that have their location component in F. Then the maximum value of reaching F from state $(l, v) \in S$ corresponds to $\mathbb{P}^{\max}_{[\![\mathcal{P}]\!],(l,v)}(\Diamond T_F)$. Similarly, the minimum value of reaching F from state $(l, v) \in S$ corresponds to $\mathbb{P}^{\min}_{[\![\mathcal{P}]\!],(l,v)}(\Diamond T_F)$. As in Sect. 2, we can define a number of quantitative and qualitative reachability problems on 1c-cdPTA, where the initial state is set as $(l, 0)$ for a particular $l \in L$. The maximal reachability problem for $\mathcal{P}$, $F \subseteq L$, $l \in L$, $\trianglerighteq \in \{\geq, >\}$ and $\lambda \in [0, 1]$ is to decide whether $\mathbb{P}^{\max}_{[\![\mathcal{P}]\!],(l,0)}(\Diamond T_F) \trianglerighteq \lambda$; similarly, the minimal reachability problem for $\mathcal{P}$, $F \subseteq L$, $l \in L$, $\trianglelefteq \in \{\leq, <\}$ and $\lambda \in [0, 1]$ is to decide whether $\mathbb{P}^{\min}_{[\![\mathcal{P}]\!],(l,0)}(\Diamond T_F) \trianglelefteq \lambda$. Furthermore, we can define analogues of the qualitative problems featured in Sect. 2: ($\forall 0$) decide whether $\Pr^{\sigma}_{(l,0)}(\Diamond T_F) = 0$ for all $\sigma \in \Sigma^{[\![\mathcal{P}]\!]}$; ($\exists 0$) decide whether there exists $\sigma \in \Sigma^{[\![\mathcal{P}]\!]}$ such that $\Pr^{\sigma}_{(l,0)}(\Diamond T_F) = 0$; ($\exists 1$) decide whether there exists $\sigma \in \Sigma^{[\![\mathcal{P}]\!]}$ such that $\Pr^{\sigma}_{(l,0)}(\Diamond T_F) = 1$; ($\forall 1$) decide whether $\Pr^{\sigma}_{(l,0)}(\Diamond T_F) = 1$ for all $\sigma \in \Sigma^{[\![\mathcal{P}]\!]}$.

Affine Clock Dependencies. In this paper, we consider distribution templates that are defined in terms of sets of affine functions in the following way.

Given probabilistic edge $p = (l, g, \wp) \in prob$, let I^p be the set of clock valuations in which p is enabled, i.e., $I^p = \{v \in \mathbb{R}_{\geq 0} \mid v \models g \wedge inv(l)\}$. Note that $I^p \subseteq \mathbb{R}_{\geq 0}$ corresponds to an interval with natural-numbered endpoints. Let $\overline{I^p}$ be the closure of I^p. We say that p is *affine* if, for each $e \in 2^{\{x\}} \times L$, there exists a pair $(c_e^p, d_e^p) \in \mathbb{Q}^2$ of rational constants, such that $\wp[v](e) = c_e^p + d_e^p \cdot v$ for all $v \in \overline{I^p}$. Note that, by the definition of distribution templates, for all $v \in \overline{I^p}$, we have $c_e^p + d_e^p \cdot v \geq 0$ for each $e \in 2^{\{x\}} \times L$, and $\sum_{e \in 2^{\{x\}} \times L} (c_e^p + d_e^p \cdot v) = 1$. A 1c-cdPTA is affine if all of its probabilistic edges are affine. Henceforth we assume that the 1c-cdPTAs we consider are affine. An affine probabilistic edge p is *constant* if, for each $e \in 2^{\{x\}} \times L$, we have $d_e^p = 0$, i.e., $\wp[v](e) = c_e^p$ for some $c_e^p \in \mathbb{Q}$, for all $v \in \overline{I^p}$. Note that, for a probabilistic edge $p \in prob$, outcome $e \in 2^{\{x\}} \times L$ and open interval $I \subseteq I^p$, if $d_e^p \neq 0$, then $\wp[v](e) > 0$ for all $v \in I$ (because the existence of $v_{=0} \in I$ such that $\wp[v_{=0}](e) = 0$, together with $d_e^p \neq 0$, would mean that there exists $v' \in I$ such that $\wp[v'](e) < 0$, which contradicts the definition of distribution templates).

Initialisation. In this paper, we also introduce a specific requirement for 1c-cdPTAs that allows us to analyse faithfully 1c-cdPTA using IMDPs in Sect. 4. A *symbolic path fragment* is a sequence $(l_0, g_0, \wp_0)(X_0, l_1)(l_1, g_1, \wp_1)$ $(X_1, l_2) \cdots (l_n, g_n, \wp_n) \in (prob \times (2^{\{x\}} \times L))^+ \times prob$ of probabilistic edges and outcomes such that $\wp_i[v](X_i, l_{i+1}) > 0$ for all $v \in I^{(l_i, g_i, \wp_i)}$ for all $i < n$. In this paper, we consider 1c-cdPTAs for which each symbolic path fragment that begins and ends with a non-constant probabilistic edge requires that the clock takes a natural numbered value, either from being reset or from passing through guards that have at most one (natural numbered) value in common. Formally, a 1c-cdPTA is *initialised* if, for any symbolic path fragment $(l_0, g_0, \wp_0)(X_0, l_1)(l_1, g_1, \wp_1)(X_1, l_2) \cdots (l_n, g_n, \wp_n)$ such that $(l_0, g_0, \wp_0)$ and $(l_n, g_n, \wp_n)$ are non-constant, either (1) $X_i = \{x\}$ or (2) $I^{(l_i, g_i, \wp_i)} \cap I^{(l_{i+1}, g_{i+1}, \wp_{i+1})}$ is empty or contains a single valuation, for some $0 < i < n$. We henceforth assume that all 1c-cdPTAs considered in this paper are initialised.

4   Translation from 1c-cdPTAs to IMDPs

In this section, we show that we can solve quantitative and qualitative problems of (affine and initialised) 1c-cdPTAs. In contrast to the approach for quantitative problems of multiple-clock cdPTAs presented in [32], which involves the construction of an *approximate* MDP, we represent the 1c-cdPTA *precisely* using an IMDP, by adapting the standard region-graph construction for one-clock (probabilistic) timed automata of [23, 26].

Let $\mathcal{P} = (L, inv, prob)$ be a 1c-cdPTA. Let $Cst(\mathcal{P})$ be the set of constants that are used in the guards of probabilistic edges and invariants of $\mathcal{P}$, and let $\mathbb{B} = Cst(\mathcal{P}) \cup \{0\}$. We write $\mathbb{B} = \{b_0, b_1, \ldots, b_k\}$, where $0 = b_0 < b_1 < \ldots < b_k$. The set $\mathbb{B}$ defines the set $\mathcal{I}_{\mathbb{B}} = \{[b_0, b_0], (b_0, b_1), [b_1, b_1], \cdots, [b_k, b_k]\}$. We define a total order on $\mathcal{I}_{\mathbb{B}}$ in the following way: $[b_0, b_0] < (b_0, b_1) < [b_1, b_1] < \cdots < [b_k, b_k]$. Given an open interval $B = (b, b') \in \mathcal{I}_{\mathbb{B}}$, its closure is written as $\overline{B}$, i.e.,

$\overline{B} = [b, b']$. Furthermore, let $\mathsf{lb}(B) = b$ and $\mathsf{rb}(B) = b'$ refer to the left- and right-endpoints of B. For a closed interval $[b, b] \in \mathcal{I}_{\mathbb{B}}$, we let $\mathsf{lb}(B) = \mathsf{rb}(B) = b$.

Let ψ be a guard of a probabilistic edge or an invariant of $\mathcal{P}$. By definition, we have that, for each $B \in \mathcal{I}_{\mathbb{B}}$, either $B \subseteq \{v \in \mathbb{R}_{\geq 0} \mid v \models \psi\}$ or $B \cap \{v \in \mathbb{R}_{\geq 0} \mid v \models \psi\} = \emptyset$. We write $B \models \psi$ in the case of $B \subseteq \{v \in \mathbb{R}_{\geq 0} \mid v \models \psi\}$ (to represent the fact that all valuations of B satisfy ψ).

Example 1. Consider the 1c-cdPTA of Fig. 1. We have $\mathbb{B} = \{0, 1, 3, 4, 5\}$ and $\mathcal{I}_{\mathbb{B}} = \{[0, 0], (0, 1), [1, 1], (1, 3), [3, 3], (3, 4), [4, 4], (4, 5), [5, 5]\}$. Consider the clock constraint $x < 3$: we have $B \models (x < 3)$ for all $B \in \{[0, 0], (0, 1), [1, 1], (1, 3)\}$. Similarly, for the clock constraint $4 < x < 5$, we have $(4, 5) \models (4 < x < 5)$.

$\mathbb{B}$-Minimal Schedulers. The following technical lemma specifies that any scheduler of the 1c-cdPTA can be made "more deterministic" in the following way: for each interval $\tilde{B} \in \mathcal{I}_{\mathbb{B}}$ and probabilistic edge $p \in prob$, if, after executing a certain finite path, a scheduler chooses (assigns positive probability to) multiple actions $(\tilde{v}_1, p), \cdots, (\tilde{v}_n, p)$ that share the same probabilistic edge p and for which $\tilde{v}_i \in \tilde{B}$ for all $1 \leq i \leq n$, then we can obtain another scheduler for which the aforementioned actions are replaced by an action $(\tilde{v}, p)$ such that $\tilde{v} \in \tilde{B}$. Formally, we say that a scheduler $\sigma \in \Sigma^{[\![\mathcal{P}]\!]}$ of $[\![\mathcal{P}]\!]$ is $\mathbb{B}$-*minimal* if, for all finite paths $r \in Paths_*^{[\![\mathcal{P}]\!]}$, for all probabilistic edges $p \in prob$, and for all pairs of actions $(\tilde{v}_1, p_1), (\tilde{v}_2, p_2) \in \mathsf{support}(\sigma(r))$, either $p_1 \neq p_2$ or v_1 and v_2 belong to distinct intervals in $\mathcal{I}_{\mathbb{B}}$, i.e., the intervals $\tilde{B}_1, \tilde{B}_2 \in \mathcal{I}_{\mathbb{B}}$ for which $\tilde{v}_1 \in \tilde{B}_1$ and $\tilde{v}_2 \in \tilde{B}_2$ are such that $\tilde{B}_1 \neq \tilde{B}_2$. Let $\Sigma_{\mathbb{B}}^{[\![\mathcal{P}]\!]}$ be the set of schedulers of $\Sigma^{[\![\mathcal{P}]\!]}$ that are $\mathbb{B}$-minimal.

Lemma 1. *Let $(l, v) \in S_{\mathcal{P}}$ and $F \subseteq L$. Then, for each $\sigma \in \Sigma^{[\![\mathcal{P}]\!]}$, there exists $\pi \in \Sigma_{\mathbb{B}}^{[\![\mathcal{P}]\!]}$ such that $\mathrm{Pr}_{(l,v)}^{\sigma}(\Diamond T_F) = \mathrm{Pr}_{(l,v)}^{\pi}(\Diamond T_F)$.*

The underlying idea of the proof of the lemma (which can be found in [34]) is that every finite path of π corresponds to a set of finite paths of σ, where all of these paths have the same length, visit the same locations in order, choose the same probabilistic edges in order, and visit the same intervals of clock valuations in order. Consider the choice of π after a finite path: to replicate the choices made at the end of the corresponding set of finite paths of σ, the choice of π is derived from a weighted average of the choices of σ, where the weights correspond to the probabilities of the finite paths of σ under consideration. Another key point for the construction of π is that, when a non-constant probabilistic edge is chosen, the clock valuation used by π when taking the probabilistic edge reflects the clock valuation used by σ when taking some probabilistic edge from the finite paths of σ under consideration: the clock valuation chosen by π is obtained as a weighted average of the clock valuations chosen by σ. Lemma 1 allows us to consider only $\mathbb{B}$-minimal schedulers in the sequel, permitting us to obtain a close correspondence between the schedulers of $[\![\mathcal{P}]\!]$ and the schedulers of the constructed IMDP, the definition of which we consider in the subsequent subsection.

Example 2. Consider the 1c-cdPTA of Fig. 1. In the following, we denote the outgoing probabilistic edges from W and F as p_W and p_F, respectively. Consider a scheduler $\sigma \in \Sigma^{[\![\mathcal{P}]\!]}$, where $\sigma(W, 0)$ (i.e., the choice of σ after the finite path comprising the single state $(W, 0)$) assigns probability $\frac{1}{2}$ to the action $(\frac{5}{4}, p_W)$ and probability $\frac{1}{2}$ to the action $(\frac{7}{4}, p_W)$ (where the two actions refer to either $\frac{5}{4}$ or $\frac{7}{4}$ time units elapsing, after which the probabilistic edge p_W is taken). Then we can construct a $\mathbb{B}$-minimal scheduler $\pi \in \Sigma_{\mathbb{B}}^{[\![\mathcal{P}]\!]}$ such that $\pi(W, 0)$ assigns probability 1 to the action $(\frac{3}{2}, p_W)$ (i.e., where $\frac{3}{2} = \frac{1}{2} \cdot \frac{5}{4} + \frac{1}{2} \cdot \frac{7}{4}$). Now consider finite paths $r = (W, 0)(\frac{5}{4}, p_W)(F, \frac{5}{4})$ and $r' = (W, 0)(\frac{7}{4}, p_W)(F, \frac{7}{4})$. Note that $\mathrm{Pr}^\sigma_{*,(W,0)}(r) = \frac{1}{2} \cdot \frac{11 - \frac{3 \cdot 5}{4}}{16}$ and $\mathrm{Pr}^\sigma_{*,(W,0)}(r') = \frac{1}{2} \cdot \frac{11 - \frac{3 \cdot 7}{4}}{16}$. Say that $\sigma(r)$ assigns probability 1 to $\frac{17}{4}$ and probability 1 to $\frac{19}{4}$. Then $\pi((W, 0)(\frac{3}{2}, p_W)(F, \frac{3}{2}))$ assigns probability 1 to action $(\tilde{v}, p_F)$, where $\tilde{v} = \mathrm{Pr}^\sigma_{*,(W,0)}(r) \cdot 1 \cdot \frac{17}{4} + \mathrm{Pr}^\sigma_{*,(W,0)}(r') \cdot 1 \cdot \frac{19}{4}$, i.e., a weighted sum of the time delays chosen by σ after r and r', where the weights correspond to the probabilities of r and r' under σ. Repeating this reasoning for all finite paths yields a $\mathbb{B}$-minimal scheduler π such that the probability of reaching a set of target states from $(W, 0)$ is the same for both σ and π.

IMDP Construction. We now present the idea of the IMDP construction. The states of the IMDP fall into two categories: (1) pairs comprising a location and an interval from $\mathcal{I}_\mathbb{B}$, with the intuition that the state $(l, B) \in L \times \mathcal{I}_\mathbb{B}$ of the IMDP represents all states (l, v) of $[\![\mathcal{P}]\!]$ such that $v \in B$; (2) triples comprising an interval from $\mathcal{I}_\mathbb{B}$, a probabilistic edge and a bit that specifies whether the state refers to the left- or right-endpoint of the interval. A single transition of the semantics of the 1c-cdPTA, which we recall represents the elapse of time (therefore increasing the value of the clock) followed by the traversal of a probabilistic edge, is represented by a sequence of *two* transitions in the IMDP: the first IMDP transition represents the choice of (i) the probabilistic edge, (ii) the interval in $\mathcal{I}_\mathbb{B}$ which contains the valuation of the clock after letting time elapse and immediately before the probabilistic edge is traversed, and (iii) in the case in which the aforementioned interval is open, the position of the clock valuation within the interval; the second IMDP transition represents the probabilistic choice made from the extreme (left and right) endpoints of the aforementioned interval with the chosen probabilistic edges.

Example 3. The IMDP construction, applied to the example of Fig. 1, is shown in Fig. 2 (note that transitions corresponding to probability 0 are shown with a dashed line). The location W, and the value of the clock being 0, is represented by the state $(W, [0, 0])$. Recall that the outgoing probabilistic edge from W is enabled when the clock is between 1 and 3: hence the single action $((1, 3), p_W)$ is available from $(W, [0, 0])$ (representing the set of actions $(\tilde{v}, p_W)$ of $[\![\mathcal{P}]\!]$ with $\tilde{v} \in (1, 3)$). The action $((1, 3), p_W)$ is associated with two target states, $((1, 3), p_W, \mathsf{lb})$ and $((1, 3), p_W, \mathsf{rb})$, each corresponding to the probability interval $(0, 1)$. The choice of probability within the interval can be done in the IMDP to represent a choice of clock valuation in $(1, 3)$: for example, the valuation $\frac{3}{2}$ would be represented by the assignment that associates

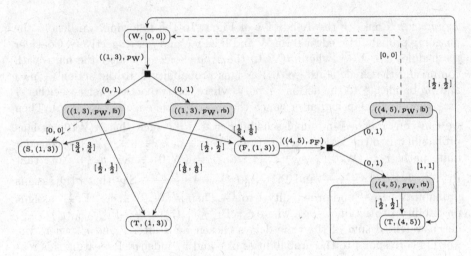

Fig. 2. Interval Markov decision process $\mathfrak{M}[\mathcal{P}]$ obtained from $\mathcal{P}$.

probability $\frac{3}{4}$ with $((1,3), p_W, \mathsf{lb})$ and $\frac{1}{4}$ with $((1,3), p_W, \mathsf{rb})$ (i.e., assigns a weight of $\frac{3}{4}$ to the lower bound of $(1,3)$, and a weight of $\frac{1}{4}$ to the upper bound of $(1,3)$, obtaining the weighted combination $\frac{3}{4} \cdot 1 + \frac{1}{4} \cdot 3 = \frac{3}{2}$). Then, from both $((1,3), p_W, \mathsf{lb})$ and $((1,3), p_W, \mathsf{rb})$, there is a probabilistic choice made regarding the target IMDP state to make the subsequent transition to, i.e., the transitions from $((1,3), p_W, \mathsf{lb})$ and $((1,3), p_W, \mathsf{rb})$ do not involve nondeterminism, because there is only one action available, and because the resulting interval distribution assigns singleton intervals to all possible target states.[2] The probabilities of the transitions from $((1,3), p_W, \mathsf{lb})$ and $((1,3), p_W, \mathsf{rb})$ are derived from the clock dependencies associated with 1 (i.e., the left endpoint of $(1,3)$) and 3 (i.e., the right endpoint of $(1,3)$), respectively. Hence the multiplication of the probabilities of the two aforementioned transitions (from $(W, [0,0])$ to either $((1,3), p_W, \mathsf{lb})$ or $((1,3), p_W, \mathsf{rb})$, and then to $(S, (1,3))$, $(T, (1,3))$ or $(F, (1,3))$) represents exactly the probability of a single transition in the 1c-cdPTA: for example, in the 1c-cdPTA, considering again the example of the clock valuation associating $\frac{3}{2}$ with x, the probability of making a transition to location S is $\frac{3x-3}{8} = \frac{3}{16}$; in the IMDP, assigning $\frac{3}{4}$ to the transition to $((1,3), p_W, \mathsf{lb})$ and $\frac{1}{4}$ to the transition to $((1,3), p_W, \mathsf{rb})$, we then obtain that the probability of making a transition to $(S, (1,3))$ from $(W, [0,0])$ is $\frac{3}{4} \cdot 0 + \frac{1}{4} \cdot \frac{3}{4} = \frac{3}{16}$. Similar reasoning applies to the transitions available from $(F, (1,3))$.

We now describe formally the construction of the IMDP $\mathfrak{M}[\mathcal{P}] = (S_{\mathfrak{M}[\mathcal{P}]},$ $\mathfrak{A}_{\mathfrak{M}[\mathcal{P}]}, \mathfrak{D}_{\mathfrak{M}[\mathcal{P}]})$. The set of states of $\mathfrak{M}[\mathcal{P}]$ is defined as $S_{\mathfrak{M}[\mathcal{P}]} = S_{\mathfrak{M}[\mathcal{P}]}^{\mathsf{reg}} \cup S_{\mathfrak{M}[\mathcal{P}]}^{\mathsf{end}}$, where $S_{\mathfrak{M}[\mathcal{P}]}^{\mathsf{reg}} = \{(l, B) \in L \times \mathcal{I}_\mathbb{B} \mid B \models inv(l)\}$ and $S_{\mathfrak{M}[\mathcal{P}]}^{\mathsf{end}} = \{(\tilde{B}, (l, g, \wp),$ $\mathsf{dir}) \in \mathcal{I}_\mathbb{B} \times prob \times \{\mathsf{lb}, \mathsf{rb}\} \mid \tilde{B} \models_{,} g \wedge inv(l)\}$. In order to distinguish states

---

[2] Given that there is only one action available from states such as $((1,3), p_W, \mathsf{lb})$ and $((1,3), p_W, \mathsf{rb})$, we omit both the action and the usual black box from the figure.

of $[\![\mathcal{P}]\!]$ and states of $\mathfrak{M}[\mathcal{P}]$, we refer to elements of $S^{\mathsf{reg}}_{\mathfrak{M}[\mathcal{P}]}$ as *regions*, and elements of $S^{\mathsf{end}}_{\mathfrak{M}[\mathcal{P}]}$ as *endpoint indicators*. The set of actions of $\mathfrak{M}[\mathcal{P}]$ is defined as $\mathfrak{A}_{\mathfrak{M}[\mathcal{P}]} = \{(\tilde{B},(l,g,\wp)) \in \mathcal{I}_\mathbb{B} \times prob \mid \tilde{B} \models g \wedge inv(l)\} \cup \{\tau\}$ (i.e., there is an action for each combination of interval from $\mathcal{I}_\mathbb{B}$ and probabilistic edge such that all valuations from the interval satisfy both the guard of the probabilistic edge and the invariant condition of its source location). For each region $(l,B) \in S^{\mathsf{reg}}_{\mathfrak{M}[\mathcal{P}]}$, let $\mathfrak{A}_{\mathfrak{M}[\mathcal{P}]}(l,B) = \{(\tilde{B},(l',g,\wp)) \in \mathfrak{A}_{\mathfrak{M}[\mathcal{P}]} \mid l = l' \text{ and } \tilde{B} \geq B\}$.[3] For each $(\tilde{B},p,\mathsf{dir}) \in S^{\mathsf{end}}_{\mathfrak{M}[\mathcal{P}]}$, let $\mathfrak{A}_{\mathfrak{M}[\mathcal{P}]}(\tilde{B},p,\mathsf{dir}) = \{\tau\}$. The transition function $\mathfrak{D}_{\mathfrak{M}[\mathcal{P}]} : S_{\mathfrak{M}[\mathcal{P}]} \times \mathfrak{A}_{\mathfrak{M}[\mathcal{P}]} \to \mathfrak{Dist}(S_{\mathfrak{M}[\mathcal{P}]}) \cup \{\bot\}$ is defined as follows[4]:

- For each $(l,B) \in S^{\mathsf{reg}}_{\mathfrak{M}[\mathcal{P}]}$ and $(\tilde{B},p) \in \mathfrak{A}_{\mathfrak{M}[\mathcal{P}]}(l,B)$, we let $\mathfrak{D}_{\mathfrak{M}[\mathcal{P}]}((l,B),(\tilde{B},p))$ be the interval distribution such that $\mathfrak{D}_{\mathfrak{M}[\mathcal{P}]}((l,B),(\tilde{B},p))(\tilde{B},p,\mathsf{lb}) = (0,1)$, $\mathfrak{D}_{\mathfrak{M}[\mathcal{P}]}((l,B),(\tilde{B},p))(\tilde{B},p,\mathsf{rb}) = (0,1)$, and $\mathfrak{D}_{\mathfrak{M}[\mathcal{P}]}((l,B),(\tilde{B},p))(s) = [0,0]$ for all $s \in S_{\mathfrak{M}[\mathcal{P}]} \setminus \{(\tilde{B},p,\mathsf{lb}),(\tilde{B},p,\mathsf{rb})\}$.
- For each $(\tilde{B},(l,g,\wp),\mathsf{dir}) \in S^{\mathsf{end}}_{\mathfrak{M}[\mathcal{P}]}$ and $(l',B') \in S^{\mathsf{reg}}_{\mathfrak{M}[\mathcal{P}]}$, let:

$$\lambda^{(\tilde{B},(l,g,\wp),\mathsf{dir})}_{(l',B')} = \begin{cases} \wp[\mathsf{dir}(\tilde{B})](\{x\},l') + \wp[\mathsf{dir}(\tilde{B})](\emptyset,l') & \text{if } B' = \tilde{B} = [0,0] \\ \wp[\mathsf{dir}(\tilde{B})](\emptyset,l') & \text{if } B' = \tilde{B} > [0,0] \\ \wp[\mathsf{dir}(\tilde{B})](\{x\},l') & \text{if } B' = 0 \text{ and } \tilde{B} > 0 \\ 0 & \text{otherwise.} \end{cases}$$

Then $\mathfrak{D}_{\mathfrak{M}[\mathcal{P}]}((\tilde{B},(l,g,\wp),\mathsf{dir}),\tau)$ is the interval distribution such that, for all $s \in S_{\mathfrak{M}[\mathcal{P}]}$:

$$\mathfrak{D}_{\mathfrak{M}[\mathcal{P}]}((\tilde{B},(l,g,\wp),\mathsf{dir}),\tau)(s) = \begin{cases} [\lambda^{(\tilde{B},(l,g,\wp),\mathsf{dir})}_s, \lambda^{(\tilde{B},(l,g,\wp),\mathsf{dir})}_s] & \text{if } s \in S^{\mathsf{reg}}_{\mathfrak{M}[\mathcal{P}]} \\ [0,0] & \text{otherwise.} \end{cases}$$

Next, we consider the correctness of the construction of $\mathfrak{M}[\mathcal{P}]$, i.e., that $\mathfrak{M}[\mathcal{P}]$ can be used for solving quantitative and qualitative properties of the 1c-cdPTA $\mathcal{P}$. The proof relies on showing that transitions of the semantic MDP $[\![\mathcal{P}]\!]$ of $\mathcal{P}$ can be mimicked by a sequence of *two* transitions of the semantic MDP $[\![\mathfrak{M}[\mathcal{P}]]\!]$ of $\mathfrak{M}[\mathcal{P}]$, and vice versa. Let $[\![\mathcal{P}]\!] = (S_\mathcal{P}, A_\mathcal{P}, \Delta_\mathcal{P})$ be the semantic MDP of $\mathcal{P}$. Given state $(l,v) \in S_\mathcal{P}$, we let $\mathsf{reg}(l,v) = (l,B) \in S^{\mathsf{reg}}_{\mathfrak{M}[\mathcal{P}]}$ be the unique region such that $v \in B$. In the following, we let $[\![\mathfrak{M}[\mathcal{P}]]\!] = (S_{\mathfrak{M}[\mathcal{P}]}, A_{\mathfrak{M}[\mathcal{P}]}, \Delta_{\mathfrak{M}[\mathcal{P}]})$ be the semantic MDP of $\mathfrak{M}[\mathcal{P}]$.

We now show that, for any scheduler of (the semantics of) the 1c-cdPTA $\mathcal{P}$, there exists a scheduler of (the semantics of) the IMDP $\mathfrak{M}[\mathcal{P}]$ such that the schedulers assign the same probability to reaching a certain set of locations from a given location with the value of the clock equal to 0. Let $\mathfrak{T}_F = \{(l,B) \in S^{\mathsf{reg}}_{\mathfrak{M}[\mathcal{P}]} \mid l \in F\}$ be the set of regions with location component in F.

---

[3] Note that $\mathfrak{A}_{\mathfrak{M}[\mathcal{P}]}(l,B) \neq \emptyset$ for each $(l,B) \in S^{\mathsf{reg}}_{\mathfrak{M}[\mathcal{P}]}$, by the assumptions that we made on 1c-cdPTA in Sect. 3 (namely, that it is always possible to take a probabilistic edge, either immediately or after letting time elapse).

[4] We recall that $\mathfrak{D}_{\mathfrak{M}[\mathcal{P}]}(s,\mathfrak{a}) = \bot$ for $s \in S_{\mathfrak{M}[\mathcal{P}]}$ and $\mathfrak{a} \in \mathfrak{A}_{\mathfrak{M}[\mathcal{P}]} \setminus \mathfrak{A}_{\mathfrak{M}[\mathcal{P}]}(s)$.

164   J. Sproston

Lemma 2. *Let $l \in L$ be a location and let $F \subseteq L$ be a set of locations. Given a $\mathbb{B}$-minimal scheduler $\pi \in \Sigma^{[\![\mathcal{P}]\!]}_{\mathbb{B}}$, there exists scheduler $\hat{\pi} \in \Sigma^{[\![\mathfrak{M}[\mathcal{P}]]\!]}$ such that $\mathrm{Pr}^{\pi}_{(l,0)}(\Diamond T_F) = \mathrm{Pr}^{\hat{\pi}}_{\mathrm{reg}(l,0)}(\Diamond \mathfrak{T}_F)$.*

The proof of Lemma 2 (see [34]) is simplified by the fact that, by Lemma 1, it suffices to consider $\mathbb{B}$-minimal schedulers: for each finite path r of π, we can identify a set of finite paths of $\hat{\pi}$ of length twice that of r, that visit the same locations in order, choose the same probabilistic edges in order, and visit the same intervals in order, both regarding the clock valuations/intervals in states and in actions. In fact, finite paths of $\hat{\pi}$ that are associated with r differ *only* in terms of the lb and rb components used in endpoint indicators. Furthermore, $\hat{\pi}$ replicates exactly the choice of π made after r in terms of interval of $\mathcal{I}_{\mathbb{B}}$ chosen and probabilistic edge in all of its finite paths associated with r. Finally, $\hat{\pi}$ chooses assignments (over edges labelled with $(0,1)$) in order to represent exactly the choices of clock valuations made by π, in the manner described in Example 3 above: more precisely, the choice of action $(\tilde{v}, p)$ by π, where $\tilde{B}$ is the unique interval such that $\tilde{v} \in \tilde{B}$, is mimicked by $\hat{\pi}$ choosing the action $((\tilde{B}, p), \alpha)$ for which $\alpha(\tilde{B}, p, \mathsf{lb}) = \frac{\mathsf{rb}(\tilde{B}) - \tilde{v}}{\mathsf{rb}(\tilde{B}) - \mathsf{lb}(\tilde{B})}$, and $\alpha(\tilde{B}, p, \mathsf{rb}) = 1 - \alpha(\tilde{B}, p, \mathsf{lb}) = \frac{\tilde{v} - \mathsf{lb}(\tilde{B})}{\mathsf{rb}(\tilde{B}) - \mathsf{lb}(\tilde{B})}$.

Example 4. Consider the 1c-cdPTA of Fig. 1. Let $\pi \in \Sigma^{[\![\mathcal{P}]\!]}_{\mathbb{B}}$ be a scheduler such that $\pi(\mathrm{W}, 0)$ assigns probability 1 to the action $(\frac{3}{2}, p_{\mathrm{W}})$. Then $\hat{\pi} \in \Sigma^{[\![\mathfrak{M}[\mathcal{P}]]\!]}$ is constructed such that $\hat{\pi}(\mathrm{W}, [0,0])$ assigns probability 1 to $(((1,3), p_{\mathrm{W}}), \alpha)$, where $\alpha((1,3), p_{\mathrm{W}}, \mathsf{lb}) = \frac{3}{4}$ and $\alpha((1,3), p_{\mathrm{W}}, \mathsf{rb}) = \frac{1}{4}$ (observe that $\alpha((1,3), p_{\mathrm{W}}, \mathsf{lb}) = \frac{3 - \frac{3}{2}}{2}$). Furthermore, $\hat{\pi}((\mathrm{W}, [0,0])(((1,3), p_{\mathrm{W}}), \alpha))$ assigns probability 1 to τ. Now consider the finite path $r = (\mathrm{W}, 0)(\frac{3}{2}, p_{\mathrm{W}})(\mathrm{F}, \frac{3}{2})$ of π: then the corresponding set of finite paths of $\hat{\pi}$ is $r' = (\mathrm{W}, [0,0])(((1,3), p_{\mathrm{W}}), \alpha)((1,3), p_{\mathrm{W}}, \mathsf{lb})(\mathrm{F}, (1,3))$ and $r'' = (\mathrm{W}, [0,0])(((1,3), p_{\mathrm{W}}), \alpha)((1,3), p_{\mathrm{W}}, \mathsf{rb})(\mathrm{F}, (1,3))$. Now say that $\pi(r)$ assigns probability 1 to the action $(\frac{9}{2}, p_{\mathrm{F}})$: then both $\hat{\pi}(r')$ and $\hat{\pi}(r'')$ assign probability 1 to the action $(((4,5), p_{\mathrm{F}}), \alpha')$, where $\alpha'((4,5), p_{\mathrm{F}}, \mathsf{lb}) = \frac{1}{2}$ and $\alpha'((4,5), p_{\mathrm{F}}, \mathsf{rb}) = \frac{1}{2}$ (note that $\alpha'((4,5), p_{\mathrm{F}}, \mathsf{lb}) = 5 - \frac{9}{2}$). Hence, regardless of whether $((1,3), p_{\mathrm{W}}, \mathsf{lb})$ or $((1,3), p_{\mathrm{W}}, \mathsf{rb})$ was visited, scheduler $\hat{\pi}$ makes the *same* choice to mimic $\pi(r)$.

The following lemma considers the converse direction, namely that (starting from a given location with the clock equal to 0) any scheduler of $[\![\mathfrak{M}[\mathcal{P}]]\!]$ can be mimicked by a $\mathbb{B}$-minimal scheduler of $[\![\mathcal{P}]\!]$ such that the schedulers assign the same probability of reaching a certain set of locations.

Lemma 3. *Let $l \in L$ be a location and let $F \subseteq L$ be a set of locations. Given a scheduler $\hat{\pi} \in \Sigma^{[\![\mathfrak{M}[\mathcal{P}]]\!]}$, there exists a $\mathbb{B}$-minimal scheduler $\pi \in \Sigma^{[\![\mathcal{P}]\!]}_{\mathbb{B}}$, such that $\mathrm{Pr}^{\pi}_{(l,0)}(\Diamond T_F) = \mathrm{Pr}^{\hat{\pi}}_{\mathrm{reg}(l,0)}(\Diamond \mathfrak{T}_F)$.*

We characterise the size of a 1c-cdPTA as the sum of the number of its locations, the size of the binary encoding of the clock constraints used in invariant conditions and guards, and the size of the binary encoding of the constants used in the distribution templates of the probabilistic edges (i.e., c^p_e and d^p_e for each $p \in prob$ and $e \in 2^{\{x\}} \times L$).

Theorem 1. *Given a 1c-cdPTA* $\mathcal{P} = (L, inv, prob)$, $l \in L$ *and* $F \subseteq L$, *the quantitative and qualitative problems can be solved in polynomial time.*

The theorem follows from Lemma 1, Lemma 2, Lemma 3, Proposition 1 and the fact that quantitative and qualitative problems for IMDPs can be solved in polynomial time, given that there exist polynomial-time algorithms for analogous problems on IMCs with the semantics adopted in this paper [9,11,30,33], and from the fact that the IMDP construction presented in this section gives an IMDP that is of size polynomial in the size of the 1c-cdPTA. We add that the quantitative problems for 1c-cdPTAs are PTIME-hard, following from the PTIME-hardness of reachability for MDPs [29], thus establishing PTIME-completeness for quantitative problems for 1c-cdPTAs.

5   Conclusion

We have presented a method for the transformation of a class of 1c-cdPTAs to IMDPs such that there is a precise relationship between the schedulers of the 1c-cdPTA and the IMDP, allowing us to use established polynomial-time algorithms for IMDPs to decide quantitative and qualitative reachability problems on the 1c-cdPTA. Overall, the results establish that such problems are in PTIME. The techniques rely on the initialisation requirement, which ensures that optimal choices for non-constant probabilistic edges correspond to the left or right endpoints of intervals that are derived from the syntactic description of the 1c-cdPTA. The initialisation requirement restricts dependencies between non-constant probabilistic edges: while this necessarily restricts the expressiveness of the formalism, the resulting model nevertheless retains the expressive power to represent basic situations in which the probability of certain events depends on the exact amount of time elapsed, such as those described in the introduction.

The IMDP construction can be simplified in a number of cases: for example, in the case in which at most two outcomes e_1, e_2 of every probabilistic edge p are non-constant, i.e., for which $d^p_{e_1} \neq 0$ and $d^p_{e_2} \neq 0$, endpoint indicators are unnecessary; instead, when a probabilistic edge is taken from an open interval $\tilde{B}$, each of e_1 and e_2 are associated with (non-singleton) intervals (other outcomes are associated with singleton intervals), and the choice of probability to assign between the two intervals represents the choice of clock valuation in $\tilde{B}$. This construction is also polynomial in the size of the 1c-cdPTA. Future work could consider lifting the initialisation requirement: we conjecture that this is particularly challenging for quantitative properties, in particular recalling that Fig. 2 of [32] provides an example of a non-initialised 1c-cdPTA for which the maximum probability of reaching a certain location is attained by choosing a time delay corresponding to an irrational number. Solutions to the qualitative problem for non-initialised 1c-cdPTAs could potentially utilise connections with parametric MDPs [19,35]. Furthermore, time-bounded reachability properties could also be considered in the context of 1c-cdPTAs.

References

1. Akshay, S., Bouyer, P., Krishna, S.N., Manasa, L., Trivedi, A.: Stochastic timed games revisited. In: Faliszewski, P., Muscholl, A., Niedermeier, R., (eds.) Proceedings of MFCS 2016 LIPIcs, vol. 58, pp. 8:1–8:14. Leibniz-Zentrum für Informatik (2016)
2. Alur, R., Dill, D.L.: A theory of timed automata. Theor. Comput. Sci. **126**(2), 183–235 (1994)
3. Baier, C., Katoen, J.-P.: Principles of Model Checking. MIT Press, Cambridge (2008)
4. Bertrand, N., Bordais, B., Hélouët, L., Mari, T., Parreaux, J., Sankur, O.: Performance evaluation of metro regulations using probabilistic model-checking. In: Collart-Dutilleul, S., Lecomte, T., Romanovsky, A. (eds.) RSSRail 2019. LNCS, vol. 11495, pp. 59–76. Springer, Cham (2019). https://doi.org/10.1007/978-3-030-18744-6_4
5. Bertrand, N., et al.: Stochastic timed automata. Log. Methods Comput. Sci. **10**(4), 1–73 (2014)
6. Bertrand, N., Brihaye, T., Genest, B.: Deciding the value 1 problem for reachability in 1-clock decision stochastic timed automata. In: Norman, G., Sanders, W. (eds.) QEST 2014. LNCS, vol. 8657, pp. 313–328. Springer, Cham (2014). https://doi.org/10.1007/978-3-319-10696-0_25
7. Bouyer, P., Fahrenberg, U., Larsen, K.G., Markey, N., Ouaknine, J., Worrell, J.: Model checking real-time systems. In: Clarke, E.M., Henzinger, T.A., Veith, H., Bloem, R. (eds.) Handbook of Model Checking, pp. 1001–1046. Springer, Cham (2018). https://doi.org/10.1007/978-3-319-10575-8_29
8. Bouyer, P., Larsen, K.G., Markey, N.: Model checking one-clock priced timed automata. Log. Methods Comput. Sci. **4**(2), 1–28 (2008)
9. Chakraborty, S., Katoen, J.-P.: Model checking of open interval markov chains. In: Gribaudo, M., Manini, D., Remke, A. (eds.) ASMTA 2015. LNCS, vol. 9081, pp. 30–42. Springer, Cham (2015). https://doi.org/10.1007/978-3-319-18579-8_3
10. Chatterjee, K., Sen, K., Henzinger, T.A.: Model-checking ω-regular properties of interval Markov chains. In: Amadio, R. (ed.) FoSSaCS 2008. LNCS, vol. 4962, pp. 302–317. Springer, Heidelberg (2008). https://doi.org/10.1007/978-3-540-78499-9_22
11. Chen, T., Han, T., Kwiatkowska, M.: On the complexity of model checking interval-valued discrete time Markov chains. Inf. Process. Lett. **113**(7), 210–216 (2013)
12. Clarke, E.M., Grumberg, O., Peled, D.A.: Model Checking. MIT Press, Cambridge (2001)
13. Feng, L., Wiltsche, C., Humphrey, L.R., Topcu, U.: Synthesis of human-in-the-loop control protocols for autonomous systems. IEEE Trans. Autom. Sci. Eng. **13**(2), 450–462 (2016)
14. Forejt, V., Kwiatkowska, M., Norman, G., Parker, D.: Automated verification techniques for probabilistic systems. In: Bernardo, M., Issarny, V. (eds.) SFM 2011. LNCS, vol. 6659, pp. 53–113. Springer, Heidelberg (2011). https://doi.org/10.1007/978-3-642-21455-4_3
15. Givan, R., Leach, S.M., Dean, T.L.: Bounded-parameter Markov decision processes. Artif. Intell. **122**(1–2), 71–109 (2000)
16. Gregersen, H., Jensen, H.E.: Formal design of reliable real time systems. Master's thesis, Department of Mathematics and Computer Science, Aalborg University (1995)

17. Haddad, S., Monmege, B.: Interval iteration algorithm for MDPs and IMDPs. Theor. Comput. Sci. **735**, 111–131 (2018)
18. Hahn, E.M.: Model checking stochastic hybrid systems. Ph.D., thesis, Universität des Saarlandes (2013)
19. Hahn, E.M., Han, T., Zhang, L.: Synthesis for PCTL in parametric Markov decision processes. In: Bobaru, M., Havelund, K., Holzmann, G.J., Joshi, R. (eds.) NFM 2011. LNCS, vol. 6617, pp. 146–161. Springer, Heidelberg (2011). https://doi.org/10.1007/978-3-642-20398-5_12
20. Hashemi, V., Hatefi, H., Krcál, J.: Probabilistic bisimulations for PCTL model checking of interval MDPs. In: André, É., Frehse, G., (eds.) Proceedings of SynCoP 2014 EPTCS, vol. 145, pp. 19–33 (2014)
21. Henzinger, T.A., Kopke, P.W., Puri, A., Varaiya, P.: What's decidable about hybrid automata? J. Comput. Syst. Sci. **57**(1), 94–124 (1998)
22. Jonsson, B., Larsen, K.G.: Specification and refinement of probabilistic processes. In: Proceedings of LICS 1991, pp. 266–277. IEEE Computer Society (1991)
23. Jurdziński, M., Laroussinie, F., Sproston, J.: Model checking probabilistic timed automata with one or two clocks. Log. Methods Comput. Sci. **4**(3), 1–28 (2008)
24. Kozine, I.O., Utkin, L.V.: Interval-valued finite Markov chains. Reliab. Comput. **8**(2), 97–113 (2002)
25. Kwiatkowska, M., Norman, G., Segala, R., Sproston, J.: Automatic verification of real-time systems with discrete probability distributions. Theor. Comput. Sci. **286**, 101–150 (2002)
26. Laroussinie, F., Markey, N., Schnoebelen, P.: Model checking timed automata with one or two clocks. In: Gardner, P., Yoshida, N. (eds.) CONCUR 2004. LNCS, vol. 3170, pp. 387–401. Springer, Heidelberg (2004). https://doi.org/10.1007/978-3-540-28644-8_25
27. Nilim, A., El Ghaoui, L.: Robust control of Markov decision processes with uncertain transition matrices. Oper. Res. **53**(5), 780–798 (2005)
28. Norman, G., Parker, D., Sproston, J.: Model checking for probabilistic timed automata. Form. Methods Syst. Des. **43**(2), 164–190 (2013)
29. Papadimitriou, C.H., Tsitsiklis, J.N.: The complexity of Markov decision processes. Math. Oper. Res. **12**(3), 441–450 (1987)
30. Puggelli, A., Li, W., Sangiovanni-Vincentelli, A.L., Seshia, S.A.: Polynomial-time verification of PCTL properties of MDPs with convex uncertainties. In: Sharygina, N., Veith, H. (eds.) CAV 2013. LNCS, vol. 8044, pp. 527–542. Springer, Heidelberg (2013). https://doi.org/10.1007/978-3-642-39799-8_35
31. Sen, K., Viswanathan, M., Agha, G.: Model-checking markov chains in the presence of uncertainties. In: Hermanns, H., Palsberg, J. (eds.) TACAS 2006. LNCS, vol. 3920, pp. 394–410. Springer, Heidelberg (2006). https://doi.org/10.1007/11691372_26
32. Sproston, J.: Probabilistic timed automata with clock-dependent probabilities. In: Hague, M., Potapov, I. (eds.) RP 2017. LNCS, vol. 10506, pp. 144–159. Springer, Cham (2017). https://doi.org/10.1007/978-3-319-67089-8_11
33. Sproston, J.: Qualitative reachability for open interval Markov chains. In: Potapov, I., Reynier, P.-A. (eds.) RP 2018. LNCS, vol. 11123, pp. 146–160. Springer, Cham (2018). https://doi.org/10.1007/978-3-030-00250-3_11
34. Sproston, J.: Probabilistic timed automata with one clock and initialised clock-dependent probabilities. CoRR (2020)

35. Winkler, T., Junges, S., Pérez, G.A., Katoen, J.: On the complexity of reachability in parametric Markov decision processes. In: Fokkink, W., van Glabbeek, R. (eds.) Proceedings of CONCUR 2019 LIPIcs, vol. 140, pp. 14:1–14:17. Leibniz-Zentrum für Informatik (2019)
36. Wu, D., Koutsoukos, X.D.: Reachability analysis of uncertain systems using bounded-parameter Markov decision processes. Artif. Intell. **172**(8–9), 945–954 (2008)

A Formal Framework for Consent Management

Shukun Tokas$^{(\boxtimes)}$ and Olaf Owe$^{(\boxtimes)}$

Department of Informatics, University of Oslo, Oslo, Norway
{shukunt,olaf}@ifi.uio.no

Abstract. The aim of this work is to design a formal framework for consent management in line with EU's General Data Protection Regulation (GDPR). To make a general solution, we consider a high-level modeling language for distributed service-oriented systems, building on the paradigm of active objects. Our framework provides a general solution for data subjects to observe and change their privacy settings and to be informed about all personal data stored about them. The solution consists of a set of predefined types for privacy related concepts, a formalization of policy compliance, a set of interfaces that forms the basis of interaction with external users for consent management, a set of classes that is used in interaction with the runtime system, and a runtime system enforcing the consented policies.

Keywords: GDPR · Data protection · Privacy policies · Policy compliance · Tagging · Runtime enforcement · Consent management

1 Introduction

In response to the emerging privacy concerns, the European Union (EU) has approved the General Data Protection Regulation (GDPR) [1] to strengthen and impose data protection rules across the EU. This regulation requires controllers that process personal data of individuals within EU and EEA, to process personal information in a "lawful, fair, and transparent manner". Article 6 and Article 9 of the regulation [1] provide the criteria for lawful processing, such as consent, fulfillment of contractual obligation, compliance with a legal obligation etc. The regulation (including several other data protection laws) recognises consent as one of the lawful principles for legitimate processing, and Article 7 sets out the conditions for the processing personal data when relying on consent.

A data subject's consent reflects his/her agreements in terms of the processing of personal data. The regulation indicates that the consent must specifically be given for the particular *purpose* of processing. It is also indicated in Recital 43 that the data subject should be given a free choice to accept or deny consent for specific purposes, rather than having one consent for several purposes. In particular our focus is on processing of personal data when *consent* is the legal

© IFIP International Federation for Information Processing 2020
Published by Springer Nature Switzerland AG 2020
A. Gotsman and A. Sokolova (Eds.): FORTE 2020, LNCS 12136, pp. 169–186, 2020.
https://doi.org/10.1007/978-3-030-50086-3_10

ground, i.e., processing is valid only if a data subject has given consent for the specific purpose, otherwise processing of the personal data should cease. Moreover, this can be extended to incorporate other applicable legal grounds, such as vital interest, legitimate interest etc, but a discussion on this will be out of scope of this work.

Furthermore, Article 15 of the regulation prescribes that the data subject has *Right of Access*, which requires the data controllers to provide the data subject with his/her personal data, the purposes of processing, the legal basis for doing so, and other relevant information (see Article 15 [1]). WP29 recommends controllers to introduce tools, such as a privacy dashboards through which the data subject can be informed and engaged regarding the processing of their personal data [2]. The regulation also introduces an obligation for data controllers to demonstrate compliance, i.e., accountability (see Article 5(2) [1]). These requirements are likely to pose substantial administrative burden. This work is an attempt to design a pragmatic solution to address these requirements, using a formal approach. In particular, our framework covers certain aspects of *privacy principles* (Article 5), *lawfulness of processing* (Article 6), *privacy by design* (Article 25) and *data subject access request* (Article 15). Due to the nature of these requirements and space constraints, we cover these requirements partially.

The privacy requirements in the data protection regulations are defined informally, therefore, to avoid ambiguity the policy language equipped with a formal semantics is essential [3]. It is essential that the policy terminology establishes a clear link between the law and the program artifacts. For this, we let privacy policies and consent specifications be expressed in terms of several predefined names, reflecting standard terminology (allowing names to be added as needed). It is necessary that the policy terminology used towards the data subject is simple but with a formal connection to the underlying programming elements. We have previously studied static aspects of privacy policies and static checking of policy compliance from a formal point of view, a brief overview is given in [4].

The aim of this work is to design a formal framework for consent management where a data subject can change his/her privacy settings through predefined interfaces, which could be part of a library system. The data subjects are seen as external system users without knowledge of the underlying program. Data subjects may interact with the system at runtime through a user-friendly interface (e.g. a privacy dashboard), to view current privacy settings and update these settings. To make a general solution, we consider a high-level modeling language for distributed service-oriented systems, building on the paradigm of *active objects* [5,6]. The method for protecting access to personal data in this setting comprises of: tagging the data with ($subject, purpose$) pairs; associating a *purpose* to each method accessing personal data; storing consented policies of a subject in a subject object; deriving an *effective* policy for the access from the executing method and data tags; and comparing the effective policy with the current consented policies to determine if it is a valid operation.

The main contribution of this research is a framework that consists of: *(i)* a policy and consent specification language; *(ii)* a formalization of runtime policy compliance; *(iii)* predefined interfaces and classes for consent management; *(iv)* a run-time system for dynamic checking of privacy compliance, with built-in generation of runtime privacy tags when new personal data is created. We prove a notion of runtime compliance with respect to the consented policies.

$$
\begin{aligned}
A &::= no \mid read \mid incr \mid write \mid rincr \mid wincr \mid full && \text{access rights} \\
\mathcal{RD} &::= \textbf{purpose } R^+ \text{ } [\textbf{where } Rel \text{ } [\textbf{and } Rel]^*] && \text{purpose declaration} \\
Rel &::= R^+ < R^+ && \text{sub-purpose declaration} \\
P &::= I \mid o && \text{principals: interface or object} \\
p &::= (P, R, A) && \text{policies} \\
C &::= pos(P, R, A) \mid neg(P, R, A) && \text{consented policies} \\
Q &::= C^* && \text{policy list}
\end{aligned}
$$

Fig. 1. BNF syntax definition of the policy language. I ranges over interface names, R over purpose names, and P over principal names. A principal is given by an object or an interface (representing all objects of that interface). Superscripts $*$ and $+$ denote general and non-empty repetition, respectively.

Paper Outline. The rest of the paper is structured as follows. Section 2 presents the policy and consent specification language, a formalization of policy compliance, and the core language. Section 3 introduces the functionality for consent management. Section 4 presents tag generation, dynamic checking and an operational semantics. Section 5 discusses related work, and Sect. 6 concludes the paper and discusses future work.

2   Language Setting

In order to formalize the management and processing of personal information, we introduce basic notions for privacy policies and consent in Sect. 2.1, and introduce a small language for interface and class definitions in Sect. 2.2.

2.1   Policy and Consent Specification

Privacy policies are often described in natural language statements. To verify formally that the program satisfies the privacy specification, the desired notions of privacy need to be expressed explicitly. To formalize such policies, we define a policy specification language. In our setting, a privacy policy is a statement that expresses permitted use of the personal information by the declared program entities. In particular, a policy is given by triples that put restrictions on what *principals* can access the personal data for specific *purposes* and *access-rights*. That being the case, a policy p is given by a triple (P, R, A), where:

i) P describes a principle that can access personal information and is given by an object representing a principal, or by an interface (representing all objects supporting that interface). Interfaces are organized in an open-ended inheritance hierarchy, letting $I < J$ denote that principal I is a subinterface of J and letting $o < I$ if object o supports I. We let $\leq$ denote the transitive and reflexive extension of $<$. As an example,

$$Specialist < Doctor < HealthWorker$$

ii) The purpose name R describe the specific purpose for which personal data can be used. Such purpose names are organized in an open-ended directed acyclic graph, reflecting specialization. For instance, the declaration

---

purpose $treatm, health\_care$ **where** $treatm < health\_care$
policy $p_{Doc} = (Doctor, treatm, rincr)$ // *general policy*
consent $pos(p_{Doc}) = (Doctor, health\_care, write)$ // *general positive consent*
consent $neg(p_{MyDoc}) = (Dr.Hansen, treatm, full)$ // *specific negative consent*

Fig. 2. Sample purpose and policy definitions. Here $Dr.Hansen$ is a principal object.

$$\textbf{purpose}\ spl\_treatm, treatm\ \textbf{where}\ spl\_treatm < treatm$$

makes spl_treatm more specialized purpose than $treatm$. If data is collected for the purpose of spl_treatm then it cannot be used for $treatm$. However, if it is collected for the purpose of $treatm$ then it can be used for spl_treatm. We let $\leq$ denote the transitive and reflexive extension of $<$, and let the predefined purpose *all* be the least specialized purpose.

iii) Access rights A describe the permitted operations on personal data, and are given by a lattice, with *full* and *no* as top and bottom and with a partial ordering $\sqsubseteq_A$: *read* gives read access, *write* gives write access (without including read access), *incr* allows addition of new information but neither read nor write is included. The join of *read* and *incr* is abbreviated *rincr*, the join of *write* and *incr* is abbreviated *wincr*, while the join of *read* and *write* is *full*.

The language syntax for policies is summarized in Fig. 1, where [ ] is used as meta-parenthesis, and superscripts * and + denote general and non-empty repetition, respectively. Sample policies are given in Fig. 2.

Definition 1 (Policy Compliance). Policy compliance, $\sqsubseteq$, *is defined by*

$$(P', R', A') \sqsubseteq (P, R, A) \triangleq P' \leq P \wedge R' \leq R \wedge A' \sqsubseteq_A A$$

Thus, a policy p' complies with p if it has the same or smaller interface, the same or more specialized purpose, and the same or weaker access rights.

In order to deal with both addition and removal of policies, we organize the policies in a list of negative and positive policies, such that the newest and most significant policy is last in the list. A positive consent has the form $pos(p)$, where p is a policy triple, meaning that access to personal data requiring p is allowed.

A negative consent has the form $neg(p)$, meaning that access to personal data requiring p is forbidden. The disjoint union of these two forms is captured by the type $Consent$. Consented policies are organized in a $Consent$ list. We define compliance of policies with respect to such a list L by:

$$p \sqsubseteq \epsilon \qquad\qquad = \textit{false}$$
$$p \sqsubseteq (L; pos(p')) = \textbf{if } p \sqsubseteq p' \textbf{ then } \textit{true} \textbf{ else } p \sqsubseteq L$$
$$p \sqsubseteq (L; neg(p')) = \textbf{if } p \sqsubseteq p' \textbf{ then } \textit{false} \textbf{ else } p \sqsubseteq L$$

where $\_;\_$ denotes list append. Thus positive or negative policies later in the list (capturing newer ones) override policies earlier in the list (capturing older ones) with smaller policy triples. This gives a simple way to upgrade and downgrade consent, and with a uniform treatment of negative as well as positive consent.

$$
\begin{array}{lll}
Pr & ::= [\mathcal{T} \mid \mathcal{RD} \mid In \mid Cl]^* & \text{program} \\
\mathcal{T} & ::= \textbf{type } N\,[\overline{T}] =\texttt{<type\_expression>} & \text{type definition} \\
T & ::= \mathsf{Int} \mid \mathsf{Any} \mid \mathsf{Bool} \mid \mathsf{String} \mid \mathsf{Void} \mid \mathsf{List}[T] \mid I \mid N & \text{interfaces and types} \\
In & ::= \textbf{interface } I\,[\textbf{extends } I^+]\,\{D^*\}[:: R] & \text{interface declaration} \\
Cl & ::= \textbf{class } C\,([T\ z]^*) & \text{class definition} \\
& \quad [\textbf{implements } I^+]\,[\textbf{extends } C] & \text{support, inheritance} \\
& \quad \{[T\ w\ [= ini]]^*\,[B\,[:: R]] & \text{fields and class constructor} \\
& \quad [[\textbf{with } I]\ M]^*\} & \text{methods} \\
D & ::= \textbf{op } T\ m([T\ y]^*)\,[:: R] & \text{method signature} \\
M & ::= \textbf{op } T\ m([T\ y]^*)\,[B]\,[:: R] & \text{method definition} \\
B & ::= \{[T\ x\ [= rhs];]^*\,[s]\,[;\,\textbf{return } rhs]\} & \text{method blocks} \\
v & ::= w \mid x & \text{assignable variable} \\
e & ::= v \mid y \mid z \mid \mathsf{this} \mid \mathsf{caller} \mid \mathsf{void} \mid f(\overline{e}) \mid (\overline{e}) & \text{pure expressions} \\
ini & ::= e \mid \textbf{new } C(\overline{e}) & \text{initial value of field} \\
rhs & ::= ini \mid e.m(\overline{e}) & \text{right-hand sides} \\
s & ::= \mathsf{skip} \mid s; s \mid v := rhs \mid v :+ e \mid e!m(\overline{e}) \mid I!m(\overline{e}) & \text{assignment and call} \\
& \quad \mid \textbf{if } e \textbf{ then } s\,[\textbf{else } s]\ \textbf{fi} \mid \textbf{while } e \textbf{ do } s \textbf{ od} & \text{if- and while-statements}
\end{array}
$$

Fig. 3. BNF syntax of the core language, extended with purpose specifications $(:: R)$. A field is denoted w, a local variable x, a method parameter y, a class parameter z, type names N, expressions e, and expression lists $\overline{e}$. The brackets in $[T]$ and $[\overline{T}]$ are ground symbols. Function symbols f range over pre-/programmer-defined functions/-constructors with prefix/mixfix notation.

```
interface PrivacySettings {
  with User
    op PolicyList seeMyPolicies() // the current policy list is sent to the user
    op Bool addPolicy(Policy p) // add a new policy (return false if redundant)
    op Bool remPolicy(Policy p) } // remove a policy (return false if redundant)
```

Fig. 4. Interface declarations for subject's privacy settings

2.2   A High-Level Language for Active Objects

In the setting of active objects, the objects are autonomous and execute in
parallel, communicating by so-called asynchronous method invocations. Object-
local data structure is defined by data types. Classes are defined by an imperative
language while data types and associated functions are defined by a functional
language. We assume interface abstraction, i.e., remote field access is illegal and
an object can only be accessed though an interface. This allows us to focus on
major challenges of modern architectures, without the complications of low-level
language constructs related to the shared-variable concurrency model.

```
interface Sensitive{
  with Subject
    op Void requestMySensitiveData() // a subject (the caller) requests to see
  }                                   // all personal data in the sensitive object about her

interface Subject extends PrivacySettings, Sensitive, Principal {
  with Sensitive
    op Void receiveMySensitiveData(List[TaggedData] tl)
  with User
    op Void collectMyData() // to initiate collection of personal data about the subject
    op List[TaggedData] seeMyData() // the received info is sent to subject user
  } :: all
```

Fig. 5. Interface declarations for sensitive objects and data subjects.

A strongly typed language for active objects based on [6] is given in Fig. 3.
The programs we consider are defined by a sequence of declarations of interfaces
(containing method declarations), classes (containing class parameters, fields,
methods and class constructors), and data type definitions. Class parameters are
like fields, but with read-only access. A subclass inherits class parameters, fields,
and methods (and the class constructor) unless redefined. A method m may
have a cointerface Co given by the with clause, **with** Co, restricting callers to
objects supporting interface Co (this is checked statically and allows type-correct
call backs). Each method dealing with personal data must have an associated
purpose, given at the end of the method definition (:: R), if any, otherwise
the one declared for the method in the interface, if any, or otherwise the one
declared for the interface. Methods may declare local variables and end with
a return statement. We include standard statements such as skip, assignment
(:=), object creation (**new**), if- and while-statements, and we allow blocking
calls ($v := o.m(\overline{e})$) where o is the callee and $\overline{e}$ is the list of actual parameters,
and asynchronous calls $o!m(\overline{e})$ and broadcasts $I!m(\overline{e})$ to all objects of interface
I. The incremental update $v :+ e$ extends a list v with one or more elements e.

We consider pure expressions, including products ($e_1, e_2, \ldots$), lists, and function applications $f(\overline{e})$ where f may be a defined function or a constructor

function (including ";" for lists and constants such as *nil*, *void*, 0, 1, 2, etc.). A value is a variable-free expression with only constructor functions, such as the list *nil*; 1; 2; 3.

3 Consent Management

The policy settings of each data subject may change dynamically during runtime in interaction with the external users. In order to handle this, we define a runtime system where personal data values are tagged with specification of data subjects and processing purposes. The runtime system will check that every access to personal data complies with the consented policies. Since there could be a huge amount of personal information in a distributed system, it is essential that the information in the tags is minimized. *Our framework includes a general solution for subjects to observe and change their privacy settings.* We chose to let the information about the consented policies be stored separately from the tags. The tags are generated by the runtime system as explained in detail in Sect. 4.1. The consented policy may change dynamically, in contrast to the information in the tags, which do not change. By combining the core information in the tags with the dynamically changing consent information, we are able to keep the information in the tags relatively small.

We let interface *Principal* correspond to a system user, be it a person, an organization, or other identifiable actor. Interface *PrivacySettings* (Fig. 4) defines methods for accessing and resetting consented policies by the data subject, while the subinterface *Subject* (Fig. 5) defines methods for consent management including functionality for requesting and updating policy settings. For each data subject there is an associated object (i.e., the subject object) supporting *Privacy-Settings* and *Subject*, and this object is used to manage the privacy settings and policies in interaction with an external user (for instance through an app on a mobile phone). The subject object will contain the consented policies and is used when personal data about the data subject is accessed, in order to check compliance with the consented policies as explained in the operational semantics. In addition, it is used to manage the collection of personal data from sensitive objects. Thus the class *SUBJECT*, supporting interface *Subject*, deals with handling of consented policies and collection of personal data.

The interface *PrivacySettings* specifies the interface for updating consent (Fig. 4). It includes methods for adding and removing consent by the user such that after successful addition/removal of a policy p, that policy (or a smaller) allows/denies access to personal data. There is also functionality for an user to check her current policy settings, through method *seeMyPolicies*, which returns all policies of that user.

Class *PRIVACYSETTINGS* in Fig. 6 implements *PrivacySettings* by storing the consented policies in a field variable *consented*, which is a *Consent* list (i.e., list of consented policies). The add operation $addPolicy(p)$ adds $pos(p)$ at the end of the consented list (unless $p \sqsubseteq consented$ holds already), and the remove operation $remPolicy(p)$ adds $neg(p)$ at the end of the list (unless $p \sqsubseteq consented$ gives false, in which case it is redundant). The consent list of a subject S can be initialized with some initial policies, including $(S, all, rincr)$ for self access.

One may also remove redundant consented policies in the list when new ones are added, using the following strategy: A positive policy $pos(p)$ occurring in a list L is *redundant* in the list if $p \sqsubseteq L'$ holds where L' is the list with this occurrence removed. Similarly, a negative policy $neg(p)$ occurring in L is *redundant* if $p \sqsubseteq L'$ gives false. In these cases L can replaced by L' in order to simplify future compliance tests by limiting the size of the *consented* list.

3.1   Data Collection from Sensitive Objects to Data Subjects

In order to restrict processing of personal information, we define an interface *Sensitive*, which will be the superinterface of all objects handling personal data. The interfaces *Subject* and *Sensitive* in Fig. 5 define the functionality for collection of personal information for subjects and define consent management. Class *SUBJECT* in Fig. 7 gives an implementation. A call to the method *collectMyData* on a subject object from the corresponding user will start a process to collect all personal information about the subject. The broadcast *Sensitive!requestMySensitiveData()* sends a *requestMySensitiveData* message to all objects implementing *Sensitive*. A sensitive object may receive a *requestMySensitiveData* request from a subject object (*caller*) and will then react by collecting the personal data tagged with the subject and send it back to the subject object through the method *receiveMySensitiveData*. This data is then collected incrementally and stored in a (tagged) list, *mydata*, which can be accessed by the corresponding user using *seeMyData* or *seeData*. This class may be used as superclass of objects supporting *Subject*. The method *requestMySensitiveData* is provided by, and implemented in, the runtime system as explained in Sect. 4.2.

```
class PRIVACYSETTINGS (User user) implements PrivacySettings {
  List[Consent] consented; // the current privacy policies
with User
  op PolicyList seeMyPolicies()
    {return (if caller = user then consented else nil fi)}
  op Bool addPolicy(Policy p) { // add a new policy (return false if redundant)
    Bool ok := (caller = user); if ok then
    if p ⊑ consented then ok := false
    else consented :+ pos(p) fi fi; return ok } // incremental update
  op Bool remPolicy(Policy p){ // add a negative policy (return false if redundant)
    Bool ok := (caller=user); if ok then
    if p ⊑ consented then consented :+ neg(p)// incremental update
    else ok := false fi fi; return ok }
...}
```

Fig. 6. The implementation of privacy settings and policy changes.

Interface *Subject* has *all* as declared purpose, and all methods in the interface and class inherit this purpose. The access to personal information in *SUBJECT* complies with the general policy $(S, all, rincr)$ for a subject object S.

4   Runtime System

The operational semantics of the considered language is given in Fig. 9. Data values are tagged with set of pairs of subject and purpose. A runtime configuration of an active object system is captured by a multiset of objects and messages (using blank-space as the binary multiset union constructor). Each object o is responsible for executing all method calls to o as well as self-calls. An object has at most one active process, reflecting the remaining part of a method execution. Objects have the form

$$o : \mathbf{ob}(\delta, \overline{s})$$

where o is the object identity, δ is the current object state, and $\overline{s}$ is a sequence of statements ending with a **return**, representing the remaining part of the active process, or **idle** when there is no active process. The state of an object δ is given by a twin mapping from variable names to tagged values, written $(\alpha|\beta)$, where α is the state of the field variables $\overline{w}$ and class parameters $\overline{z}$ (including this), and β is the state of the local variables $\overline{x}$ and formal parameters $\overline{y}$ of the current process. Look-up in a twin mapping, $(\alpha|\beta)[v]$, is simply given by **if** v in β **then** $\beta[v]$ **else** $\alpha[v]$, where in is used for testing domain membership. The notation $\alpha[v \mapsto e]$ denotes map update, and the notation $(\alpha|\beta)[v := e]$ abbreviates **if** v in β **then** $(\alpha \mid \beta[v \mapsto (\alpha|\beta)[e]])$ **else** $(\alpha[v \mapsto (\alpha|\beta)[e]] \mid \beta)$.

```
class SUBJECT implements Subject // thereby also PrivacySettings
    extends PRIVACYSETTINGS {
  List[TaggedData] mydata; // personal data collected about subject
  op Void receiveMySensitiveData(List[TaggedData] tl){
    mydata :+ tl } // could also include info of caller, i.e., mydata :+ (caller,d)
with User
  op Void collectMyData(){
    if caller = user then
      mydata := nil; // clear list
      Sensitive!requestMySensitiveData() fi } // broadcast to all sensitive objects
  op List[TaggedData] seeMyData(){
    return (if caller = user then mydata else nil fi)}
}
```

Fig. 7. The implementation of subject.

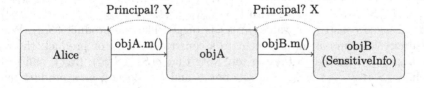

Fig. 8. Call chain. Here Alice is the principal of the method execution on objB.

178 S. Tokas and O. Owe

In addition, the operational semantics defines the system variables *pcs* and nextFut, which appear in the state of each object (in α). The "program counter stack" *pcs* is used for storing the stack of tags on the conditions corresponding to the nesting of enclosing if/while statements, and nextFut is used for generating unique identities for calls. Furthermore, the self reference this is handled as an implicit class parameter, while myfuture and caller appear as implicit method parameters, holding the identity of a call and its caller, respectively.

Example. Consider some personal health data with the tag $\{(Alice, treatm)\}$, and assume the consented policies $(\ldots; pos(Doctor, treatm, full))$ in object *Alice*. A Doctor can then read the data since there is a matching positive policy with at least read access where Doctor is the principal and the purpose of the current method is *treatm* or less. However, for the consented list $(\ldots; pos(Doctor, treatm, full); neg(Bob, treatm, read))$, where *Bob* is a doctor object, read access will be denied due to the presence of negative policy.

4.1 Runtime Tagging of Values

The runtime checking uses two special notions: The *current purpose*, denoted $R_{current}$, is the purpose of the enclosing method, which we assume is statically specified, as in [4]. (Alternatively one could take the purpose defined in some other way, for instance by data-flow graphs as in [7].) Secondly, we define the *current principal*, denoted $P_{current}$, as the first principal object found by following the dynamic call chain from a method execution as illustrated in Fig. 8 (ignoring non-principals such as *objA*).

The runtime evaluation of an expression e gives a tagged value c of form d_l with a tag l. In a method execution the evaluation of an expression e in a state δ and with policy context *pcs* is denoted $\Delta[e]$, where the data value is evaluated (as explained in the next subsection) ignoring tags, resulting in a ground term, i.e., a term d with only constructor functions (g), and where the tag is given by the *tag* function defined below: For tagged data values, the tag function is given by $tag(d_l) = l$, and for untagged values it is given by:

$$
\begin{aligned}
tag() &= flatten(\delta[pcs]) & tag(d_l, \overline{c}) &= l \cup tag(\overline{c}) \\
tag(g(S)) &= \{(S, R_{current})\} \cup tag() & tag(S, \overline{c}) &= \{(S, R_{current})\} \cup tag(\overline{c}) \\
tag(g(\overline{c})) &= tag(\overline{c}), \textbf{otherwise} & tag(d, \overline{c}) &= tag(d) \cup tag(\overline{c}), \textbf{otherwise}
\end{aligned}
$$

Note that the tag includes $flatten(\delta[pcs])$, defined as the *union* of all tags in the stack *pcs*. An untagged product $(\ldots, S, \ldots)$ will also include the tag $(S, R_{current})$. A pair (S, S') will be tagged with $\{(S, R_{current}), (S', R_{current}), flatten(\delta[pcs])\}$. An untagged constructor value $g(S, \overline{c})$ is tagged like the product $(S, \overline{c})$. When a subject S occurs as an argument to a constructor term or product, the pair $(S, R_{current})$ is added to the tag set. Note that $g(S)$, (S, S'), (S, c), and (c, S) include $(S, R_{current})$ in the tag set, but S and (S) do not, as a product must have at least two arguments. A tag (S, R) is redundant in a tag set l, and may be removed, if there is another tag (S, R') in l such that $R < R'$. Non-personal data will have an empty tag set. Policies are considered non-personal.

4.2 Runtime Checking of Privacy Compliance

The runtime system keeps track of the current consented policy list for each subject, specifying the policies for accessing personal data concerning the subject. In the runtime system there is a mapping from subjects to policy lists

$$\mathcal{M} : Subject \rightarrow PolicyList$$

given by $\mathcal{M}[S] == S.consented$ where each *consented* is maintained by the runtime system. Note that even though remote field access is not possible within the program syntax, this restriction does not apply to the runtime system.

The evaluation of expressions, $\Delta[e]$, is done depth-first, left-to-right. Thus $\Delta[f(\bar{e})]$ is $[f(\Delta\bar{e})]$, $\Delta[\text{if } b \text{ then } e \text{ else } e']$ is $\Delta[e]$ if $\Delta[b]$ is true and $\Delta[e']$ if $\Delta[b]$ is false, and for a value c, $\Delta[c]$ is c. (Here b is a boolean expression.) For a defined function f, $\Delta[f(\bar{c})]$ is obtained by the definition of f replacing the formal parameters by the actual values $\bar{c}$. We let the evaluation of a variable v have a built-in compliance check of read access:

$$\Delta[v] = \delta[v], \quad \textbf{if } \forall(S,R) \in tag(\delta[v]) : (P_{current}, R, read) \sqsubseteq \mathcal{M}[S]$$
$$\Delta[v] = error, \textbf{ otherwise}$$

In the first line, the tag is defined by the *tag* function in Sect. 4.1. A policy $(S, all, rincr)$ is initially added to the consented list of each subject object S, to allow the data subject to read and increment his/her own data.

For write access, we define a modified state update function $\Delta[v := c]$ so that it includes the appropriate checks for assignments, and similarly for incremental assignments. Note that there is no check on local variables since they form the local work space, i.e., a method has always write access to the local variables.

$$\Delta[x := c] = \delta[x := c],$$
$$\Delta[w := c] = \delta[w := c], \quad \textbf{if } \forall(S,R) \in tag(c) : (P_{current}, R, write) \sqsubseteq \mathcal{M}[S]$$
$$\Delta[w := c] = \delta[w := error], \textbf{ otherwise}$$

This definition is lifted to expressions e, letting $\Delta[x := e]$ denote $\Delta[x := \Delta[e]]$. Similarly, $\Delta[v :+ c]$ requires $(P_{current}, R, incr) \sqsubseteq \mathcal{M}[S]$ for $(S,R) \in tag(c)$. Non-personal data can be accessed without restrictions since the tag is empty.

Implementation of method *requestMySensitiveData* is provided by the runtime system by making the call *caller!receiveMySensitiveData(tl)* where *tl* is given by $\Delta[\bar{w}]/caller$, i.e., the tagged values of fields with *caller* in the tag.

Runtime Overhead. We have given a solution for compliance checking by a runtime system formulated at a high-level of abstraction. We here discuss the overhead in tagging and checking with this solution, and how it can be reduced. By combining the core information in the tags with the dynamically changing consent information, we are able to keep the information in the tags relatively small, and moreover the tags are not changed when the consent is changed, which is a crucial property. Thus the main overhead is in accessing the consented list for the subjects in the tag. Note that the updates on each consent list is atomic, so there is no need for critical regions nor object synchronization at the runtime level. Thus a compliance check made by one object will not slow down the other objects. This processing can easily be made more efficient by letting each principal pull a copy of a subject's consent setting when needed. However, as this could lead to outdated consent information, one could use a version number for each subject's consent list, and let a principal check that it has the latest version before applying its local copy of a consent list. A further method of reducing overhead, would be to re-represent each consent list by means of a mapping (from principal and purpose of a given subject to access right) thereby the list traversal is reduced to direct look-up. This method has a cost whenever a consent list is updated. A further discussion is beyond the scope of this paper.

4.3 Operational Rules

Each rule in the operational semantics deals with only one object o, and possibly messages, reflecting the nature of concurrent distributed active objects, communicating asynchronously. Remote calls and replies are handled by message passing. When a subconfiguration $\mathcal{C}$ can be rewritten to a $\mathcal{C}'$, this means that the whole configuration $\ldots \mathcal{C} \ldots$ can be rewritten to $\ldots \mathcal{C}' \ldots$, reflecting interleaving semantics. The operational rules reflect small-step semantics. For instance, the rule for *skip* is given by

$$o : \mathbf{ob}(\delta, skip; \overline{s}) \longrightarrow o : \mathbf{ob}(\delta, \overline{s})$$

saying that the execution of *skip* has no effect on the state δ of the object.

Each method call will have a unique identity u. A message has the form

$$\mathbf{msg}\ o \rightarrow o'.m(u, \overline{c})$$

representing a call to m with o as caller, o' callee, and $\overline{c}$ actual parameters, or

$$\mathbf{msg}\ o \leftarrow o'.(u, c)$$

representing a completion event where c is the returned value and u the identity of the call. In addition, $\mathbf{msg}\ o \rightarrow I.m(u, \overline{c})$ denotes a broadcast to all I objects.

The semantics in Fig. 9 formalizes the notion of idleness, and generation of objects and messages, including a rule (*no-query*) for garbage collection of unused reply messages. Generation of identities for objects and method calls is handled by underlying semantic functions and implicit attributes.

The operational semantics uses an additional *query* statement, **get** u, for dealing with the termination of call statements. A synchronous call is treated as an asynchronous call followed by a **get** query. The query **get** u is blocking while waiting for the method response with identity u.

Assignment is handled by updating the state, requiring that there is read access to any personal data (using Δ). An if-statement requires read access to personal data in the condition and the resulting tag set l is pushed on the policy stack pcs, ensuring that all evaluations in the taken branch implicitly includes

assign : $o : \mathbf{ob}(\delta, v := e; \overline{s})$
                $\longrightarrow o : \mathbf{ob}(\Delta[v := e], \overline{s})$

if-true : $o : \mathbf{ob}(\delta, \mathbf{if}\ b\ \mathbf{then}\ \overline{s1}\ \mathbf{else}\ \overline{s2}\ \mathbf{fi}; \overline{s})$
                $\longrightarrow o : \mathbf{ob}(\delta[pcs := push(pcs, l)], \overline{s1}; pcs := pop(pcs); \overline{s})$
                $\mathbf{if}\ \Delta[b] = true_l$

if-false : $o : \mathbf{ob}(\delta, \mathbf{if}\ b\ \mathbf{then}\ \overline{s1}\ \mathbf{else}\ \overline{s2}\ \mathbf{fi}; \overline{s})$
                $\longrightarrow o : \mathbf{ob}(\delta[pcs := push(pcs, l)], \overline{s2}; pcs := pop(pcs); \overline{s})$
                $\mathbf{if}\ \Delta[b] = false_l$

while : $o : \mathbf{ob}(\delta, \mathbf{while}\ b\ \mathbf{do}\ \overline{s1}\ \mathbf{od}; \overline{s})$
                $\longrightarrow o : \mathbf{ob}(\delta, \mathbf{if}\ b\ \mathbf{then}\ \overline{s1};\ \mathbf{while}\ b\ \mathbf{do}\ \overline{s1}\ \mathbf{od}\ \mathbf{fi}; \overline{s})$

new : $o : \mathbf{ob}(\delta, v := \mathbf{new}\ C(\overline{e}); \overline{s})$
                $\longrightarrow o : \mathbf{ob}(\delta[v := o'], \overline{s})$
                $o' : \mathbf{ob}(\delta_C[\mathrm{this} \mapsto o', \mathrm{nextFut} \mapsto initialFut(o'), \overline{z} \mapsto \Delta[\overline{e}]], init_C)$
                $\mathbf{where}\ o' = (fresh, C)$, with $fresh$ a fresh reference relative to C

async. call: $o : \mathbf{ob}(\delta, a!m(\overline{e}); \overline{s})$
                $\longrightarrow o : \mathbf{ob}(\delta[\mathrm{nextFut} := next(\mathrm{nextFut})], \overline{s})$
                $\mathbf{msg}\ o \to \Delta[a].m(\Delta[\mathrm{nextFut}, \overline{e}])$

sync. call : $o : \mathbf{ob}(\delta, v := a.m(\overline{e}); \overline{s})$
                $\longrightarrow o : \mathbf{ob}(\delta, a!m(\overline{e}); v := \mathbf{get}\ \delta[\mathrm{nextFut}]; \overline{s})$

start : $\mathbf{msg}\ o' \to o.m(u, \overline{c})$
                $o : \mathbf{ob}((\alpha|\beta'), \mathbf{idle})$
                $\longrightarrow o : \mathbf{ob}((\alpha|(\beta[\mathrm{caller} \mapsto o', \mathrm{myfuture} \mapsto u, \overline{y} \mapsto \Delta[\overline{c}], pcs \mapsto nil])), \overline{s})$
                $\mathbf{where}\ (m, \overline{y}, \beta, \overline{s})$ is the body of m in the class of this

return : $o : \mathbf{ob}(\delta, \mathbf{return}\ e)$
                $\longrightarrow o : \mathbf{ob}(\delta, \mathbf{idle})$
                $\mathbf{msg}\ \delta[\mathrm{caller}] \leftarrow \delta[\mathrm{this}].(\delta[\mathrm{myfuture}], \Delta[e])$

query : $\mathbf{msg}\ o \leftarrow o'.(u, c)$
                $o : \mathbf{ob}(\delta, v := \mathbf{get}\ u; \overline{s})$
                $\longrightarrow o : \mathbf{ob}(\delta, v := c; \overline{s})$

no-query : $\mathbf{msg}\ o \leftarrow o'.(u, c)$
                $o : \mathbf{ob}(\delta, \overline{s})$
                $\longrightarrow o : \mathbf{ob}(\delta, \overline{s})$
                $\mathbf{if}\ \mathbf{get}\ u \notin \overline{s}$

Fig. 9. Operational rules defining small-step semantics with privacy tags. Unique future identities are ensured by functions $initialFut$, parameterized with the parent, and $next$.

l in the tag set. A while loop is handled by expanding **while** b **do** s **od** to
if b **then** s; **while** b **do** s **od fi** upon execution of the while-statement.
Void methods return the value *void*. We assume all methods end in a return
statement, including class constructors, which end in **return** *void* (although
omitted in the examples). An assignment of the form $v : + e$ is treated as an
atomic operation at runtime. (When lists are implemented by linked lists, this
operation can be executed by a single pointer assignment, since the value of e is
not affected by other objects.) Semantically, $v : + e$ is the same as $v := v + e$,
and we do not show a special rule for it. This means that a consent update can
also be considered atomic. Furthermore, we assume that initial values given to
fields or local variables are expanded to assignments, as described earlier.

For simplicity, rules for broadcasting (similar to that for asynchronous calls)
and local synchronous calls (i.e., queries on local calls) are omitted, since such
calls do not pose additional privacy challenges. In the current semantics, a query
on a local call will lead to deadlock. The handling of local queries would require
addition of a stack in the object state in order to be able to push and pop
unfinished local method frames, for instance as in [6].

The theorem below ensures that every access to a data subject's personal
information will comply with the consented policy.

Theorem 1 (Runtime Compliance). *After a policy is successfully removed,
all further variable accesses that need this policy will fail by giving a runtime
error until the policy, or a stronger one, is added again.*

Proof. Consider an object state δ where $(S, R) \in tag(\delta[v])$. Let policy p denote
$(P_{current}, R, read)$. We must prove that a runtime look-up of v in such a state
gives error after a policy p' such that $p \sqsubseteq p'$ is removed from the consented list
of S and before a policy p'' such that $p \sqsubseteq p''$ is added to the consented list of S.

Every variable look-up is made through one of the operational rules, by means
of δ or Δ. By inspection of these rules, we observe that all program variables are
evaluated by Δ apart from caller and this in rule RETURN, but here the *pcs* stack
is empty (since a return statement occurs last in a body), so evaluation by δ in
this case is the same as by Δ. It remains to show the theorem for variable access
through Δ, and for an access to v we must show that $p \not\sqsubseteq \mathcal{M}[S]$.

By induction on the length of the execution we show that $\Delta[v]$ gives error
between the successful removal of p' and addition of p'' to $\mathcal{M}[S]$. A successful
removal must perform the atomic operation *consented* $: + neg(p')$ in S. Right
afterwards, $neg(p')$ is the last element in $\mathcal{M}[S]$ and therefore $\Delta[v]$ gives error.
If a consent $neg(p''')$ is added, $p \sqsubseteq \mathcal{M}[S]$ remains false. If a consent $pos(p''')$ is
added, we may assume that $p \not\sqsubseteq p'''$ (otherwise p''' can be used as p'' and there
is nothing to prove) and by the induction hypothesis $p \sqsubseteq \mathcal{M}[S]$ remains false. □

5   Related Work

This paper focuses on the intersection between compliance formalization and
programming languages. This line of work is relatively recent, featuring several

threads of active research such as policy specification, policy enforcement, monitoring, privacy by design, language-based privacy, and role-based access control.

The work presented in [8] provides a privacy management framework for the definition of privacy agents (such as subject, controller) acting as representatives of individuals. These privacy agents play a specific role as "representative" or "proxy" of the user in order to manage personal data and ensure privacy-compliant interactions among agents. We share with [8] the objective of privacy compliant interactions, but we use an integrated style, i.e., including compliance checks within objects and actors accessing personal data. In addition, we use the same policy language for different actors and consented policies are maintained in subject objects. Cunche et al. [9] present a generic information and consent framework for IoT that allows the data subject to express privacy requirements as well as receive the information and associated privacy policy. The privacy policies for subjects and controllers are based on the PILOT semantics [10]. Privacy policies in [10] are more expressive than ours as they also encapsulate contextual information, but the semantics of policy compliance is not discussed in particular. We define fewer privacy requirements and focus on compliance formalization. The approach followed in [9] makes use of dedicated privacy agents, while we integrate the compliance checks in actor objects.

Sen et al. [11] demonstrate techniques for compliance checking in big data systems. Privacy policies are specified using a policy specification language, *LEGALEASE*, where policies can be expressed using *allow* and *deny* clauses to permit and prohibit access. Policies can be expressed using nested allow-deny rules. Policy clauses use data store, purpose, role, and data type attributes to specify information flow restrictions. Then, a data inventory tool *GROK* maps data types in code to high-level policy concepts, and the compliance checking then reduces to a form of information flow analysis. This is similar to our approach in [4] where we associate policy with the *types* carrying sensitive information, but the difference is that the type-policy mapping is integrated in the language. The policy specification language in [11] has some similarities with our work: the semantics of policies is compositional and policies are expressed as lists of positive and negative policies. However, for the sake of simplicity, we do not consider nested-policies. All information flow restrictions (policy attributes) are encoded as a lattice in [11], while in our setting that is not the case. However, in [11] the concept lattice does not seem to distinguish with information about other subjects, which we do and in addition we can generate tags at runtime when new information (involving a subject or personal information) is created.

Yang et al. [12] propose a *policy-agnostic programming* model. Sensitive data values are associated with policies and then the programmer may implement the rest of the program in a policy agnostic manner. The language's [13] runtime system enforces these policies to ensure that only policy compliant values are used in computations. In contrast, we use generalized polices for each subject (including purpose) and minimize the information in the tags.

Other examples of language-based approaches relying on information-flow control include the role-based approach in [14] and the purpose-based approach in [15]. Myers and Liskov present a model of decentralized information flow labels, where *principals* and *labels* are the essentials of the model [14]. Principals are the entities that own, update and release (to other principals) information. A label is a set of *owner: reader* policy pairs, where *owner* is the data owner (i.e., subject in our approach), and *reader* is the principal that has read access to this data. Programs and data are annotated with such labels, and information flow restrictions are enforced by type checking. For an access to be valid, all the policy requirements of the label should be enforced, which holds in our approach as all the tags must comply with the consented policies. There are no generalized policies, and the tags will take more space than in our case. In [15], Hayati and Abadi describe an approach to model and verify aspects of privacy policies in the Jif (Java Information Flow) programming language. Data collected for a specific purpose is annotated with Jif principals and then the methods needed for a specific purpose are also annotated with Jif principals. Explicitly declaring purposes for data and methods ensures that the labeled data will be used only by the methods with connected purposes. However, this representation of purpose is not sufficient to guarantee that principals will perform actions compliant with the declared purpose. In contrast, this can be checked at runtime in our approach.

Basin et al. [7] propose an approach that relates a purpose with a business process and use formal models of inter-process communication to demonstrate GDPR compliance. Process collection is modeled as data-flow graphs which depict the data collected and the data used by the processes. Then these processes are associated with a data purpose and are used to algorithmically generate data purpose statements, i.e., specifying which data is used for which purpose and detect violation of data minimization. A main challenge tackled by this work is to automatically generate compliant privacy policies from the model. We share with this work an explicit specification of *purpose*. In [7], a purpose is associated with a process, while in our approach a method accessing personal information is tagged with a purpose and personal data is tagged with sets of (*subject, purpose*) pairs. This tagging is useful in generating privacy policies to check compliance.

6   Conclusion

We propose a consent management framework that allows a data subject to communicate and update consent policies to the controller and to view all personal data about her in the system along with the purposes for which they are used. We have considered a core language for distributed active object systems and formalized the notion of policy compliance and given an operational semantics for the considered programming language. The runtime system ensures that every access to personal data complies with the currently consented polices.

We have illustrated the feasibility of formalizing GDPR specific privacy requirements, including *privacy by design* by providing explicit specifications of *purpose* and policy constructs; *lawfulness and transparency* of processing based on consented purposes; *data subject access request* by providing predefined interfaces and classes to assist in providing the data subject with the personal data and purposes for which it is being processed.

Our framework includes a general solution for subjects to observe and change their privacy settings and for subjects to be informed about all personal data stored about them. The solution consists of a set of predefined types for privacy related concepts and a set of interfaces that forms the basis for interaction with external users, a set of classes that is used in interaction with the runtime system, and runtime checking of all access to personal data to ensure that it complies with the current privacy settings. The same framework can be reused for another language, as long as the assumption of interface abstraction is respected and as long as the purpose of any method handling personal data is identified.

Future Work: The framework can be extended to accommodate for other legal bases by having separate policy lists for each legal basis, and a logic to chose from these bases as required. More information can be included in the tags for a richer compliance check, for instance, the *data creator* can be recorded as the current principal of the method instance creating the data. More information can be included in the policy specification, for example restrictions on temporal validity, data collectors, and data creators. Furthermore, we could add cases of non-personal tag information as exceptions to the generated tags, for instance to deal with encryption. We can easily add more fine-grained methods for selection of policies/personal data in the interfaces/classes for privacy settings and data collection (from sensitive objects), for instance using purpose and principal to limit the selection.

References

1. European Parliament and Council of the European Union: The General Data Protection Regulation (GDPR). https://eur-lex.europa.eu/eli/reg/2016/679/oj. Accessed 24 Nov 2019
2. Article 29 Working Party: Guidelines on Consent under Regulation 2016/679. https://ec.europa.eu/newsroom/article29/item-detail.cfm?item_id=623051. Accessed 05 Feb 2020
3. Métayer, D.: Formal methods as a link between software code and legal rules. In: Barthe, G., Pardo, A., Schneider, G. (eds.) SEFM 2011. LNCS, vol. 7041, pp. 3–18. Springer, Heidelberg (2011). https://doi.org/10.1007/978-3-642-24690-6_2
4. Tokas, S., Owe, O., Ramezanifarkhani, T.: Language-based mechanisms for privacy-by-design. In: Friedewald, M., Önen, M., Lievens, E., Krenn, S., Fricker, S. (eds.) Privacy and Identity 2019. IAICT, vol. 576, pp. 142–158. Springer, Cham (2020). https://doi.org/10.1007/978-3-030-42504-3_10
5. Nierstrasz, O.: A tour of hybrid - a language for programming with active objects. In: Advances in Object-Oriented Software Engineering, pp. 67–182. Prentice-Hall, Upper Saddle River (1992)
6. Johnsen, E.B., Owe, O.: An asynchronous communication model for distributed concurrent objects. Softw. Syst. Model. **6**, 39–58 (2007)

7. Basin, David, Debois, Søren, Hildebrandt, Thomas: On purpose and by necessity: compliance under the GDPR. In: Meiklejohn, Sarah, Sako, Kazue (eds.) FC 2018. LNCS, vol. 10957, pp. 20–37. Springer, Heidelberg (2018). https://doi.org/10.1007/978-3-662-58387-6_2

8. Métayer, D.: A formal privacy management framework. In: Degano, P., Guttman, J., Martinelli, F. (eds.) FAST 2008. LNCS, vol. 5491, pp. 162–176. Springer, Heidelberg (2009). https://doi.org/10.1007/978-3-642-01465-9_11

9. Morel, V., Cunche, M., Le Métayer, D.: A generic information and consent framework for the IoT. In: 2019 18th IEEE International Conference on Trust, Security and Privacy in Computing and Communications/13th IEEE International Conference on Big Data Science and Engineering (TrustCom/BigDataSE), pp. 366–373. IEEE (2019)

10. Pardo, R., Le Métayer, D.: Analysis of privacy policies to enhance informed consent. In: Foley, S.N. (ed.) DBSec 2019. LNCS, vol. 11559, pp. 177–198. Springer, Cham (2019). https://doi.org/10.1007/978-3-030-22479-0_10

11. Sen, S., Guha, S., Datta, A., Rajamani, S.K., Tsai, J., Wing, J.M.: Bootstrapping privacy compliance in big data systems. In: 2014 IEEE Symposium on Security and Privacy, pp. 327–342. IEEE (2014)

12. Yang, J., et al.: Preventing information leaks with policy-agnostic programming. Ph.D. thesis, Massachusetts Institute of Technology (2015)

13. Yang, J., Yessenov, K., Solar-Lezama, A.: A language for automatically enforcing privacy policies. ACM SIGPLAN Not. 47(1), 85–96 (2012)

14. Myers, A.C., Liskov, B.: Protecting privacy using the decentralized label model. ACM Trans. Softw. Eng. Methodol. (TOSEM) 9(4), 410–442 (2000)

15. Hayati, K., Abadi, M.: Language-based enforcement of privacy policies. In: Martin, D., Serjantov, A. (eds.) PET 2004. LNCS, vol. 3424, pp. 302–313. Springer, Heidelberg (2005). https://doi.org/10.1007/11423409_19

Tutorials

Tutorial: Parameterized Verification with Byzantine Model Checker

Igor Konnov[1]([✉]), Marijana Lazić[2], Ilina Stoilkovska[1,3], and Josef Widder[1]

[1] Informal Systems, Vienna, Austria
{igor,ilina,josef}@informal.systems
[2] TU Munich, Munich, Germany
lazic@in.tum.de
[3] TU Wien, Vienna, Austria

Abstract. Threshold guards are a basic primitive of many fault-tolerant algorithms that solve classical problems of distributed computing, such as reliable broadcast, two-phase commit, and consensus. Moreover, threshold guards can be found in recent blockchain algorithms such as Tendermint consensus. In this tutorial, we give an overview of the techniques implemented in Byzantine Model Checker (ByMC). ByMC implements several techniques for automatic verification of threshold-guarded distributed algorithms. These algorithms have the following features: (1) up to t of processes may crash or behave Byzantine; (2) the correct processes count messages and make progress when they receive sufficiently many messages, e.g., at least $t + 1$; (3) the number n of processes in the system is a parameter, as well as t; (4) and the parameters are restricted by a resilience condition, e.g., $n > 3t$. Traditionally, these algorithms were implemented in distributed systems with up to ten participating processes. Nowadays, they are implemented in distributed systems that involve hundreds or thousands of processes. To make sure that these algorithms are still correct for that scale, it is imperative to verify them for all possible values of the parameters.

1 Introduction

The recent advent of blockchain technologies [2,20,23,30,68,81] has brought fault-tolerant distributed algorithms to the spotlight of computer science and software engineering. In particular, due to the huge amount of funds managed by blockchains, it is crucial that their software is free of bugs. At the same time, these systems are characterized by a large number of participants. Thus, automated verification methods face the well-known state space explosion problem.

Supported by Interchain Foundation (Switzerland) and by the European Research Council (ERC) under the European Union's Horizon 2020 research and innovation programme under grant agreement No 787367 (PaVeS). Partially supported by the Austrian Science Fund (FWF) via the Doctoral College LogiCS W1255.

A. Gotsman and A. Sokolova (Eds.): FORTE 2020, LNCS 12136, pp. 189–207, 2020.
https://doi.org/10.1007/978-3-030-50086-3_11

Furthermore, the well-known undecidability results for the verification of parameterized systems [4,15,37,38,79] apply in this setting. One way to circumvent these problems is to develop domain specific methods that work for a specific subclass of systems.

In this tutorial, we consider verification techniques for fault-tolerant distributed algorithms. As an example, consider a blockchain system, where a blockchain algorithm ensures coordination of the processes participating in the system. We observe that to do so, the processes need to solve a coordination problem called *atomic (or, total order) broadcast* [43], that is, every process delivers the same transactions in the same order. To achieve that, we typically need a *resilience condition* that restricts the fraction of processes that may be faulty [70]. The techniques we survey in this tutorial deal with the concepts of broadcast and atomic broadcast under resilience conditions.

While Bitcoin [68] was a new approach to consensus, several Blockchain systems like Tendermint [20] and HotStuff [81] are modern implementations that are built on these classic Byzantine fault tolerance concepts. While the techniques we describe here address in part the challenges for the verification of such systems. We discuss open challenges in Sect. 5.

In addition to practical importance, the reasons for the long-standing interest [39,58,61,70] in distributed systems is that distributed consensus is non-trivial in two aspects:

1. Most coordination problems are impossible to solve without imposing constraints on the environment, e.g., an upper bound on the fraction of faulty processes, assumptions on the behavior of faulty processes, or bounds on message delays and processing speeds (i.e., restricting interleavings) [33,39,70].
2. Designing correct solutions is hard, owing to the huge state and execution space, and the complex interplay of assumptions mentioned in Point 1. Thus, even published protocols may contain bugs, as reported, e.g., by [62,64].

Due to the impossibility of asynchronous fault-tolerant consensus [39], much of the research focuses one what kinds of problems are solvable in asynchronous systems (e.g., some forms of reliable broadcast) or what kinds of systems allow to solve consensus. In Sect. 2 we will survey some of the most fundamental system assumptions that allow to solve problems in the presence of faults and example algorithms, and in Sect. 3 we will discuss how these algorithms can be modeled and how they can be automatically verified.

2   Threshold-Guarded Distributed Algorithms

In a classic survey, Schneider [73] explains replicated state machines by the following notion of replica coordination that consists of two properties:

Agreement. "Every non-faulty state machine replica receives every request."
Order. "Every non-faulty state machine replica processes the requests it receives in the same relative order."

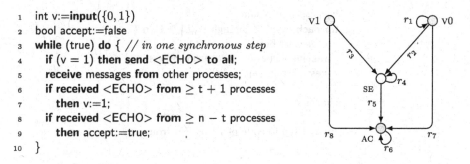

```
1   int v:=input({0, 1})
2   bool accept:=false
3   while (true) do { // in one synchronous step
4       if (v = 1) then send <ECHO> to all;
5       receive messages from other processes;
6       if received <ECHO> from ≥ t + 1 processes
7           then v:=1;
8       if received <ECHO> from ≥ n − t processes
9           then accept:=true;
10  }
```

Fig. 1. Pseudo code of reliable broadcast à la [77] and its threshold automaton.

In Schneider's approach [73], the specification of *Agreement* can be solved using an algorithm for reliable broadcast [43]. The processes can use a consensus algorithm [25, 27, 35] to establish the *Order* property. For instance, the atomic broadcast algorithm from [25] contains these two sub-algorithms.

The simplest canonical system model that allows one to solve consensus is the synchronous one, and we discuss it in Sect. 2.1. A second elegant way to circumvent the impossibility of [39] is by replacing liveness with almost sure termination, that is, a probabilistic guarantee. We review this approach in Sect. 2.3. In fact, reliable broadcast can be solved with an asynchronous distributed algorithm. We discuss their characteristics in Sect. 2.2.

2.1   Synchronous Algorithms

A classic example of a fault-tolerant distributed algorithm is the broadcasting algorithm by Srikanth & Toueg [76]. The description of its code is given in Fig. 1. As is typical for distributed algorithms, the semantics are not visible from the pseudo code. In fact, we use the same pseudo-code to describe its asynchronous variant later in Sect. 2.2.

The algorithm satisfies the Agreement property mentioned above. In a distributed system comprising reliable servers, which do not fail and do not lose messages, this property is easy to achieve. If a server receives a requests it sends the request to all other servers. As messages are delivered reliably, every request will eventually be received by every server. The problems comes with faults. Srikanth and Toueg studied Byzantine failures, where faulty servers may send messages only to a subset of the servers (or even send conflicting data). Then two servers may receive different requests. The algorithm in Fig. 1 addresses this problem, by forwarding message content received from other servers and only accepting a message content when it was received from a quorum of servers. For each message content m, one instance of this algorithm is executed. Initially the variable v captures whether a process has received m, it is 1 if this is the case. Then a process sends ECHO to all. In an implementation, the message would be of the form (ECHO,m), that is, it would be tagged with ECHO, and carry the content m to distinguish different instances running in parallel; also it would

```
best := input_value
for each round 1 through ⌊t/k⌋ + 1 do {
    broadcast best;
    receive values b₁, ... bₗ from others;
    best := min {b₁, ... bₗ};
}
choose best
```

Fig. 2. Pseudo code of *FloodMin* from [28]

suffice to send the message once instead of sending it in each iteration. Then if
the second guard in line 6 evaluates to true at a server p, then p has received $t+1$
ECHO messages, which means that at least one correct process has forwarded
the message, so it also forwards it. If a server receives $n - t$ ECHO messages, it
finally accepts the request stored in m due to line 8. The reason this algorithm
works is that the combination of $n - t$, $t + 1$, and $n > 3t$ ensures that if one
correct processes has $n - t$ ECHO messages, every other correct process will eventually received at least $t + 1$ (there are $t + 1$ correct processes among any $n - t$
processes) so that every correct process will forward, and since there are at least
$n - t$ correct processes, every one will accept. However, this arithmetics over
parameters is subtle and error-prone. To this end, our verification techniques
focus on threshold expressions and resilience conditions.

In the above discussion, we were imprecise about the code semantics. In this
section we consider the synchronous semantics: All correct processes execute the
code line-by-line in lock-step. One loop iteration is called one *round*. A message sent by a correct process to a correct process is received within the same
round. Then after sending and receiving messages in lock-step, all correct processes continue by evaluating the guards, before they all proceed to the next
round. Because this semantics ensures that all processes move together, and all
messages are received within the next rounds, no additional fairness needed to
ensure liveness. In practice, this approach is often considered slow and expensive,
as it has to be implemented with timeouts that are aligned to worst case message delays (which can be very slow in real networks). However, synchronous
semantics offers a high-level abstraction that allows one to design algorithms
easier.

Figure 2 shows an example of another synchronous algorithm. This algorithm
is run by n replicated processes, up to t of which may fail by crashing, that is,
by prematurely halting. It solves the k-set agreement problem, that is, out of
the n initial values each process decides on one value, so that the number of
different decision values is at most k. By setting $k = 1$, we obtain that there can
be exactly one decision value, which coincides with the definition of consensus.
In contrast to the reliable broadcast above, it runs for a finite number of rounds.
The number of loop iterations $⌊t/k⌋ + 1$ of the FloodMin algorithm has been
designed such that it ensures that there is at least one clean round in which at
most $k - 1$ processes crash. When we consider consensus, this means there is a

```
1   bool v := input_value({0, 1});            10   if received at least t + 1
2   int r := 1;                                11       messages (P,r,w,D) then {
3   while (true) do                            12   v := w;
4     send (R,r,v) to all;                     13   if received at least (n + t) / 2
5     wait for n − t messages (R,r,∗);         14     messages (P,r,w,D)
6     if received (n + t) / 2 messages (R,r,w) 15     then decide w;
7     then send (P,r,w,D) to all;              16   } else v := random({0, 1});
8     else send (P,r,?) to all;                17   r := r + 1;
9     wait for n − t messages (P,r,∗);         18   od
```

Fig. 3. Pseudo code of Ben-Or's algorithm for Byzantine faults

round in which no process crashes, so that all processes receive the same values $b_1, \ldots b_\ell$. As a result, during that round all processes set *best* to the same value.

2.2   Asynchronous Algorithms

We now discuss the asynchronous semantics of the code in Fig. 1: at each time, exactly one processes performs a step. That is, the steps of the processes are interleaved. In the example one may interpret this as one code line being an atomic unit of executions at a process. In the "receive" statement, a process takes some messages out of the incoming message buffer: possibly no message, and not necessarily all messages that are in the buffer. The "send to all" then places one message in the message buffers of all the other processes. Often asynchronous semantics is considered more coarse-grained, e.g., a step consists of receiving, updating the state, and sending one or more messages.

As we do not restrict which messages are taken out of the buffer during a step, we cannot bound the time needed for message transmission. Moreover, we do not restrict the order, in which processes have to take steps, so we cannot bound the time between two steps of a single process. Typically, we are interested in verifying safety (nothing bad ever happens) under these conditions.

However, for liveness this is problematic. We need messages to be delivered eventually, and correct processes to take steps from time to time. So liveness is typically preconditioned by fairness guarantees: every correct processes takes infinitely many steps and every message sent from a correct process to a correct process is eventually received. For broadcast these constraints are sufficient, while for consensus they are not.

2.3   Randomized Algorithms

A prominent example is Ben-Or's fault-tolerant binary consensus [7] algorithm in Fig. 3. It circumvents the impossibility of asynchronous consensus [39] by relaxing the termination requirement to almost-sure termination, i.e., termination with probability 1. Here processes execute an infinite sequence of asynchronous rounds. While the algorithm is executed under asynchronous semantics, the processes have a local variable r that stores the round number. Processes essages that they send in round r with the round number. Observe that the algorithm only operates on messages from the current round (the guards only count messages tagged with r). Asynchronous algorithms with this feature are called *communication closed* [29,36]. Each round consists of two stages where the processes first exchange messages tagged with R, wait until the number of received messages reaches a certain threshold (the expression over parameters in line 5) and then exchange messages tagged with P. As in the previous examples, n is the number of processes, among which at most t may crash or be Byzantine. The thresholds $n - t$, $(n + t)/2$ and $t + 1$ in combination with the resilience condition $n > 5t$ ensure that no two correct processes ever decide on different values. If there is no "strong majority" for a value in line 13, a process chooses a new value by tossing a coin in line 16.

3   Parameterized Verification

3.1   Synchronous Algorithms

In [78], we introduced the synchronous variant of threshold automata, and studied their applicability and limitations for verification of synchronous fault-tolerant distributed algorithms. We showed that the parameterized reachability problem for synchronous threshold automata is undecidable. Nevertheless, we observed that counter systems of many synchronous fault-tolerant distributed algorithms have bounded diameters, even though the algorithms are parameterized by the number of processes. Hence, bounded model checking can be used for verifying these algorithms. We briefly discuss these results in the following.

Synchronous Threshold Automata. In a synchronous algorithm, the processes execute the send, receive, and local computation steps in lock-step. Consider the synchronous reliable broadcast algorithm from [77], whose pseudocode is given in Fig. 1 (left). A *synchronous threshold automaton (STA)* that encodes the pseudocode of this algorithm is given in Fig. 1 (right). The STA models the loop body of the pseudo code: one iteration of the loop is expressed as an STA edge that connects the locations before and after a loop iteration.

The semantics of the synchronous threshold automaton is defined in terms of a counter system. For each location $\ell_i \in \{\text{V0, V1, SE, AC}\}$ (a node in the graph), we have a counter κ_i that stores the number of processes located in ℓ_i. The counter system is parameterized in two ways: (i) in the number of processes n, the number of faults f, and the upper bound on the number of faults t, (ii) the expressions in the guards contain n, t, and f. Every system transition moves all processes simultaneously; potentially using a different rule for each process (depicted by an edge in the figure), provided that the rule guards evaluate to true. The guards compare a sum of counters to a linear combination of parameters. Processes send messages based on their current locations. Hence, we use the number of processes in given locations to test how many messages of a certain type have been sent in the previous round. However, the pseudo code in Fig. 1 is predicated by received messages rather than by sent messages. This algorithm

Table 1. A long execution of reliable broadcast and the short representative.

Process	σ_0	σ_1	σ_2	...	σ_{t+1}	σ_{t+2}	σ_{t+3}
1	v1	SE	SE	...	SE	SE	AC
2	v0	v0	SE	...	SE	SE	AC
...				...			
$t+1$	v0	v0	v0	...	SE	SE	AC
...				...			
$n-f$	v0	v0	v0	...	v0	SE	AC

Process	σ_0'	σ_1'	σ_2'
1	v1	SE	AC
2	v0	SE	AC
...			
$t+1$	v0	SE	AC
...			
$n-f$	v0	SE	AC

is designed to tolerate Byzantine-faulty processes, which may send corrupt messages to some correct processes. Thus, the number of received messages may deviate from the number of correct processes that sent a message. For example, if the guard in line 6 evaluates to true, the $t+1$ received messages may contain up to f messages from the faulty processes. If i correct processes send <ECHO>, for $1 \leq i \leq t$, the faulty processes may "help" some correct processes to pass over the $t+1$ threshold. That is, the effect of the f faulty processes on the correct processes is captured by the "$-f$" component in the guards. As a result, we run only the correct processes, so that a system consists of $n - f$ copies of the STA.

For example, in the STA in Fig. 1, processes send a message if they are in a location v1, SE, or AC. Thus, the guards compare the number of processes in a location v1, SE, or AC, which we denote by $\#\{\text{v1}, \text{SE}, \text{AC}\}$, to some linear expression over the parameters, called a threshold. The assignment v:=1 in line 6 is modeled by the rule r_2, guarded with $\phi_1 \equiv \#\{\text{v1}, \text{SE}, \text{AC}\} \geq t+1-f$. This guard evaluates to true if he number of processes in location v1, SE, or AC is greater than or equal to $t+1-f$. The implicit "else" branch between lines 6 and 8 is modeled by the rule r_1, guarded with $\phi_3 \equiv \#\{\text{v1}, \text{SE}, \text{AC}\} < t+1$. The effect of the faulty processes is captured by both the rules r_1 and r_2 being enabled. Similarly, the rules r_5, r_7, r_8 are guarded with the guard $\phi_2 \equiv \#\{\text{v1}, \text{SE}, \text{AC}\} \geq n-t-f$, which is true when the number of process in one of v1, SE, or AC is greater or equal to $n-t-f$, while the rules r_3, r_4 are guarded with $\phi_4 \equiv \#\{\text{v1}, \text{SE}, \text{AC}\} < n-t$. The rule r_6 is unguarded, i.e., its guard is $\top$.

Bounded Diameter. An example execution of the synchronous reliable broadcast algorithm is depicted in Table 1 on the left. Observe that the guards of the rules r_1 and r_2 are both enabled in the configuration σ_0. One STA uses r_2 to go to SE while the others use the self-loop r_1 to stay in v0. As both rules remain enabled, in every round one copy of STA can go to SE. Hence, the configuration σ_{t+1} has $t+1$ correct STA in location SE and the rule r_1 becomes disabled. Then, all remaining STA go to SE and then finally to AC. This execution depends on the parameter t, which implies that the length of this execution grows with t and is thus unbounded. (We note that we can obtain longer executions, if some STA use the rule r_4). On the right, we see an execution where all copies of STA immediately move to SE via rule r_2. That is, while the configuration σ_{t+3} is reached by a long execution on the left, it is reached in just two steps on the right (observe that $\sigma_2' = \sigma_{t+3}$). We are interested in whether there is a natural number k (independent of n, t and f) such that we can always shorten executions to executions of length $\leq k$. (By length, we mean the number of transitions in an execution.) In such a case, we say that the STA has *bounded diameter*. We adapt the definition of diameter from [14], and introduce an SMT-based procedure for computing the diameter of the counter system. The procedure enumerates candidates for the diameter bound, and checks (by calling an SMT solver) if the number is indeed the diameter; if it finds such a bound, it terminates.

Bounded Model Checking. The existence of a bounded diameter motivates the use of bounded model checking, as safety verification can be reduced to checking the violation of a safety property in executions with length up to the diameter. Crucially, this approach is complete: if an execution reaches a bad configuration, this bad configuration is already reached by an execution of bounded length. Thus, once the diameter is found, we encode the violation of a safety property using a formula in Presburger arithmetic, and use an SMT to check for violations.

The SMT queries that are used for computing the diameter and encoding the violation of the safety properties contain quantifiers for dealing with the parameters symbolically. Surprisingly, performance of the SMT solvers on these queries is very good, reflecting the recent progress in dealing with quantified queries. We found that the diameter bounds of synchronous algorithms in the literature are tiny (from 1 to 8), which makes our approach applicable in practice. The verified algorithms are given in Sect. 4.

Undecidability. In [78], we showed that the parameterized reachability problem is in general undecidable for STA. In particular, this implies that some STA have unbounded diameters. We identified a class of STA which in theory have bounded diameters. For some STA outside of this class, our SMT-based procedure still can automatically find the diameter. Remarkably, the SMT-based procedure gives us the diameters that are independent of the parameters.

3.2   Asynchronous Algorithms

Asynchronous Threshold Automata. Similarly as in STAs, nodes in asynchronous threshold automata (TAs) represent locations of processes, and edges represent local transitions. What makes a difference between an STA and a TA are shared variables and labels on edges that have a form $\gamma \mapsto$ act. A process moves along an edge labelled by $\gamma \mapsto$ act and performs an action act, only if the condition γ, called a *threshold guard*, evaluates to true.

We model reliable broadcast [76] using the same threshold automaton from Fig. 1 but with different edge labels in comparison to the STA. We use a shared variable x to capture the number of <ECHO> messages sent by correct processes. We have two threshold guards: $\gamma_1 \colon x \geq (t+1) - f$ and $\gamma_2 \colon x \geq (n-t) - f$. Depending on the initial value of a correct process, 0 or 1, the process is initially either in location v0 or in v1. If its value is 1 a process broadcasts <ECHO>, and executes the rule r_3: TRUE $\mapsto$ x++. This is modelled by a process moving from V1 to SE and increasing the value of x. If its value is 0, it has to wait to receive enough messages, i.e., it waits for γ_1 to become true, and then it broadcasts the <ECHO> message and moves to location SE. Thus, r_2 is labelled by $\gamma_1 \mapsto x$++. Finally, once a process has γ_2-enough <ECHO> messages, it sets accept to true and moves to AC. Thus, r_5 is labelled by γ_2, whereas r_7 and r_8 by $\gamma_2 \mapsto x$++.

Counter Systems. The semantics of threshold automata is captured by counter systems. Instead of storing the location of each process, we count the number of processes in each location, as all processes are identical. Therefore, a configuration comprises (i) values of the counters for each location, (ii) values of the shared variables, and (iii) parameter values. A configuration is initial if all processes are in initial locations, here V0 or V1, and all shared variables have value 0 (here $x = 0$). A transition of a process along an edge from location ℓ to location ℓ' — labelled by $\gamma \mapsto$ act — is modelled by the configuration update as follows: (i) the counter of ℓ is decreased by 1, and the counter of ℓ' is increased by 1, (ii) shared variables are updated according to the action act, and (iii) parameter values are unchanged. The key ingredient of our technique is acceleration of transitions, that is, many processes may move along the same edge simultaneously. In the resulting configuration, counters and shared variables are changed depending on the number of processes that participate in the transition. It is important to notice that any accelerated transition can be encoded in SMT.

Reachability. In [49], we determine a finite set of execution "patterns", and then analyse each pattern separately. These patterns restrict the order in which threshold guards become true (if ever). Namely, we observe how the set of guards that evaluate to true changes along each execution. In our example, there are two (non-trivial) guards, γ_1 and γ_2. Initially, both are false as $x = 0$. During an execution, none, one, or both of them become true, but note that once they become true, they never return to false, as the number of sent messages x cannot decrease. Thus, there is a finite set of execution patterns.

For instance, a pattern $\{\} \ldots \{\gamma_1\} \ldots \{\gamma_1, \gamma_2\}$ captures all finite executions τ that can be represented as $\tau = \tau_1 \cdot t_1 \cdot \tau_2 \cdot t_2 \cdot \tau_3$, where τ_1, τ_2, τ_3 are sub-executions of τ, and t_1 and t_2 are transitions. No threshold guard is enabled in a configuration visited by τ_1, and only γ_1 is enabled in all configurations visited by τ_2. Both guards are enabled in configurations visited by τ_3, and t_1 and t_2 change the evaluation of the guards. Another pattern $\{\} \ldots \{\gamma_2\} \ldots \{\gamma_1, \gamma_2\}$ enables γ_2 before γ_1. Third pattern $\{\} \ldots \{\gamma_1\}$ never enables γ_2.

To perform verification, we have to analyse all execution patterns. For each pattern we construct a so-called *schema*: A sequence of accelerated transitions that have as free variables: the number of processes that execute the transitions and the parameter values. In Fig. 1 transitions are modelled by edges denoted with r_i, $i \in 1..8$. For instance, the pattern $\{\} \ldots \{\gamma_1\}$ produces the schema:

$$\mathcal{S} = \{\} \underbrace{r_1, r_3, r_3}_{\tau_1} \underbrace{r_3}_{t_1} \{\gamma_1\} \underbrace{r_1, r_2, r_3, r_4}_{\tau_2} \{\gamma_1\} .$$

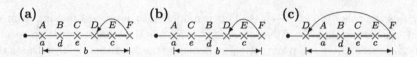

Fig. 4. Three out of 18 shapes of lassos that satisfy the formula $\mathbf{F}(a \wedge \mathbf{F}d \wedge \mathbf{F}e \wedge \mathbf{G}b \wedge \mathbf{G}\mathbf{F}c)$. The crosses show cut points for: (A) formula $\mathbf{F}(a \wedge \mathbf{F}d \wedge \mathbf{F}e \wedge \mathbf{G}b \wedge \mathbf{G}\mathbf{F}c)$, (B) formula $\mathbf{F}d$, (C) formula $\mathbf{F}e$, (D) loop start, (E) formula $\mathbf{F}c$, and (F) loop end.

There are two segments τ_1 and τ_2 corresponding to $\{\}$ and $\{\gamma_1\}$, respectively. In each of them we list all the rules that can be executed according to the true guards, in a fixed natural order: only r_1 and r_3 can be executed if no guard is enabled, and r_1, r_2, r_3, r_4 if only γ_1 holds true. Additionally, we have to list all the candidate rules for t_1 that can change the evaluation of the guards. In our example only r_3 can enable the guard γ_1.

We say that an execution follows the schema $\mathcal{S}$ if its transitions appear in the same order as in $\mathcal{S}$, but they are accelerated (every transition is executed by a number of processes, possibly zero). For example, if (r, k) denotes that k processes execute the rule r simultaneously, then the execution $\rho = (r_1, 2)(r_3, 3)(r_2, 2)(r_4, 1)$ follows $\mathcal{S}$, where the transitions of the form $(r, 0)$ are omitted. In this case, we prove that for each execution τ of pattern $\{\} \ldots \{\gamma_1\}$, there is an execution τ' that follows the schema $\mathcal{S}$, and τ and τ' reach the same configuration (when executed from the same initial configuration). This is achieved by *mover analysis*: inside any segment in which the set of enabled guards is fixed, we can swap adjacent transitions (that are not in a natural order); in this way we gather all transitions of the same rule next to each other, and transform them into a single accelerated transition. For example, $\tau = (r_3, 2)(r_1, 1)(r_3, 1)(r_1, 1)(r_2, 1)(r_4, 1)(r_2, 1)$ can be transformed into $\tau' = \rho$ from above, and they reach the same configurations. Therefore, instead of checking reachability for all executions of the pattern $\{\} \ldots \{\gamma_1\}$, it is sufficient to analyse reachability only for the executions that follow the schema $\mathcal{S}$.

Every schema is encoded as an SMT query over linear integer arithmetic with free variables for acceleration factors, parameters, and counters. An SMT model gives us an execution of the counter system, which typically disproves safety.

For example, consider the following reachability problem: Can the system reach a configuration with at least one process in ℓ_3? For each SMT query, we add the constraint that the counter of ℓ_3 is non-zero in the final configuration. If the query is satisfiable, then there is an execution where at least one process reaches ℓ_3. Otherwise, there is no such execution following the particular schema, where a process reaches ℓ_3. That is why we have to check all schemas.

Safety and Liveness. In [50] we introduced a fragment of Linear Temporal Logic called $\mathsf{ELTL_{FT}}$. Its atomic propositions test location counters for zero. Moreover, this fragment only uses only two temporal operators: $\mathbf{F}$ (eventually) and $\mathbf{G}$ (globally). Our goal is to check whether there exists a counterexample to a

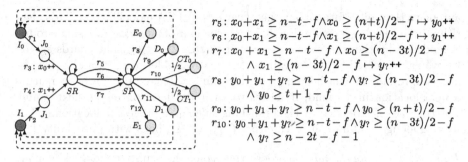

$$r_5 : x_0 + x_1 \geq n - t - f \wedge x_0 \geq (n+t)/2 - f \mapsto y_0\text{++}$$
$$r_6 : x_0 + x_1 \geq n - t - f \wedge x_1 \geq (n+t)/2 - f \mapsto y_1\text{++}$$
$$r_7 : x_0 + x_1 \geq n - t - f \wedge x_0 \geq (n - 3t)/2 - f$$
$$\wedge\ x_1 \geq (n - 3t)/2 - f \mapsto y_?\text{++}$$
$$r_8 : y_0 + y_1 + y_? \geq n - t - f \wedge y_? \geq (n - 3t)/2 - f$$
$$\wedge\ y_0 \geq t + 1 - f$$
$$r_9 : y_0 + y_1 + y_? \geq n - t - f \wedge y_0 \geq (n + t)/2 - f$$
$$r_{10} : y_0 + y_1 + y_? \geq n - t - f \wedge y_? \geq (n - 3t)/2 - f$$
$$\wedge\ y_? \geq n - 2t - f - 1$$

Fig. 5. Ben-Or's alorithm as PTA with resilience condition $n > 3t \wedge t > 0 \wedge t \geq f \geq 0$.

temporal property, and thus formulas in this fragment represent negations of safety and liveness properties.

Our technique for verification of safety and liveness properties uses the reachability method as its basis. As before, we want to construct schemas that we can translate to SMT queries and check their satisfiability. Note that violations of liveness properties are infinite executions of a lasso shape, that is, $\tau \cdot \rho^{\omega}$, where τ and ρ are finite executions. Hence, we have to enumerate the patterns of lassos. These shapes depend not only on the values of thresholds, but also on the evaluations of atomic propositions that appear in temporal properties. We single out configurations in which atomic propositions evaluate to true, and call them *cut points*, as they "cut" an execution into finitely many segments (see Fig. 4).

We combine these cut points with those "cuts" in which threshold guards become enabled (as in the reachability analysis). All the possible orderings in which thresholds and formulas become true, give us a finite set of lasso patterns. We construct a schema for each shape by first defining schemas for each of the segments between two adjacent cut points. On one hand, for reachability it is sufficient to execute all enabled rules of that segment exactly once in the natural order. Thus, each sub-execution τ_i can be transformed into τ_i' that follows the segment's schema, so that τ_i and τ_i' reach the same final configuration. On the other hand, safety and liveness properties reason about atomic propositions inside executions. To this end, we introduced a *property specific mover analysis* that allows us to construct schemas by executing all enabled rules a fixed number of times in a specific order. The number of rule repetitions depends on a temporal property; it is typically two or three.

For each lasso pattern we encode its schema in SMT and check its satisfiability. As ELTL$_{\mathsf{FT}}$ formulas are negations of specifications, an SMT model gives us a counterexample. If no schema is satisfiable, the temporal property holds true.

3.3 Asynchronous Randomized Multi-round Algorithms

Probabilistic Threshold Automata. Randomized algorithms typically have an unbounded number of asynchronous rounds and randomized choices. Probabilistic threshold automata (PTAs) are extensions of asynchronous threshold automata that allow formalizing these features. A PTA modelling Ben-Or's algorithm from Fig. 3 is shown in Fig. 5. The behaviour of a process in a single round is modelled by the solid edges. Note that in this case threshold guards should be evaluated according to the values of shared variables, e.g., x_0 and x_1, in the observed round. The dashed edges model round switches: once a process reaches a final location in a round, it moves to an initial location of the next round. The coin toss is modelled by the branching rule r_{10}: a process in location SP by moving along this fork can reach either CT_0 or CT_1, both with probability $1/2$.

Unboundedly Many Rounds. In order to overcome the issue of unboundedly many rounds, we prove that we can verify PTAs by analysing a one-round automaton that fits in the framework of Sect. 3.2. In [11], we prove that one can reorder transitions of any fair execution such that their round numbers are in a non-decreasing order. The obtained ordered execution is stutter equivalent to the original one. Thus, the both execution satisfy the same LTL$_X$ properties over the atomic propositions of one round. In other words, the distributed system can be transformed to a sequential composition of one-round systems.

The main problem with isolating a one-round system is that consensus specifications often talk about at least two different rounds. In this case we need to use round invariants that imply the specifications. For example, if we want to verify agreement, we have to check that no two processes decide different values, possibly in different rounds. We do this in two steps: (i) we check the round invariant that no process changes its decision from round to round, and (ii) we check that within a round no two processes disagree.

Probabilistic Properties. The semantics of a probabilistic threshold automaton is an infinite-state Markov decision process (MDP), where the non-determinism is traditionally resolved by an adversary. In [11], we restrict our attention to so-called *round-rigid adversaries*, that is, fair adversaries that generate executions in which a process enters round $r + 1$ only after all processes finished round r.

Verifying almost-sure termination under round-rigid adversaries calls for distinct arguments. Our methodology follows the lines of the manual proof of Ben Or's consensus algorithm by Aguilera and Toueg [3]. However, our arguments are not specific to Ben Or's algorithm, and apply to other randomized distributed algorithms (see Table 2). Compared to their paper-and-pencil proof, the threshold automata framework required us to provide a more formal setting and a more informative proof, also pinpointing the needed hypotheses. The crucial parts of our proof are automatically checked by the model checker ByMC.

4   ByMC: Byzantine Model Checker

Overview of the Techniques Implemented in ByMC. Table 2 shows coverage of various asynchronous algorithms with the techniques that are implemented in ByMC. In the following, we give a brief description of these techniques.

We started development of ByMC in 2012. We extended the classic $\{0, 1, \infty\}$-counter abstraction to threshold-guarded algorithms [41,46,47]. Instead of using

Table 2. Asynchronous fault-tolerant distributed algorithms that are verified by different generations of ByMC. For every technique and algorithm we show, whether the technique could verify the properties: safety (S), liveness (L), almost-sure termination under round-rigid aversaries (RRT), or none of them (-).

Algorithm	CA+SPIN[47]	CA+BDD[55]	CA+SAT[55]	SMT-S [52]	SMT-L [50]	SMT+MR[11]
FRB [26]	S+L	S+L	S	S	S+L	-
STRB [77]	S+L	S+L	S	S	S+L	-
ABA [18]	-	S+L	-	S	S+L	-
NBACG [42]	-	-	-	S	S+L	-
NBACR [71]	-	-	-	S	S+L	-
CBC [66]	-	-	-	S	S+L	-
CF1S [32]	-	S+L	-	S	S+L	-
C1CS [19]	-	-	-	S	S+L	-
BOSCO [75]	-	-	-	S	S+L	-
Ben-Or [7]	-	-	-	-	-	S+RRT
RABC [17]	-	-	-	-	-	S+RRT
kSet [65]	-	-	-	-	-	S+RRT
RS-BOSCO [75]	-	-	-	-	-	S+RRT

the predefined intervals $[0, 1)$ and $[1, \infty)$, the tool was computing parametric intervals by simple static analysis, for instance, the intervals $[0, 1)$, $[1, t + 1)$, $[t+1, n-t)$, and $[n-t, \infty)$. ByMC was automatically constructing the finite-state counter abstraction from protocol specifications in Parameterized Promela. This finite abstraction was automatically checked with Spin [45]. As this abstraction was typically too coarse for liveness checking, we have implemented a simple counterexample-guided abstraction refinement loop for parameterized systems. This technique is called CA+SPIN in Table 2.

Spin scaled only to two broadcast algorithms. Thus, we extended ByMC with the abstraction/checking loop that used nuXmv [24] instead of Spin. This technique is called CA+BDD in Table 2. Although this extension scaled better than CA+SPIN, we could only check two more benchmarks with it. Detailed discussions of the techniques CA+SPIN and CA+BDD can be found in [41,53].

By running the abstraction/checking loop in nuXmv, we found that the bounded model checking algorithms of nuXmv could check long executions of our benchmarks. However, bounded model checking in general does not have completeness guarantees. In [51,55], we have shown that the counter systems of (asynchronous) threshold automata have computable bounded diameters, which gave us a way to use bounded model checking as a complete verification approach for reachability properties. This technique is called CA+SAT in Table 2. Still, the computed upper bounds were too high for achieving complete verification.

The SMT-based techniques of Sect. 3.2 are called SMT-S (for safety) and SMT-L (for liveness) in Table 2. These techniques accept either threshold automata or Parametric Promela on their input. As one can see, these techniques are the most efficient techniques that are implemented in ByMC. More details on the experiments can be found in the tool paper [54].

Table 3. Synchronous fault-tolerant distributed algorithms verified with the bounded model checking approach from [78]. With ✓ we show that: the SMT based procedure finds a diameter bound with Z3 (DIAM+Z3) and CVC4 (DIAM+CVC4); there is a theoretical bound on the diameter (DIAM+THM). We verify safety (S) by bounded model checking with Z3 (BMC+Z3) and CVC4 (BMC+CVC4).

Algorithm	DIAM+Z3	DIAM+CVC4	DIAM+THM	BMC+Z3	BMC+CVC4
FloodSet [63]	✓	✓	–	S	S
FairCons [72]	✓	✓	–	S	S
PhaseKing [10]	✓	✓	–	S	S
PhaseQueen [9]	✓	✓	–	S	S
HybridKing [13]	✓	✓	–	S	S
ByzKing [13]	✓	✓	–	S	S
OmitKing [13]	✓	✓	–	S	S
HybridQueen [13]	–	–	–	–	–
ByzQueen [13]	✓	✓	–	S	S
OmitQueen [13]	✓	✓	–	S	S
FloodMin [63]	✓	✓	–	S	S
kSetOmit [72]	✓	✓	–	S	S
RB [77]	✓	✓	✓	S	S
HybridRB [13]	✓	✓	✓	S	S
OmitRB [13]	✓	✓	✓	S	S

Finally, the technique for multi-round randomized algorithms is called SMT-MR in Table 2. This technique is explained in Sect. 3.3.

Model Checking Synchronous Threshold Automata. The bounded model checking approach for STA introduced in Sect. 3.1 is not yet integrated into ByMC. It is implemented as a stand-alone tool, available at [1]. In [78], we encoded multiple synchronous algorithms from the literature, such as consensus [9,10,13,63,72], k-set agreement (from [63], whose pseudocode is given in Fig. 2 and [72]), and reliable broadcast (from [13,77]) algorithms. We use Z3 [67] and CVC4 [6] as back-end SMT solvers. Table 3 gives an overview of the verified synchronous algorithms. For further details on the experimental results, see [78].

5   Towards Verification of Tendermint Consensus

Tendermint consensus is a fault-tolerant distributed algorithm for proof-of-stake blockchains [22]. Tendermint can handle Byzantine faults under the assumption of partial synchrony. It is running in the Cosmos network, where currently over 100 validator nodes are committing transactions and are managing the ATOM cryptocurrency [21]. Tendermint consensus heavily relies on threshold guards, as can be seen from its pseudo-code in [22] [Algorithm 1]. For instance, one of the Tendermint rules has the following precondition:

$$\textbf{upon } \langle \text{PROPOSAL}, h_p, round_p, v, * \rangle \textbf{ from } proposer(h_p, round_p)$$
$$\textbf{AND } 2f + 1 \langle \text{PREVOTE}, h_p, round_p, id(v) \rangle$$
$$\textbf{while } valid(v) \wedge step_p \geq \textsf{prevote for the first time} \qquad (1)$$

The rule 1 requires two kinds of messages: (1) a single message of type PRO-POSAL carrying a proposal v from the process $proposer(h_p, round_p)$ that is identified by the current round $round_p$ and consensus instance h_p, and (2) messages of type PREVOTE from several nodes. Here the term $2f + 1$ (taken from the original paper) in fact does not refer to a number of processes. Rather each process has a voting power (an integer that expresses how many votes a process has), and $2f + 1$ (in combination with $n = 3t + 1$) expresses that nodes that have sent PREVOTE have more than two-thirds of voting power. Although this rule bears similarity with the rules of threshold automata, Tendermint consensus has the following features that cannot be directly modelled with threshold automata:

1. In every consensus instance h_p and round $round_p$, a single proposer sends a value that the nodes vote on. The identity of the proposer can be accessed with the function $proposer(h_p, round_p)$. *This feature breaks symmetry among individual nodes,* which is required by our modelling with counter systems. Moreover, the proposer function should be fairly distributed among the nodes, e.g., it can be implemented with round robin.
2. Whereas the classical example algorithms in this paper count messages, Tendermint evaluates the voting power of the nodes from which messages where received. This adds an additional layer of complexity.
3. Liveness of Tendermint requires the distributed system to reach a global stabilization period, when every message could be delivered not later than after a bounded delay. This model of partial synchrony lies between synchronous and asynchronous computations and requires novel techniques for parameterized verification.

As a first step towards parameterized verification, we are specifying Tendermint consensus in TLA$^+$ [59] and check its properties with the symbolic model checker APALACHE [48]. As Apalache currently supports only non-parameterized verification — the specification parameters must be fixed — we are planning to use automatic abstractions to build a bridge between Apalache and ByMC.

6 Conclusions

Computer-aided verification of distributed algorithms and systems is a lively research area. Approaches range from mechanized verification [44,74,80] over deductive verification [8,29,31,34,69] to automated techniques [5,16,40,56]. In our work, we follow the idea of identifying fragments of automata and logic that are sufficiently expressive for capturing interesting algorithms and specifications, while these fragments are amenable for completely automated verification. We introduced threshold automata for that and implemented our verification techniques in the open source tool ByMC [54]. By doing so, we verified several challenging distributed algorithms; most of them were verified for the first time.

The threshold automata framework has proved to be both of practical relevance as well as of theoretical interest. There are several ongoing projects that consider automatic generation of threshold automata from code, complexity theoretic analysis of verification problems, and more refined probabilistic reasoning.

Acknowledgments. This survey is based on the results of a long-lasting research agenda [12,47,49,50,57,60,78]. We are grateful to our past and present collaborators Nathalie Bertrand, Roderick Bloem, Annu Gmeiner, Jure Kukovec, Ulrich Schmid, Helmut Veith, and Florian Zuleger, who contributed to many of the described ideas that are now implemented in ByMC.

References

1. Bounded Model Checking of STA. https://github.com/istoilkovska/syncTA
2. Abraham, I., Malkhi, D., Nayak, K., Ren, L., Spiegelman, A.: Solidus: an incentive-compatible cryptocurrency based on permissionless Byzantine consensus. CoRR abs/1612.02916 (2016). http://arxiv.org/abs/1612.02916
3. Aguilera, M., Toueg, S.: The correctness proof of Ben-Or's randomized consensus algorithm. Distributed Computing pp. 1–11 (2012)
4. Apt, K., Kozen, D.: Limits for automatic verification of finite-state concurrent systems. IPL **15**, 307–309 (1986)
5. Bakst, A., von Gleissenthall, K., Kici, R.G., Jhala, R.: Verifying distributed programs via canonical sequentialization. PACMPL **1(OOPSLA)**, 110:1–110:27 (2017)
6. Barrett, C., et al.: CVC4. In: CAV, pp. 171–177 (2011)
7. Ben-Or, M.: Another advantage of free choice: Completely asynchronous agreement protocols (extended abstract), In: PODC, pp. 27–30 (1983)
8. Berkovits, I., Lazić, M., Losa, G., Padon, O., Shoham, S.: Verification of threshold-based distributed algorithms by decomposition to decidable logics. In: Dillig, I., Tasiran, S. (eds.) CAV 2019. LNCS, vol. 11562, pp. 245–266. Springer, Cham (2019). https://doi.org/10.1007/978-3-030-25543-5_15
9. Berman, P., Garay, J.A., Perry, K.J.: Asymptotically optimal distributed consensus. Technical report, Bell Labs (1989). http://plan9.bell-labs.co/who/garay/asopt.ps
10. Berman, P., Garay, J.A., Perry, K.J.: Towards optimal distributed consensus (Extended Abstract). In: FOCS, pp. 410–415 (1989)
11. Bertrand, N., Konnov, I., Lazic, M., Widder, J.: Verification of randomized consensus algorithms under round-rigid adversaries. In: CONCUR 2019, LIPIcs, vol. 140, pp. 33:1–33:15 (2019)
12. Bertrand, N., Konnov, I., Lazić, M., Widder, J.: Verification of randomized consensus algorithms under round-rigid adversaries. In: CONCUR, pp. 33:1–33:15 (2019)
13. Biely, M., Schmid, U., Weiss, B.: Synchronous consensus under hybrid process and link failures. Theor. Comput. Sci. **412**(40), 5602–5630 (2011)
14. Biere, A., Cimatti, A., Clarke, E.M., Zhu, Y.: Symbolic Model Checking without BDDs. TACAS. LNCS **1579**, 193–207 (1999)
15. Bloem, R., et al..: Decidability of Parameterized Verification. Morgan & Claypool, Synthesis Lectures on Distributed Computing Theory (2015)
16. Bouajjani, A., Enea, C., Ji, K., Qadeer, S.: On the completeness of verifying message passing programs under bounded asynchrony. In: CAV. pp. 372–391 (2018)
17. Bracha, G.: Asynchronous Byzantine agreement protocols. Inf. Comput. **75**(2), 130–143 (1987)
18. Bracha, G., Toueg, S.: Asynchronous consensus and broadcast protocols. J. ACM **32**(4), 824–840 (1985)
19. Brasileiro, F.V., Greve, F., Mostéfaoui, A., Raynal, M.: Consensus in one communication step PaCT. LNCS **2127**, 42–50 (2001)

20. Buchman, E.: Tendermint: Byzantine Fault Tolerance in the Age of Blockchains. Master's thesis, University of Guelph (2016). http://hdl.handle.net/10214/9769
21. Buchman, E., Kwon, J.: Cosmos whitepaper: a network of distributed ledgers (2018). https://cosmos.network/resources/whitepaper
22. Buchman, E., Kwon, J., Milosevic, Z.: The latest gossip on BFT consensus. arXiv preprint arXiv:1807.04938 (2018). https://arxiv.org/abs/1807.04938
23. Buterin, V.: A next-generation smart contract and decentralized application platform (2014)
24. Cavada, R., et al.: The NUXMV symbolic model checker, In: CAV. pp. 334–342 (2014)
25. Chandra, T.D., Toueg, S.: Unreliable failure detectors for reliable distributed systems. J. ACM **43**(2), 225–267 (1996)
26. Chandra, T.D., Toueg, S.: Unreliable failure detectors for reliable distributed systems. JACM **43**(2), 225–267 (1996)
27. Charron-Bost, B., Schiper, A.: The heard-of model: computing in distributed systems with benign faults. Distrib. Comput. **22**(1), 49–71 (2009)
28. Chaudhuri, S., Herlihy, M., Lynch, N.A., Tuttle, M.R.: Tight Bounds for k-set Agreement. J. ACM **47**(5), 912–943 (2000)
29. Damian, A., Drăgoi, C., Militaru, A., Widder, J.: Communication-closed asynchronous protocols, In: CAV. pp. 344–363 (2019)
30. Decker, C., Seidel, J., Wattenhofer, R.: Bitcoin meets strong consistency, In: ICDCN. pp. 13:1–13:10 (2016). https://doi.org/10.1145/2833312.2833321
31. Desai, A., Garg, P., Madhusudan, P.: Natural proofs for asynchronous programs using almost-synchronous reductions, In: OOPSLA, pp. 709–725 (2014)
32. Dobre, D., Suri, N.: One-step consensus with zero-degradation, In: DSN. pp. 137–146 (2006)
33. Dolev, D., Dwork, C., Stockmeyer, L.: On the minimal synchronism needed for distributed consensus. J. ACM **34**, 77–97 (1987)
34. Drăgoi, C., Henzinger, T.A., Veith, H., Widder, J., Zufferey, D.: A logic-based framework for verifying consensus algorithms VMCAI. LNCS **8318**, 161–181 (2014)
35. Dwork, C., Lynch, N., Stockmeyer, L.: Consensus in the presence of partial synchrony. J. ACM **35**(2), 288–323 (1988)
36. Elrad, T., Francez, N.: Decomposition of distributed programs into communication-closed layers. Sci. Comput. Program. **2**(3), 155–173 (1982)
37. Emerson, E., Namjoshi, K.: Reasoning about rings, In: POPL, pp. 85–94 (1995)
38. Esparza, J.: Decidability of model checking for infinite-state concurrent systems. Acta Informatica **34**(2), 85–107 (1997)
39. Fischer, M.J., Lynch, N.A., Paterson, M.S.: Impossibility of distributed consensus with one faulty process. J. ACM **32**(2), 374–382 (1985)
40. Gleissenthall, K.V., Gökhan Kici, R., Bakst, A., Stefan, D., Jhala, R.: Pretend synchrony. In: POPL (2019), (to appear)
41. Gmeiner, A., Konnov, I., Schmid, U., Veith, H., Widder, J.: Tutorial on parameterized model checking of fault-tolerant distributed algorithms. In: Bernardo, M., Damiani, F., Hähnle, R., Johnsen, E.B., Schaefer, I. (eds.) SFM 2014. LNCS, vol. 8483, pp. 122–171. Springer, Cham (2014). https://doi.org/10.1007/978-3-319-07317-0_4
42. Guerraoui, R.: Non-blocking atomic commit in asynchronous distributed systems with failure detectors. Distrib. Comput. **15**(1), 17–25 (2002)
43. Hadzilacos, V., Toueg, S.: Fault-tolerant broadcasts and related problems. In: Mullender, S. (ed.) Distributed systems (2nd Ed.) pp. 97–145 (1993)

44. Hawblitzel, C., et al.: Ironfleet: proving safety and liveness of practical distributed systems. Commun. ACM **60**(7), 83–92 (2017)
45. Holzmann, G.: The SPIN Model Checker. Addison-Wesley, Boston (2003)
46. John, A., Konnov, I., Schmid, U., Veith, H., Widder, J.: Counter attack on byzantine generals: parameterized model checking of fault-tolerant distributed algorithms, October 2012. http://arxiv.org/abs/1210.3846
47. John, A., Konnov, I., Schmid, U., Veith, H., Widder, J.: Parameterized model checking of fault-tolerant distributed algorithms by abstraction, In: FMCAD. pp. 201–209 (2013)
48. Konnov, I., Kukovec, J., Tran, T.: TLA+ model checking made symbolic. PACMPL **3(OOPSLA)**, 123:1–123:30 (2019)
49. Konnov, I., Lazić, M., Veith, H., Widder, J.: Para²: Parameterized path reduction, acceleration, and SMT for reachability in threshold-guarded distributed algorithms. Formal Methods Syst. Des. **51**(2), 270–307 (2017)
50. Konnov, I., Lazić, M., Veith, H., Widder, J.: A short counterexample property for safety and liveness verification of fault-tolerant distributed algorithms. In: POPL, pp. 719–734 (2017)
51. Konnov, I., Veith, H., Widder, J.: On the completeness of bounded model checking for threshold-based distributed algorithms: reachability. CONCUR. LNCS **8704**, 125–140 (2014)
52. Konnov, I., Veith, H., Widder, J.: SMT and POR beat counter abstraction: parameterized model checking of threshold-based distributed algorithms. In: CAV (Part I). LNCS, vol. 9206, pp. 85–102 (2015)
53. Konnov, I., Veith, H., Widder, J.: What you always wanted to know about model checking of fault-tolerant distributed algorithms. In: Mazzara, M., Voronkov, A. (eds.) PSI 2015. LNCS, vol. 9609, pp. 6–21. Springer, Cham (2016). https://doi.org/10.1007/978-3-319-41579-6_2
54. Margaria, T., Steffen, B. (eds.): ISoLA 2018. LNCS, vol. 11246. Springer, Cham (2018). https://doi.org/10.1007/978-3-030-03424-5
55. Konnov, I.V., Veith, H., Widder, J.: On the completeness of bounded model checking for threshold-based distributed algorithms: reachability. Inf. Comput. **252**, 95–109 (2017)
56. Kragl, B., Qadeer, S., Henzinger, T.A.: Synchronizing the asynchronous. In: CONCUR. pp. 21:1–21:17 (2018)
57. Kukovec, J., Konnov, I., Widder, J.: Reachability in parameterized systems: all flavors of threshold automata. In: CONCUR. LIPIcs, vol. 118, pp. 19:1–19:17 (2018)
58. Lamport, L.: Time, clocks, and the ordering of events in a distributed system. Commun. ACM **21**(7), 558–565 (1978)
59. Lamport, L.: Specifying Systems: The TLA+ Language and Tools for Hardware and Software Engineers. Addison-Wesley, Boston (2002)
60. Lazić, M., Konnov, I., Widder, J., Bloem, R.: Synthesis of distributed algorithms with parameterized threshold guards. In: OPODIS. LIPIcs, vol. 95, pp. 32:1–32:20 (2017). https://doi.org/10.4230/LIPIcs.OPODIS.2017.32
61. Le Lann, G.: Distributed systems - towards a formal approach. In: IFIP Congress, pp. 155–160 (1977). http://www-roc.inria.fr/novaltis/publications/IFIP%20Congress%201977.pdf
62. Lincoln, P., Rushby, J.: A formally verified algorithm for interactive consistency under a hybrid fault model. In: FTCS, pp. 402–411 (1993)
63. Lynch, N.: Distributed Algorithms. Morgan Kaufman, San Francisco (1996)

64. Malekpour, M.R., Siminiceanu, R.: Comments on the "Byzantine self-stabilizing pulse synchronization". protocol: Counterexamples. Tech. rep., NASA, February 2006. http://shemesh.larc.nasa.gov/fm/papers/Malekpour-2006-tm213951.pdf
65. Mostéfaoui, A., Moumen, H., Raynal, M.: Randomized k-set agreement in crash-prone and Byzantine asynchronous systems. Theor. Comput. Sci. **709**, 80–97 (2018)
66. Mostéfaoui, A., Mourgaya, E., Parvédy, P.R., Raynal, M.: Evaluating the condition-based approach to solve consensus. In: DSN, pp. 541–550 (2003)
67. de Moura, L., Bjørner, N.: Z3: an efficient SMT solver. In: TACAS, pp. 337–340 (2008)
68. Nakamoto, S.: Bitcoin: a peer-to-peer electronic cash system (2008). https://bitcoin.org/bitcoin.pdf
69. Padon, O., McMillan, K.L., Panda, A., Sagiv, M., Shoham, S.: Ivy: safety verification by interactive generalization. In: PLDI, pp. 614–630 (2016)
70. Pease, M.C., Shostak, R.E., Lamport, L.: Reaching agreement in the presence of faults. J. ACM **27**(2), 228–234 (1980)
71. Raynal, M.: A case study of agreement problems in distributed systems: Non-blocking atomic commitment. In: HASE, pp. 209–214 (1997)
72. Raynal, M.: Fault-tolerant agreement in synchronous message-passing systems. Morgan & Claypool Publishers, Synthesis Lectures on Distributed Computing Theory (2010)
73. Schneider, F.B.: Implementing fault-tolerant services using the state machine approach: a tutorial. ACM Comput. Surv. **22**(4), 299–319 (1990)
74. Sergey, I., Wilcox, J.R., Tatlock, Z.: Programming and proving with distributed protocols. PACMPL **2(POPL)**, 281–2830 (2018)
75. Song, Y.J., van Renesse, R.: Bosco: one-step Byzantine asynchronous consensus. DISC. LNCS **5218**, 438–450 (2008)
76. Srikanth, T.K., Toueg, S.: Optimal clock synchronization. J. ACM **34**(3), 626–645 (1987)
77. Srikanth, T., Toueg, S.: Simulating authenticated broadcasts to derive simple fault-tolerant algorithms. Dist. Comp. **2**, 80–94 (1987)
78. Stoilkovska, I., Konnov, I., Widder, J., Zuleger, F.: Verifying safety of synchronous fault-tolerant algorithms by bounded model checking. In: Vojnar, T., Zhang, L. (eds.) TACAS 2019. LNCS, vol. 11428, pp. 357–374. Springer, Cham (2019). https://doi.org/10.1007/978-3-030-17465-1_20
79. Suzuki, I.: Proving properties of a ring of finite-state machines. Inf. Process. Lett. **28**(4), 213–214 (1988)
80. Wilcox, J.R., et al.: Verdi: a framework for implementing and formally verifying distributed systems. In: PLDI, pp. 357–368 (2015)
81. Yin, M., Malkhi, D., Reiter, M.K., Golan-Gueta, G., Abraham, I.: Hotstuff: BFT consensus with linearity and responsiveness. In: PODC, pp. 347–356 (2019)

Typechecking Java Protocols
with [St]Mungo

A. Laura Voinea$^{(\boxtimes)}$ (ID), Ornela Dardha (ID), and Simon J. Gay (ID)

School of Computing Science, University of Glasgow, Glasgow, UK
a.voinea.1@research.gla.ac.uk, {Ornela.Dardha,Simon.Gay}@glasgow.ac.uk

Abstract. This is a tutorial paper on [St]Mungo, a toolchain based on *multiparty session types* and their connection to *typestates* for safe distributed programming in Java language.

The StMungo ("Scribble-to-Mungo") tool is a bridge between multiparty session types and typestates. StMungo translates a *communication protocol*, namely a sequence of sends and receives of messages, given as a multiparty session type in the Scribble language, into a typestate specification and a Java API skeleton. The generated API skeleton is then further extended with the necessary logic, and finally typechecked by Mungo. The Mungo tool extends Java with (optional) typestate specifications. A typestate is a state machine specifying a *Java object protocol*, namely the permitted sequence of method calls of that object. Mungo statically typechecks that method calls follow the object's protocol, as defined by its typestate specification. Finally, if no errors are reported, the code is compiled with `javac` and run as standard Java code.

In this tutorial paper we give an overview of the stages of the [St]Mungo toolchain, starting from Scribble communication protocols, translating to Java classes with typestates, and finally to typechecking method calls with Mungo. We illustrate the [St]Mungo toolchain via a real-world case study, the HTTP client-server request-response protocol over TCP. During the tutorial session, we will apply [St]Mungo to a range of examples having increasing complexity, with HTTP being one of them.

Keywords: Multiparty session types · Typestate · Mungo · StMungo · HTTP protocol

1 Introduction

The concept of an *application programming interface* (API) is central to software architecture and implementation. An API is a specification of a collection

---

Supported by the UK EPSRC grant EP/K034413/1, "From Data Types to Session Types: A Basis for Concurrency and Distribution (ABCD)", by the EU HORIZON 2020 MSCA RISE project 778233 "BehAPI: Behavioural Application Program Interfaces", and by an EPSRC PhD studentship.

© IFIP International Federation for Information Processing 2020
Published by Springer Nature Switzerland AG 2020
A. Gotsman and A. Sokolova (Eds.): FORTE 2020, LNCS 12136, pp. 208–224, 2020.
https://doi.org/10.1007/978-3-030-50086-3_12

of related programming language operations that enable the use of a particular kind of functionality. For example, in a typical programming language, the functionality for implementing graphical user interfaces is organised and described as an API. In an object-oriented language, an API is presented as a collection of classes, each with methods for a range of related operations. A specific example is the JavaFX API, which provides graphics and media functionality—in fact JavaFX is so large that it is better described as a collection of APIs for more specific purposes, such as media streaming and web rendering.

Nowadays, APIs are not only used to present the library functions of programming language implementations. They can also package up the functionality of distributed services, and be called remotely in networked applications. A significant trend is the development and publication of APIs to allow access to functions that were previously internal to a software application. For example, the developer of a student records database might publish an API to allow programmatic access to the data, and this could be used by third-party developers to produce applications that make use of student records to provide additional services. This evolution of the API concept has become a key aspect of open software development and service-oriented system architectures. In a commercial setting it has enabled the birth of an API economy in which the provision of APIs can be monetised. APIs have thus become a key focus of the software industry.

Typical methods in an API require parameters, and these can be specified using standard type-theoretic techniques. In a statically typed language, each method in an API has its type signature, specifying the types of its parameters and the type of any result that it returns. The standard techniques of typechecking, especially when implemented in an integrated development environment (IDE), are effective in supporting programmers to use APIs correctly, identifying errors during development rather than waiting until the testing phase when they are much more expensive to correct.

The description of an API as a collection of typed method signatures however, does not capture any constraints on the sequence in which methods can be called. For example, an API for working with files requires that a file must be successfully opened before it can be read or written. After the file has been closed, it cannot be read or written any more, and the only available method is open. Another standard example is the `Iterator` class in Java, in which the `hasNext` method must be called (and return `true`) before the `next` method can be called.

Another category of examples arises in APIs for communication, in concurrent or distributed systems. Typically the communication within a system is structured around various *communication protocols*, each of which specifies a permitted sequence of messages and the format (type) of each message. An API whose operations allow sending and receiving of messages in a given protocol has constraints so that the operation calls follow the protocol specification. These constraints cannot be expressed purely within the framework of typed method signatures, more expressive types and type systems are needed. In general, we can speak of *behavioural APIs*, a term based on the term *behavioural types* for type systems that specify sequence-related properties involving multiple method calls.

Two established lines of research are relevant in this context. One is *typestates* [42], which is the idea of using static type systems to specify permitted sequences of method calls. The other is *session types* [26, 28, 44], which are type-theoretic descriptions of communication protocols. The StMungo and Mungo tools are the result of convergence between these two lines of research [2, 17, 34, 35]. On the one hand, APIs for communication protocols are clearly a special case of behavioural APIs in general. On the other hand, transferring the concepts of session types from process calculi or functional languages to object-oriented languages requires embedding them in a more general setting that supports typestates. This is because it is natural to define methods that each perform several communication steps, and then the original communication protocol (session type) gives rise to different, although related, sequencing constraints on the methods.

StMungo is a bridge between session types and typestates, by translating multiparty session types (MPST) [29] written in the Scribble language [41] into typestate specifications for Java classes. The key steps are given in the following:

- Scribble is used as a specification language for *global protocols* (or global types) describing communication among all involved participants in a communication protocol in a distributed system.
- The Scribble tools are used to *validate* and *project* a global type into *local protocols* (or local types) for each participant involved.
- StMungo translates Scribble local types into typestate specifications for Java classes, describing the Java object protocols, namely the permitted sequences of method calls of an object.
- StMungo also generates an API implementation for each participant, which follows its typestate specification, described in the previous step.

At this stage we can run the Mungo tool. The key ideas and steps behind Mungo are given in the following:

- Typestate specifications are expressed as annotations of Java classes, so there is no change to the language itself.
- Linear typing is used to control aliasing, so that there is no possibility of inconsistent views of an object's state.
- The Mungo typechecker checks that method calls are performed following the object's protocol, as specified by its associated typestate.
- If Mungo typechecking is successful and no errors are reported, then the code is compiled with `javac` and run as standard Java code.
- The Mungo typechecker is formalised inspired by session types theory and the resulting type system is proved correct via the standard theorems of progress and subject reduction [34, 35].

In the remainder of this tutorial paper we will describe the StMungo Sect. 2 and Mungo Sect. 3 tools via a real-world case study, the HTTP protocol.

In Sect. 4 we give step-by-step instructions on how to run the tools. In Sect. 5 we discuss related work and in Sect. 6 we conclude the paper and discuss future work.

2   StMungo

The StMungo tool is a Java-based transpiler implemented using the ANTLR v4.5 framework [6]. StMungo acts as a bridge between multiparty session types and typestate specifications. In particular it is the link between the Scribble specification language [27,41] and the Mungo tool Sect. 3. StMungo is the *first* tool to provide a practical embedding of Scribble multiparty session types into an object-oriented language with typestates.

In order to better understand the StMungo tool, we need to describe both the Scribble language and the typestate specifications. Let's start with Scribble.

The Scribble specification language is an implementation of multiparty session types (MPST) [29,41]. Participants in a distributed system communicate among each other by sending and receiving messages and following a predefined communication protocol. Such protocol is given as a *global protocol* (or global type) in Scribble. The Scribble tools can perform *validation* and *projection* of a global protocol. First, we must check if the specified global protocol is valid, meaning if it is correct with respect to transmitted data; there are no deadlocks within the global protocol; there are no un-notified participants for example, regarding session termination, and so on. These checks follow the MPST theory [29]. Once a global protocol is validated, with Scribble tools we can project it into *local protocols* (or local types) for each participant in the system.

The HTTP Protocol Case Study. Let us illustrate the notions of global and local protocols using our HTTP case study. HTTP (HyperText Transfer Protocol) [22] is the underlying data protocol used by the World Wide Web defining how messages are formatted and transmitted, and what actions servers and clients may take in response to various methods, such as GET, PUT or POST. An HTTP session is a sequence of network request-response transactions, initiated by the client sending a request over a TCP connection to a particular port of a server. Upon receiving the request, the server listening on that port sends back a status line, such as "HTTP/1.1 200 OK", and a message of its own. The structure of the request and response messages exchanged is rich and complex, lending itself to be further specified through session types. Hence, we represent the HTTP global protocol in the style of Hu [31] where an HTTP request and response are broken down respectively into sending and receiving a request line – request, followed by zero or more header-fields – host or usera terminated by a new-line. This fine grained representation of the protocol is made possible by the message being broken down via TCP bit streams, in a manner that is transparent to the parties involved.

The global protocol for HTTP specified in Scribble is given in Listing 1.1. Line 1 contains the module declaration, made up of an optional package prefix i.e., `http`, and the name of the file containing the module, `Http`. Line 2 contains a payload type declaration `type <java>...`, which gives an alias (`str`) to a data type (`String`) from an external language `java` which can be used in the payload of a message signature. A module can contain zero or more *global protocol declarations*, consisting of a protocol signature (line 4), choices (lines 5 and 27), message passing (line 6), and recursion (line 7). Lines 11–46 model a correctly formatted client request and lines 49–91 a server response.

```
1  module http.Http;
2  type <java> "java.lang.String" from "rt.jar" as str;
3
4  global protocol Http(role C, role S){
5    choice at C{ // Request
6      request(str) from C to S;  //GET / HTTP/1.1
7      rec X{ choice at C{
8              host(str) from C to S;//Host: www.google.co.uk
9              continue X;
10            }or{
11            userA(str) from C to S;//User-Agent:...
12            continue X;
13            }or{
14            acceptT(str) from C to S;//Accept: text/html...
15            continue X;
16            }or{
17            ... //other header fields
18            body(str) from C to S;
19            }}}
20    //Response
21    httpv(str) from S to C;//HTTP/1.1
22    choice at S{
23      200(str) from S to C;//200 OK
24    }or{
25      404(str) from S to C;//404 Bad Request
26    }
27    rec Y{
28      choice at S{
29        date(str) from S to C;//Date: ...
30        continue Y;
31      }or{
32        server(str) from S to C;//Server:...
33        continue Y;
34      }or{
35        strictTS(str) from S to C;//Strict-Transport-Security
36        continue Y;
37      }or{
38        ...//other header fields
39        body(str) from S to C;
40      }}}
```

Listing 1.1. HTTP Global Protocol

Using the Scribble tools, we can project the HTTP global protocol onto local protocols for the server S and the client C. In this tutorial we will focus only on the client side as we will interact with real-world HTTP servers. The local protocol for the HTTP client C, given in Listing 1.2, describes the behaviour of this role. The _C in the protocol name indicates that C is the local endpoint. For simplicity, we limit this protocol to the GET command only, with the rest being represented in a similar manner.

```
1  ...
2  local protocol Http_C(role C, role S) {
3    choice at C {
4      request(str) to S;
5      rec X { choice at C {
6                host(str) to S;
7                continue X;
8            } or {
9                userA(str) to S;
10               continue X;
11           } or {
12               acceptT(str) to S;
13               continue X;
14           } or {
15               ...//other header fields
16               body(str) to S;
17           }}}
18   httpv(str) from S;
19   choice at S {
20      200(str) from S;
21   } or {
22      404(str) from S;
23   }
24   rec Y { choice at S {
25               date(str) from S;
26               continue Y;
27           } or {
28               server(str) from S;
29               continue Y;
30           } or {
31               strictTS(str) from S;
32               continue Y;
33           } or {
34               ...//other header fields
35               body(str) from S;
36           }}}
```

Listing 1.2. HTTP Client Protocol

The client can send a request line **request** (line 4), followed by zero or more header-fields—**host**, or **userA** and so on. The server responds with a line containing the HTTP version—**httpv** (line 18) followed by the status of the request, either—**200** for a found resource, or—**404** for a bad request. The server can choose zero or more header-fields to follow this message with. The StMungo tool takes in input a Scribble local protocol for a **role** and translates it into a typestate specification for a Java API skeleton. This translation is based on the principle that each **role** in the multiparty session communication following its local protocol, can be abstracted as a Java class following its typestate specification. A typestate is a state machine defining the permitted sequence of method calls of a Java object, thus defining the object's protocol.

The HTTP Protocol Case Study (Continued). Running StMungo on the HTTP client protocol Listing 1.2 produces the following files, where C at the beginning of each file name stands for client.

1. CProtocol.protocol: the typestate specification representing the HTTP client's local protocol. The send and receive operations are translated as Java methods (Listing 1.3 below in this section).
2. CRole.java: the Java API implementing the HTTP client. This class implements the typestate CProtocol over Java sockets (Listing 1.4, Sect. 3).
3. CMain.java: this can be an optional file. It gives a minimum logic of the client CRole and provides a main() method (Listing 1.5, Sect. 3).

The typestate specification CProtocol.protocol for the HTTP client is given in Listing 1.3.

```
 1 typestate CProtocol {
 2    State0 = {void send_REQUESTToS(): State1}
 3    State1 = {void send_requestStrToS(String): State2}
 4    State2 = {void send_HOSTToS(): State3,
 5             void send_USERAToS(): State4,
 6             void send_ACCEPTTToS(): State5,
 7             ... //send other labels
 8             void send_BODYToS(): State12}
 9    State3 = {void send_hostStrToS(String): State2}
10    State4 = {void send_userAStrToS(String): State2}
11    ... //send other main messages
12    State12 = {void send_bodyStrToS(String): State13}
13    State13 = {String receive_httpvStrFromS(): State14}
14    State14 = {Choice1 receive_Choice1LabelFromS():
15             <_200: State15, _404: State16>}
16    State15 = {String receive_200StrFromS(): State17}
17    State16 = {String receive_404StrFromS(): State17}
18    State17 = {Choice2 receive_Choice2LabelFromS():
19             <DATE: State18, SERVER: State19,
20             STRICTTS: State20, ..., BODY: State28>}
21    State18 = {String receive_dateStrFromS(): State17}
22    State19 = {String receive_serverStrFromS(): State17}
23    State20 = {String receive_strictTSStrFromS(): State17}
24    ...
25    State28 = {String receive_BODYStrFromS(): end}}
```

Listing 1.3. Typestate Specification

A typestate is a state machine (Fig. 1) with states labelled State0 (initial state), State1, State2 ... Each state offers a set of methods that must be a subset of the methods defined by the class; each method specifies a transition to a successor state, such that when called at runtime allows the object to change state as specified by its typestate.

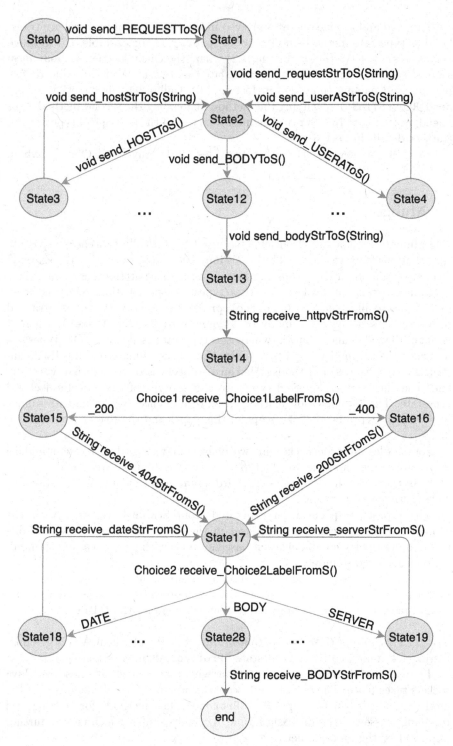

Fig. 1. State machine for CProtocol

The send and receive operations given in the client's local protocol are translated as typestate methods in `CProtocol.protocol`. For example, the message `request(str) to S` (line 4, Listing 1.2) where the client sends a `request` message of type `str` to the server, is translated as two method calls due to formatting and parsing (lines 2–3 in Listing 1.3). Calling the first method `void send_REQUESTToS()` specifying the method and calling the second method `void send_requestStrToS(String)` requests the rest of the message of type `String` (further details in Sect. 3).

We will comment on the other two files `CRole.java` and `CMain.java` in Sect. 3.

3   Mungo

The Mungo tool is a Java front-end tool used to statically typecheck typestate specifications for Java classes. The tool is implemented in Java using the ExtendJ framework [25,38], a meta-compiler based on reference attribute grammars.

Mungo extends a Java class with a typestate specification, which is saved in a separate file (such as `CProtocol.protocol` in Sect. 2) and is attached to a Java class using the annotation `@Typestate("ProtocolName")`, where "ProtocolName" names the file where the typestate is defined. The typestate inference algorithm given by the formalisation of the Mungo tool in [34,35] constructs the sequences of methods called on all objects associated with a typestate, and then checks if the inferred typestate is a subtype of the object's declared typestate. The formalisation of the typestate inference system and its soundness properties are beyond the scope of this paper and the reader is referred to [34,35].

Source files are typechecked in two phases: first, according to the standard Java type system, and then to the typestate type system via Mungo. The source files can then be compiled using standard `javac` and executed in the standard Java runtime environment.

The typestate specification generated from StMungo together with the Mungo typechecker can guide the user in the design and development of distributed multiparty communication-based systems with guarantees of communication safety and soundness.

We will now describe the use of Mungo via our running example, the HTTP protocol, and in particular we will do so by commenting on the last two files `CRole.java` and `CMain.java` generated by StMungo for the HTTP client C.

The HTTP Protocol Case Study (Continued). The HTTP client API is given by Listing 1.4 annotated by the typestate `CProtocol`, defined in Listing 1.3.

Lines 3–9 define the client's constructor where the connection phase over Java sockets takes place. The rest of `CRole` contains a minimal implementation of the methods specified in the typestate `CProtocol`. The methods for sending and receiving messages contain basic formatting and parsing, which can be further improved by the programmer.

```
1  @Typestate("CProtocol")
2  public class CRole {
3    public CRole() { ...//Bind the sockets and accept a client
4      connection
5      try { // Create the read and write streams
6          socketSIn = new BufferedReader(...);
7          socketSOut = new PrintWriter(...);}
8      catch (IOException e) {...}}
9    public void send_REQUESTToS(){this.socketSOut.print("GET")
       ;}
10   public void send_requestStrToS(String payload){this.
       socketSOut.println(payload);}
11   ... // Define all other send methods in CProtocol
12   public String receive_httpvStrFromS()() {
13     String line = "";
14     try {line = this.socketSIn.readLine();}
15     catch (IOException e) {...}
16     return line;}
17   public Choice1 receive_Choice1LabelFromS() {
18     try {stringLabelChoice1 = this.socketSIn.readLine();}
19     catch (IOException e) {...}
20     switch (stringLabelChoice1) {
21       case "200":
22         return Choice1._200;
23       case "404":
24       default:
25         return Choice1._404;}}
26   public String receive_200StrFromS() {
27     String line = "";
28     try {line = this.socketSIn.readLine();}
29     catch (IOException e) {...}
30     return line;}
31   public String receive_404StrFromS() {
32     String line = "";
33     try {line = this.socketSIn.readLine();}
34     catch (IOException e) {...}
35     return line;}
36     .../*Define all other receive methods in CProtocol*/}}}
```

Listing 1.4. Client API

Lines 8–9 define the two methods for sending the initial, mandatory, request line—send_REQUESTToS (for the method, i.e. "GET") and send_requestStrToS (for the rest of the message). Lines 11–34 define methods for receiving the first line in a response, composed of the HTTP version—receive_httpvStrFrom and the status. The method in line 16 Choice1 receive_Choice1LabelFromS captures the status. This method returns a Choice1 type, which is an enumerated type defined as:

```
1  enum Choice1 {_200, _404;}
```

For each choice there is an enumerated type, named by StMungo according to the position of the choice in the sequence of choices within the local protocol.

The values of the enumerated type are the names of the first message in each branch of the choice, for example for `Choice1` they are `_200` or `_400`. Thus, the method `receive_Choice1LabelFromS` receives a message which represents one of the two status codes, and it returns the corresponding `enum` value.

Let's move now onto the `CMain.java` given in Listing 1.5. `CMain.java` contains a minimal implementation of the client endpoint using the `CRole` class to communicate with the server endpoint. Below we give the main method, omitting any auxiliary methods generated by StMungo. The code is modified from the generated version by adding the request and host messages needed to request the home page from `www.google.co.uk`.

```
1   public static void main(String[] args) {
2     CRole currentC = new CRole();
3     String sread = //input REQUEST
4     if ("REQUEST".equals(sread)) {
5       currentC.send_REQUESTToS();
6       currentC.send_requestStrToS("/ HTTP/1.1");
7       _X: do { sread = //input header choice
8         switch (sread) {
9           case ("HOST"):
10            currentC.send_HOSTToS();
11            currentC.send_hostStrToS("www.google.co.uk");
12            continue _X;
13            ... //other cases corresponding to header fields
14          case ("BODY"):
15            currentC.send_BODYToS();
16            currentC.send_bodyStrToS("/r/n");
17            break _X;
18        }} while (true);}
19    currentC.receive_httpvStrFromS();
20    switch (currentC.receive_Choice1LabelFromS()) {
21      case _200:
22        currentC.receive_200StrFromS();
23        break;
24      case _404:
25        currentC.receive_404StrFromS();
26        break;}
27    _Y:do {
28      switch (currentC.receive_Choice2LabelFromS()) {
29        case DATE:
30          currentC.receive_dateStrFromS();
31          continue _Y;
32          ... //other cases corresponding to the header fields
33        case BODY:
34          currentC.receive_bodyStrFromS();
35          break _Y;}
36    } while (true);}
```

Listing 1.5. Client Implementation

In line 2 we create a new HTTP client, `currentC`, and proceed by showing the code for a small correctly formatted request, with the initial, mandatory request line messages being sent first (lines 5–6); then among the recursive choice cases we show the code for sending the the host field (lines 10–11), before concluding the request by an empty body (lines 15–16). Then `currentC` will receive the response status line (lines 19–26) followed by recursive choice cases for the fields to be received from the server (lines 27–36).

To ensure that methods of the protocol are called in a valid sequence and that all possible responses are handled, the `CMain` implementation is checked by computing the sequences of method calls that are made on the `currentC` object, inferring the minimal typestate specification that allows them, and then comparing it with the specification declared in `CProtocol`.

4   How to Run [St]Mungo: A Step-by-Step Tutorial

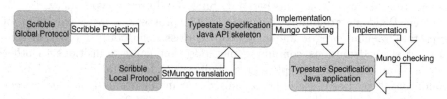

The tools together with the HTTP example and further examples can be obtained from the [St]Mungo repository [1].

The tools come prebuilt and ready to use as runnable jar files: `stmungo.jar` and `mungo.jar`. In the same repository we also provide the latest release—0.4.3, of the command line tool for Scribble.

We show how to use these tools via the HTTP example, assuming the root folder of the repository linked above.

To run the Scribble tool on the global protocol for validation only: `./scribble-0.4.3/scribblec.sh demos/http/Http.scr`

To run the Scribble tool on the global protocol and project the client role: `./scribble-0.4.3/scribblec.sh demos/http/Http.scr -project http C`

To run StMungo and obtain the Java prototype implementation: `java -jar stmungo.jar demos/http/Http_C.scr`

To run Mungo: `java -jar mungo.jar demos/http/CMain.java`

Finally, if no errors are reported, the code can be compiled with `javac` and run as standard Java code.

5   Related Work

There is a huge and growing literature on session types and other forms of behavioural types, going back to the original papers on binary session types [26,28,44] and multiparty session types [29,30]. The BETTY project[1] produced three survey articles: one on foundations of behavioural types [33], one on behavioural types and security [13] and one on behavioural types in programming

---

[1] COST Action IC1201: Behavioural Types for Reliable Large-Scale Software Systems (BETTY), www.behavioural-types.eu.

languages [5]. The project also produced a book [24] describing implementations of programming languages and tools based on behavioural types. The ABCD project[2] has produced a list of implementations of session types in programming languages.

Since the introduction of typestate [42], there have been several projects to add the concept to practical programming languages. Vault [18,21] is an extension of C, and Fugue [19] applies similar ideas to C#. Plural [10] is based on Java and has been used to study access control systems [9] and transactional memory [8], and to evaluate the effectiveness of typestate in Java APIs [10]. Sing# [20] is an extension of C# which was used to implement Singularity, an operating system based on message-passing. It incorporates typestate-like contracts, which are a form of session type, to specify protocols. Bono et al. [12] have formalised a core calculus based on Sing# and proved type safety.

The Plaid programming language [3,43] proposes a new paradigm of typestate-oriented programming. Instead of class definitions, a program consists of state definitions containing methods that cause transitions to other states. Transitions are specified in a similar way to Plural's pre- and post-conditions. Like classes, states are organised into an inheritance hierarchy. Recent work [23,45] uses gradual typing to integrate static and dynamic typestate checking.

Bodden and Hendren [11] developed the Clara framework, which combines static typestate analysis with runtime monitoring. The monitoring is based on the *trace matches* approach [4], using regular expressions to define allowed sequences of method calls. The static analysis attempts to remove the need for runtime monitoring, but if this is not possible, the runtime monitor is optimised.

A challenge in typestate systems is aliasing. State changes to a given object must be reflected in all references that point to that object, otherwise inconsistency can result in violations of type safety. The literature includes several approaches to alias control. Some work, including ours, uses linear typing to forbid aliasing completely. The *adoption and focus* approach of Vault and Fugue, and the permission-based approaches of Plural and Plaid, are more flexible. Militão et al. [36] present an expressive fine-grained system. Crafa and Padovani [16,40] present an approach to concurrent typestate-oriented programming, allowing objects to be accessed and modified concurrently by several processes, each potentially changing only part of their state. Some work [32,39] combines static checking of typestate (or session type) properties with dynamic monitoring of (non-)aliasing properties. Balzer et al. [7] augment session types with points at which locks need to be acquired in order to perform state-changing operations; this approach has not yet been applied to a typestate system.

There is relatively little work combining behavioural types and typestate in the way that Mungo and StMungo do. The only other research we are aware of is the *API generation* approach of Hu [31]. The idea is to translate a Scribble protocol into a collection of classes for a standard language such as Java [32],

[2] EPSRC EP/K034413/1 From Data Types to Session Types: A Basis for Concurrency and Distribution (ABCD), groups.inf.ed.ac.uk/abcd/.

F# [37] or Go [15]. Each class represents a particular state in a protocol, with the methods available in that state. Each method returns the object on which it was called, but with a different class corresponding to the new state of the object. Because each state has its own class, standard IDEs can show the programmer which methods are available; however, for a complex protocol there can be a large number of classes. Runtime monitoring is used to check absence of aliasing.

For this tutorial we have used an example based on a standard internet protocol, HTTP. In previous work with Mungo and StMungo we have analysed SMTP [34,35] and POP3 [17]. Hu et al. also use SMTP [32,37] and HTTP [31] as case studies.

6   Conclusion and Future Work

We have presented a tutorial on using the [St]Mungo toolchain for static type-checking of a communication protocols. StMungo connects the Scribble specification language, used to define communication protocols, to Mungo by translating multiparty session types into typestate specifications. Mungo extends Java with typestate specifications, which annotate classes and define the permitted sequence of method calls of Java objects. We illustrate the workflow of both tools through implementing a substantial case study, an HTTP client. We use this client to communicate with a real-world server, the www.google.co.uk server.

While the toolchain is effective for statically typechecking the correct implementation of communication protocols, we intend to further improve its features for distributed programming in Java. On the StMungo side, we will keep it up to date with any changes in the Scribble specification language. On the Mungo side, we aim to offer static typechecking of generics and exceptions. To support generics, method calls on an object whose type is a generic parameter must be type-checked against the typestate specification of the parameter's upper bound. To support typechecking of exception handlers, typestate specifications must define the state transitions corresponding to exceptions, and check the transitions are consistent with the states of fields at the point where an exception is thrown. While existing work on exceptions in session types [14] provides inspiration, the complexities of Java's exception mechanism need to be accounted for as well. Another aim is to improve Mungo's error messages to better allow debugging.

References

1. Mungo Repository. https://bitbucket.org/abcd-glasgow/mungo-tools/src/master/
2. Mungo Webpage. http://www.dcs.gla.ac.uk/research/mungo/
3. Aldrich, J., Sunshine, J., Saini, D., Sparks, Z.: Typestate-oriented programming. In: OOPSLA Companion, pp. 1015–1022. ACM (2009). https://doi.org/10.1145/1639950.1640073
4. Allan, C., et al.: Adding trace matching with free variables to AspectJ. In: OOPSLA, pp. 345–364. ACM (2005). https://doi.org/10.1145/1094811.1094839
5. Ancona, D., et al.: Behavioral types in programming languages. Found. Trends Program. Lang. 3(2–3), 95–230 (2016). https://doi.org/10.1561/2500000031

6. ANTLR Project Homepage. www.antlr.org

7. Balzer, S., Toninho, B., Pfenning, F.: Manifest deadlock-freedom for shared session types. In: Caires, L. (ed.) ESOP 2019. LNCS, vol. 11423, pp. 611–639. Springer, Cham (2019). https://doi.org/10.1007/978-3-030-17184-1_22

8. Beckman, N.E., Bierhoff, K., Aldrich, J.: Verifying correct usage of atomic blocks and typestate. In: OOPSLA, pp. 227–244. ACM (2008). https://doi.org/10.1145/1449764.1449783

9. Bierhoff, K., Aldrich, J.: Modular typestate checking of aliased objects. In: OOPSLA, pp. 301–320. ACM (2007). https://doi.org/10.1145/1297027.1297050

10. Bierhoff, K., Beckman, N.E., Aldrich, J.: Practical API protocol checking with access permissions. In: Drossopoulou, S. (ed.) ECOOP 2009. LNCS, vol. 5653, pp. 195–219. Springer, Heidelberg (2009). https://doi.org/10.1007/978-3-642-03013-0_10

11. Bodden, E., Hendren, L.J.: The clara framework for hybrid typestate analysis. STTT **14**(3), 307–326 (2012). https://doi.org/10.1007/s10009-010-0183-5

12. Bono, V., Messa, C., Padovani, L.: Typing copyless message passing. In: Barthe, G. (ed.) ESOP 2011. LNCS, vol. 6602, pp. 57–76. Springer, Heidelberg (2011). https://doi.org/10.1007/978-3-642-19718-5_4

13. Capecchi, S., Castellani, I., Dezani-Ciancaglini, M.: Information flow safety in multiparty sessions. Math. Struct. Comput. Sci. **26**(8), 1352–1394 (2016). https://doi.org/10.1017/S0960129514000619

14. Carbone, M., Honda, K., Yoshida, N.: Structured interactional exceptions in session types. In: van Breugel, F., Chechik, M. (eds.) CONCUR 2008. LNCS, vol. 5201, pp. 402–417. Springer, Heidelberg (2008). https://doi.org/10.1007/978-3-540-85361-9_32

15. Castro-Perez, D., Hu, R., Jongmans, S., Ng, N., Yoshida, N.: Distributed programming using role-parametric session types in go: statically-typed endpoint APIs for dynamically-instantiated communication structures. PACMPL **3**(POPL), 29:1–29:30 (2019). https://doi.org/10.1145/3290342

16. Crafa, S., Padovani, L.: The chemical approach to typestate-oriented programming. In: OOPSLA, pp. 917–934. ACM (2015). https://doi.org/10.1145/2814270.2814287

17. Dardha, O., Gay, S.J., Kouzapas, D., Perera, R., Voinea, A.L., Weber, F.: Mungo and StMungo: tools for typechecking protocols in Java. In: Behavioural Types: From Theory to Tools. River Publishers (2017)

18. DeLine, R., Fähndrich, M.: Enforcing high-level protocols in low-level software. In: Proceedings of the ACM SIGPLAN Conference on Programming Language Design and Implementation (PLDI), pp. 59–69. ACM (2001). https://doi.org/10.1145/378795.378811

19. DeLine, R., Fähndrich, M.: Typestates for objects. In: Odersky, M. (ed.) ECOOP 2004. LNCS, vol. 3086, pp. 465–490. Springer, Heidelberg (2004). https://doi.org/10.1007/978-3-540-24851-4_21

20. Fähndrich, M., et al.: Language support for fast and reliable message-based communication in singularity OS. In: EuroSys, pp. 177–190. ACM (2006). https://doi.org/10.1145/1217935.1217953

21. Fähndrich, M., DeLine, R.: Adoption and focus: practical linear types for imperative programming. In: PLDI, pp. 13–24. ACM (2002). https://doi.org/10.1145/512529.512532

22. Fielding, R.T., Reschke, J.F.: Hypertext transfer protocol (HTTP/1.1): message syntax and routing. RFC 7230, pp. 1–89 (2014)

23. Garcia, R., Tanter, É., Wolff, R., Aldrich, J.: Foundations of typestate-oriented programming. ACM Trans. Program. Lang. Syst. **36**(4), 12:1–12:44 (2014). https://doi.org/10.1145/2629609
24. Gay, S.J., Ravara, A. (eds.): Behavioural Types: From Theory to Tools. River Publishers, Denmark (2017)
25. Hedin, G.: An introductory tutorial on JastAdd attribute grammars. In: Fernandes, J.M., Lämmel, R., Visser, J., Saraiva, J. (eds.) GTTSE 2009. LNCS, vol. 6491, pp. 166–200. Springer, Heidelberg (2011). https://doi.org/10.1007/978-3-642-18023-1_4
26. Honda, K.: Types for dyadic interaction. In: Best, E. (ed.) CONCUR 1993. LNCS, vol. 715, pp. 509–523. Springer, Heidelberg (1993). https://doi.org/10.1007/3-540-57208-2_35
27. Honda, K., Mukhamedov, A., Brown, G., Chen, T.-C., Yoshida, N.: Scribbling interactions with a formal foundation. In: Natarajan, R., Ojo, A. (eds.) ICDCIT 2011. LNCS, vol. 6536, pp. 55–75. Springer, Heidelberg (2011). https://doi.org/10.1007/978-3-642-19056-8_4
28. Honda, K., Vasconcelos, V.T., Kubo, M.: Language primitives and type discipline for structured communication-based programming. In: Hankin, C. (ed.) ESOP 1998. LNCS, vol. 1381, pp. 122–138. Springer, Heidelberg (1998). https://doi.org/10.1007/BFb0053567
29. Honda, K., Yoshida, N., Carbone, M.: Multiparty asynchronous session types. In: POPL, pp. 273–284. ACM (2008). https://doi.org/10.1145/1328438.1328472
30. Honda, K., Yoshida, N., Carbone, M.: Multiparty asynchronous session types. J. ACM **63**(1), 9:1–9:67 (2016). https://doi.org/10.1145/2827695
31. Hu, R.: Distributed programming using Java APIs generated from session types. Behavioural Types: from Theory to Tools, pp. 287–308 (2017)
32. Hu, R., Yoshida, N.: Hybrid session verification through endpoint API generation. In: Stevens, P., Wąsowski, A. (eds.) FASE 2016. LNCS, vol. 9633, pp. 401–418. Springer, Heidelberg (2016). https://doi.org/10.1007/978-3-662-49665-7_24
33. Hüttel, H., et al.: Foundations of session types and behavioural contracts. ACM Comput. Surv. **49**(1), 3:1–3:36 (2016). https://doi.org/10.1145/2873052
34. Kouzapas, D., Dardha, O., Perera, R., Gay, S.J.: Typechecking protocols with mungo and StMungo. In: PPDP, pp. 146–159. ACM (2016). https://doi.org/10.1145/2967973.2968595
35. Kouzapas, D., Dardha, O., Perera, R., Gay, S.J.: Typechecking protocols with Mungo and StMungo: a session type toolchain for java. Sci. Comput. Program. **155**, 52–75 (2018). https://doi.org/10.1016/j.scico.2017.10.006
36. Militão, F., Aldrich, J., Caires, L.: Aliasing control with view-based typestate. In: FTfJP@ECOOP, pp. 7:1–7:7. ACM (2010). https://doi.org/10.1145/1924520.1924527
37. Neykova, R., Hu, R., Yoshida, N., Abdeljallal, F.: A session type provider: compile-time API generation of distributed protocols with refinements in F#. In: CC, pp. 128–138. ACM (2018). https://doi.org/10.1145/3178372.3179495
38. Öqvist, J.: ExtendJ: extensible java compiler. In: Programming, pp. 234–235. ACM (2018). https://doi.org/10.1145/3191697.3213798
39. Padovani, L.: A simple library implementation of binary sessions. J. Funct. Program. **27**, e4 (2017). https://doi.org/10.1017/S0956796816000289
40. Padovani, L.: Deadlock-free typestate-oriented programming. Program. J. **2**(3), 15 (2018). https://doi.org/10.22152/programming-journal.org/2018/2/15
41. Scribble Project Homepage. www.scribble.org

42. Strom, R.E., Yemini, S.: Typestate: a programming language concept for enhancing software reliability. IEEE Trans. Softw. Eng. **12**(1), 157–171 (1986). https://doi.org/10.1109/TSE.1986.6312929

43. Sunshine, J., Naden, K., Stork, S., Aldrich, J., Tanter, É.: First-class state change in Plaid. In: OOPSLA, pp. 713–732 (2011). https://doi.org/10.1145/2048066.2048122

44. Takeuchi, K., Honda, K., Kubo, M.: An interaction-based language and its typing system. In: Halatsis, C., Maritsas, D., Philokyprou, G., Theodoridis, S. (eds.) PARLE 1994. LNCS, vol. 817, pp. 398–413. Springer, Heidelberg (1994). https://doi.org/10.1007/3-540-58184-7_118

45. Wolff, R., Garcia, R., Tanter, É., Aldrich, J.: Gradual typestate. In: Mezini, M. (ed.) ECOOP 2011. LNCS, vol. 6813, pp. 459–483. Springer, Heidelberg (2011). https://doi.org/10.1007/978-3-642-22655-7_22

Short Paper

Towards a Hybrid Verification Methodology for Communication Protocols (Short Paper)

Christian Bartolo Burlò[1]([⊠]) (iD), Adrian Francalanza[1]([⊠]) (iD),
and Alceste Scalas[2]([⊠]) (iD)

[1] University of Malta, Msida, Malta
{christian.bartolo.16,adrian.francalanza}@um.edu.mt
[2] Aston University, Birmingham, UK
a.scalas@aston.ac.uk

Abstract. We present our preliminary work towards a comprehensive solution for the hybrid (static + dynamic) verification of open distributed systems, using session types. We automate a solution for binary sessions where one endpoint is statically checked, and the other endpoint is dynamically checked by a *monitor* acting as an intermediary between typed and untyped components. We outline our theory, and illustrate a tool that *automatically synthesises* type-checked session monitors, based on the Scala language and its session programming library (`lchannels`).

Keywords: Session types · Static and dynamic verification · Monitors

1 Introduction

Session Types [12,13,27] have emerged as a central formalism for the verification of concurrent and distributed programs. Session-types-based analysis ensures that a program correctly implements some predetermined *communication protocol*, stipulating the desired exchange of messages [4,16]. The analysis is typically performed *statically*, via type checking, before the programs are deployed. However, full static analysis is not always possible (*e.g.,* when the source code of third-party programs and components is unavailable); in such cases, session types are checked at runtime via *monitors* [6,10,17,19]. We view these approaches as two extremes on a continuum: our aim is to develop practical *hybrid* (static and dynamic) verification methodologies and tools for distributed programs in *open* settings. In particular, our aim is to verify distributed systems where:

The research was partly supported by the EU H2020 RISE programme under the Marie Skłodowska-Curie grant agreement No. 778233.

A. Gotsman and A. Sokolova (Eds.): FORTE 2020, LNCS 12136, pp. 227–235, 2020.
https://doi.org/10.1007/978-3-030-50086-3_13

(i) we make no assumptions on how messages are delivered between components;

(ii) the components available prior-deployment are checked statically; and

(iii) the components that are unavailable for checking prior-deployment are verified at runtime, by deploying *autogenerated, type-checked monitors.*

To achieve this aim, we present a methodology with three key features, presented
as contributions in this paper:

F1. Open systems are prone to malicious attacks and data corruption. Thus, we
describe protocols via *augmented session types* including *runtime data assertions* (reminiscent of interaction refinements [18]), and synthesise *monitors*
that automate such data checks. Unlike [6,18], our monitors are independent, type-checked processes, that can be deployed over any network.

F2. We develop a tool that, given a session type S, can synthesise the Scala code
of *(1)* a *type-checked monitor* that verifies at run-time whether an interaction
abides by S (aim *(iii)*), and *(2)* the *signatures* usable to implement a process
that interacts according to S, in a correct-by-construction manner (aim *(ii)*).

F3. Our monitor synthesis can *abstract over low-level communication protocols,*
bridging across a variety of message transports (*e.g.,* TCP/IP, REST, *etc.*):
this is key to facilitate the interaction with third-party (untyped) components in open systems (aim *(i)*); this is also unlike previous work on session
monitoring (theoretical [6] or practical [19]) that focus on a specific technology and runtime system, or assume a centralised message routing medium.

2   Binary Sessions with Assertions

A session type defines the intended behaviour of a participant that communicates
with another over a *channel.* Our work is based on *session types with assertions*:

$$\text{Assertions}\quad A ::= v_1 == v_2 \mid v_1 >= v_2 \mid A_1 \text{ \&\& } A_2 \mid !A \mid \dots$$

$$\text{Base types}\quad B ::= \text{Int} \mid \text{Str} \mid \text{Boolean} \mid \dots$$

$$\text{Session types}\quad R, S ::= \&_{i \in I}?l_i(V_i : B_i)[A_i].S_i \mid \oplus_{i \in I}!l_i(V_i : B_i)[A_i].S_i$$
$$\mid \text{rec } X.S \mid X \mid \text{end} \quad (\text{with } I \neq \emptyset, \ l_i \text{ pairwise distinct})$$

We assume a set of *base types* B, and introduce *payload identifiers* V (with
their types) and *assertions* A (*i.e.,* predicates on payload values). *Branching* (or
external choice) $\&_{i \in I}?l_i(V_i : B_i)[A_i].S_i$ requires the participant to receive one
message of the form $l_i(v_i)$, where v_i is of (base) type B_i for some $i \in I$; the value
v_i (i.e., the message payload) is bound to the variable V_i in the continuation. If
the assertion $A_i[v_i/V_i]$ holds, the participant must proceed according to the *continuation type* $S_i[v_i/V_i]$, but if the assertion fails, a violation is raised. *Selection*
(or *internal choice*) $\oplus_{i \in I}!l_i(V_i : B_i)[A_i].S_i$ requires the participant to choose and
send one message $l_i(v_i)$ where v_i is of (base) type B_i for some $i \in I$; a violation
is raised if the assertion $A_i[v_i/V_i]$ does *not* hold, otherwise the protocol proceeds
as $S_i[v_i/V_i]$. The *recursive* session type rec $X.S$ binds the recursion variable X

in S (we assume guarded recursion), while end is the *terminated* session. For brevity, we often omit $\oplus$ and $\&$ for singleton choices, end, and trivial assertions (*i.e.*, true). A process implementing a session type S can correctly interact with a process implementing the *dual type of S*, denoted $\overline{S}$—where each selection (resp. branching) of S is a branching (resp. selection), with the same choices:

$$\overline{\&_{i\in I}?l_i(V_i : B_i)[A_i].S_i} = \oplus_{i\in I}!l_i(V_i : B_i)[A_i].\overline{S_i} \qquad \overline{\text{end}} = \text{end} \qquad \overline{X} = X$$

$$\overline{\oplus_{i\in I}!l_i(V_i : B_i)[A_i].S_i} = \&_{i\in I}?l_i(V_i : B_i)[A_i].\overline{S_i} \qquad \overline{\text{rec } X.S} = \text{rec } X.\overline{S}$$

Example 1. The type S_{login} below describes the protocol of a server handling *authorised logins*. Notice that the type uses two assertion predicates:

- *validAuth()* checks if an OAuth2-style token [20] authorises a given user;
- *validId()* checks whether an authentication id is correct for a given user.

$$S_{login} = \text{rec } X.?\text{Login}(uname\text{:Str}, pwd\text{:Str}, tok\text{:Str})[validAuth(uname, tok)].$$
$$\oplus\{!\text{Success}(id\text{:Str})[validId(id, uname)].R , !\text{Retry}().X\}$$

The server waits to receive $\text{Login}(uname\text{:Str}, pwd\text{:Str}, tok\text{:Str})$, where tok is a token obtained by the client from an authorisation service. Once received, the values of $uname$ and tok are passed to the predicate $validAuth()$ which checks whether tok contains a desired cryptographically-signed authorisation for $uname$: if it evaluates to true, the server can either send Success including an id, or Retry. If the server chooses the former, then id and $uname$ must be validated by $validId()$: if it succeeds, the message is sent and the server continues along session type R. If the server chooses to send Retry, the session loops. ∎

3   Design and Implementation

We now give an overview (Sect. 3.2) and an example-driven tour (Sect. 3.3) of our methodology; but first, we summarise the toolkit underlying its implementation (Sect. 3.1).

3.1   Background: Session Programming with lchannels

lchannels [21,24,25] is a library implementation of session types in the Scala programming language. Its API is inspired by the continuation-passing encoding of session types into the linear π-calculus [9]. lchannels allows to implement a program that communicates according to a session type S by *(1)* translating S into a set of *Continuation-Passing Style Protocol classes* (CPSPc), capturing the order of send/receive operations in S; and *(2)* communicating via "one-shot" channel objects, having type $\text{Out}[A]$ or $\text{In}[A]$—where A is a CPSP class. We show an example of CPSPc in Sect. 3.3. The main payoffs of lchannels are that *(1)* the CPSP classes restrict the usage the $\text{In}[A]/\text{Out}[A]$ channel objects to receive/send messages according to S, letting the Scala compiler check *safety* (*i.e.,* only messages allowed by S are sent) and *exhaustiveness* (*i.e.,* all inputs allowed by S are handled); and *(2)* the library provides run-time linearity enforcement: *e.g.*, if a "one-shot" channel object is used twice to send messages, then the program is not advancing along S, hence lchannels discards the message and raises an error.

3.2   Hybrid Verification via Static and Dynamic Checking

We now illustrate how our methodology is implemented, as a tool [7] targeting the Scala programming language. Consider the scenario on the right: a client C exchanges messages with a server Srv over a network. Srv implements the session type S_{login} outlined in Example 1, and expects each client C to follow the dual, $\overline{S_{login}}$. However, in an open system, we cannot guarantee that C abides by $\overline{S_{login}}$.

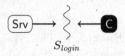

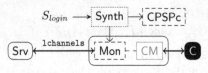

Our approach is outlined on the left. The accessible participant Srv is *statically* checked, and the behaviour of the inaccessible participant C is *dynamically* monitored at runtime. Given S_{login}, the synthesiser Synth generates *(1)* the *Continuation-Passing-Style Protocol classes* (CPSPc) for representing S_{login} in Scala and lchannels (see Sect. 3.1), and *(2)* the source code of a runtime monitor (Mon), based on the CPSPc above. Below are the CPSPc generated from S_{login} by our synthesiser: notably, they can be used to write a type-checked version of Srv.

```
1  case class Login(uname: String, pwd: String, tok: String)(val cont: Out[Choice1])
2  sealed abstract class Choice1
3  case class Success(id: String)(val cont: Out[R]) extends Choice1
4  case class Retry()(val cont: Out[Choice1]) extends Choice1
5  case class R(...) // This is the continuation of the session (omitted)
```

The messages sent from Srv to C (and *vice versa*) must pass through the monitor Mon. As Srv and Mon use lchannels to interact, they are statically typed according to S_{login} and $\overline{S_{login}}$; instead, there is no assumption on the interaction between Mon and C: it is handled by a user-supplied *connection manager* (CM), which acts as a *translator* and *gatekeeper* by transforming messages from the transport protocol supported by C to the Mon's CPSP classes, and *vice versa*. Hence, CM provides a message transport abstraction for Mon and Srv: to support new clients and message transports, only CM needs extending.

When the monitor is initialised, it invokes CM to set up the communication channel with client C, through a suitable message transport: *e.g.*, in the case of TCP/IP, CM creates a socket and initialises the I/O buffers. Each message sent from Srv to Mon via lchannels is analysed by Mon, and if it conforms to S_{login} and its assertions, it is translated by CM and forwarded to C. Dually, each message sent from C to Mon is translated by CM and analysed by Mon, and if it conforms to $\overline{S_{login}}$ and its assertions, it is forwarded to Srv. Mon's assertion checks provide additional verification against incorrect values from Srv or C.

3.3   A Step-by-Step Example

To illustrate our approach and implementation, we now follow the message exchanges prescribed by S_{login}, showing how they engage with the elements of our design. Roughly, Mon acts as a state machine: it transitions by receiving and forwarding messages between Srv and CM, abiding by the type S_{login} and its dual. CM, in turn, provides a send/receive interface to Mon, and delivers messages to/from client C. The monitor also maintains a mapping, called payloads, that associates the payload identifiers of S_{login} to their current values.

```
1   val loginR = """"LOGIN (.+) (.+) (.+)""".r
2   def receive(): Any = inBuf.readLine() match {
3     case loginR(uname, pwd, tok) => Login(uname, pwd, tok)(null)
4     case other => other
5   }
```

We begin with the login request sent from a client over TCP/IP. The client's message is initially handled by the connection manager CM, which provides a receive method like the one shown above: it is invoked by Mon to retrieve messages. When invoked, receive checks the socket input buffer inBuf: if a new supported message is found (line 3, where the message matches the regex loginR), the corresponding CPSP class is returned to the monitor; otherwise, the unaltered message is returned (line 4).

```
1    def receiveLogin(srv: Out[Login], client: ConnManager): Unit = {
2      client.receive() match {
3        case msg @ Login(_, _, _) =>
4          if (validateAuth(msg.uname, msg.tok)) {
5            val cont = srv !! Login(msg.uname, msg.pwd, msg.tok)_
6            payloads.Login.uname = msg.uname
7            sendChoice1(msg.cont, client) // Protocol continues
8          } else { /* log and halt: Incorrect values received */ }
9        case _ => /* log and halt: Unexpected message received */
10   } }
```

On the left is the synthesised code for Mon that handles the beginning of S_{login}. The monitor invokes CM's method receive (shown above) to retrieve the latest message (line 2). Depending on the type of message, the monitor will perform a series of actions. By default, a catch-all case (line 9) handles any messages violating the protocol. If Login is received, the monitor initially invokes the function validateAuth() with the values of uname and tok; *i.e.*, the assertion predicate in S_{login} corresponds to a Scala function (imported from a user-supplied library). If the function returns true, the message is forwarded to the server Srv (line 5), otherwise the monitor logs the violation and halts. The function used to forward the message (!!), which is part of lchannels, returns a continuation channel that is stored in cont. The value of uname is stored in a mapping (line 6) since it is used later on in S_{login}. Finally, the monitor moves to the next state, by calling the synthesised method sendChoice1, passing cont to continue the protocol.

```
1  def sendChoice1(srv: In[Choice1], Client: ConnManager): Unit = {
2    srv ? {
3      case msg @ Success(_) =>
4        if (validateId(msg.id, payloads.Login.uname)) {
5          Client.send(msg)
6          /* Continue according to R */
7        } else {
8          /* log and halt: Sending incorrect values. */
9        }
10     case msg @ Retry() =>
11       Client.send(msg)
12       receiveLogin(msg.cont, Client)
13   } }
```

On the left is the synthesised code of Mon that handles the server's response to the client. According to S_{login}, the server can choose to send either Success or Retry; correspondingly, the monitor waits to receive either of the options from Srv, using the function ? from lchannels (line 2).

- If the server sends Success, including the value id as specified in S_{login}, the first case is selected (line 3). The monitor evaluates the assertion on id and $uname$ (stored in receiveLogin above, and now retrieved from the payloads mapping): if it is satisfied, the message is sent to the client (line 5) via CM's send method (explained below), and the monitor continues according to session type R. Otherwise, the monitor logs a violation and halts (line 8).
- Instead, if the server sends Retry (line 10), the message is forwarded directly to the client using the method send of the CM (see below); notice that there are no dynamic checks at this point, as there is no assertion after $Retry$ in S_{login}. The monitor then goes back to the previous state receiveLogin.

Notably, unlike the synthesised code of receiveLogin (that handles the previous external choice), there is no catch-all case for unexpected messages from Srv. In fact, here we assume that Srv is written in Scala and lchannels, hence statically checked, and conforming to S_{login}; hence, it can only send one of the expected messages (as per Sect. 3.1). The monitor only checks the assertions on Srv's messages.

```
1  def send(msg: Any): Unit = msg match {
2    case Success(id) => outB.write(f"SUCCESS ${id}\n")
3    case Retry() => outB.write(f"RETRY\n")
4    case _ => { close();
5                throw new Exception("Invalid message") }
6  }
```

Finally, we review the send method of CM: it translates messages from a CPSP class instance to the format accepted by the client's transport protocol. In this case, the format is a textual representation of the session type. The catch-all case (lines 4–5) is for debugging purposes.

4   Conclusion

We presented our preliminary work on the hybrid verification of open distributed systems, based on *session types with assertions* and *automatically syntehsised monitors*—with a supporting tool [7] based on the Scala programming language.

Future Work. Our approach adheres to the *"fail-fast"* design methodology: if an assertion fails, the monitor logs the violation and halts. In the practice of distributed systems, "fail-fast" is advocated as an alternative to defensive programming [8]; it is also in line with existing literature on runtime verification [5]. Our further rationale for this design choice is that we intend to investigate *monitorability* properties of session types, along the lines of recent work [1,2,11], and identify any limits, in terms of what can be verified at runtime. We plan to extend our approach to multiparty sessions [14,15], in connection to existing work [22,23] based on lchannels and Scribble [26,28]. Finally, we plan to investigate how to handle assertion violations by adding *compensations* to our session types, formalising how the protocol should proceed whenever an assertion fails.

Related Work. The work in [6] formalises a theory of monitored (multiparty) session types, based on a global, centralised router providing a *safe transport network* that dispatches messages between participant processes. The main commonality with our work is that session types are used to synthesise monitors. The main differences (besides our focus on a tool implementation) are that *(1)* we do not assume a centralised message routing system, and consider the network adversarial (as per contribution F1) and use monitors to also protect typed participants; *(2)* our monitors can enforce data constraints, through assertions; and *(3)* in our setting, if a participant sends an invalid message, the monitor will flag violations (and stop computation) whereas [6] drops the invalid message, but will continue forwarding the rest, akin to runtime enforcement via suppressions [3]. Our protocol assertions are reminiscent of *interaction refinements* in [18], that are also statically generated (by an F# type provider), and dynamically enforced when messages are sent/received. However, we enforce our assertions by synthesising well-typed monitoring processes that can be deployed over a network, whereas [18] injects dynamic checks in the local executable of a process.

References

1. Aceto, L., Achilleos, A., Francalanza, A., Ingólfsdóttir, A., Lehtinen, K.: Adventures in monitorability: from branching to linear time and back again. PACMPL **3**(POPL), 1–29 (2019). https://doi.org/10.1145/3290365
2. Aceto, L., Achilleos, A., Francalanza, A., Ingólfsdóttir, A., Lehtinen, K.: An operational guide to monitorability. In: Ölveczky, P.C., Salaün, G. (eds.) SEFM 2019. LNCS, vol. 11724, pp. 433–453. Springer, Cham (2019). https://doi.org/10.1007/978-3-030-30446-1_23
3. Aceto, L., Cassar, I., Francalanza, A., Ingólfsdóttir, A.: On runtime enforcement via suppressions. In: CONCUR, LIPIcs, vol. 118. Schloss Dagstuhl - Leibniz-Zentrum für Informatik (2018). https://doi.org/10.4230/LIPIcs.CONCUR.2018.34
4. Ancona, D., et al.: Behavioral types in programming languages. Found. Trends Program. Lang. **3**(2–3), 95–230 (2016). https://doi.org/10.1561/2500000031
5. Bartocci, E., Falcone, Y., Francalanza, A., Reger, G.: Introduction to runtime verification. In: Bartocci, E., Falcone, Y. (eds.) Lectures on Runtime Verification. LNCS, vol. 10457, pp. 1–33. Springer, Cham (2018). https://doi.org/10.1007/978-3-319-75632-5_1

6. Bocchi, L., Chen, T.-C., Demangeon, R., Honda, K., Yoshida, N.: Monitoring networks through multiparty session types. In: Beyer, D., Boreale, M. (eds.) FMOODS/FORTE - 2013. LNCS, vol. 7892, pp. 50–65. Springer, Heidelberg (2013). https://doi.org/10.1007/978-3-642-38592-6_5

7. Burlò, C.B., Francalanza, A., Scalas, A.: STMonitor implementation (February 2020). https://github.com/chrisbartoloburlo/stmonitor

8. Cesarini, F., Thompson, S.: ERLANG Programming, 1st edn. O'Reilly Media Inc., Sebastopol (2009)

9. Dardha, O., Giachino, E., Sangiorgi, D.: Session types revisited. Inf. Comput. **256**, 253–286 (2017). https://doi.org/10.1016/j.ic.2017.06.002

10. Demangeon, R., Honda, K., Hu, R., Neykova, R., Yoshida, N.: Practical interruptible conversations: distributed dynamic verification with multiparty session types and Python. Form. Methods Syst. Des. **46**(3), 197–225 (2014). https://doi.org/10.1007/s10703-014-0218-8

11. Francalanza, A., Aceto, L., Ingolfsdottir, A.: Monitorability for the Hennessy–Milner logic with recursion. Form. Methods Syst. Des. **51**(1), 87–116 (2017). https://doi.org/10.1007/s10703-017-0273-z

12. Honda, K.: Types for dyadic interaction. In: Best, E. (ed.) CONCUR 1993. LNCS, vol. 715, pp. 509–523. Springer, Heidelberg (1993). https://doi.org/10.1007/3-540-57208-2_35

13. Honda, K., Vasconcelos, V.T., Kubo, M.: Language primitives and type discipline for structured communication-based programming. In: Hankin, C. (ed.) ESOP 1998. LNCS, vol. 1381, pp. 122–138. Springer, Heidelberg (1998). https://doi.org/10.1007/BFb0053567

14. Honda, K., Yoshida, N., Carbone, M.: Multiparty asynchronous session types. In: POPL. ACM (2008). https://doi.org/10.1145/1328438.1328472. Full version in [15]

15. Honda, K., Yoshida, N., Carbone, M.: Multiparty asynchronous session types. J. ACM **63**(1), 1–67 (2016). https://doi.org/10.1145/2827695

16. Hüttel, H., et al.: Foundations of session types and behavioural contracts. ACM Comput. Surv. **49**(1), 1–36 (2016). https://doi.org/10.1145/2873052

17. Jia, L., Gommerstadt, H., Pfenning, F.: Monitors and blame assignment for higher-order session types. In: POPL. ACM (2016). https://doi.org/10.1145/2837614.2837662

18. Neykova, R., Hu, R., Yoshida, N., Abdeljallal, F.: A session type provider: Compile-time API generation of distributed protocols with refinements in f#. In: Proceedings of the 27th International Conference on Compiler Construction, CC 2018. ACM (2018). https://doi.org/10.1145/3178372.3179495

19. Neykova, R., Yoshida, N.: Let it recover: multiparty protocol-induced recovery. In: Proceedings of the 26th International Conference on Compiler Construction. ACM (2017). https://doi.org/10.1145/3033019.3033031

20. OAuth Working Group: RFC 6749: OAuth 2.0 framework (2012). http://tools.ietf.org/html/rfc6749

21. Scalas, A.: lchannels (2017). https://alcestes.github.io/lchannels

22. Scalas, A., Dardha, O., Hu, R., Yoshida, N.: A linear decomposition of multiparty sessions for safe distributed programming. In: ECOOP, Leibniz International Proceedings in Informatics (LIPIcs), vol. 74. Schloss Dagstuhl-Leibniz-Zentrum fuer Informatik (2017). https://doi.org/10.4230/LIPIcs.ECOOP.2017.24

23. Scalas, A., Dardha, O., Hu, R., Yoshida, N.: A linear decomposition of multiparty sessions for safe distributed programming (artifact). DARTS **3**(2) (2017). https://doi.org/10.4230/DARTS.3.2.3

24. Scalas, A., Yoshida, N.: Lightweight session programming in scala. In: ECOOP, LIPIcs, vol. 56. Schloss Dagstuhl - Leibniz-Zentrum fuer Informatik (2016). https://doi.org/10.4230/LIPIcs.ECOOP.2016.21
25. Scalas, A., Yoshida, N.: Lightweight session programming in scala (artifact). DARTS 2(1) (2016). https://doi.org/10.4230/DARTS.2.1.11
26. Scribble Homepage (2020). http://www.scribble.org
27. Takeuchi, K., Honda, K., Kubo, M.: An interaction-based language and its typing system. In: Halatsis, C., Maritsas, D., Philokyprou, G., Theodoridis, S. (eds.) PARLE 1994. LNCS, vol. 817, pp. 398–413. Springer, Heidelberg (1994). https://doi.org/10.1007/3-540-58184-7_118
28. Yoshida, N., Hu, R., Neykova, R., Ng, N.: The scribble protocol language. In: Abadi, M., Lluch Lafuente, A. (eds.) TGC 2013. LNCS, vol. 8358, pp. 22–41. Springer, Cham (2014). https://doi.org/10.1007/978-3-319-05119-2_3

Author Index

Printed in the United States
By Bookmasters